T0265584

1001

Series 7 Exam

Practice Questions

2nd Edition

A Wiley Brand

by Steven M. Rice

Series 7 Exam: 1001 Practice Questions For Dummies®, 2nd Edition

Published by: **John Wiley & Sons, Inc.,** 111 River Street, Hoboken, NJ 07030-5774, www.wiley.com

Copyright © 2023 by John Wiley & Sons, Inc., Hoboken, New Jersey

Media and software compilation copyright © 2023 by John Wiley & Sons, Inc. All rights reserved.

Published simultaneously in Canada

For general information on our other products and services, please contact our Customer Care Department within the U.S. at 877-762-2974, outside the U.S. at 317-572-3993, or fax 317-572-4002. For technical support, please visit https://hub.wiley.com/community/support/dummies.

Wiley publishes in a variety of print and electronic formats and by print-on-demand. Some material included with standard print versions of this book may not be included in e-books or in print-on-demand. If this book refers to media such as a CD or DVD that is not included in the version you purchased, you may download this material at http://booksupport.wiley.com. For more information about Wiley products, visit www.wiley.com.

Library of Congress Control Number: 2023940076

ISBN 978-1-394-19288-5 (pbk); ISBN 978-1-394-19289-2 (ebk); ISBN 978-1-394-19290-8 (ebk)

SKY10049344_062123

Contents at a Glance

INTRODUCTION 1

PART 1: PRACTICING THE QUESTIONS 3

CHAPTER 1: Underwriting Securities 5
CHAPTER 2: Equity Securities 15
CHAPTER 3: Corporate and U.S. Government Debt Securities 25
CHAPTER 4: Municipal Bonds 39
CHAPTER 5: Margin Accounts 59
CHAPTER 6: Packaged Securities 67
CHAPTER 7: Direct Participation Programs 79
CHAPTER 8: Options 85
CHAPTER 9: Portfolio and Securities Analysis 107
CHAPTER 10: Orders and Trades 119
CHAPTER 11: Taxes and Retirement Plans 129
CHAPTER 12: Rules and Regulations 141

PART 2: CHECKING YOUR ANSWERS 161
CHAPTER 13: Answers and Explanations 163

INDEX 347

Table of Contents

INTRODUCTION 1

   What You'll Find.. 1

   Beyond the Book.. 2

   Where to Go for Additional Help 2

PART 1: PRACTICING THE QUESTIONS 3

CHAPTER 1: Underwriting Securities 5

   The Problems You'll Work On 5

   What to Watch Out For 5

   1–22 Bringing New Issues to Market 6

   23–47 Agreement Among Underwriters 8

   48–64 Reviewing Exemptions 11

CHAPTER 2: Equity Securities 15

   The Problems You'll Work On 15

   What to Watch Out For 15

   65–87 Common Stock 16

   88–103 Preferred Stock 19

   104–118 ADRs, Rights, and Warrants............................. 21

CHAPTER 3: Corporate and U.S. Government Debt Securities 25

   The Problems You'll Work On 25

   What to Watch Out For 26

   119–138 Bond Terms, Types, and Traits 27

   139–156 Price and Yield Calculations............................ 29

   157–176 Comparing Bonds.. 31

   177–200 U.S. Government Securities............................. 34

   201–206 Money Market Instruments............................... 37

   207–208 Structured Products 38

CHAPTER 4: Municipal Bonds 39

   The Problems You'll Work On 39

   What to Watch Out For 39

   209–227 General Obligation Bonds............................... 40

   228–244 Revenue Bonds.. 42

   245–260 The Primary Market 44

   261–284 Other Types of Municipal Bonds 46

   285–296 Municipal Notes 49

   297–300 Municipal Fund Securities 51

   301–313 Taxes on Municipal Bonds............................... 51

   314–331 Municipal Bond Rules.................................... 53

   332–352 Gathering Municipal Bond Info........................... 55

CHAPTER 5: Margin Accounts 59

The Problems You'll Work On 59

What to Watch Out For 60

353–359 Margin Paperwork 61

360–362 FRB Rules Relating to Margin Accounts 62

363–368 Initial Margin Requirements 62

369–370 Calculating Debt and Equity in Long Margin Accounts 63

371–374 Calculating Debt and Equity in Short Margin Accounts 63

375–381 Excess Equity 64

382–392 Restricted Accounts and Minimum Maintenance 65

CHAPTER 6: Packaged Securities 67

The Problems You'll Work On 67

What to Watch Out For 68

393–427 Management Investment Companies 69

428–432 Face-Amount Certificate Companies, UITs, and ETFs 73

433–437 Real Estate Investment Trusts 74

438–449 Fixed and Variable Annuities 74

450–453 Variable Life and Variable Universal Life Insurance 76

454–456 Investment Company Rules 77

CHAPTER 7: Direct Participation Programs 79

The Problems You'll Work On 79

What to Watch Out For 79

457–465 DPPs, General Partners, and Limited Partners 80

466–471 Partnership Paperwork 81

472–473 Types of DPP Offerings 81

474–476 Passive Income and Losses 82

477–496 Evaluating Direct Participation Programs 82

CHAPTER 8: Options 85

The Problems You'll Work On 85

What to Watch Out For 86

497–509 Option Basics 87

510–529 Option Basics 88

530–571 Straddles, Combinations, and Spreads 90

572–604 Stock and Options 96

605–615 Non-equity Options 100

616–636 Registered Options Principal (ROP), the OCC, the ODD, and the OAA 102

637–640 Additional Option Rules 104

CHAPTER 9: Portfolio and Securities Analysis 107

The Problems You'll Work On 107

What to Watch Out For 108

641–673 Portfolio Analysis 109

674–705 Fundamental Analysis 113

706–720 Technical Analysis 117

CHAPTER 10: Orders and Trades 119
The Problems You'll Work On 119
What to Watch Out For 119
721–726 Primary and Secondary Markets 120
727–736 Exchanges and the OTC Market 120
737–741 Broker-Dealer 121
742–771 Order Types and Features 122
772–792 Designated Market Maker 126

CHAPTER 11: Taxes and Retirement Plans 129
The Problems You'll Work On 129
What to Watch Out For 129
793–830 Taxes on Investments 130
831–836 Gift and Estate Tax Rules 135
837–864 Retirement Plans 136

CHAPTER 12: Rules and Regulations 141
The Problems You'll Work On 141
What to Watch Out For 141
865–870 Securities Regulatory Organizations 142
871–919 Opening Accounts 142
920–973 Trading by the Book Once the Account Is Open 149
974–1001 Other Important Rules 156

PART 2: CHECKING YOUR ANSWERS 161

CHAPTER 13: Answers and Explanations 163
Chapter 1 Answers 163
Chapter 2 Answers 174
Chapter 3 Answers 184
Chapter 4 Answers 202
Chapter 5 Answers 227
Chapter 6 Answers 238
Chapter 7 Answers 249
Chapter 8 Answers 255
Chapter 9 Answers 288
Chapter 10 Answers 302
Chapter 11 Answers 314
Chapter 12 Answers 326

INDEX 347

Introduction

This book is designed for people like you who are getting prepared to tackle the Series 7 exam. Make no mistake, the Series 7 can be a gorilla of an exam if you don't prepare adequately. It is not enough for you to have a good grasp on the material covered on the Series 7; you also need to have completed enough practice questions to go in to take the *real deal* with confidence.

No doubt tackling test questions is a skill. I have tutored many students who could just about recite a Series 7 book, but when it came down to answering questions, they were lost. The only way to get better is to answer a lot of questions. You need to learn how to break questions down, focus on the last sentence in the question, and eliminate wrong answers.

Although the book is broken down into chapters and sections, you can jump around the book to whatever topic you need help with. Even though the book is broken down into logical chapters, when you take the real Series 7 exam, the questions are not going to be in chapter order; they will be jumbled. If you would like to get somewhat of a feel for the real exam, you may want to randomly grab 125 questions or so encompassing all of the different chapters and subchapters. You may want to answer every eighth question starting with number 1 the first time, 2 the second time, and so on.

This is your book, so feel free to either take a question and go look at the answer and explanation or complete a section before looking at the answers and explanations. Either way you do it, make sure that you give your best effort in answering each question before looking at the answer. Also, keep your eyes from wandering to the answers and explanations for questions you haven't completed yet.

Work hard and give yourself the best opportunity to pass the Series 7 exam on the first (or next) attempt.

What You'll Find

The 1,001 Series 7 exam practice problems in the book are divided into 12 chapters with several subsections. Each chapter provides an abundance of question types you are likely to face when facing the real exam. As on the real exam, some questions will take you a few seconds to answer, and some will take you a couple of minutes.

The last chapter of the book provides the answers and detailed explanations to all the problems. If you get an answer wrong, give it a second attempt before reading the explanation. Eliminating answers that you know are wrong will have a big impact on your score as compared to just "C"ing your way through (just choosing the answer "C" for every answer you're not sure of).

Beyond the Book

This product also comes with an online Cheat Sheet that helps you increase your odds of performing well. Go to www.dummies.com.com and type "Series 7 Exam: 1001 Practice Questions For Dummies cheat sheet" in the search box. Here, you'll find articles on how to prepare for the Series 7.

Where to Go for Additional Help

I wouldn't say that any part of the Series 7 is overly difficult, but the exam itself is tough. The problem is that there is soooo much to remember. Remembering everything and not confusing rules and numbers makes it one of the tougher exams you can take.

In addition to getting help from people who have recently passed the Series 7, Series 7 teachers (like me), or tutors (like me), you can find a variety of questions and study materials online. A simple online search often turns up heaps of information. You can also head to www.dummies.com to see the many articles and books that can help you in your studies.

Series 7 Exam: 1001 Practice Questions For Dummies gives you just that — 1,001 practice questions and answers in order for you to prepare yourself for the Series 7 exam. If you need more in-depth study and direction, check out the latest edition of *Series 7 Exam For Dummies*, which I also wrote. This book provides you with the background info you need along with coverage of all the topics and concepts that are tested on the Series 7 exam. In addition, you get full-length exams to prepare yourself for test day.

1

Practicing the Questions

IN THIS PART . . .

Underwriting Securities (Chapter 1)

Equity Securities (Chapter 2)

Corporate and U.S. Government Debt Securities (Chapter 3)

Municipal Bonds (Chapter 4)

Margin Accounts (Chapter 5)

Packaged Securities (Chapter 6)

Direct Participation Programs (Chapter 7)

Options (Chapter 8)

Portfolio and Securities Analysis (Chapter 9)

Orders and Trades (Chapter 10)

Taxes and Retirement Plans (Chapter 11)

Rules and Regulations (Chapter 12)

Chapter 1

Underwriting Securities

A good place to start is at the beginning. Prior to corporations "going public," they must register and have a way of distributing their securities. The Series 7 exam tests your ability to understand the registration process, the entities involved in bringing new issues to market, and types of offerings. In addition, you're expected to know which securities are exempt from Securities and Exchange Commission (SEC) registration.

The Problems You'll Work On

As you work through this chapter, be sure you can recognize, understand, and, in some cases, calculate the following:

>> The process involved with bringing new issues to market

>> Who gets what (distribution of profits)

>> The different types of offerings

>> Exempt securities and transactions

What to Watch Out For

Read the questions and answer choices carefully and make sure that you

>> Watch out for words that can change the answer you're looking for, such as EXCEPT, NOT, ALWAYS, and so on.

>> Recognize that there's a difference between *exempt securities* and *exempt transactions*.

>> If you're not certain of the correct answer, try to eliminate any answers that you can. Doing so may make the difference between passing and failing.

1–22 Bringing New Issues to Market

1. For an entity to become a corporation, they must file a _____ with their home state of business.

   (A) registration statement

   (B) statement of additional information (SAI)

   (C) corporate charter

   (D) prospectus

2. GNU Corporation is planning to issue new shares to the public. GNU has not yet filed a registration statement with the SEC. An underwriter for GNU may do which of the following?

   (A) Accept money from investors for payment of the new issue of GNU.

   (B) Send a red herring to investors.

   (C) Accept indications of interest.

   (D) None of the above.

3. Which of the following information must be included in the registration statement to the SEC when registering new securities?

   I. The issuer's name and description of its business

   II. What the proceeds of sale will be used for

   III. Financial statements

   IV. The company's capitalization

   (A) I and III

   (B) I, II, and III

   (C) I, III, and IV

   (D) I, II, III, and IV

4. What is the underwriting arrangement that allows an issuer whose stock is already trading publicly to time the sales of an additional issue?

   (A) Shelf registration

   (B) A standby underwriting

   (C) A negotiated offering

   (D) An Eastern account underwriting

5. SEC Rule 415 outlines rules for

   (A) primary offerings

   (B) shelf offerings

   (C) secondary offerings

   (D) IPOs

6. The cooling-off period for a new issue lasts approximately how many days?

   (A) 20

   (B) 30

   (C) 40

   (D) 60

7. All of the following terms apply to a new issue of securities EXCEPT

   (A) stabilization

   (B) due diligence

   (C) matching orders

   (D) cooling-off period

8. Under the Securities Act of 1933, the SEC has the authority to

   I. approve new issues of common stock

   II. issue stop orders

   III. review registration statements

   (A) I and II

   (B) II and III

   (C) I and III

   (D) all of the above

9. Which of the following MAY NOT occur during the cooling-off period?

    (A) Having a due diligence meeting
    (B) Obtaining indications of interest
    (C) The publishing of a tombstone ad
    (D) Soliciting sales of the new security

10. If AylDec Corporation wishes to have a public offering of common stock, they must

    I.   issue a prospectus
    II. publish a tombstone advertisement
    III. register the securities with the SEC

    (A) I and II
    (B) II and III
    (C) I and III
    (D) I, II, and III

11. A tombstone ad would include all of the following names EXCEPT

    (A) selling group members
    (B) syndicate members
    (C) the syndicate manager
    (D) the issuer

12. All of the following would be included on a tombstone ad EXCEPT

    (A) the name of the issuer
    (B) the names of the selling groups
    (C) the names of the syndicate members
    (D) the name of the syndicate manager

13. Zamzow, Inc., has filed a registration statement and is currently in the cooling-off period. Zowie Broker-Dealer is the lead underwriter for Zamzow and is in the process of taking indications of interest. Which TWO of the following are TRUE regarding indications of interest?

    I.   They are binding on Zowie.
    II. They are binding on customers.
    III. They are not binding on Zowie.
    IV. They are not binding on customers.

    (A) I and II
    (B) III and IV
    (C) I and IV
    (D) II and III

14. Which of the following are types of state securities registration?

    I.   Filing
    II. Communication
    III. Qualification
    IV. Coordination

    (A) I, III, and IV
    (B) II, III, and IV
    (C) I, II, and III
    (D) I, II, III, and IV

15. This type of state securities registration is used for established companies that have previously sold securities in the state.

    (A) Notification
    (B) Coordination
    (C) Indemnification
    (D) Qualification

16. This type of state securities registration is used for securities that are exempt from SEC registration but must register with the state.

    (A) Notification
    (B) Coordination
    (C) Indemnification
    (D) Qualification

17. All of the following may be determined by the managing underwriter EXCEPT

    (A) the takedown
    (B) the public offering price
    (C) the effective date
    (D) the allocation of orders

18. The SEC has ruled that an offering has become effective. This means that

    (A) the SEC has approved the issue
    (B) the SEC has cleared the issue
    (C) the SEC has verified the accuracy of the information provided on the registration statement
    (D) all of the above

19. Which of the following securities acts covers the registration and disclosure requirements of new issues?

    (A) Securities Act of 1933
    (B) Securities Exchange Act of 1934
    (C) Trust Indenture Act of 1939
    (D) All of the above

20. Which of the following are covered under the Securities and Exchange Act of 1934?

    I.   Margin accounts
    II. Trust indentures
    III. Proxies
    IV. Short sales

    (A) I, II, and III
    (B) II and IV
    (C) III and IV
    (D) I, III, and IV

21. The Trust Indenture Act of 1939 prohibits corporate bond issues valued greater than _____ from being offered to investors without an indenture.

    (A) $5 million
    (B) $10 million
    (C) $50 million
    (D) $75 million

22. The main function of an investment banker is to

    (A) advise an issuer on how to raise capital
    (B) raise capital for issuers by selling securities
    (C) help issuers comply with the laws of the Securities Act of 1933
    (D) all of the above

23–47 Agreement Among Underwriters

23. Which of the following documents details the liabilities and responsibilities of each firm involved in the distribution of new securities?

    (A) The registration statement
    (B) The letter of intent
    (C) The syndicate agreement
    (D) The code of procedure

24. Which of the following documents would contain the allocation of orders?

    (A) Official statement
    (B) Trust indenture
    (C) Syndicate agreement
    (D) Preliminary prospectus

25. Which of the following types of underwriting agreements specify that any unsold securities are retained by the underwriters?

    (A) Mini-max
    (B) Firm commitment
    (C) All-or-none (AON)
    (D) Best efforts

26. An investment banking firm has won a competitive bid for a corporate underwriting of ABCDE common stock. The investment banking firm has agreed to purchase the shares from the issuer. This type of offering is a(n)

   (A) all-or-none underwriting
   (B) best efforts underwriting
   (C) standby underwriting
   (D) firm commitment underwriting

27. Which of the following is NOT a type of bond underwriting?

   (A) Mini-max
   (B) Best efforts
   (C) Standby
   (D) AON

28. Silversmith Securities is the lead underwriter for 2 million shares of HIJ common stock. Silversmith has entered into an agreement with HIJ to sell as many shares of their common stock as possible, but HIJ will cancel the offering if the entire 2 million shares are not sold. What type of offering is this?

   (A) Firm commitment
   (B) All-or-none
   (C) Mini-max
   (D) Best efforts

29. Selling group members are required to sign a

   (A) syndicate agreement
   (B) letter of intent
   (C) selling group agreement
   (D) repurchase agreement

30. Stabilizing bids may be entered at

   (A) a price at or below the public offering price
   (B) the stabilizing price stated in the final prospectus
   (C) a price at or slightly above the public offering price
   (D) a price deemed reasonable by the Fed

31. The public offering price to purchase a new issue of DEF Corporate bonds is $1,000. However, the issuer receives only $989 per bond. What is the $11 difference called?

   (A) The takedown
   (B) The underwriting spread
   (C) The additional takedown
   (D) The concession

32. Place the following in order from largest compensation to smallest compensation in an underwriting spread.

   I.   Concession
   II. Manager's fee
   III. Reallowance
   IV. Takedown

   (A) IV, I, III, II
   (B) II, III, I, IV
   (C) I, II, III, IV
   (D) III, II, I, IV

33. What is the profit syndicate members make when selling shares of a new issue?

   (A) The concession
   (B) The takedown
   (C) The reallowance
   (D) The spread

34. The smallest portion of a corporate underwriting spread is the

   (A) concession
   (B) takedown
   (C) reallowance
   (D) manager's fee

35. During an underwriting the profit made by syndicate members on shares or bonds sold by the selling group is called

   (A) the selling group concession
   (B) the takedown
   (C) the additional takedown
   (D) the reallowance

36. Armbar common stock is being sold to a syndicate during an underwriting for $13.50 per share. The public offering price is $15.00 per share, and the manager's fee is $0.25 per share. If the concession is $0.80 per share, what is the additional takedown?

(A) $0.45 per share

(B) $1.15 per share

(C) $1.25 per share

(D) $1.50 per share

37. TUV Corp. is offering 6 million new shares to the public. The shares are being sold to a syndicate for $15 and are being reoffered to the public at $16. The compensation to the underwriters for each share sold is $0.75. The selling group receives $0.30 a share for each share it sells, and the managing underwriter retains $0.25 in fees for each share sold by anybody. The selling group will assist in selling 1 million of the 6 million shares offered. If the selling group sells its entire allotment, how much does the syndicate make on shares sold by the selling group?

(A) $200,000

(B) $300,000

(C) $450,000

(D) $750,000

38. Faber Hughes Corporation is offering 2 million new shares to the public. The shares are being sold to a syndicate for $8 and are being reoffered to the public at $9. The takedown for each share sold is $0.85. The concession is $0.55 a share, and the managing underwriter retains $0.15 in fees for each share sold by anybody. The selling group will assist in selling 500,000 of the 2 million shares offered. If the selling group sells its entire allotment, how much does it make in profits?

(A) $425,000

(B) $150,000

(C) $350,000

(D) $275,000

39. A municipality is offering $20 million of new bonds through a syndicate in a negotiated offering. A firm in a syndicate that is established as a Western account is responsible for selling $2 million of the bonds. After the firm sells $1.8 million of the firm's allotment, the manager of the syndicate determines that there are $4 million of bonds left unsold. How much of the unsold bonds is the firm responsible for selling?

(A) 0

(B) 200,000

(C) 400,000

(D) 600,000

40. Liddell Securities is part of a syndicate that is offering new shares of SLAM Corporation common stock to the public. There are 8 million shares being offered to the public, and Liddell Securities is allocated 1 million shares. After selling its allotment, 800,000 shares remain unsold by other members. How much of the remaining shares would Liddell Securities be responsible for?

I. 100,000 shares if the offering was on an Eastern account basis

II. 100,000 shares if the offering was on a Western account basis

III. 0 shares if the offering was on an Eastern account basis

IV. 0 shares if the offering was on a Western account basis

(A) I and IV

(B) II and III

(C) I and II

(D) III and IV

41. A syndicate is offering 10 million new shares to the public on an Eastern account basis. A member of the syndicate is responsible for selling 2.5 million shares. After selling its entire allotment, 1 million shares are left unsold by other members. How many additional shares is the firm responsible for selling to the public?

(A) 0

(B) 100,000

(C) 250,000

(D) 1 million

42. A registered rep may use a preliminary prospectus to

(A) solicit orders from clients to purchase a new issue

(B) show prospective investors that the issue has been approved by the SEC

(C) obtain indications of interest from investors

(D) accept orders and payments from investors for a new issue

43. All of the following are included in the preliminary prospectus EXCEPT

I. the public offering price

II. the financial history of the issuer

III. the effective date

(A) I only

(B) I and II

(C) II and III

(D) I and III

44. When is a red herring available to potential customers?

(A) Prior to the issuer filing a registration statement

(B) During the cooling-off period

(C) For 45 days after the issue has become effective

(D) For 60 days after the issue has become effective

45. The key difference between a preliminary prospectus and a final prospectus is that the final prospectus includes

(A) the offering price

(B) the issuer's income statement

(C) the issuer's balance sheet

(D) the issuer's income statement and balance sheet

46. HIJ Corporation is issuing common stock through an IPO that will trade on the OTCBB when it is first issued. Broker-dealers who execute orders for clients in HIJ common stock must have a copy of a final prospectus available for how long?

(A) 25 days after the effective date

(B) 30 days after the effective date

(C) 40 days after the effective date

(D) 90 days after the effective date

47. Pluto Broker-Dealer is offering an IPO that will not be listed on the NYSE, NASDAQ, or any other exchange. How long after the effective date must Pluto provide a final prospectus to all purchasers?

(A) 20 days

(B) 30 days

(C) 40 days

(D) 90 days

48–64 Reviewing Exemptions

48. Which TWO of the following are considered securities under the Securities Act of 1933?

I. Variable annuities

II. Fixed annuities

III. FDIC insured negotiable CDs

IV. Oil and gas limited partnerships

(A) I and III

(B) I and IV

(C) II and III

(D) II and IV

49. Which of the following securities are exempt from the full registration requirements of the Securities Act of 1933?

(A) Corporate convertible bonds

(B) Closed-end funds

(C) Real estate limited partnerships

(D) Commercial paper

50. Which of the following are non-exempt securities?

I. Municipal GO bonds

II. Treasury notes

III. Blue chip stocks

IV. Variable annuities

(A) I and II

(B) II and III

(C) III and IV

(D) I and IV

51. Which of the following securities is NOT exempt from SEC registration?

(A) Limited partnership public offerings

(B) Treasury notes sold at auction

(C) Rule 147 offerings

(D) Private placements

52. All of the following are exempt securities under the Act of 1933 EXCEPT

(A) treasury bonds

(B) municipal general obligation bonds

(C) REITs

(D) public utility stocks

53. Which of the following are exempt transactions?

I. Private placements

II. Securities issued by the U.S. government

III. Municipal bonds

IV. Intrastate offerings

(A) II and III

(B) II, III, and IV

(C) I and IV

(D) I, II, III, and IV

54. Which of the following Securities Act of 1933 exemptions may be used for an initial offering of securities?

I. Rule 144

II. Rule 147

III. Regulation D

IV. Regulation S

(A) I, II, and III

(B) II and IV

(C) III and IV

(D) II, III, and IV

55. A Rule 147 offering is

(A) an offering of securities only within the issuer's home state

(B) an offering of securities worth no more than $5 million within a one-year period

(C) an offering of securities to no more than 35 unaccredited investors within a one-year period

(D) also known as an interstate offering

56. Which of the following is TRUE of Regulation A+ Tier 1 offerings?

    (A) They are limited to 35 unaccredited investors each year.
    (B) They are issued without using a prospectus.
    (C) They are limited to raising up to $10 million per year.
    (D) They are also known as private placements.

57. Which of the following exempt transactions deals with an offering of $75,000,000 worth of securities or less in a 12-month period?

    (A) Regulation A+ Tier 1
    (B) Regulation A+ Tier 2
    (C) Regulation D
    (D) Regulation S

58. A Regulation S exemption under the Securities Act of 1933 is for

    (A) a non-U.S. issuer issuing new securities to U.S. investors
    (B) a U.S. issuer issuing new securities to non-U.S. investors
    (C) a U.S. issuer issuing new securities to U.S. investors
    (D) a non-U.S. issuer issuing new securities to non-U.S. investors

59. One of your clients purchased unregistered securities overseas from a U.S. corporation under Regulation S. Which of the following is TRUE?

    I.   They are exempt transactions.
    II. They are exempt securities.
    III. The securities must be held for 270 days before they can be resold in the United States.
    IV. The securities must be held for one year before they can be resold in the United States.

    (A) I and III
    (B) I and IV
    (C) II and III
    (D) II and IV

60. A Regulation D private placement is

    (A) an offering of securities to no more than 35 unaccredited investors in a 12-month period
    (B) an intrastate offering
    (C) an offering of securities worth no more than $5 million in a 12-month period
    (D) a large offering of commercial paper

61. Mike Steelhead and his wife, Mary, would like to open a joint account at your firm. They are interested in purchasing a private placement under Regulation D. You should inform them that to be considered accredited investors, they must have a combined annual income of at least

    (A) $200,000
    (B) $300,000
    (C) $500,000
    (D) $1 million

62. One of your clients wants to purchase a private placement. According to Regulation D, which of the following are the minimum standards for an accredited investor?

I. A net worth exceeding $1 million excluding primary residence

II. A net worth exceeding $300,000 excluding primary residence

III. An annual income exceeding $100,000 in each of the two most recent years and a reasonable expectation of the same income level in the current year

IV. Annual income exceeding $200,000 in each of the two most recent years and a reasonable expectation of the same income level in the current year

(A) I and III

(B) I and IV

(C) II and III

(D) II and IV

63. Derrick Diamond has held restricted stock for six months. When must Derrick file a Form 144 with the SEC to sell the stock publicly?

(A) At the time of sale

(B) 30 days after the sale

(C) 60 days after the sale

(D) 90 days after the sale

64. Sig Hillstrand has held shares of Greenhorn restricted stock for more than one year. Greenhorn has 4 million shares outstanding. The most recently reported weekly trading volumes for Greenhorn are as follows:

Week Ending	Trading Volume
May 27	35,000
May 20	50,000
May 13	40,000
May 6	45,000
Apr 29	50,000

What is the maximum number of shares that Sig can sell under Rule 144?

(A) 35,000

(B) 46,250

(C) 44,000

(D) 42,500

Chapter **2**

Equity Securities

To be a corporation, you must have stockholders. Both common and preferred stock are considered equity securities because they represent ownership of the corporation. A majority of most registered representatives' commission is earned by selling equity securities because, historically, equity securities have outpaced inflation.

Although this isn't the largest section on the Series 7 exam, it does relate to many other chapters, such as packaged securities and options.

The Problems You'll Work On

In this chapter, you're expected to understand and calculate questions regarding the following:

>> The specifics of common stock

>> Voting rights and dividends

>> The difference between common stock and preferred stock

>> The reason for American depositary receipts (ADRs)

>> What rights and warrants are

What to Watch Out For

Read the questions and answer choices carefully and be sure you

>> Don't assume an answer without reading each question and answer choice completely (twice if necessary).

>> Watch out for key words that can change the answer (EXCEPT, NOT, and so on).

>> Eliminate any incorrect answer choice that you can.

>> Look at questions from the corporation's or the investor's point of view depending on how the question is worded.

65–87 Common Stock

65. Which of the following would be owners of a corporation?

    I.   Common stockholders

    II. Debenture holders

    III. Participation preferred stockholders

    IV. Equipment trust bondholders

    (A) I and III

    (B) II and IV

    (C) I, III, and IV

    (D) II, III, and IV

66. You have a new client who is new to investing. They are concerned about taking too much risk. Which of the following investments could you tell them is the riskiest?

    (A) Common stock

    (B) Preferred stock

    (C) Debentures

    (D) GO bonds

67. Which of the following investments exposes an investor to the greatest risk?

    (A) TUV subordinated debentures

    (B) TUV mortgage bonds

    (C) TUV common stock

    (D) TUV preferred stock

68. Common stockholders have which of the following rights and privileges?

    I.   The right to receive monthly audited financial reports

    II. The right to vote for cash dividends

    III. The right to vote for stock splits

    IV. A residual claim to assets at dissolution

    (A) I and II

    (B) III and IV

    (C) I, III, and IV

    (D) II, III, and IV

69. Common stockholders have the right to vote for all of the following EXCEPT

    I.   cash dividends

    II. stock dividends

    III. stock splits

    IV. members of the board of directors

    (A) I, II, and III

    (B) III and IV

    (C) I and II

    (D) IV only

70. An investor owns 200 shares of JKL common stock. JKL stockholders can vote only by way of statutory voting. If JKL holds an election in which six candidates are running for three seats on the board, this investor could cast

    (A) 600 votes for any one candidate

    (B) 100 votes each for any six candidates

    (C) 200 votes for each of the three positions

    (D) Any of the above

71. Which type of voting benefits minority shareholders?

    (A) Cumulative

    (B) Statutory

    (C) Regular

    (D) Senior

72. An individual owns 2,000 shares of TUV common stock. TUV has four vacancies on the board of directors. If the voting is cumulative, the investor may vote in any of the following ways EXCEPT

    (A) 4,000 votes for two candidates each

    (B) 5,000 votes for one candidate and 3,000 votes for another candidate

    (C) 3,000 votes each for three candidates

    (D) 2,000 votes for four candidates each

73. Cain Weidman owns 1,000 shares of HIT Corp. HIT issues stock with cumulative voting. What is the maximum number of votes that Cain can cast for one candidate if the board of directors of HIT has four vacancies?

(A) 100

(B) 250

(C) 1,000

(D) 4,000

74. Macrohard Corp. was authorized to issue 2 million shares of common stock. Macrohard issued 1.1 million shares and subsequently repurchased 150,000 shares. How many of Macrohard's shares remain outstanding?

(A) 150,000

(B) 900,000

(C) 950,000

(D) 1.85 million

75. MKR Corporation's by laws have authorized 20 million shares of common stock. MKR has issued 12 million shares of common stock and has 2 million shares of treasury stock. How many shares of MKR common stock are authorized but still unissued?

(A) 2 million

(B) 6 million

(C) 10 million

(D) 8 million

76. Which of the following does NOT describe treasury stock?

(A) It has no voting rights.

(B) It is stock that was previously authorized but still unissued.

(C) It is issued stock that has been repurchased by the company.

(D) It has no dividends.

77. Treasury stock is

(A) U.S. government stock

(B) local government stock

(C) authorized but unissued stock

(D) repurchased stock

78. The par value of a common stock is

I. used for bookkeeping purposes

II. one dollar

III. adjusted for stock splits

IV. the amount investors receive at maturity

(A) I and III

(B) I, II, and III

(C) II, III, and IV

(D) I, II, III, and IV

79. Which of the following changes the par value of a stock?

(A) a rights offering

(B) the issuer repurchasing some of its outstanding stock

(C) a stock split

(D) a cash dividend

80. The ex-dividend date as related to cash dividends is

I. the date that the stock price is reduced by the dividend amount

II. the date that the stock price is increased by the dividend amount

III. 2 business days before the record date

IV. 2 business days after the trade date

(A) I and III

(B) I and IV

(C) II and III

(D) II and IV

81. A listed stock closed at $24.95 on the business day prior to the ex-dividend date. If the company previously announced a $0.30 dividend, what will be the opening price on the next business day?

(A) $24.35

(B) $24.65

(C) $24.95

(D) $25.25

82. One of your customers owns 1,000 shares of DIM common stock at $24. DIM declares a 20% stock dividend. On the ex-dividend date, your customer will own

I.   1,000 shares

II. 1,200 shares

III. stock at $20 per share

IV. stock at $24 per share

(A) I and III

(B) I and IV

(C) II and III

(D) II and IV

83. EYEBM Corp. shares are trading at $55 per share when it declares a 5% stock dividend. After EYEBM pays the dividend, one of your clients who owned 500 shares now owns

(A) 500 shares valued at $57.73 per share

(B) 525 shares valued at $55.00 per share

(C) 550 shares valued at $55.00 per share

(D) 525 shares valued at $52.38 per share

84. Rule 145 applies to reclassification of securities in which of the following situations?

(A) Stock splits

(B) The issuance of convertible securities

(C) The issuance of non-voting common stock

(D) Consolidations

85. Unless otherwise exempt, all investors of penny stocks must receive

(A) a quarterly account statement

(B) a risk disclosure document

(C) an ODD

(D) a statement of additional information (SAI)

86. Which TWO of the following are TRUE regarding penny stocks?

I.   They are Nasdaq securities.

II. They are non-Nasdaq securities.

III. They are stocks that trade under $1 per share.

IV. They are stocks that trade under $5 per share.

(A) I and III

(B) I and IV

(C) II and III

(D) II and IV

87. An investor is recommended by a registered rep to purchase stock of DDDD Corporation. Currently, DDDD trades at $3 per share on the OTCBB. According to the "penny stock rule," a registered rep usually needs a written suitability statement signed by the investor. All of the following are exemptions from the suitability statement requirement EXCEPT

(A) unsolicited transactions

(B) accredited investors

(C) a one-year customer of the broker-dealer

(D) a customer who has purchased two different penny stocks previously through the broker-dealer of the rep

88–103 Preferred Stock

88. Which of the following are TRUE about both preferred and common stock?

    I.   They are equity securities.

    II.   Dividends are determined by the issuer's board of directors.

    III. Holders have the right to vote for members of the board of directors.

    (A) I and II

    (B) I and III

    (C) II and III

    (D) I, II, and III

89. Which of the following are advantages of holding straight preferred stock over common stock?

    I.   A fixed dividend

    II.   More voting power

    III. Preference in the event of issuer bankruptcy

    IV. The ability to receive par value at maturity

    (A) I and II

    (B) II and IV

    (C) I and III

    (D) I, III, and IV

90. Preferred dividends may be paid in the form of

    I.   cash

    II.   stock

    III. product

    (A) I only

    (B) I and II

    (C) I and III

    (D) I, II, and III

91. Which TWO of the following are TRUE of preferred stock?

    I.   Holders have voting rights.

    II.   Holders do not have voting rights.

    III. In the event of corporate bankruptcy, preferred stock is senior to common stock.

    IV. In the event of corporate bankruptcy, preferred stock is junior to common stock.

    (A) I and III

    (B) I and IV

    (C) II and III

    (D) II and IV

92. Interest rates have just increased. Investors would expect that the prices of their straight preferred stock would

    (A) increase

    (B) decrease

    (C) remain the same

    (D) first increase then decrease

93. A company has previously issued 4% of $100 par cumulative preferred stock. Over the first three years, the company paid out $9 in dividends. If the company announces a common dividend in the following year, how much does it owe preferred stockholders?

    (A) $3

    (B) $4

    (C) $7

    (D) $16

94. One of your customers wants to purchase preferred stock that would help them reduce inflation risk. Which of the following types of preferred stock would you recommend?

    (A) Participating

    (B) Convertible

    (C) Cumulative

    (D) Noncumulative

95. One of your clients wants to purchase preferred stock but wants to reduce the risk of inflation. You should recommend

(A) straight preferred stock

(B) callable preferred stock

(C) cumulative preferred stock

(D) convertible preferred stock

96. If DEF preferred stock ($100 par) is convertible into common stock for $20, what is the conversion ratio?

(A) 1 share

(B) 5 shares

(C) 20 shares

(D) 100 shares

97. An investor purchases a DEF 4% convertible preferred stock at $90. The conversion price is $25. If the common stock is trading one point below parity, what is the price of DEF common stock?

(A) $21.50

(B) $22.50

(C) $24.00

(D) $26.00

98. With everything else being equal, a preferred stockholder would expect _____ preferred stock to pay the highest dividend.

(A) convertible

(B) straight

(C) callable

(D) cumulative

99. What is the advantage to a corporation issuing callable preferred stock as compared to non-callable preferred stock?

(A) It allows the issuer to take advantage of high interest rates.

(B) The dividend rate on callable preferred stock is lower than that of non-callable preferred stock.

(C) It allows the issuer to issue preferred stock with a lower fixed dividend after the call date.

(D) Callable preferred stock usually has a longer maturity date.

100. Callable preferred stock is most advantageous to the issuer because

(A) the issuer can issue high-dividend stock

(B) the issuer can issue stock with a lower dividend

(C) the issuer can call in the stock at a price less than par value

(D) the issuer can replace stock with a higher dividend with stock with a lower dividend

101. Platinum Edge Corp. is offering 5% participating preferred stock. The 5% represents the

(A) minimum yearly dividend payment

(B) average yearly dividend payment

(C) maximum yearly dividend payment

(D) exact yearly dividend payment

102. In the event of corporate bankruptcy, which of the following preferred shareholders would be paid first?

(A) Variable preferred shareholders

(B) Prior preferred shareholders

(C) Participation preferred shareholders

(D) Callable preferred shareholders

103. The dividend rate on adjustable-rate preferred stock will vary depending on the

(A) Treasury bill rate

(B) Treasury note rate

(C) Treasury bond rate

(D) CPI

104–118 ADRs, Rights, and Warrants

104. Which of the following may be paid dividends?

(A) Right holders

(B) Warrant holders

(C) ADR holders

(D) All of the above

105. An ADR is

(A) a receipt for a foreign security trading in the United States

(B) a receipt for a foreign security trading in the United States and overseas

(C) a receipt for a U.S. security trading overseas

(D) a receipt for a U.S. security trading in the United States and overseas

106. All of the following are benefits of investing in ADRs EXCEPT

(A) the dividends are received in U.S. currency

(B) transactions are completed in U.S. currency

(C) it has low currency risk

(D) it allows U.S. investors to invest overseas

107. All of the following are characteristics of American depositary receipts EXCEPT

(A) they help U.S. companies gain access to foreign dollars

(B) investors do not receive the actual certificates

(C) investors can't vote

(D) dividends are paid in U.S. dollars

108. Holders of American depositary receipts assume which of the following risks?

I.   Liquidity risk

II.   Foreign currency risk

III. Market risk

IV.   Political risk

(A) I, III, and IV

(B) II, III, and IV

(C) I, II, and III

(D) II and III

109. A corporation needs to raise additional capital. Which of the following would help the corporation meet its goal?

(A) Declaring a stock dividend to existing shareholders

(B) A rights distribution to existing shareholders

(C) Calling in their convertible bonds

(D) Splitting their stock 2 for 1

110. All of the following are TRUE about rights offerings EXCEPT

(A) they are short-term

(B) each share of outstanding common stock receives one right

(C) they typically have a standby underwriter

(D) rights are automatically received by preferred stockholders

111. A corporation offering additional shares to existing shareholders would be made through a(n)

    (A) secondary offering

    (B) offering of warrants

    (C) rights offering

    (D) offering of convertible preferred stock

112. The Hanson Hilstrand Corp. is issuing new stock through a rights offering. If the stock trades at $30 and it costs $24 plus two rights to buy a new share, what is the theoretical value of a right cum-rights (prior to ex-rights)?

    (A) $0.50

    (B) $0.75

    (C) $1.00

    (D) $2.00

113. One of your clients owns 80 shares of common stock of a company issuing new shares in a rights offering. The stock trades at $12 per share. The company requires that investors must submit nine rights plus $10 to purchase a new share of stock. Fractional shares automatically become whole shares. How many additional shares may your client purchase, and what is the amount of money that needs to be paid for the new shares?

    I.   8 shares

    II.   9 shares

    III. $80 paid

    IV. $90 paid

    (A) I and III

    (B) I and IV

    (C) II and III

    (D) II and IV

114. Global International World Corporation is proposing an additional public offering of its common stock. According to the terms of its rights offering, current shareholders can purchase the stock for $35 per share plus five rights. If the market price of Global International is $45 after the ex-right date, what is the value of one right?

    (A) $1.00

    (B) $1.50

    (C) $2.00

    (D) $5.00

115. All of the following are TRUE of warrants EXCEPT

    I.   they pay dividends quarterly

    II.   they are equity securities

    III. they are used to buy common stock at a fixed price

    IV. they give the holder a leveraged position

    (A) I and II

    (B) II and III

    (C) II, III, and IV

    (D) III and IV

116. Which of the following is NOT TRUE regarding warrants?

    (A) They are marketable securities.

    (B) They offer investors a long-term right to buy stock at a fixed price.

    (C) They have voting rights.

    (D) Investors do not receive dividends.

117. All of the following are TRUE of warrants EXCEPT

(A) they have a longer life than rights

(B) they are non-marketable securities

(C) they are typically issued in units

(D) the exercise price is above the current market price of the common stock when issued

118. Which of the following are TRUE regarding warrants?

I. Warrants are often issued with a corporation's other securities to make an offering more attractive to investors.

II. Warrants provide a perpetual interest in an issuer's common stock.

III. Holders of warrants have no voting rights.

(A) I and II

(B) I and III

(C) II and III

(D) I, II, and III

Chapter **3**

Corporate and U.S. Government Debt Securities

Whenissuers want to borrow money from the public, they issue debt securities. These issuers include corporations, local governments (municipal bonds), and the U.S. government. Unlike equity securities, holders of debt securities are creditors, not owners.

The Problems You'll Work On

In this chapter, you'll work on questions regarding the following:

>> Understanding the different types of bonds

>> Determining bond prices and yields

>> Comparing the different types of bonds

>> Seeing the benefits and risks of convertible bonds

>> Recognizing the different types of U.S. government securities and their tax benefits

>> Comparing money market instruments

>> Calculating accrued interest when bonds are sold between coupon dates

>> Understanding collateralized mortgage obligations (CMOs) and collateralized debt obligations (CDOs)

What to Watch Out For

Keep the following tips in mind as you answer questions in this chapter:

» Be aware of words that can change the answer you're looking for, such as EXCEPT or NOT.

» Don't jump too quickly to answer a question. Make sure you read each question and answer choice completely before choosing an answer.

» Make sure you understand which type of bond the question is talking about prior to answering because many differences exist.

» Double-check your math when doing calculations.

119–138 Bond Terms, Types, and Traits

119. Which of the following securities is exempt from the Trust Indenture Act of 1939?

  I. T-bonds

  II. GO bonds

  III. Equipment trust bonds

  IV. Revenue bonds

  (A) I only

  (B) II and III

  (C) I, II, and IV

  (D) I, III, and IV

120. Dee Plump, an investor, owns a TUB 5% convertible bond purchased at 103 with five years until maturity. If they hold the bond until maturity, Dee will receive

  (A) $970 plus any outstanding interest

  (B) $1,000 plus any outstanding interest

  (C) $1,015 plus any outstanding interest

  (D) $1,030 plus any outstanding interest

121. One of your clients purchased a 4% ABC convertible bond yielding 5% and convertible at $50. If your client holds the bond until maturity, how much will they receive?

  (A) $1,000

  (B) $1,020

  (C) $1,025

  (D) $1,050

122. ABC Corporate Bonds are quoted at 101⅜. How much would an investor purchasing ten of these bonds pay?

  (A) $1,013.75

  (B) $1,013.80

  (C) $10,137.50

  (D) $10,138.00

123. A bond has increased in value by 50 basis points, which is equal to which TWO of the following?

  I. 0.50%

  II. 5%

  III. $5

  IV. $50

  (A) I and III

  (B) I and IV

  (C) II and III

  (D) II and IV

124. An investor purchased a 4% corporate bond at 98 with ten years to maturity. If the bond is currently trading at 101, how much interest will the investor receive next time they get paid?

  (A) $19.60

  (B) $20.00

  (C) $20.20

  (D) $40.00

125. A corporate bond indenture would include which of the following?

  I. The nominal yield

  II. The rating

  III. Any collateral backing the bond

  IV. The yield to maturity

  (A) I and II

  (B) I and III

  (C) I, III, and IV

  (D) III and IV

126. The indenture of a corporate bond includes the

  (A) current yield

  (B) yield to maturity

  (C) yield to call

  (D) nominal yield

127. One of your clients is interested in bonds with a relatively high level of regular income with only a moderate amount of risk. Which of the following would you recommend?

(A) High-yield bonds

(B) Convertible bonds

(C) Mortgage bonds

(D) Income bonds

128. HIJ Corp. has issued $30 million worth of convertible mortgage bonds, which are convertible for $25. The bonds are callable beginning in March 2020, while the maturity date is March 2040. The bond trades at 98, and the stock trades at $24. The bonds are secured by

(A) rolling stock

(B) the full faith and credit of HIJ Corp.

(C) securities owned by HIJ Corp.

(D) a lien on property owned by HIJ Corp.

129. Corporations may issue which of the following debt securities?

I. Equipment trust bonds

II. Mortgage bonds

III. Double-barreled bonds

IV. Revenue bonds

(A) I and IV

(B) I and II

(C) II, III, and IV

(D) I, II, III, and IV

130. The type of secured bond typically issued by transportation companies is called

(A) a guaranteed bond

(B) a mortgage bond

(C) an equipment trust bond

(D) a collateral trust bond

131. A collateral trust bond is

(A) mainly issued by transportation companies

(B) backed by stocks and bonds owned by the issuer

(C) issued by corporations in bankruptcy

(D) backed by the assets of a parent company

132. Which of the following BEST describes a guaranteed bond?

(A) one that is mainly issued by transportation companies

(B) one that is backed by the assets of another company

(C) one that is issued by corporations in bankruptcy

(D) one that is backed by stocks and bonds held by the issuer

133. Which of the following bonds normally trades without accrued interest?

(A) Treasury notes

(B) Subordinated debentures

(C) Debentures

(D) Income bonds

134. Which type of corporate bond is not backed by any collateral?

(A) Mortgage bonds

(B) Guaranteed bonds

(C) Debentures

(D) Collateral trusts

135. You have a customer who is risk-averse and wants to start investing in bonds. Which of the following should you NOT recommend?

(A) TIPS

(B) Income bonds

(C) AAA rated corporate bonds

(D) T-bonds

136. Mrs. Jones wants to put away money for an 8-year-old child's college tuition. Which of the following investments would be MOST suitable to meet their needs?

(A) Zero-coupon bonds

(B) Growth company common stocks

(C) Growth company preferred stocks

(D) Certificates of deposit

137. Which of the following are TRUE regarding Eurodollar bonds?

I. They must be registered with the SEC.

II. They are U.S.-dollar denominated.

III. They are issued by non-American companies outside of the United States and the issuer's home state.

IV. They are subject to currency risk.

(A) II, III, and IV

(B) I, II and IV

(C) I, II, and III

(D) I, III, and IV

138. Bonds issued by national governments are referred to as

(A) ADRs

(B) sovereign bonds

(C) Eurodollar bonds

(D) global bonds

139–156 Price and Yield Calculations

139. Due to an increase in the money supply, inflation has been running rampant. As a way of combatting the high inflation, the Fed decides to increase the discount rate. Holders of bonds with fixed coupon rates would expect the prices of their bonds to

(A) increase

(B) decrease

(C) remain the same

(D) fluctuate

140. The coupon rate of a bond is the same as the

(A) current yield

(B) nominal yield

(C) yield to call

(D) yield to maturity

141. A 4% bond is purchased at 92 with 25 years until maturity. What is the current yield?

(A) 3.65%

(B) 4%

(C) 4.35%

(D) 4.66%

142. What is the current yield on a T-bond with an initial offering price of $1,000, a current market price of $101.16, and a coupon rate of 4.25%?

(A) 4.19%

(B) 4.25%

(C) 4.37%

(D) 4.41%

143. The basis of a bond is its

(A) yield to call

(B) current yield

(C) yield to maturity

(D) nominal yield

144. An investor buys a 5% callable corporate bond at 95 with 20 years until maturity. The bond was called five years later at 105. What is the yield to call?

(A) 4.3%

(B) 5.7%

(C) 6.3%

(D) 7.0%

145. The discount yield formula would be used for all of the following EXCEPT

(A) Treasury bills

(B) Treasury strips

(C) zero-coupon bonds

(D) Eurodollar bonds

146. A 4% bond has a basis of 3.30%. The bond is trading at

(A) a discount

(B) a premium

(C) par

(D) a price that could be at a discount, at a premium, or at par value depending on the maturity

147. A 6% corporate bond is trading at 101. What yield could an investor expect if purchasing the bond at the current price and holding it ten years until maturity?

(A) 4.76%

(B) 5%

(C) 5.24%

(D) 6%

148. Which of the following is TRUE of bonds selling at a discount?

I. The market price is lower than par value.

II. The current yield is greater than the coupon rate.

III. Interest rates most likely declined after the bonds were issued.

IV. The yield to maturity is greater than the current yield.

(A) I and III

(B) II and III

(C) II, III, and IV

(D) I, II, and IV

149. An investor purchases a bond with a 6% coupon. The bond is callable in ten years at par. The maturity of the bond is 15 years. If the bond is purchased at 102, which of the following is TRUE?

(A) The yield to maturity is higher than the yield to call.

(B) The yield to call is higher than the yield to maturity.

(C) Because the bond is callable at par, the yield to maturity and the yield to call are the same.

(D) The current yield is higher than the nominal yield.

150. The dated date is best described as

(A) the trade date

(B) the settlement date

(C) the date on which a bond begins accruing interest

(D) the issue date

151. An investor buys a new municipal bond on Tuesday, February 18, with coupon dates March 1 and September 1 and a dated date of January 1. How many days of accrued interest does the investor owe?

(A) 47 days

(B) 48 days

(C) 49 days

(D) 50 days

152. One of your clients buys a corporate bond on Monday, May 10, with coupon dates February 15 and August 15. How many days of accrued interest does your client owe?

(A) 85 days

(B) 86 days

(C) 87 days

(D) 88 days

153. Accrued interest is calculated

(A) from the previous coupon date up to but not including the settlement date

(B) from the settlement date up to the following coupon date

(C) from the previous coupon date up to and including the settlement date

(D) from the trade date up to and including the next coupon date

154. Accrued interest on U.S. government securities is calculated by using

I. actual day per month

II. 30-day months

III. a 360-day year

IV. actual days in a year

(A) I and III

(B) I and IV

(C) II and III

(D) II and IV

155. On Thursday, October 19, one of your customers purchases one 4.6% U.S. government bond maturing in 2035. If the coupon dates are January 15 and July 15, how many days of accrued interest does your customer owe?

(A) 94 days

(B) 95 days

(C) 97 days

(D) 101 days

156. If an official statement has a dated date of January 15 but the first coupon payment is set at August 1, the first payment is a(n)

(A) short coupon

(B) intermediate coupon

(C) long coupon

(D) discount payment

157–176 Comparing Bonds

157. Which of the following would affect the liquidity of a bond?

I. The rating

II. The coupon rate

III. The maturity

IV. Call features

(A) I and II

(B) I, II, and III

(C) II, III, and IV

(D) I, II, III, and IV

158. Which of the following is rated by Moody's and Standard & Poor's?

(A) Default risk

(B) Market risk

(C) Systematic risk

(D) All of the above

159. Which of the following Moody's bond ratings are considered investment grade?

I. Aa

II. A

III. Baa

IV. Ba

(A) I and II

(B) I and III

(C) I, II, and III

(D) I, II, III, and IV

160. An investor has $10,000 to invest. Which of the following investments would expose the investor to the LEAST amount of capital risk?

(A) Blue chip stocks

(B) Warrants

(C) Investment grade bonds

(D) Call options

161. One of your clients wants to purchase a corporate bond with a high degree of safety. You have recommended four different bonds with varying credit ratings. Place the following S&P bond ratings from highest to lowest:

    I.   A+

    II. AA–

    III. AA

    IV. AAA

    (A) IV, III, II, I

    (B) IV, I, III, II

    (C) I, IV, III, II

    (D) I, II, III, IV

162. Which of the following is the highest S&P credit rating for high-yield bonds?

    (A) AAA

    (B) BBB

    (C) BB

    (D) C

163. Which of the following is the MOST appealing to the issuer of a corporate bond?

    (A) A high coupon rate

    (B) A put feature

    (C) A high call premium

    (D) Little call protection

164. Which of the following BEST describes the call premium for debt securities?

    (A) The amount that investors paid above par value to purchase the bond in the primary market

    (B) The amount that investors paid above par value to purchase the bond in the secondary market

    (C) The amount that investors must pay to the issuer for having the bond called early

    (D) The amount that the issuer must pay to investors for calling its bonds early

165. The call premium on a callable bond is

    (A) the amount an investor must pay above par value when calling the bonds early

    (B) the amount an issuer must pay above par value when calling its bonds early

    (C) the amount of interest an issuer must pay on its callable bonds

    (D) the difference in interest an issuer must pay on its callable bonds over its non-callable bonds

166. If a bond's YTM is 5%, which of the following would MOST likely be refunded by the issuer?

    I.   Coupon 5.5%, maturing in 2040, callable in 2031 at 103

    II. Coupon 4.5%, maturing in 2040, callable in 2030 at 103

    III. Coupon 4.5%, maturing in 2040, callable in 2030 at 100

    IV. Coupon 5.5%, maturing in 2040, callable in 2031 at 100

    (A) I and II

    (B) II and IV

    (C) III only

    (D) IV only

167. With all else being equal, put bonds would have a coupon rate that is _____ callable bonds.

    (A) lower than

    (B) the same as

    (C) higher than

    (D) cannot be determined

168. MKR Corporation issued 7% callable bonds. In which of the following situations would MKR be most likely to call their bonds?

    (A) If interest rates have decreased

    (B) If interest rates have remained the same

    (C) If interest rates have increased

    (D) If interest rates are fluctuating

169. An anti-dilution clause is important to holders of which of the following debt securities?

(A) Adjustment bonds

(B) Convertible bonds

(C) Income bonds

(D) Zero-coupon bonds

170. DUD Corp. previously issued $5 million par value of convertible bonds. The bonds are convertible at $25 and are issued with an anti-dilution covenant. If DUD Corp. declares a 5% stock dividend, which of the following are TRUE on the ex-dividend date?

I.   The conversion price will increase.

II. The conversion price will decrease.

III. The conversion ratio will increase.

IV. The conversion ratio will decrease.

(A) I and III

(B) I and IV

(C) II and III

(D) II and IV

171. TUV convertible bonds are trading at 98. TUV is convertible into common stock at $20. If the common stock is 10% below parity, what is the price of the common stock?

(A) $8.82

(B) $9.80

(C) $17.64

(D) $19.60

172. Curly Fry Lighting Corporation bonds are convertible at $50. If DIM's common stock is trading in the market for $42 and the bonds are trading for 83, which of the following statements are TRUE?

I.   The bonds are trading below parity.

II. The stock is trading below parity.

III. Converting the bonds would be profitable.

IV. Converting the bonds would not be profitable.

(A) I and III

(B) I and IV

(C) II and III

(D) II and IV

173. A bond is convertible into 25 shares of common stock. The bond trades at 98, and the stock trades at $40. If the bond is called at 102, which of the following is the BEST alternative for an investor?

(A) Allow the bond to be called.

(B) Sell the bond in the market.

(C) Convert the bond and sell the stock.

(D) None of the above.

174. TUV Corp. has issued $10 million worth of convertible mortgage bonds, which are convertible for $40. The bonds are callable beginning in March 2020, while the maturity date is March 2030. The bond trades at 110, and the stock trades at $48. What is the conversion ratio of the bonds?

(A) 10

(B) 16.66

(C) 20

(D) 25

175. A bond is convertible into common stock for $25. If the stock trades at $28, what is the parity price of the bond?

(A) $990

(B) $1,020

(C) $1,040

(D) $1,120

176. One of your clients holds ABC convertible bonds in their portfolio. ABC bonds are convertible into 40 shares of ABC common stock. Your client has the choice of converting the bonds while ABC common stock is trading at $28.50 or allowing the bond to be called at 104. The situation being faced by your client is called

(A) a forced conversion

(B) an arbitrage situation

(C) risk arbitrage

(D) a refunding call

177–200 U.S. Government Securities

177. Treasury bonds issued by the U.S. government are issued in what form?

(A) Book entry

(B) Bearer

(C) Fully registered

(D) Partially registered

178. All of the following are TRUE of T-bills EXCEPT

I. they make semiannual interest payments

II. they are issued with 4-, 13-, and 26-week maturities

III. most T-bills are callable

IV. they are traded on a discount yield basis

(A) I and II

(B) I, II, and III

(C) II and IV

(D) II, III, and IV

179. A security is quoted as follows:

1.933 – 1.835

This is the quote for a

(A) Ginnie Mae

(B) Treasury bill

(C) Treasury note

(D) Treasury bond

180. Which of the following securities earns interest?

I. Treasury bills

II. Treasury bonds

III. Treasury stock

IV. Treasury STRIPS

(A) II only

(B) I, II, and IV

(C) II and III

(D) II and IV

181. Place the following U.S. government securities in order of initial maturity from shortest term to longest term.

I. Treasury notes

II. Treasury bonds

III. Treasury bills

(A) I, II, III

(B) III, II, I

(C) III, I, II

(D) II, I, III

182. Which TWO of the following are TRUE regarding T–STRIPS?

I. Holders do not pay taxes on the interest earned until maturity.

II. Holders must pay taxes on the interest earned annually.

III. Holders receive the principal and interest at maturity.

IV. Holders receive interest semiannually, and principal is paid at maturity.

(A) I and III

(B) I and IV

(C) II and III

(D) II and IV

183. All of the following are benefits of investing in TIPS EXCEPT

(A) a guaranteed profit

(B) they are low-risk investments

(C) the principal keeps pace with inflation

(D) they can be purchased directly through the Treasury Direct system

184. Treasury bonds have initial maturities of

(A) 1 month to 1 year

(B) more than 1 year to 10 years

(C) either 20 or 30 years

(D) between 1 and 30 years

185. The maximum maturity on a T-note is

(A) one year

(B) two years

(C) five years

(D) ten years

186. Which of the following is TRUE of GNMAs?

I. They are considered safer than FHLMCs.

II. They are backed by the U.S. government.

III. They pay interest semiannually.

IV. The interest received by investors is state tax-free.

(A) I and II

(B) II, III, and IV

(C) I and IV

(D) I, II, III, and IV

187. Which of the following agency securities are a direct obligation of the U.S. government?

(A) FHLMC

(B) GNMA

(C) FNMA

(D) FCS

188. Which of the following is NOT TRUE about GNMAs?

(A) They issue pass-through certificates.

(B) They are backed by commercial, FHA, and VA mortgages.

(C) They pay interest semiannually.

(D) The interest received is subject to federal, state, and local taxes.

189. Which of the following are part of the Farm Credit System (FCS)?

I. Federal Home Loan Banks

II. Federal Intermediate Credit Banks

III. Bank for Cooperatives

IV. Federal Land Banks

(A) II, III, and IV

(B) I, III, and IV

(C) I, II, and III

(D) I, II, and IV

190. CMOs typically have one of these TWO S&P ratings:

I. AAA

II. AA

III. A

IV. BBB

(A) I and II

(B) II and III

(C) III and IV

(D) II and IV

191. All of the following are part of a CMO EXCEPT

(A) GNMA

(B) FNMA

(C) SLMA

(D) FHLMC

192. Which TWO of the following are TRUE regarding prepayment of CMOs?

I. As interest rates rise, prepayments increase.

II. As interest rates rise, prepayments decrease.

III. As interest rates fall, prepayments increase.

IV. As interest rates fall, prepayments decrease.

(A) I and III

(B) I and IV

(C) II and III

(D) II and IV

193. One of your customers is interested in investing in collateralized mortgage obligations for the first time. You should disclose to your customer that

(A) because they are made up of GNMA, FNMA, and FHLMC securities, they are guaranteed by the U.S. government

(B) all CMOs carry an equal amount of risk

(C) they are triple tax-free investments

(D) they are subject to prepayment and extension risk

194. Which of the following CMO tranches is supported by a companion tranche?

(A) PAC

(B) Z

(C) PO

(D) IO

195. One of your clients is interested in investing in CMOs for the first time. If your client's main concern is safety, which of the following tranches would you recommend?

(A) Z

(B) TAC

(C) Companion

(D) PAC

196. Companion tranches support

I. PO tranches

II. PAC tranches

III. TAC tranches

IV. IO tranches

(A) I only

(B) II only

(C) II and III

(D) II, III, and IV

197. You are making recommendations to a client. If your client is interested in CMOs, you may compare them to which of the following?

(A) Certificates of deposit

(B) Mortgage bonds

(C) Other CMOs only

(D) FNMAs

198. All of the following are TRUE of collateralized debt obligations EXCEPT

(A) they are known as asset-backed securities

(B) they are always backed by mortgages

(C) they are backed by credit cards, auto loans, and so on

(D) they are liquid investments

199. When recommending CDOs to one of your clients, you may state which of the following?

I.   The loans that determine the value of the CDOs are liquid.

II. CDOs have tranches that have different forms of prepayment and extension risk.

III. CDOs are not suitable for all investors.

IV. They represent the securitization of non-mortgage loans, including credit cards and auto loans.

(A) I only

(B) I and III

(C) II and IV

(D) II, III, and IV

200. One of your smaller clients is interested in purchasing negotiable CDs. You may tell them that this may not be an appropriate investment because the minimum denomination for negotiable CDs is

(A) $25,000

(B) $50,000

(C) $100,000

(D) $500,000

201–206 Money Market Instruments

201. Money market instruments are

(A) short-term debt

(B) long-term debt

(C) common stock

(D) preferred stock

202. Which of the following is NOT TRUE regarding Eurodollar deposits?

(A) They pay a higher rate of interest than U.S. banks.

(B) The interest rate is determined from the discount rate set by the Federal Reserve Board (FRB).

(C) The deposit is denominated in U.S. dollars but held in foreign banks.

(D) The risk is higher than depositing money in U.S. banks.

203. Corporate commercial paper has a maximum maturity of

(A) 30 days

(B) 45 days

(C) 90 days

(D) 270 days

204. Which of the following money market instruments trades with accrued interest?

(A) Treasury bills

(B) Bankers' acceptance

(C) Jumbo CDs

(D) Commercial paper

205. Which of the following is TRUE about commercial paper?

    I.   It trades without accrued interest.

    II. It is backed by the issuer's assets.

    III. It is an exempt security.

    IV. It matures in 270 days or less.

    (A) I, III, and IV

    (B) II and IV

    (C) II, III, and IV

    (D) I, II, and III

206. This money market instrument is guaranteed by a bank and provides capital for importing and exporting.

    (A) American depositary receipts

    (B) Bankers' acceptance

    (C) Eurodollar bonds

    (D) Fed funds

207–208 Structured Products

207. Which of the following debt securities are issued by banks where the amount paid back to investors at maturity depends on the performance of a stock index?

    (A) HOLDR

    (B) ECN

    (C) ETF

    (D) ETN

208. Which TWO of the following are TRUE of equity linked notes?

    I.   They are traded on an exchange.

    II. They are not traded on an exchange.

    III. They have fixed interest payments.

    IV. They have variable interest payments.

    (A) I and II

    (B) I and III

    (C) II and III

    (D) II and IV

Chapter 4

Municipal Bonds

Municipal bonds are ones issued by state governments, local governments, or U.S. territories. Municipalities may issue many types of municipal bonds, but the two main types are GO (general obligation) bonds and revenue bonds. Municipal bonds may be backed by taxes or by a revenue–producing facility.

After you become a licensed registered rep, you may not spend a lot of time selling municipal bonds, but you need to know about them for the Series 7 exam and expect to be tested heavily.

The Problems You'll Work On

When working through the questions in this chapter, be prepared to

>> Compare the differences between GO bonds and revenue bonds.

>> Compare other municipal bonds and notes.

>> Understand the tax treatment of municipal bonds.

>> Determine how new issues of municipal bonds come to market (primary market).

>> Analyze municipal bonds and make recommendations.

>> Remember rules relating to municipal bonds.

What to Watch Out For

This chapter includes a lot of municipal bond questions, so watch out for questions that require you to

>> Recognize the difference between taxable and non-taxable municipal bonds.

>> Understand an investor's needs when answering questions regarding recommendations.

>> Pay attention to key words, like EXCEPT and NOT, that would change your answer choice.

209–227 General Obligation Bonds

209. One of your new clients is interested in purchasing municipal bonds for the first time. Which of the following information should you take into consideration prior to making a recommendation?

    I.   Your client's tax bracket

    II. Your client's home state

    III. The bond's rating

    IV. The bond's maturity

    (A) I and III

    (B) I, II and III

    (C) II, III, and IV

    (D) I, II, III, and IV

210. One of your clients is interested in purchasing municipal GO bonds and is looking for guidance. You can inform them that

    I.   they are issued to fund revenue-producing facilities

    II. they are backed by the taxing power of the municipality

    III. they need approval of voters to be issued

    IV. they are subject to a debt ceiling

    (A) I and IV

    (B) II, III, and IV

    (C) II and III

    (D) I, III, and IV

211. Which of the following municipal securities is backed by the full faith and credit of the issuer?

    I.   GO

    II. Revenue

    III. Double-barreled

    IV. Moral obligation

    (A) I and II

    (B) I and III

    (C) II and IV

    (D) I, III, and IV

212. All of the following are factors that may be examined in analyzing a general obligation bond EXCEPT

    (A) net overall debt per capita

    (B) flow of funds

    (C) assessed property valuations

    (D) traffic fines

213. All of the following are factors that would affect the marketability of municipal bonds EXCEPT

    (A) the credit rating

    (B) the dated date

    (C) the maturity

    (D) the issuer's name

214. Which of the following factors affect the marketability of municipal bonds?

    I.   The maturity

    II. The rating

    III. The issuer's name

    IV. The dated date

    (A) II and III

    (B) II, III, and IV

    (C) I, II, and III

    (D) I, II, III, and IV

215. Park City, Utah, decides to issue general obligation bonds to build an expansive children's park. Which of the following characteristics of the issuer should an investor consider when analyzing this issue of bonds?

  I. Overall debt

  II. Efficiency of the government

  III. Rate covenants

  IV. Flow of funds

  (A) I and II

  (B) II, III, and IV

  (C) III and IV

  (D) I, II, III, and IV

216. Plano, Texas, is issuing $30 million worth of callable general obligation bonds. All of the following are TRUE about the call feature of these bonds EXCEPT

  (A) the call feature makes the bonds less marketable

  (B) callable bonds have a higher coupon rate than non-callable bonds

  (C) the call feature makes the bonds more marketable

  (D) callable bonds are issued with certain degree of call protection

217. Municipal bond insurance protects investors against

  (A) market risk

  (B) liquidity risk

  (C) default risk

  (D) inflation risk

218. Municipal revenue bonds are often insured because

  (A) revenue bond issues in excess of $10 million are required to be insured under MSRB rules

  (B) it increases the credit rating and marketability of the bonds

  (C) it is required under most state laws

  (D) revenue bond issues in excess of $10 million are required to be insured under SEC rules

219. When helping a client compare municipal general obligation bonds from different issuers, you should compare

  I. population trends

  II. the home state

  III. wealth of the community

  IV. diversity of industry within its tax base

  (A) II and III

  (B) II, III, and IV

  (C) I and II

  (D) I, II, III, and IV

220. All of the following could have overlapping debt EXCEPT

  (A) a town

  (B) a city

  (C) a county

  (D) a state

221. Coterminous debt is synonymous with

  (A) direct debt

  (B) overlapping debt

  (C) overall debt

  (D) none of the above

222. Fort Myers has $50 million in debt, while Florida has $1 billion in debt. Fort Myers has a population of 92,000 and has an assessed property value that is 3% of Florida's. What is Fort Myers's direct debt per capita?

(A) $769.23

(B) $1,230.77

(C) $15,384.62

(D) $16,153.85

223. In which of the following instances would a municipal issuer require voter approval prior to bonds being issued?

I. Bonds being issued to build a public school

II. Bonds being issued to build a county jail

III. Bonds being issued to build a toll road

IV. Bonds being issued to build a new airport

(A) II and IV

(B) I and II

(C) III and IV

(D) I, III, and IV

224. Which of the following municipal bodies receives no revenue from ad valorem taxes?

(A) School districts

(B) County governments

(C) State governments

(D) Town governments

225. The largest source of backing for a local GO bond is

(A) property tax

(B) sales tax

(C) income tax

(D) traffic fines and parking tickets

226. An individual owns property with a market value of $220,000 and an assessed value of $235,000. If the tax rate of the municipality is 14 mills, what is the ad valorem tax?

(A) $3,080

(B) $30,800

(C) $3,290

(D) $32,900

227. Which of the following is true about bank-qualified municipal bonds?

(A) Investors may claim a 20% tax deduction of the amount of interest charges for purchases in margin accounts.

(B) Banks may claim a 20% tax deduction of the amount of interest charges for purchases in margin accounts.

(C) Investors may claim an 80% tax deduction of the amount of interest charges for purchases in margin accounts.

(D) Banks may claim an 80% tax deduction of the amount of interest charges for purchases in margin accounts.

228–244 Revenue Bonds

228. Which of the following is NOT a source of funding for municipal revenue bonds?

(A) Airports

(B) Tolls

(C) Property taxes

(D) User fees

229. Municipal revenue bonds may be issued to fund which of the following projects?

I. A toll road

II. A sports stadium

III. A public library

IV. An airport

(A) I, II, and III

(B) I, III, and IV

(C) I and IV

(D) I, II, and IV

230. Which of the following is NOT an important factor when evaluating a revenue bond?

(A) Feasibility study

(B) Property taxes

(C) Flow of funds

(D) Rate covenants

231. New Jersey decides to issue revenue bonds to construct a new highway. The highway will charge tolls to pay off the revenue bond debt. Which of the following are important factors in assessing the safety of the revenue bond being issued?

I. Feasibility reports

II. Debt limitations

III. Flow of funds

IV. Debt per capita

(A) I and III

(B) II and IV

(C) I, III, and IV

(D) II, III, and IV

232. All of the following statements regarding municipal revenue bonds are TRUE EXCEPT

(A) the maturity date of the issue will typically exceed the useful life of the facility backing the bonds

(B) they are not subject to a debt ceiling

(C) they may be issued by interstate authorities

(D) the principal and interest are paid from revenues received from the facility backing the bonds

233. All of the following are factors that may be examined in analyzing a revenue bond EXCEPT

(A) rate covenants

(B) the debt service coverage ratio

(C) the tax base of the municipality

(D) the flow of funds

234. With all else being equal, revenue bonds usually have _____ yields than general obligation bonds.

(A) higher

(B) lower

(C) equal

(D) cannot be determined

235. A bond resolution includes the covenants between the issuer and the

(A) trustee acting for the bondholders

(B) MSRB

(C) syndicate manager

(D) bond counsel

236. All of the following are important in analyzing a general obligation bond issued by a school district EXCEPT

(A) debt ceiling

(B) traffic fines

(C) insurance covenants

(D) property taxes

237. All of the following are important factors when examining the rating of a general obligation bond EXCEPT

(A) the debt ceiling

(B) overlapping debt

(C) debt per capita

(D) covenants

238. Which of the following would NOT affect the credit rating of a general obligation bond?

(A) Rate covenants

(B) Per capita debt

(C) Assessed property values

(D) The tax collection history of the municipality

239. The flow of funds found on the trust indenture is used for municipal

(A) revenue anticipation notes

(B) general obligation bonds

(C) industrial development revenue bonds

(D) revenue bonds

240. An investor is comparing several different issues of revenue bonds and sees that most of them have a net revenue pledge. The first priority under a net revenue pledge is

(A) debt service

(B) operation and maintenance

(C) the sinking fund

(D) the reserve fund

241. When comparing municipal revenue bonds, your client found one that's covered by a gross revenue pledge. This means that the FIRST expense to be paid is

(A) bond principal and interest

(B) operation and maintenance

(C) debt service reserve

(D) renewal and replacement

242. Which of the following is important when analyzing the credit of a municipal revenue bond?

I. Direct debt per capita

II. Net debt to assessed valuation

III. Debt service coverage ratio

IV. Flow of funds

(A) I and II

(B) III and IV

(C) I, II and III

(D) I, III, and IV

243. A municipal revenue bond was issued under a net revenue pledge. The following numbers are reported for the current year:

$76 million in gross revenues

$40 million in operating and maintenance expenses

$10 million in interest expenses

$2 million in principal repayment

What is the debt service coverage ratio?

(A) 2 to 1

(B) 3 to 1

(C) 4 to 1

(D) 5 to 1

244. A municipality generates $30 million in revenues from a facility. The municipality must pay bond interest of $1.5 million, principal of $3 million, and operating and maintenance expenses of $12 million. What is the debt service coverage ratio?

(A) 4 to 1

(B) 6.67 to 1

(C) 10 to 1

(D) 20 to 1

245–260 The Primary Market

245. In a municipal underwriting, which of the following are the most likely scenarios?

I. Revenue bonds sold on a negotiated basis

II. Revenue bonds sold on a competitive basis

III. General Obligation bonds (GO) sold on a negotiated basis

IV. General Obligation (GO) bonds sold on a competitive basis

(A) I and III

(B) I and IV

(C) II and III

(D) II and IV

246. Which of the following must be found on the confirmation of a premium municipal bond transaction that was issued through a negotiated offering?

   I.   The spread of the offering
   II. Yield-to-maturity
   III. Yield-to-call
   IV. The rating

   (A) I and II
   (B) I and III
   (C) I, II, and IV
   (D) I, III, and IV

247. If an issuer wants to choose a syndicate directly to underwrite a new municipal bond issue, what type of underwriting is this?

   (A) Competitive
   (B) Negotiated
   (C) All-or-none
   (D) Fill-or-kill

248. Suffolk County, New York, is issuing bonds through a competitive offering; how do they determine the winning syndicate?

   (A) The proposal with the highest payment
   (B) The proposal with the longest maturity
   (C) The proposal with the lowest interest cost
   (D) The proposal with the lowest spread

249. An official notice of sale contains all of the following EXCEPT

   (A) the bond rating
   (B) interest and payment dates
   (C) method and place of settlement
   (D) the name of the bond counsel

250. Smithtown, New York, is auctioning a block of new bonds to underwriters. What document will Smithtown use to notify potential underwriters about the auction?

   (A) The indenture
   (B) Official statement
   (C) Notice of sale
   (D) Agreement among underwriters

251. Which of the following items can be found on the official notice of sale?

   I.   Call provisions
   II. The name of the bond counsel providing the legal opinion
   III. Maturity structure
   IV. Type of bond

   (A) II and IV
   (B) I, II, and IV
   (C) II and III
   (D) I, II, III, and IV

252. When accepting bids for a municipal bond offering, what is the municipality looking for?

   (A) A syndicate that could sell the issue at the highest price
   (B) A syndicate that could sell the issue at the lowest price
   (C) A syndicate that could sell the issue with the lowest cost to the municipality
   (D) A syndicate that could help the issuer with day-to-day operations

253. A municipality placed a notice of sale in *The Bond Buyer*. The municipal issuer will take into consideration the timing of interest payments when comparing bids. Which of the following methods of interest cost is the issuer using?

   (A) Net interest cost
   (B) True interest cost
   (C) Actual interest cost
   (D) Approximate interest cost

254. A municipality decides to call its general obligation bonds due to mature in 2030 and to finance the call by issuing bonds with a maturity date of 2050. This is known as

(A) pre-refunding

(B) advance refunding

(C) redeeming

(D) refunding

255. Which of the following is the BEST source of information about municipal bonds in the primary market?

(A) the Blue List

(B) *The Bond Buyer*

(C) Thomson Municipal News

(D) EMMA

256. A make whole call provision on a municipal bond means that the issuer must pay bondholders

(A) par value if the entire issue is called

(B) par value plus any accrued interest due if the entire issue is called

(C) a lump sum payment that includes the par value of the bond plus the net present value of future coupon payments that will not be paid as a result of the call

(D) par value plus the next two coupon payments due if the entire issue is called

257. A benefit of adding a sinking fund provision to an issue of municipal bonds generally means that

(A) the bonds can be issued with a lower coupon rate

(B) the bonds can be issued with a shorter maturity

(C) the bonds can be issued with a longer maturity

(D) the bonds can be issued without a call provision

258. This redemption provision on municipal bonds requires an issue to redeem all or a portion of the bond issue in accordance with the prepayment provisions outlined on the bond indenture.

(A) Extraordinary

(B) In-whole

(C) Optional

(D) Mandatory

259. This call provision allows the issuer to call a portion or all of the outstanding bonds on or after a specified date at the redemption price plus accrued interest until the redemption date.

(A) Extraordinary

(B) In-whole

(C) Optional

(D) Mandatory

260. In which of the following circumstances may the issuer of a municipal revenue bond issue an (extraordinary) catastrophe call?

(A) A drop in interest rates occurred.

(B) The facility backing the bond has been condemned due to a hurricane.

(C) The revenues from the facility backing the bonds have dropped by 20% or more from the previous year's revenues.

(D) The bonds have reached the first call date.

261–284 Other Types of Municipal Bonds

261. Special tax bonds are

(A) backed by charges on the property that benefits

(B) backed by excise taxes

(C) types of general obligation bonds

(D) types of moral obligation bonds

262. Which of the following is TRUE of special assessment bonds?

(A) They are backed by charges on the benefitted property.

(B) They are backed by excise taxes.

(C) They require legislative approval to be issued.

(D) They are backed by a revenue-producing facility.

263. A municipality issues revenue bonds. The revenues are not sufficient to meet the debt service payments. If the municipality is able to meet the debt service obligation of the revenue bonds by backing it with its taxing power, the debt is termed

(A) moral obligation bonds

(B) special situation bonds

(C) special tax bonds

(D) double-barreled bonds

264. Which of the following is TRUE of industrial development revenue bonds?

(A) They are backed by municipal taxes.

(B) They are backed by municipal revenues.

(C) They are backed by a corporation.

(D) None of the above.

265. A double-barreled bond is a combination of

I. revenue bonds

II. special tax bonds

III. build America bonds

IV. general obligation bonds

(A) I and II

(B) II and III

(C) II and IV

(D) I and IV

266. Which of the following is TRUE of municipal certificates of participation?

I. They require voter approval prior to being issued.

II. They do not require voter approval prior to being issued.

III. They are a type of revenue bond.

IV. They are a type of GO bond.

(A) I and III

(B) I and IV

(C) II and III

(D) II and IV

267. When purchasing a limited tax general obligation bond, what is limited?

(A) The number of taxpayers backing the bond issue

(B) The type of tax that can be used to back the bond issue

(C) The number of investors who are able to purchase the bond issue

(D) The number of syndicate members who are allowed to sell the bond issue

268. Clint, one of your clients, is interested in investing in municipal bonds for the first time. They are primarily interested in safety. Which of the following should you recommend?

(A) Moral obligation bonds

(B) Public housing authority bonds

(C) Special assessment bonds

(D) Double-barreled bonds

269. An Industrial Development Bond is

(A) backed by charges on the benefitted property

(B) backed by a private user

(C) backed by excise taxes

(D) a bond that requires legislative approval

270. For clients looking for a safe investment, new housing authority bonds would be acceptable because

(A) they are backed by U.S. government subsidies

(B) they are backed by the taxing power of the municipal issuer

(C) they are backed by rental income, which remains constant

(D) they are typically backed by AMBAC insurance

271. Akron, Ohio, has issued revenue bonds to build a local stadium. The indenture of the bonds states that emergency funding from the Ohio State legislature would be pursued in the event that the debt service exceeds revenues. What type of bond is this?

(A) A moral obligation bond

(B) A double-barreled bond

(C) Debentures

(D) BABs

272. A moral obligation bond is

(A) backed by charges on the benefitted property

(B) backed by a private user

(C) backed by excise taxes

(D) a bond that requires legislative approval

273. Uriah Silva is interested in purchasing Miami municipal general obligation bonds. The bonds were originally issued with a serial maturity. If Uriah believes that interest rates are going to drop over the next 20 to 30 years, which maturity would you advise Uriah to buy?

(A) Short-term

(B) Intermediate-term

(C) Long-term

(D) A combination of long-term, short-term, and intermediate-term

274. Municipalities issue _____ bonds.

(A) term, series, and serial

(B) series and serial

(C) term and series

(D) term and serial

275. This type of bond issue has all bonds issued at one time and all maturing at the same time.

(A) Series

(B) Serial

(C) Term

(D) Balloon

276. This type of bond issue has all bonds issued at one time but an equal portion of the issue matures in successive years.

(A) Series

(B) Serial

(C) Term

(D) Balloon

277. A customer purchased an OID 4% municipal bond with ten years to maturity at 90. If the bond is held to maturity, what are the tax consequences?

(A) $900 return of capital, $400 federally tax-free interest, and $100 of taxable accretion over the life of the bond

(B) $900 return of capital and $500 federally tax-free interest over the life of the bond

(C) $1,000 return of capital and $400 federally tax-free interest over the life of the bond

(D) $900 return of capital, $400 taxable interest, and $100 of non-taxable accretion over the life of the bond

278. An investor purchases a 30-year municipal zero-coupon bond on the original issue date 60. The investor holds the bond until maturity and receives $1,000. What are her federal tax consequences?

(A) A long-term capital gain of $400

(B) $400 taxable interest

(C) No tax liability

(D) A short-term capital gain of $400

279. This type of long-term variable-rate municipal bond, which is sold in $25,000 increments, uses a Dutch auction to reset the interest rates on the bonds.

(A) Capital-appreciation bonds

(B) Variable-rate demand obligations

(C) Term bonds

(D) Auction-rate securities

280. One of your clients is interested in adding additional bonds to their portfolio. You may suggest variable rate municipal bonds over other municipal bonds because

(A) they are non-callable

(B) the bond price should remain stable

(C) they are typically puttable bonds

(D) the interest is exempt from federal taxes

281. Variable rate municipal bonds are subject to which of the following risks?

I. Interest rate

II. Liquidity

III. Market

IV. Default

(A) I only

(B) II and IV

(C) II, III, and IV

(D) I, II, III, and IV

282. Which of the following types of municipal bonds would MOST likely be issued to build a bridge?

(A) BABs

(B) PHAs

(C) IDRs

(D) LRBs

283. Investors of this type of bond receive a tax credit equal to 35% of the coupon rate.

(A) IDRs

(B) Direct payment BABs

(C) Tax credit BABs

(D) Special assessment bonds

284. Which of the following municipal bonds allows a municipality to receive from the U.S. government tax credit payments of 35% of the amount of interest paid?

(A) IDRs

(B) Direct payment BABs

(C) Tax credit BABs

(D) Special assessment bonds

285–296 Municipal Notes

285. Which of the following are types of municipal notes?

I. PNs

II. TRANs

III. GANs

IV. RANs

(A) II and IV

(B) I, III, and IV

(C) III and IV

(D) I, II, III, and IV

286. RANs, BANs, TANs, and CLNs are issued by municipalities to

  (A) provide short-term financing
  (B) provide intermediate-term financing
  (C) provide long-term financing
  (D) provide flexible-term financing

287. All of the following are types of municipal notes EXCEPT

  (A) PNs
  (B) AONs
  (C) TRANs
  (D) CLNs

288. Suffolk County is experiencing a temporary cash flow shortage that is expected to last about three months. Which of the following would Suffolk County MOST likely issue to meet its current obligations?

  (A) Construction loan notes
  (B) Tax anticipation notes
  (C) Revenue bonds
  (D) General obligation bonds

289. Which of the following municipal notes are backed by money to be received from a federal grant provided by the U.S. Government?

  (A) RAN
  (B) TAN
  (C) CLN
  (D) GAN

290. Which of the following securities is subject to the LEAST market risk?

  (A) GNMA
  (B) AAA rated GO bonds
  (C) AAA rated corporate bonds
  (D) Bond anticipation notes

291. Which of the following is the highest rating for a bond anticipation note?

  (A) AAA
  (B) Aaa
  (C) MIG1
  (D) MIG4

292. All of the following municipal securities could have a rating of MIG3 EXCEPT

  (A) PNs
  (B) TRANs
  (C) CLNs
  (D) GOs

293. MIG ratings are applied to

  (A) municipal GO bonds
  (B) municipal notes
  (C) municipal revenue bonds
  (D) build America bonds

294. One of your clients is interested in purchasing municipal securities for the first time. You would like to help them purchase a diversified portfolio of municipal securities. All of the following factors are important in municipal diversification EXCEPT

  (A) type
  (B) rating
  (C) amount
  (D) geographical

295. Geographical diversification of municipal bonds would protect against which of the following risks?

  I.   Interest rate
  II. Business
  III. Purchasing power
  IV. Economic

  (A) I, II, and IV
  (B) I and III
  (C) II and IV
  (D) I, II, III, and IV

296. Mr. Mullahy owns the following investments:

> 25 New Jersey 5% GO bonds maturing in 2040 and rated AA
>
> 25 Florida University 6% revenue bonds maturing in 2041 and rated AA
>
> 25 Utah turnpike 6% revenue bonds maturing in 2040 and rated AA

What type of diversification does Mr. Mullahy have?

(A) Maturity

(B) Quality

(C) Quantity

(D) Geographical

297–300 Municipal Fund Securities

297. Qualified tuition plans, ABLE accounts, and local government investment pools are types of

(A) retirement plans

(B) mutual funds

(C) annuities

(D) municipal fund securities

298. Which of the following is NOT TRUE regarding Section 529 educational savings plans?

(A) Contributions are tax-deductible on the state level.

(B) The plan only allows for after-tax contributions on the federal level.

(C) There are no income limits placed on investors of the plan.

(D) Contribution levels vary from state to state.

299. Which of the following municipal fund securities is designed for individuals with provable disabilities and their families?

(A) Section 529 plans

(B) QTPs

(C) ABLE accounts

(D) LGIPs

300. Which TWO of the following are TRUE regarding local government investment pools (LGIPs)?

I. They are exempt from SEC registration.

II. They are not exempt from SEC registration.

III. There is a prospectus requirement.

IV. There is no prospectus requirement.

(A) I and III

(B) I and IV

(C) II and III

(D) II and IV

301–313 Taxes on Municipal Bonds

301. Dallas, Texas, is issuing $100 million general obligation bonds at a discount from par with a coupon rate of 2.5%. If the bonds are issued at 90 and there are 30 years until maturity, how is the discount treated to purchasers of the new issue if the bond is held to maturity?

(A) The discount is accreted annually and not taxed on the federal level.

(B) The discount is accreted annually and treated as federally taxable income each year.

(C) The discount is not accreted annually but treated as taxable income at maturity.

(D) The amount of the discount is treated as a long-term capital gain subject to tax on both the state and federal level.

302. All of the following is subject to federal taxation EXCEPT

    I.   interest on municipal bonds

    II. interest on U.S. government bonds

    III. capital gain on municipal bonds

    IV. cash dividends on stocks

    (A) I only

    (B) I and III

    (C) II, III, and IV

    (D) II and III

303. Which of the following bonds generally have the lowest yields?

    (A) AA rated corporate bonds

    (B) GO bonds

    (C) T–bonds

    (D) Cannot be determined

304. You have a client who is in a high income tax bracket and is looking for income for their investment account. Which of the following should you recommend?

    (A) Municipal zero-coupon bonds

    (B) Municipal GO bonds

    (C) AAA rated corporate bonds

    (D) Aggressive growth funds

305. Tito Sonnen lives in Oregon and is considering purchasing a bond. Tito has settled on either a 4% municipal bond offered by Oregon or a 6% corporate bond offered by Ground and Pound Corp., which has headquarters in Oregon. Tito needs some guidance and would like you to help determine which bond will provide the greatest return. Which of the following information do you need before you can make the appropriate recommendation?

    (A) Tito's place of employment

    (B) Tito's tax bracket

    (C) How long Tito has lived in Oregon

    (D) Tito's other holdings

306. Which of the following investments would provide the BEST after-tax return for an individual in the 28% tax bracket?

    (A) 4.25% treasury bond

    (B) 5% AA rated corporate bond

    (C) 4% GO bond

    (D) 5.5% preferred stock

307. One of your clients who is in the 28% tax bracket is interested in two different debt securities. One of them is a 6% corporate bond, and the other is a 5% municipal general obligation bond. Which of the following is TRUE regarding their investment choices?

    (A) The general obligation bond has a higher after-tax yield.

    (B) The corporate bond has a higher after-tax yield.

    (C) The corporate bond and municipal bond have an equivalent after-tax yield.

    (D) There is not enough information given to determine the after-tax yield.

308. Mr. Jones is in the 31% tax bracket and owns a 6% corporate bond. What is the municipal equivalent yield?

    (A) 3.96%

    (B) 4.14%

    (C) 5.11%

    (D) 5.42%

309. You are in the process of convincing one of your clients to invest in triple tax-free municipal bonds. Which of the following U.S. territories issues municipal bonds that are triple tax-free?

    I.   U.S. Virgin Islands

    II. Puerto Rico

    III. Guam

    IV. Hawaii

    (A) I and IV

    (B) I, II, and IV

    (C) I, II, and III

    (D) I, II, III, and IV

310. Gary Golden is a resident of Atlantic City, New Jersey. Gary purchased 20 New Jersey municipal bonds. What is the tax treatment of the interest that Gary earns on his New Jersey bonds?

(A) It is exempt from local taxes only.

(B) It is exempt from state taxes only.

(C) It is exempt from federal taxes only.

(D) It is exempt from federal, state, and local taxes.

311. One of your customers purchased a pre-refunded municipal bond. The bond will be called in two years at 101. What yield must be shown on the customer's confirmation?

(A) Yield to maturity or yield to call, whichever is lower

(B) Yield to maturity or yield to call, whichever is higher

(C) Yield to call

(D) Yield to maturity

312. A basis point on a $1,000 par value bond is equal to

(A) $0.01

(B) $0.10

(C) $1.00

(D) $10.00

313. A $5,000 par value municipal bond is currently trading at 99. This translates to a dollar price of

(A) $99

(B) $990

(C) $4,950

(D) $4,990

314–331 Municipal Bond Rules

314. Confirmations of trades of municipal bonds must be sent or given to customers at or prior to the settlement date. The regular settlement date for municipal bonds is

(A) on the trade date

(B) 1 business day after the trade date

(C) 2 business days after the trade date

(D) 3 business days after the trade date

315. All of the following would be found on a municipal bond confirmation EXCEPT

(A) the bond rating

(B) the customer's name

(C) the capacity of the trade

(D) the trade date

316. If each of the following municipal bonds is callable at par, which confirmation must show yield to call?

(A) 4% bond trading at a 4.5% basis maturing in 2035

(B) 5% bond trading at a 5.5% basis maturing in 2040

(C) 5% bond trading at a 4.5% basis maturing in 2035

(D) 4.5% bond trading at a 4.5% basis maturing in 2040

317. Which of the following must be included on a customer's confirmation of a municipal securities transaction?

I. The customer's name

II. The capacity of the broker–dealer

III. Par value

IV. Trade date and time of execution

(A) I and IV

(B) I, II and III

(C) I, II, and IV

(D) I, II, III, and IV

318. Advertisements relating to municipal GO bonds must be approved by

(A) the Fed

(B) the SEC

(C) the MSRB

(D) a municipal securities principal

319. All of the following are governed by MSRB rules EXCEPT

(A) issuers

(B) registered reps

(C) broker–dealers

(D) bank–dealers

320. According to MSRB rules, disputes between a customer and a member should be decided by

(A) arbitration

(B) litigation

(C) mediation

(D) code of procedure

321. Under MSRB Rules G–8 and G–9, all brokers, dealers, and municipal securities dealers must keep which of the following records related to municipal securities transactions?

(A) Records concerning primary offerings

(B) Customer complaints

(C) Records relating to political contributions

(D) All of the above

322. According to MSRB Rule G–9, complaints must be maintained by brokerage firms for

(A) 3 years

(B) 4 years

(C) 6 years

(D) a lifetime

323. A quote on municipal securities between one municipal dealer and another is assumed to be

(A) a subject quote

(B) a workout quote

(C) a bona fide quote

(D) a nominal quote

324. Under MSRB Rule G–19, all recommendations to customers must take into consideration which of the following?

I. The customer's time horizon

II. The customer's risk tolerance

III. The customer's liquidity needs

IV. The customer's other investments

(A) I, II, III, and IV

(B) I, III, and IV

(C) II and III

(D) II, III, and IV

325. Which of the following is considered a gift violation according to MSRB Rule G–20?

(A) A $320 round-trip airline ticket for a client to come to the firm

(B) Spending $120 on business lunch with a client

(C) Buying a client season passes to the Yankees

(D) Sending a client a picture of yourself in an $80 frame

326. According to MSRB rules, a municipal securities broker-dealer opening an account for the employee of another firm must

I. notify the employing firm in writing

II. notify the SEC at the time of each trade

III. obtain the approval of the employing firm prior to each trade

IV. send the employing firm a duplicate confirmation after each trade

(A) I and IV

(B) I, III, and IV

(C) II and III

(D) I, II, III, and IV

327. When a municipal securities dealer sells securities from its inventory to a customer, the price must include a markup that is

(A) in line with the 5% markup policy

(B) no more than 1% of the sale if the trade is more than $100,000

(C) fair and reasonable

(D) must be reviewed by the MSRB

328. If a security is being issued to the public through a negotiated offering, confirmations of trades must include

(A) the spread

(B) the rating

(C) the spread and the rating

(D) neither the spread nor the rating

329. A municipal securities dealer pays an unaffiliated person to solicit business on their behalf. According to MSRB Rule G-38, this is allowable

(A) as long as the payment does not exceed 1% of the market price of any sales derived from the solicitor's action

(B) as long as the payment does not exceed 1/2% of the market price of any sales derived from the solicitor's action

(C) under no circumstances

(D) only with prior approval from a municipal securities principal

330. According to MSRB Rule G-37, what is the maximum contribution allowed for a municipal finance professional to a person running for local government office?

(A) $250 per year

(B) $250 per election

(C) $2,500 per year

(D) $2,500 per election

331. According to MSRB rules, which of the following constitutes a control relationship?

(A) More than one employee of a broker-dealer lives in the issuer's municipality.

(B) At least one officer of a broker-dealer lives in the issuer's municipality.

(C) An employee of a broker-dealer holds a position of authority over the municipal issuer.

(D) All of the above.

332–352 Gathering Municipal Bond Info

332. Which of the following would be found on the indenture of a revenue bond?

I. The legal opinion

II. The rating

III. Covenants

IV. Flow of funds

(A) I, II, and III

(B) I, III, and IV

(C) II, III, and IV

(D) I, II, III, and IV

333. The legal opinion for municipal bonds is prepared by the

(A) trustee

(B) municipal issuer

(C) syndicate manager

(D) bond counsel

334. All of the following are responsibilities of the bond counsel EXCEPT

(A) to validate the bond certificate

(B) rating the bonds

(C) to determine that the bond is tax-exempt

(D) to state that any obligation on the indenture is binding on the issuer

335. An unqualified legal opinion for a municipal bond indicates that

(A) a bond attorney did not examine the indenture

(B) the bond attorney guarantees all interest payments will be made

(C) the issuer meets conditions with restrictions

(D) the issuer meets all conditions without restrictions

336. Investors would be able to find information about a municipal issuer's financial condition by examining the

(A) official statement

(B) indenture

(C) notice of sale

(D) prospectus

337. Where would you tell a potential investor that they can find the most information about a municipal bond issue?

(A) The official notice of sale

(B) The final prospectus

(C) The bond indenture

(D) The official statement

338. A municipal bond counsel is responsible for all of the following EXCEPT

(A) making sure the issue is valid and binding on the issuer

(B) making sure that the issue will be federally tax-free

(C) preparing the legal opinion

(D) guaranteeing timely payment of interest

339. A principal at a municipal securities firm must approve all of the following EXCEPT

(A) each new account

(B) each transaction

(C) advertisements sent out by the firm

(D) the preliminary official statement

340. Which of the following BEST describes the visible supply?

(A) 20-year general obligation bonds with 30-year maturities

(B) 20-year general obligation bonds rated AA or better

(C) 30-year revenue bonds with 25-year maturities

(D) The total dollar amount of municipal bonds expected to reach the market in the next 30 days

341. Where would a municipal securities broker-dealer find the visible supply?

(A) *The Bond Buyer*

(B) the Blue List

(C) the Yellow Sheets

(D) Munifacts

342. The BEST indication for the demand for new municipal issues would be found by analyzing

(A) the placement ratio

(B) the visible supply

(C) *The Bond Buyer's* Index

(D) the 11-Bond Index

343. If a municipal issuer is auctioning a block of new bonds to underwriters, what document will the issuer publish to announce the auction?

(A) Syndicate agreement

(B) Indenture

(C) Official statement

(D) Notice of sale

344. A municipal issuer is auctioning a block of new G.O. bonds to underwriters, what would the issuer compare to determine the winning bid?

(A) NIC or TIC

(B) Good faith deposit

(C) Official statement

(D) Syndicate agreement

345. All of the following are found in the Notice of Sale EXCEPT

(A) whether NIC or TIC will be used to determine the winning syndicate

(B) good faith deposit

(C) the rating of the bonds being auctioned

(D) maturity and call provisions of the bonds

346. *The Bond Buyer's* Index is

(A) 25 bonds with 30-year maturities

(B) 20-year GO bonds rated AAA and AA

(C) 20, 20-year GO bonds in the investment grade category

(D) the amount of new issues expected to be offered in the next 30 days

347. *The Bond Buyer's* 11-Bond Index shows the average yield of 11 general obligation bonds rated

I.   AAA

II. AA

III. A

IV. BBB

(A) I only

(B) I and II

(C) I, II, and III

(D) I, II, III, and IV

348. *The Bond Buyer's* 11-Bond Index is comprised of which of the following grades of bonds?

I.   AAA

II. AA

III. A

IV. BBB

(A) I only

(B) I and II

(C) I, II, and III

(D) I, II, III, and IV

349. All of the following could be used to help measure the marketability of a new municipal general obligation bond EXCEPT

(A) credit ratings

(B) the placement ratio

(C) the RevDex

(D) the visible supply

350. *The Bond Buyer* Municipal Bond Index is an index of 40 revenue and GO bonds with an average maturity of

(A) 15 years

(B) 20 years

(C) 25 years

(D) 30 years

351. Which of the following provides a free online site that stores key information about municipal securities for retail, non-professional investors?

(A) EMMA

(B) RTRS

(C) *The Bond Buyer*

(D) The Blue List

352. One of your customers is interested in getting the latest up-to-the-minute pricing information on municipal securities. This information can best be found on

(A) Thomson Municipal News

(B) EMMA

(C) the National Quotation Bureau

(D) MSRB RTRS

Chapter 5

Margin Accounts

Instead of paying for securities in full, investors may buy (or sell short) certain securities on margin. Margin accounts are ones in which the broker–dealer covers a percentage of the securities purchased by investors. The good news is that it gives investors leverage to purchase more securities than they might without margin accounts. In turn, that means a larger commission or markup for you, the registered rep.

Margin isn't a huge topic on the Series 7 exam, but you can score some quick points if you're familiar with its nuances and the math.

The Problems You'll Work On

In this chapter, you'll need to have a good handle on the following:

>> The paperwork required to open a margin account

>> The initial margin required when opening a margin account

>> Long account calculations

>> Short account calculations

>> How to deal with customers who have combined margin accounts

>> How to determine the amount of excess equity

>> Rules for restricted accounts

What to Watch Out For

This chapter involves more math than most of the other chapters, so you have to be careful of

»» Using the correct formula for long accounts and short accounts

»» Making careless math mistakes

»» Remembering the Regulation T requirement and minimum maintenance requirements

»» Making sure you read each question thoroughly before attempting to answer the question

353–359 Margin Paperwork

353. Which of the following securities are exempt from the Regulation T margin requirement?

(A) U.S. Treasury bills

(B) Municipal bonds

(C) U.S. government agency securities

(D) All of the above

354. Which of the following entities determines which securities are marginable?

(A) FINRA

(B) The FRB

(C) The SEC

(D) The OCC

355. Which of the following documents must be sent to a margin customer prior to the signing of the margin agreement?

(A) Credit agreement

(B) Hypothecation agreement

(C) Loan consent form

(D) Risk disclosure document

356. One of your clients opens a long margin account and fills out the required paperwork. Which of the following are TRUE regarding this account?

I. The securities in the account will be held in street name.

II. Your client will be required to pay interest on the debit balance.

III. A decrease in market value would lower the debit balance.

IV. A portion of the securities may be pledged as collateral for a loan.

(A) II and III

(B) I and IV

(C) II, III, and IV

(D) I, II, and IV

357. You are opening a long margin account for one of your customers. You should inform them that they will have to sign

I. a credit agreement

II. a risk disclosure document

III. a hypothecation agreement

IV. a loan consent form

(A) I and II

(B) I, II, and IV

(C) I, III, and IV

(D) II, III, and IV

358. Which of the following margin documents discloses the interest rate to be charged on the debit balance?

(A) The credit agreement

(B) The hypothecation agreement

(C) The loan consent form

(D) The margin interest rate form

359. A margin loan consent form

(A) allows the broker-dealer to provide a loan to the customer

(B) allows the broker-dealer to loan a customer's margined securities to other investors

(C) allows the broker-dealer to borrow money from a bank for margin accounts

(D) is required for both cash and margin accounts

360–362 FRB Rules Relating to Margin Accounts

360. Which of the following securities can be purchased on margin by depositing the Regulation T margin requirement?

I.   Exchange-listed stocks

II. Exchange-listed bonds

III. Mutual funds

IV. IPOs

(A) I and II

(B) III and IV

(C) I and III

(D) III only

361. The deadline for meeting margin calls is

(A) on the trade date

(B) 1 business day after the trade date

(C) 3 business days after the trade date

(D) 5 business days after the trade date

362. An investor opens a margin account by purchasing 100 shares of UPP at $50 per share. What is the margin call if the house margin requirement is 60% and house maintenance is set at 30%?

(A) $1,250

(B) $1,500

(C) $2,500

(D) $3,000

363–368 Initial Margin Requirements

363. What is the minimum equity requirement for a pattern day trader?

(A) $5,000

(B) $10,000

(C) $25,000

(D) $50,000

364. Portfolio margin accounts can be set up for investors who have at least _____ invested in marginable securities?

(A) $25,000

(B) $50,000

(C) $75,000

(D) $100,000

365. In an initial transaction in a margin account, a customer purchases 100 shares of RRR at $18 per share. What is the margin call?

(A) $900

(B) $1,800

(C) $2,000

(D) $2,900

366. One of your customers wants to open a margin account by selling short 100 shares of GHI at $15. What is the margin call?

(A) $750

(B) $1,500

(C) $2,000

(D) $3,000

367. An investor opens a margin account by selling short $5,000 worth of securities. What is the margin call?

(A) $1,500

(B) $2,000

(C) $2,500

(D) $5,000

368. An investor opens a margin account by selling short 100 shares of TV at 30. What is the margin call if Regulation T is 50%?

(A) $750

(B) $1,500

(C) $2,000

(D) $3,000

369–370 Calculating Debt and Equity in Long Margin Accounts

369. One of your clients has a margin account with $30,000 in securities, a $22,000 debit balance, and $3,000 SMA. How much equity does your client have in her account?

(A) $3,000

(B) $5,000

(C) $8,000

(D) $11,000

370. Mr. Flanagan's margin account holds the following securities:

> 100 shares of CSA at $60 per share
>
> 200 shares of TUV at $24 per share
>
> 100 shares of LMN at $18 per share

How much equity is in Mr. Flanagan's margin account if the debit balance is $7,200?

(A) $5,400

(B) $6,300

(C) $7,200

(D) $7,450

371–374 Calculating Debt and Equity in Short Margin Accounts

371. An investor sells short 1,000 shares of LMN at $30. What is the credit balance?

(A) $15,000

(B) $30,000

(C) $45,000

(D) $60,000

372. One of your clients has a combined margin account with the following dollar figures:

> Long market value = $30,000
>
> Short market value = $25,000
>
> Debit balance = $18,000
>
> Credit balance = $40,000
>
> Long account SMA = $1,500

With Regulation T set at 50%, what is the combined equity in your client's account?

(A) $25,500

(B) $27,000

(C) $28,500

(D) $30,000

373. An investor has a combined margin account with a long market value of $35,000 and a short market value of $28,000. The long market value increased to $38,000, and the short market value decreased to $26,000. What change occurs to the equity in the account?

(A) $1,000 increase in equity

(B) $1,000 decrease in equity

(C) $5,000 increase in equity

(D) $5,000 decrease in equity

374. As an initial purchase in a margin account, an investor purchases 1,000 shares of HIJ at $20 per share. With Regulation T at 50%, what is the loan value?

(A) $5,000

(B) $10,000

(C) $15,000

(D) $20,000

375–381 Excess Equity

375. All of the following would increase the SMA in a long margin account EXCEPT

    (A) a cash withdrawal

    (B) a liquidation of securities in the account

    (C) a receipt of cash dividends or earned interest

    (D) a deposit of fully paid marginable securities

376. An investor receives a cash dividend of $2,000 for securities held in a long margin account. How much of the dividend will go to the special memorandum account?

    (A) $0

    (B) $500

    (C) $1,000

    (D) $2,000

377. Mrs. Diamond sells short 1,000 shares of HIJ at $80. If HIJ drops to $70, what is the buying (shorting) power?

    (A) $0

    (B) $7,500

    (C) $15,000

    (D) $30,000

378. Mr. Jones has a margin account with $60,000 market value and $22,000 debit balance. If Mr. Jones wants to purchase an additional $30,000 of stock in this account, what amount must Mr. Jones deposit?

    (A) $5,500

    (B) $7,000

    (C) $8,000

    (D) $15,000

379. One of your clients wants to use the excess equity in their margin account and wants to know what will happen to the debit balance. You can inform them that the debit balance will

    (A) increase

    (B) decrease

    (C) remain the same

    (D) fluctuate

380. An investor has a margin account with $50,000 market value and $18,000 debit balance. If the investor wants to purchase an additional $25,000 of stock in this account, what amount must the investor deposit?

    (A) $5,500

    (B) $7,000

    (C) $12,500

    (D) Cannot be determined

381. An investor has a margin account with market value $46,000 and debit balance $19,500. What is the buying power?

    (A) $3,500

    (B) $7,000

    (C) $8,500

    (D) $17,000

382–392 Restricted Accounts and Minimum Maintenance

382. The margin account of one of your customers is restricted. This means that

  I. the equity in their margin account has fallen below 50% of the long market value

  II. the equity in their margin account has fallen below 25% of the long market value

  III. they cannot borrow any additional money until the margin account is taken out of restricted status

  IV. they have 24 hours to deposit funds to bring it out of restricted status

  (A) I only

  (B) I, III, and IV

  (C) II and III

  (D) II, III, and IV

383. Mr. Steyne sells short 1,000 shares of LMN at $42. If LMN goes up to $44.50, how much is the account restricted?

  (A) 0

  (B) $2,500

  (C) $3,100

  (D) $3,750

384. An investor buys 1,000 shares of LMN at $50 in a margin account. If LMN drops to $40, by how much is the account restricted?

  (A) $1,000

  (B) $3,000

  (C) $5,000

  (D) $10,000

385. Mr. Jones sold short 400 shares of MKR common stock on margin at $40 per share. If MKR is currently trading at $44 per share, how much is the account restricted?

  (A) $2,400

  (B) $6,400

  (C) $8,800

  (D) $16,000

386. Maintenance calls must be paid:

  (A) on demand

  (B) within 1 business day

  (C) within 3 business days

  (D) within 5 business days

387. One of your clients has a long margin account with the following positions:

> 100 TUV at $15
> 200 XYZ at $30
> 500 LMN at $25

What is the minimum maintenance for his account?

  (A) $4,000

  (B) $5,000

  (C) $6,667

  (D) $10,000

388. An investor has a long margin account with a current market value of $12,000, a debit balance of $6,000, and equity of $6,000. How low would the equity have to drop before the investor receives a maintenance call?

  (A) $6,667

  (B) $8,000

  (C) $8,500

  (D) $10,000

389. Under Regulation T, what are the initial and maintenance requirements for long margin accounts?

(A) 50% initial and 25% maintenance

(B) 50% initial and 30% maintenance

(C) 75% initial and 25% maintenance

(D) 70% initial and 30% maintenance

390. What is the minimum maintenance requirement for a short account with a current market value of $25,000?

(A) $6,250

(B) $7,500

(C) $10,000

(D) $12,500

391. Ayla K. sold short 1,000 shares of MKR common stock on margin at $50 per share. If MKR is currently trading at $60 per share, what is the maintenance call?

(A) $0

(B) $2,000

(C) $3,000

(D) $8,000

392. An investor has a short margin account. To determine how high the short market value can rise before the investor receives a maintenance call, you can divide the credit balance by

(A) 70% or 0.7

(B) 80% or 0.8

(C) 120% or 1.2

(D) 130% or 1.3

Chapter 6

Packaged Securities

Packaged securities include investment companies (mutual funds and closed-end funds), real estate investment trusts, annuities, and so on. The idea is to provide investors a way to diversify their portfolios with a relatively small outlay of cash. Pretty much all investors have packaged securities in their portfolio. What's also nice about packaged securities for investors is that usually the funds are professionally managed, and the management fee is relatively small.

In this chapter, you should be aware of which funds are best for which investors according to their investment objectives.

The Problems You'll Work On

In this chapter, you'll work on questions that deal with the following:

» Understanding the different types of funds and making appropriate investment recommendations

» Knowing when investors are eligible for discounts and different methods of investing

» Determining the sales charge and public offering price

» Figuring out how funds are taxed and the rules

» Understanding information about real estate investment trusts (REITs)

» Comparing the differences between fixed and variable annuities

What to Watch Out For

Keep the following tips in mind as you work through this chapter:

>> When you're dealing with questions regarding investment recommendations, make sure you take the customer's investment objectives into consideration first.

>> Know the difference between open- and closed-end funds.

>> Make sure you have a good handle on variable annuities.

>> Get a good grasp of what the question is asking and read all the answer choices before picking an answer.

393–427 Management Investment Companies

393. An investor decides to redeem shares of a mutual fund; at what price will the trade be executed?

(A) The current bid price

(B) The current ask price

(C) The next computed bid price

(D) The next computed ask price

394. Which of the following is TRUE about closed-end funds?

I. They may issue only common stock.

II. They are generally listed on an exchange.

III. They have a fixed number of shares outstanding.

IV. They are redeemable.

(A) II and III

(B) I and IV

(C) I, III, and IV

(D) II, III, and IV

395. While reading a newspaper, an investor notices that the NAV of a fund increased by $0.80 while the POP decreased by $0.20. What type of fund does this have to be?

(A) Open-end

(B) Closed-end

(C) No-load

(D) Balanced

396. Redemptions of mutual fund shares take place at the

(A) next computed NAV

(B) next computed POP

(C) current NAV

(D) current POP

397. Which of the following is NOT TRUE of open-end investment companies?

(A) They offer shares to the public continuously.

(B) Their public offering price can't be below the net asset value.

(C) They charge commissions to customers who purchase shares.

(D) They may not lend money to customers to purchase shares.

398. You may tell one of your clients that closed-end investment companies

I. continuously issue new shares

II. make a one-time offering of new shares

III. may issue preferred stock

IV. may issue bonds

(A) II only

(B) I only

(C) I, III, and IV

(D) II, III, and IV

399. One of your clients would like to purchase a mutual fund on margin. You should inform them that

(A) mutual funds can't be purchased on margin

(B) to purchase on margin, they must sign a letter of intent

(C) the minimum deposit to purchase mutual funds on margin is $25,000

(D) the minimum deposit to purchase mutual funds on margin is $100,000

400. Blommerman closed-end fund has an NAV of $27.65 and a POP of $27.52. Purchasers of this fund would pay

(A) $27.52

(B) $27.52 plus a sales charge

(C) $27.52 plus a commission

(D) $27.65

401. Which TWO of the following are TRUE regarding open-end funds?

I. They allow for conversion privileges within the family of funds.

II. The do not allow for conversion privileges.

III. They allow for automatic reinvestment of dividends and capital gains.

IV. They do not allow for automatic reinvestment of dividends and capital gains.

(A) I and III

(B) I and IV

(C) II and III

(D) II and IV

402. Systematic withdrawal plans may be set up to redeem

(A) a fixed number of shares periodically or a fixed dollar amount periodically

(B) a fixed number of shares periodically or for a fixed period of time

(C) a fixed dollar amount periodically or a fixed period of time

(D) shares over a fixed period of time, a fixed number of shares periodically, or a fixed dollar amount periodically

403. For an investment company to avoid being taxed as a corporation, it must distribute _____ % of its net investment income to shareholders.

(A) 70

(B) 75

(C) 90

(D) 95

404. For an investment company to be considered diversified, it must meet

(A) the 75-5-10 test

(B) the 80-20 test

(C) the 90-5-5 test

(D) the 70-20-5 test

405. All of the following are TRUE about money market funds EXCEPT

(A) they offer a check-writing feature as a way of redeeming shares

(B) investors are prohibited from redeeming the money market fund for a year

(C) they are no-load

(D) they compute dividends daily and credit them monthly

406. You have a client who has never invested in mutual funds and doesn't know where to start. You should inform them that the MOST important thing is a fund's

(A) sales charge

(B) 12b1 fees

(C) management fees

(D) investment objectives

407. An investor is looking to invest in a mutual fund that has a high rate of current income. Their BEST choice would be a

(A) hedge fund

(B) growth fund

(C) aggressive growth fund

(D) income fund

408. Which of the following investments would be MOST suitable for a married couple in their mid-20s who have already maxed out their IRA contributions?

(A) DPPs

(B) Commodities

(C) Growth funds

(D) Buying index call options

409. One of your clients would like to invest in a mutual fund that has capital appreciation as its main investment objective. Which of the following types of funds should you recommend?

(A) Specialized

(B) Income

(C) Balanced

(D) Money market

410. An individual primarily interested in current income would be LEAST likely to buy which of the following funds?

(A) A municipal bond fund

(B) A sector fund investing in high-tech stocks

(C) A high-yield bond fund

(D) An income fund

411. A mutual fund holds a portfolio of securities that consists of stocks of corporations in the process of releasing new products. This type of fund is a

(A) specialized fund

(B) dual-purpose fund

(C) special situation fund

(D) life-cycle fund

412. An investor is concerned about the U.S. economy and wishes to add diversification to their stock portfolio. Which of the following funds should a rep recommend?

(A) A global fund

(B) An aggressive growth fund

(C) An international fund

(D) A specialized fund that invests in household appliance companies

413. After a mutual fund's tenth year, performance statistics must show results for which of the following periods?

I. One year

II. Three years

III. Five years

IV. Ten years

(A) II and III

(B) I, III, and IV

(C) I, II, and IV

(D) II, III, and IV

414. You have a new 35-year-old client who is interested in investing in a mutual fund. They are looking to invest $400 per month and want a fund that will minimize risk as they get older. You should recommend a(n)

(A) aggressive growth fund

(B) life-cycle fund

(C) money market fund

(D) tax-free municipal bond fund

415. One of your clients is interested in purchasing a fund. If liquidity is high on their list of investment objectives, which of the following would be the LEAST suitable recommendation?

(A) ETFs

(B) Inverse ETFs

(C) Hedge funds

(D) Money market funds

416. A 60-year-old investor is interested in purchasing a fund that provides tax-free income and a high degree of safety. Which of the following funds would you recommend?

(A) An insured municipal bond fund

(B) A high-yield bond fund

(C) A money market fund

(D) A fund of hedge funds

417. You have a client who has a high current income and is in the top federal income tax bracket. They are interested in purchasing a bond fund. The BEST suggestion would be

(A) a U.S. government bond fund

(B) a municipal bond fund

(C) a money market fund

(D) cannot be determined

418. An investor who purchases 50 shares of the same mutual fund each month is executing which method of investment?

(A) Dollar cost averaging

(B) Fixed share averaging

(C) A constant dollar plan

(D) Market timing

419. A letter of intent may be backdated up to

(A) 30 days

(B) 60 days

(C) 90 days

(D) 120 days

420. A client invests $15,000 into ABC Balance Fund and signs a letter of intent for $20,000 to qualify for a breakpoint. ABC has been doing quite well, and, even without additional investments, 12 months later, your client's shares are worth $22,000. Which of the following is TRUE?

(A) ABC will sell shares held in escrow to make up for the lost sales charge revenue.

(B) Because your client has more than $20,000 invested, their letter of intent contract is satisfied.

(C) You should remind your client that they have another month to invest an additional $5,000 into ABC.

(D) All shares will be redeemed at the NAV, and the proceeds less the adjusted sales charge will be returned to your client.

421. One of your clients deposits $1,000 on the first of each month into AGG Aggressive Growth Fund. The purchase price per share for AGG Aggressive Growth Fund on the first of each month for the time the client has been purchasing is as follows:

Month 1: $20

Month 2: $25

Month 3: $40

Month 4: $50

Month 5: $50

What is the average cost per share paid by your client?

(A) $32.26

(B) $35.22

(C) $37.00

(D) $40.00

422. What is the maximum sales charge for mutual funds?

(A) 5% of the NAV

(B) 8.5% of the NAV

(C) 5% of the amount invested

(D) 8.5% of the amount invested

423. DIMCO Growth Fund has an NAV of $13.20 and a POP of $14.00. What is the sales charge percent?

(A) 4.3%

(B) 5.7%

(C) 6.9%

(D) 7.8%

424. The public offering price of a mutual fund is

(A) the net asset value + the sales charge

(B) the net asset value − the sales charge

(C) the net asset value × the sales charge

(D) the net asset value + the sales charge

425. AMP Growth Fund has a net asset value (NAV) of $29.26 and a public offering price of $31.40. If there is a 5% sales charge for investments of $20,000 and up, how many shares can an investor who is depositing $40,000 purchase?

(A) 1,273.885 shares

(B) 1,298.701 shares

(C) 1,301.956 shares

(D) 1,311.423 shares

426. For investors who intend to purchase and hold mutual funds for many years, which load would be most advantageous?

(A) Class A

(B) Class B

(C) Class C

(D) Class D

427. Which class of mutual fund shares charge investors a level load?

(A) Class A

(B) Class B

(C) Class C

(D) Class D

428–432 Face-Amount Certificate Companies, UITs, and ETFs

428. This type of investment company is most similar to a zero-coupon bond.

(A) Open-end fund

(B) Closed-end fund

(C) Unit investment trust

(D) Face-amount certificate company

429. Which of the following types of investment companies invests in a fixed portfolio of securities and charges no management fees?

(A) UIT

(B) REIT

(C) Face amount certificate company

(D) Mutual fund

430. All of the following are TRUE about exchange traded funds (ETFs) EXCEPT

(A) they may be sold short

(B) they may trade on an exchange or over the counter

(C) they offer new securities only once

(D) they offer redeemable securities

431. One of your clients is bearish on the market. Which of the following investment choices would be appropriate for this client?

(A) Selling short an index fund

(B) An inverse exchange-traded fund

(C) A hedge fund

(D) Selling short a dual-purpose fund

432. When explaining the difference between exchange-traded funds and mutual funds, you can say that unlike mutual funds, exchange-traded funds

I.   can be sold short

II. can be purchased on margin

III. represent a basket of securities

IV. provide real-time pricing

(A) I, II, and III

(B) II and III

(C) II, III, and IV

(D) I, II, and IV

433–437 Real Estate Investment Trusts

433. Which of the following securities is actively traded in the secondary market?

(A) open-end funds

(B) unit investment trusts

(C) REITs

(D) all of the above

434. All of the following are types of REITs EXCEPT

(A) equity

(B) mortgage

(C) double-barreled

(D) hybrid

435. Which of the following is TRUE of mortgage real estate investment trusts (REITs)?

(A) The REIT must generate at least 75% of income from construction and mortgage loans.

(B) The REIT must generate at least 75% of income from ownership of properties.

(C) The REIT must generate at least 75% of income from a combination of ownership of properties and construction loans.

(D) The REIT may not invest in securities such as stocks and bonds.

436. A REIT must distribute at least _____ of its income to shareholders to avoid being taxed as a corporation.

(A) 25%

(B) 75%

(C) 90%

(D) 95%

437. Which of the following are TRUE about REITs?

I. At least 75% of the trust's gross income must be earned from real estate–related projects.

II. They may not use any of their assets to purchase securities.

III. They don't have to be registered with the SEC.

IV. They are redeemable securities.

(A) I only

(B) I, II, and III

(C) II, III, and IV

(D) I, III, and IV

438–449 Fixed and Variable Annuities

438. Variable annuities must be registered with

I. the SEC

II. the State Banking Commission

III. the State Insurance Commission

IV. the NYSE

(A) I and II

(B) II and IV

(C) I and III

(D) II, III, and IV

439. All of the following securities are covered under the Investment Company Act of 1940 EXCEPT

(A) open-end funds

(B) fixed annuities

(C) closed-end funds

(D) variable annuities

440. The investment risk in a variable annuity is assumed by

(A) the holder of the policy

(B) the insurance company

(C) 60% by the insurance company and 40% by the policyholder

(D) none of the above

441. All of the following are TRUE of variable annuities EXCEPT

(A) the securities held in the separate account are professionally managed

(B) securities held in the separate account may be mutual funds

(C) investors are protected against capital loss

(D) they are more likely to keep pace with inflation than fixed annuities

442. One of your clients has a variable annuity contract with an AIR of 4.25%. Last month, the actual net return to the separate account was 5.75%. If your client is currently in the payout phase, how would this month's payment compare to the AIR?

(A) It will be the same.

(B) It will be higher.

(C) It will be lower.

(D) It cannot be determined until this month is over.

443. Which of the following annuity options would hold accumulation units?

I.   Single payment deferred annuity

II. Periodic payment deferred annuity

III. Immediate annuity

(A) II only

(B) I and II

(C) II and III

(D) I, II, and III

444. A 25-year-old investor has just received a very large inheritance and wants to purchase a variable annuity. Which of the following purchase options would be BEST for this investor?

(A) Immediate annuity with deferred payment

(B) Periodic payment deferred annuity

(C) Single payment immediate annuity

(D) Single payment deferred annuity

445. John Silverhouse has been investing in a variable annuity for 30 years and is about to retire. When receiving payouts from his variable annuity, John will receive

(A) a variable number of accumulation units based on the value of his annuity units

(B) a variable number of annuity units based on the value of his accumulation units

(C) a fixed number of accumulation units based on the value of his annuity units

(D) a fixed number of annuity units based on the value of his accumulation units

446. One of your clients is interested in purchasing a variable annuity that would provide the largest monthly payment. Which of the following options would be MOST suitable for this client?

(A) Life income annuity

(B) Life with period certain annuity

(C) Joint and last survivor annuity

(D) Not enough information given to answer this question

447. Which of the following payout options for variable annuities would provide the largest monthly payment to annuitants?

(A) Straight life annuity

(B) Life annuity with period certain

(C) Joint and survivor annuity

(D) Unit refund

448. Investors holding a variable annuity receive payments for life. This is called a

(A) life-payment guarantee

(B) mortality guarantee

(C) deferred guarantee

(D) post-payment guarantee

449. The owner of a variable annuity dies during the accumulation phase; the death benefit will be paid to

(A) the IRS

(B) the account holder's estate

(C) the insurance company

(D) the designated beneficiary

450–453 Variable Life and Variable Universal Life Insurance

450. Individuals selling the following must have not only the appropriate securities license but also an insurance license.

I. Variable annuities

II. Variable life policies

III. Variable universal life policies

(A) I and II

(B) II and III

(C) I and III

(D) I, II, and III

451. Which TWO of the following are TRUE about variable life insurance policies?

I. The minimum death benefit is guaranteed.

II. The minimum death benefit is not guaranteed.

III. The minimum cash value is guaranteed.

IV. The minimum cash value is not guaranteed.

(A) I and III

(B) II and III

(C) I and IV

(D) II and IV

452. Which TWO of the following are TRUE about variable universal life insurance policies?

I. The minimum death benefit is guaranteed.

II. The minimum death benefit is not guaranteed.

III. The minimum cash value is guaranteed.

IV. The minimum cash value is not guaranteed.

(A) I and III

(B) II and III

(C) I and IV

(D) II and IV

453. All of the following are possible 1035 tax free exchanges EXCEPT

(A) variable annuity to variable life insurance

(B) whole life to universal life

(C) fixed annuity to variable annuity

(D) whole life to fixed annuity

454–456 Investment Company Rules

454. According to Section 10 of the Investment Company Act of 1940, the board of directors of an investment company must be made up of

(A) no more than 10% insiders

(B) no more than 30% insiders

(C) less than 50% insiders

(D) no more than 60% insiders

455. Under what circumstances may an investment company change its classification from diversified to non-diversified?

(A) If voted for by a majority of its outstanding voting securities

(B) If voted on by a majority of shareholders

(C) If voted for by at least 60% of its outstanding voting securities

(D) Under no circumstances

456. Mutual funds must send financial statements to shareholders

(A) monthly

(B) quarterly

(C) semiannually

(D) annually

Chapter 7

Direct Participation Programs

Direct participation programs (DPPs) are more commonly known as limited partnerships. DPPs raise money to invest in projects such as real estate, oil and gas, and equipment leasing. DPPs aren't for everyone because investors (limited partners) need to be prescreened by the registered representative and then accepted by the general partner.

DPPs are unique to other investments and even have their own tax category (passive). You should be prepared to answer questions about what makes these investments different.

The Problems You'll Work On

In this chapter, you should be ready to answer questions regarding

>> The roles and responsibilities of the general partner and limited partners

>> The different partnership paperwork

>> The difference between partnership taxes and other investment taxes

>> The three main types of partnerships

What to Watch Out For

Be careful not to get tripped up by common mistakes, such as the following:

>> Mixing up the roles of the general and limited partners

>> Not reading each question thoroughly before choosing an answer

>> Not understanding that the limited partnerships have their own unique tax category

>> Thinking that everyone is eligible to (or should) invest in a direct participation program

457–465 DPPs, General Partners, and Limited Partners

457. Marge is a 54-year-old investor from Utah who is looking to add some liquidity to their portfolio. All of the following investments would help Marge meet that goal EXCEPT

(A) an aggressive growth fund

(B) an oil and gas limited partnership

(C) blue chip stocks

(D) Treasury bills

458. Which TWO of the following corporate characteristics are the easiest for a limited partnership to avoid?

I. Having perpetual life

II. Providing limited liability

III. Having a centralized management

IV. Having free transferability

(A) I and III

(B) I and IV

(C) II and III

(D) II and IV

459. Which of the following is a benefit of investing in a direct participation program?

(A) Limited liability

(B) Pass through of income and losses

(C) Professional management

(D) All of the above

460. Which of the following is TRUE regarding a limited partner assisting a general partner to solicit new investors to the partnership?

(A) It is permitted as long as the limited partner is not compensated.

(B) It could jeopardize the status of the limited partner.

(C) It is allowed as long as outlined in the agreement of limited partnership.

(D) None of the above.

461. The general partner of an oil and gas developmental program is responsible for all of the following EXCEPT

(A) paying the partnership's expenses

(B) managing the partnership

(C) providing a bulk of the capital for the partnership

(D) accepting new limited partners

462. The ones who assume the most risk in an oil and gas limited partnership are

(A) limited partners

(B) general partners

(C) limited partners and general partners assume equal amount of risk

(D) it depends on how the partnership is set up

463. A general partner has

(A) an active role and unlimited liability

(B) an active role and limited liability

(C) an inactive role and unlimited liability

(D) an inactive role and limited liability

464. Which of the following partnerships are limited partners allowed to claim non-recourse debt as a tax deduction?

(A) Equipment leasing

(B) Oil and gas wildcatting

(C) Oil and gas developmental

(D) Real estate

465. Limited partners may

I. compete with the partnership

II. inspect the partnership books

III. vote to terminate the partnership

IV. make management decisions for the partnership

(A) I, II, and III

(B) I, III, and IV

(C) II, III, and IV

(D) I, II, and IV

466–471 Partnership Paperwork

466. Which of the following documents are required by a limited partnership?

  I.   Subscription agreement

  II. Certificate of limited partnership

  III. Registration form

  IV. Partnership agreement

  (A) I, II, and III

  (B) II, III, and IV

  (C) I, II, and IV

  (D) I, II, III, and IV

467. Which of the following partnership documents outlines the rights and responsibilities of the general and limited partners?

  (A) Certificate of limited partnership

  (B) Partnership agreement

  (C) Subscription agreement

  (D) Both (A) and (B)

468. Which of the following would require an amendment to a certificate of limited partnership?

  I.   A change in the sharing arrangements between the limited and general partners

  II. A typographical error on the exiting certificate of limited partnership

  III. An increase in the contributions made by the limited and/or general partner

  (A) I and II

  (B) II and III

  (C) I and III

  (D) I, II, and III

469. Which of the following partnership documents needs to be filed with the SEC prior to making a public offering?

  (A) Certificate of limited partnership

  (B) Agreement of limited partnership

  (C) Subscription agreement

  (D) All of the above

470. Which of the following investments would require written proof of the client's net worth?

  (A) A variable annuity contract

  (B) An aggressive growth fund

  (C) A face amount certificate company

  (D) An oil and gas limited partnership

471. Which of the following documents must a general partner sign to accept a new limited partner?

  (A) A prospectus

  (B) A certificate of limited partnership

  (C) An agreement of limited partnership

  (D) A subscription agreement

472–473 Types of DPP Offerings

472. Which of the following is TRUE regarding DPP private placements?

  (A) The amount of accredited limited partners is limited.

  (B) It is considered an exempt offering under Regulation D.

  (C) It is considered a nonexempt offering.

  (D) They are not allowed under SEC rules.

473. Which of the following is TRUE regarding DPP public offerings?

   (A) Initial limited partner contributions are typically lower than that of DPP private placements.

   (B) Limited partners need to be prescreened.

   (C) Investors must receive a prospectus.

   (D) All of the above.

474–476 Passive Income and Losses

474. Losses from a real estate direct participation program can be used to offset which of the following?

   I.   Income from an oil and gas partnership

   II. Earned income

   III. Portfolio income

   IV. Capital gains from a REIT

   (A) I only

   (B) IV only

   (C) II and III

   (D) I, II, III, and IV

475. Which of the following does NOT describe the tax status of a limited partnership?

   (A) Any gains generated are taxed as capital gains.

   (B) Any income generated is taxed as ordinary income.

   (C) The partnership is fully taxed by the IRS.

   (D) The tax liability flows through to the limited and general partners.

476. Losses from an oil and gas DPP can be used to offset

   (A) earned income

   (B) capital gains distributions from a mutual fund

   (C) losses from an equipment leasing DPP

   (D) income from a real estate DPP

477–496 Evaluating Direct Participation Programs

477. When evaluating a direct participation program for a customer, you should look at

   I.   the economic soundness of the program

   II. the experience and/or expertise of the general partner(s)

   III. the objectives of the program

   IV. the startup costs involved

   (A) I, II, and III

   (B) II and IV

   (C) II and III

   (D) I, II, III, and IV

478. One of your wealthy clients would like to invest in a real estate partnership that provides stability of income. Which of the following should you recommend?

   (A) Raw land

   (B) Condominiums

   (C) Section 8

   (D) New construction

479. All of the following are risks associated with investing in a new construction real estate DPP EXCEPT

(A) competing projects

(B) increases in building costs

(C) economic downturns

(D) depletion

480. An investor in an undeveloped land limited partnership is mostly concerned with

(A) depletion

(B) depreciation

(C) appreciation

(D) cash flow

481. Which of the following is TRUE of a real estate program blind pool offering?

(A) Income is mainly produced from Section 8 housing.

(B) At least 25% of the partnerships properties are not specified.

(C) They typically only invest in commercial properties.

(D) None of the above, blind pool offerings are only associated with oil and gas programs.

482. Which of the following types of real estate DPPS have the fewest write-offs?

(A) Raw land

(B) New construction

(C) Existing properties

(D) Public housing

483. All of the following are likely to be part of an equipment leasing partnership EXCEPT

(A) computers

(B) oil well drill heads

(C) construction equipment

(D) moving trucks

484. Which of the following is NOT a benefit of investing in a long-term equipment leasing program?

(A) A steady stream of income

(B) Depreciation deductions

(C) Capital appreciation potential

(D) Operating expenses to help offset revenues

485. Which of the following is TRUE regarding equipment leasing programs?

(A) An operating lease is riskier than a full payout lease and allows for depreciation write-offs.

(B) A full payout lease is riskier than an operating lease and allows for depreciation write-offs.

(C) An operating lease is riskier than a full payout lease and does not allow for depreciation write-offs.

(D) A full payout lease is riskier than an operating lease and does not allow for depreciation write-offs.

486. Which of the following are considered intangible drilling costs (IDCs) of an oil and gas wildcatting program?

I.   Wages

II. Earned income

III. Storage tanks

IV. Insurance

(A) I, III, and IV

(B) II and IV

(C) II and III

(D) I, II, III, and IV

487. Which of the following would be considered a tangible drilling cost (TDC) of an oil and gas partnership?

(A) Fuel costs

(B) Equipment hauling expenses

(C) Wages for employees

(D) Well equipment

488. Which of the following partnerships could claim depletion deductions?

    I.   Real estate

    II. Oil and gas

    III. Equipment leasing

    (A) I only

    (B) II only

    (C) I and III

    (D) II and III

489. Oil and gas program depletion deductions are based on the amount of oil

    (A) stored

    (B) extracted

    (C) lost

    (D) sold

490. All of the following are advantages of investing in a real estate limited partnership EXCEPT

    (A) appreciation potential

    (B) depreciation deductions

    (C) depletion deductions

    (D) cash flow

491. Which of the following types of partnerships has the highest IDCs?

    (A) Exploratory

    (B) Raw land

    (C) Existing property

    (D) Income

492. John Wegner is a limited partner in a real estate DPP that invests in public housing. John receives passive income that exceeds the passive deductions by a significant amount, and John would like to shelter more of his passive income. Which of the following recommendations would be appropriate for John?

    (A) Oil and gas exploratory program

    (B) Oil and gas developmental program

    (C) Oil and gas income program

    (D) Real estate program that invests in existing properties

493. Rank the following oil and gas limited partnerships from safest to riskiest.

    I.   Income

    II. Developmental

    III. Exploratory

    (A) I, II, III

    (B) II, I, III

    (C) III, I, II

    (D) III, II, I

494. Frack-for-Life Oil and Gas partnership drills only in proven areas. This is considered a(n)

    (A) exploratory program

    (B) developmental program

    (C) income program

    (D) combination program

495. The main tax benefit for investors of an oil and gas income program is

    (A) depletion deductions

    (B) depreciation deductions

    (C) intangible drilling costs (IDCs)

    (D) tangible drilling costs (TDCs)

496. Tito Rousey wants a diversified oil and gas investment portfolio. Which of the following oil and gas partnerships offers the MOST diversification?

    (A) An exploratory program

    (B) An income program

    (C) A combination program

    (D) A developmental program

Chapter 8

Options

O ptions are also known as derivatives because they derive their value from the value of an underlying security. Options give the holder the right to buy or sell the underlying security at a fixed price for a fixed period of time. Options give holders a leveraged position because they have an interest in a large amount of securities for a relatively small outlay of cash. Options are risky investments and aren't for everyone because of the likelihood of losing all the money invested.

Options are one of the more heavily tested areas on the Series 7 exam. Although you may have heard horror stories about how tough options are, using an options chart makes life much easier. You can expect at least as many questions in which you don't need an options chart as ones that you do, so don't spend all your time just practicing calculations.

The Problems You'll Work On

To work the problems in this chapter, you need to

>> Be familiar with the option basics, such as what is a put and what is a call.

>> Figure out questions related to straddles and combinations.

>> Understand option spreads, recognize option markets, and remember option rules.

>> Recognize the best option positions for someone who already owns the stock.

>> Calculate maximum gains, losses, and break-even points for investors who own multiple option contracts.

>> Determine what happens when an underlying stock splits or receives a dividend.

>> Know the basics of currency, LEAPS, yield, and index options.

What to Watch Out For

Here are a couple things to watch out for when working with option questions:

>> Don't focus entirely on the calculations; you're likely going to get more questions that don't require an options chart than do.

>> When using an options chart, make sure you put the numbers on the correct side of the chart.

497–509 Option Basics

497. Which of the following transactions may be executed in a cash account?

I. The purchase of a call option

II. The sale of a covered call option

III. The short sale of a stock

IV. The sale of a naked option

(A) I only

(B) I and II

(C) I and III

(D) III and IV

498. Unless otherwise stated, a stock option contract represents

(A) 1 share of the underlying security

(B) 10 shares of the underlying security

(C) 100 shares of the underlying security

(D) 1,000 shares of the underlying security

499. Standard option contracts are issued with an expiration of

(A) 6 months

(B) 9 months

(C) 12 months

(D) 39 months

500. An October 40 call option is two days away from expiration. The current market value of the underlying stock is 52. What is the most likely premium?

(A) 0.754

(B) 2

(C) 12.25

(D) 16

501. An ABC call option premium increased by 0.65. What is the dollar amount of the increase?

(A) $0.65

(B) $6.50

(C) $65.00

(D) $650.00

502. Bullish option strategies include

I. buying calls

II. buying puts

III. writing in-the-money calls

IV. writing in-the-money puts

(A) I and III

(B) I and IV

(C) II and III

(D) II and IV

503. One of your clients is convinced that DWN common stock will decline in value over the next few months. Which investment strategy would you recommend to your client that would allow them to take advantage of the expected decline with the smallest cash investment?

(A) Buying a DWN call option

(B) Buying a DWN put option

(C) Shorting DWN stock

(D) Buying a DWN straddle

504. A call option is in the money when the market price of the underlying security is

(A) above the strike price

(B) above the strike price plus the premium

(C) below the strike price

(D) below the strike price minus the premium

505. Which of the following option contracts are in the money when UPP is trading at 43.50?

I. Short UPP 35 call

II. Short UPP 40 put

III. Long UPP 40 call

IV. Long UPP 50 put

(A) I, III, and IV

(B) II and IV

(C) III and IV

(D) I, II, and III

506. Which option is out of the money if ABC is at $40?

(A) ABC May 45 put

(B) ABC May 35 call

(C) ABC May 50 call

(D) ABC May 55 put

507. Which of the following would affect the premium of an option?

I. Volatility of the underlying security

II. The amount of time until the option expires

III. The intrinsic value

(A) I and II

(B) II and III

(C) I and III

(D) I, II, and III

508. A QRS Dec 50 call is trading for 9 when QRS is at $55. What is the time value of this option?

(A) 0

(B) 4

(C) 5

(D) 9

509. A LMN Dec 45 put is trading for 3.5 when LMN is at $47.50. What is the time value of this option?

(A) 0

(B) 1

(C) 2.5

(D) 3.5

510–529 Option Basics

510. An investor would face an unlimited maximum loss potential if

I. writing 3 XYZ Dec 25 puts

II. shorting 200 shares of XYZ

III. writing 4 XYZ Dec 30 naked calls

IV. writing 2 XYZ Dec 30 covered calls

(A) I and II

(B) I and III

(C) II and III

(D) II and IV

511. Which of the following is the riskiest option strategy?

(A) Buying calls

(B) Buying puts

(C) Selling uncovered calls

(D) Selling uncovered puts

512. An investor who is long a call option realizes a profit if exercising the option when the underlying stock price is

(A) above the exercise price plus the premium paid

(B) below the exercise price

(C) below the exercise price minus the premium paid

(D) above the exercise price

513. Mr. Couture is long one MMA Feb 40 call at 1.75. If MMA is currently trading at $39.50, what is Mr. Couture's break-even point?

(A) $37.75

(B) $38.25

(C) $41.25

(D) $41.75

514. An investor writes an RST Dec 60 call for 7. What is this investor's maximum potential gain?

(A) $700

(B) $5,300

(C) $6,700

(D) Unlimited

515. An investor who writes a put has the

(A) right to buy stock at a fixed price

(B) right to sell stock at a fixed price

(C) obligation to buy stock at a fixed price if exercised

(D) obligation to sell stock at a fixed price if exercised

516. When selling an uncovered put, an investor would realize a profit in all of the following situations EXCEPT

(A) the price of the underlying stock increases in value above the strike price of the option

(B) the premium of the put option decreases

(C) the option expires unexercised

(D) the option is exercised when the price of the underlying stock is below the strike price minus the premium

517. Use the following exhibit to answer this question:

RST	Strike	Jun	Sep	Dec
50.50	40	12.20	14.40	15.90
50.50	40p	a	0.60	1.30
50.50	50	2.10	3.35	5.10
50.50	50p	1.50	2.80	4.15

p = put   a = not traded

What is the maximum potential gain for an investor who sells an RST Dec 50 put?

(A) $150

(B) $415

(C) $4,585

(D) Unlimited

518. Declan K. writes a naked put option on WIM common stock. What is the maximum loss per share that Mr. Drudge can incur?

(A) Strike price minus the premium

(B) Strike price plus the premium

(C) The entire premium received

(D) Unlimited

519. An investor sells one HIJ Jun 40 put at 6; what is the break-even point?

(A) 34

(B) 40

(C) 46

(D) Cannot be determined

520. An investor is sold one WXYZ Jan 35 put at 3.5 when WXYZ was trading at $36.10. What is the investor's break-even point as a result of this transaction?

(A) 31.5

(B) 32.6

(C) 38.5

(D) 39.6

521. With no previous positions in an account, Mr. Jones writes an XYZ May 75 put for 6.62 while XYZ trades at 63.25. If XYZ later closes at 60.88, what is Mr. Jones's break-even point?

(A) 54.25

(B) 56.63

(C) 68.38

(D) 81.63

522. The break-even point for an investor who is short a put is

(A) the market price minus the premium

(B) the market price plus the premium

(C) the strike price minus the premium

(D) the strike price plus the premium

523. If holding which of the following positions would an investor deliver the stock if exercised?

(A) Long a call or short a call

(B) Long a call or short a put

(C) Long a put or short a call

(D) Long a put or short a put

524. With no other positions, an investor writes one LMN Dec 60 call at 5. This is a (n)

(A) opening purchase

(B) opening sale

(C) closing purchase

(D) closing sale

525. A customer buys one HIJ Oct 40 call at 6 and one HIJ Oct 40 put at 2. Six months later, the call is closed for 1, and the put is closed for 4. What is the customer's gain or loss?

(A) $100 gain

(B) $100 loss

(C) $300 gain

(D) $300 loss

526. One of your customers wants to liquidate a long option. How would you mark the option order ticket?

(A) Opening purchase

(B) Opening sale

(C) Closing purchase

(D) Closing sale

527. An investor purchases an EFG May 70 put for 4 and writes an EFG May 90 put for 12. If the investor closes the 70 put for 6 and the 90 put for 15, what is the gain or loss?

(A) $100 gain

(B) $100 loss

(C) $500 gain

(D) $500 loss

528. An investor with no other position in RST writes one RST Dec 40 put at 3.25. If the put option is exercised when RST is trading at 37.50 and the investor immediately sells the stock in the market, what is their gain or loss excluding commissions?

(A) $75 loss

(B) $75 gain

(C) $575 loss

(D) $575 gain

529. One of your clients purchases 100 shares of DEFG at 45.10 and 1 OEX Sep 790 put at 4.50. A few months later, DEFG is trading at 43.55, and the OEX index is trading at 779. If your client closes the stock position and exercises their OEX put, what is their gain?

(A) $155

(B) $495

(C) $1,100

(D) $3,535

530–571 Straddles, Combinations, and Spreads

530. Which of the following option positions is a long straddle?

(A) Buying a call and selling a call

(B) Buying a put and selling a put

(C) Selling a call and selling a put

(D) Buying a call and buying a put

531. An investor who sees a stock with a high beta would most likely apply which of the following option strategies?

(A) Bullish spread

(B) Short combination

(C) Long straddle

(D) Short a put

532. Investors who own a long-straddle or long-combination position are hoping for the underlying stock to be

(A) bullish

(B) bearish

(C) volatile

(D) stable

533. An investor buys one LMN Sep 55 call at 6.5 and one LMN Sep 55 put at 3.2. This investor would see a profit with LMN trading at

(A) $44.70

(B) $55.00

(C) $57.30

(D) $64.70

534. Holders of which of the following option positions are looking for volatility?

I.   Long straddle

II. Short straddle

III. Long combination

IV. Short combination

(A) I and II

(B) III and IV

(C) I and III

(D) II and IV

535. An investor buys a DDD Jun 50 put for 5 and buys a DDD Jun 45 call for 2. This investor has created a

(A) long straddle

(B) long combination

(C) short straddle

(D) diagonal spread

536. An investor is long one CDE Nov 35 call for 4 and one CDE Nov 35 put for 7. CDE drops to 22 just prior to expiration. The investor buys the stock in the market and exercises the put. After the call expires, what is the gain or loss?

(A) $200 gain

(B) $200 loss

(C) $1,600 gain

(D) $1,600 loss

537. What is the maximum potential gain for an investor who purchased a straddle?

(A) The premiums

(B) The difference between the exercise price minus the premiums

(C) The difference between the premiums minus the difference between the exercise prices

(D) Unlimited

538. An investor buys an ABC May 40 call for 9 and buys an ABC May 40 put for 5 when ABC trades at $45. ABC increases to $60, and the investor exercises the call and allows the put to expire. Two weeks later, the investor sold the stock in the market for $58. What is the gain or loss?

(A) $400 gain

(B) $400 loss

(C) $600 gain

(D) $600 loss

539. An investor sells a DEF at-the-money straddle. This investor is

(A) bullish on DEF

(B) bearish on DEF

(C) neutral on DEF

(D) cannot be determined

540. These investors are looking for the price of the underlying security to remain stable.

I. Buyers of an at-the-money straddle

II. Sellers of an at-the-money straddle

III. Buyers of an out-of-the-money combination

IV. Sellers of an out-of-the-money combination

(A) I and III

(B) I and IV

(C) II and III

(D) II and IV

541. One of your clients is holding DUD common stock. You and your client believe that DUD's market price will stay at roughly the same price for the next year. Which of the following option positions would you recommend for the client to be able to generate some additional income on DUD?

(A) Buy a DUD combination.

(B) Write a DUD straddle.

(C) Buy a DUD call.

(D) Buy a DUD put.

542. One of your customers wants to create a short straddle on TUV common stock. Your customer is already short one TUV Sep 40 call. What other position would you tell your customer they need?

(A) Long one TUV Sep 45 put

(B) Long one TUV Sep 40 put

(C) Short one TUV Sep 35 put

(D) Short one TUV Sep 40 put

543. An investor with no other positions shorts an XYZ Dec 35 straddle while XYZ is trading at 35. This investor is looking for XYZ to

(A) increase in value

(B) decrease in value

(C) remain stable

(D) either Choice (A) or (B)

544. Holders of which of the following option positions face the greatest risk?

(A) Long straddle

(B) Short combination

(C) Short (credit) spread

(D) Long (debit) spread

545. An investor shorts one TUB Aug 40 call for 7 and shorts one TUB Aug 35 put for 3. What are the investor's break-even points?

(A) 32 and 47

(B) 30 and 45

(C) 25 and 50

(D) 28 and 43

546. Which of the following positions would be profitable to an investor who is long a straddle?

I. When the market value of the underlying security is above the combined premiums added to the strike price

II. When the market value of the underlying security is below the combined premiums subtracted from the strike price

III. When the market value of the underlying security is above the strike price minus the premiums

IV. When the market value of the underlying security is below the strike price plus the premiums

(A) I or II

(B) I or III

(C) II or III

(D) II or IV

547. An investor buys 1 TUV Aug 60 put for 7 and buys 1 TUV Aug 55 call for 2. What are the investor's break-even points?

(A) 53 and 57

(B) 51 and 64

(C) 55 and 60

(D) 46 and 69

548. Which of the following are spreads?

I.   Long 1 ABC Jun 30 call/short 1 ABC Jun 40 call

II.   Long 1 ABC Jun 30 call/long 1 ABC Jun 40 call

III. Long 1 ABC Sep 30 call/short 1 ABC Jun 30 call

IV.   Long 1 ABC Sep 30 call/short 1 ABC Sep 40 put

(A) I and III

(B) I and II

(C) II and III

(D) II and IV

549. An investor sells an HIJ May 50 call and buys an HIJ May 60 call. Which TWO of the following describe this spread?

I.   Bullish

II.   Bearish

III. Debit

IV.   Credit

(A) I and III

(B) I and IV

(C) II and III

(D) II and IV

550. Use the following exhibit to answer this question:

	BID	OFFER
ZAM Dec45 call	5	5.25
ZAM Dec45 put	4	4.25
ZAM Dec50 call	1	1.25
ZAM Dec50 put	7	7.25

How much would an investor creating a long (debit) call spread have to pay?

(A) $200

(B) $225

(C) $300

(D) $325

551. A customer is long one DEF Aug 80 call at 2 and writes one DEF Aug 70 call at 5. This position is called a

(A) bullish call spread

(B) bearish call spread

(C) long straddle

(D) short combination

552. A client shorts one LMN Feb 55 put at 6 and longs one LMN Feb 45 put at 1 while LMN is trading at 55. Your client is

(A) bullish on LMN

(B) bearish on LMN

(C) bullish/neutral on LMN

(D) bearish/neutral on LMN

553. What is the market attitude of a client who establishes a debit put spread?

(A) Bullish

(B) Bearish

(C) Neutral

(D) Speculative

554. Which of the following would create a short spread?

(A) Buying a call at a low strike price and selling a call at a high strike price

(B) Buying a put at a high strike price and selling a put at a low strike price

(C) Buying a call with a long expiration and selling a call with a short expiration

(D) Buying a put at a low strike price and selling a put at a high strike price

555. Which of the following is a credit spread?

(A) Long 1 ABC Dec 60 call/short 1 ABC Dec 70 call

(B) Long 1 DEF Nov 70 put/short 1 GHI Nov 55 put

(C) Long 1 JKL Sep 40 call/short 1 JKL Sep 30 call

(D) Long 1 MNO May 30 put/short 1 MNO May 20 put

556. An investor buys a WXY Dec 40 call for 9 and writes a WXY Oct 60 call for 2. What is the maximum gain?

(A) $300

(B) $700

(C) $1,300

(D) $2,000

557. Mr. Levin writes one JKL Aug 60 put for 6 and buys one Aug 75 put for 12. What is Mr. Levin's maximum potential gain?

(A) $600

(B) $900

(C) $1,500

(D) Unlimited

558. Use the following exhibit to answer this question:

	BID	OFFER
GHI Sep 40 call	5	5.25
GHI Sep 40 put	4	4.25
GHI Sep 50 call	2	2.25
GHI Sep 50 put	8	8.25

How much would an investor creating a debit call spread have to pay (disregarding commissions)?

(A) $300

(B) $325

(C) $375

(D) $425

559. One of your clients purchased one DEF May 40 call at 8 and sold one DEF May 50 call at 2. You can inform her that her break-even point is

(A) $34

(B) $42

(C) $46

(D) $50

560. Stan Goldhouse sold one XYZ Jul 65 put at 5 and purchased one XYZ Jul 60 put at 2. What is Stan's break-even point?

(A) $53

(B) $62

(C) $67

(D) $72

561. An investor is short one LMN Oct 60 put at 6 and long one LMN Oct 50 put at 2. What is the investor's break-even point?

(A) 46

(B) 54

(C) 56

(D) 64

562. Mrs. Jones bought one DEF Oct 40 put and wrote one DEF Nov 50 put. Mrs. Jones has created a

(A) vertical spread

(B) horizontal spread

(C) diagonal spread

(D) long combination

563. Which of the following is a bearish spread?

(A) Long one DEF Feb 40 call/short one DEF Feb 50 call

(B) Long one XYZ Oct 30 put/short one XYZ Dec 40 put

(C) Long one TUV Aug 60 put/short one QRS Aug 50 put

(D) Long one HIJ Dec 80 call/short one HIJ Nov 70 call

564. Mrs. Smith buys one HIJ June 60 call for 8 and sells one HIJ June 80 call for 3. Mrs. Smith has established a

(A) vertical spread

(B) horizontal spread

(C) diagonal spread

(D) long straddle

565. A client who wants to create a spread on XYZ and is bullish on XYZ would

I. create a vertical long call spread on XYZ

II. create a vertical short call spread on XYZ

III. create a vertical long put spread on XYZ

IV. create a vertical short put spread on XYZ

(A) I and III

(B) I and IV

(C) II and III

(D) II and IV

566. An ABC horizontal call spread has

(A) different expiration months

(B) different strike prices

(C) different securities

(D) Choices (A) and (B)

567. An investor who writes an ABC August 40 put for 9 and buys an ABC October 50 put for 13 has taken which TWO of the following positions?

I. Vertical spread

II. Diagonal spread

III. Credit spread

IV. Debit spread

(A) I and III

(B) I and IV

(C) II and III

(D) II and IV

568. Mr. Silver purchased an STU Sep 30 put at 2 and also wrote an STU Sep 40 put at 7. Mr. Silver will be able to make a profit if

I. both options expire unexercised

II. both options are exercised

III. the premium difference narrows to less than 5

IV. the premium difference widens to more than 5

(A) I or III

(B) I or IV

(C) II or III

(D) II or IV

569. What is the maximum potential gain on a debit call spread?

(A) The difference between the exercised strike prices minus the difference between the premiums

(B) The difference between the exercised premiums less the premium received plus the premium paid

(C) The difference between the premium paid less the premium received

(D) The difference between the strike prices plus the cost of the two premiums

570. An investor has created a long (debit) spread. In order to make a profit, this investor wants the

   I.   option premium difference to narrow

   II.   option premium difference to widen

   III.   options to be exercised

   IV.   options to remain unexercised

(A) I and III

(B) I and IV

(C) II and III

(D) II and IV

571. An individual is long 1 DEF Jun 40 call and short 1 DEF Jun 50 call. This is a

(A) debit bull spread

(B) credit bull spread

(C) credit bear spread

(D) debit bear spread.

572–604 Stock and Options

572. If an investor sells a covered call on stock owned in an account, which of the following is TRUE?

(A) The premium increases the cost basis.

(B) The premium decreases the cost basis.

(C) The investor has unlimited risk.

(D) The trade must be executed in a margin account.

573. Which of the following would cover the sale of an XYZ Aug 60 put?

(A) Long 100 shares of XYZ

(B) Long 1 XYZ Aug 50 call

(C) Long 1 XYZ Aug 50 put

(D) Long 1 XYZ Aug 70 put

574. An investor who writes a DEF call option would be considered covered if owning any of the following positions EXCEPT

(A) DEF convertible bonds convertible into 100 shares of DEF common stock

(B) an escrow receipt for the stock from a bank

(C) a DEF call option with the same expiration month and a lower strike price

(D) 100 shares of DLQ stock

575. Which of the following is TRUE regarding an investor who purchased 100 shares of MKR at 50 and wrote 1 Oct 55 call at 3?

(A) The investor is bullish on MKR, and they have a maximum gain potential that is unlimited.

(B) The investor is bullish on MKR, and their upside is limited.

(C) The investor is bearish on MKR, and they have a maximum gain potential that is unlimited.

(D) The investor is bearish on MKR, and their upside is unlimited.

576. Mr. Goldshack purchases 100 shares of RST at 47.50 per share and sells 1 RST Oct 50 call at 3.25. What is Mr. Goldshack's maximum potential loss?

(A) $250

(B) $4,425

(C) $5,175

(D) Unlimited

577. Zeb Zeldin purchased 1 RST 45 put at 2.75 and 100 shares of RST at 51. A few months later, with RST trading at 53.50, Zeb closes their put for 0.50 and sells their stock at the market. What is Zeb's gain or loss as a result of these transactions?

(A) $25 gain

(B) $25 loss

(C) $475 gain

(D) $475 loss

578. One of your clients purchases 100 shares of DEF at $54 per share and subsequently writes a DEF May 60 call for 5. If DEF increases to 73 and the call is exercised, what is your client's gain?

(A) $100

(B) $1,100

(C) $2,400

(D) $2,900

579. One of your clients is long 100 shares of WIZ stock originally purchased at $32.50 per share. Your client subsequently wrote a WIZ Jun 35 call at 3.25 when WIZ was trading at $34.10 per share. What is your client's maximum potential loss?

(A) $2,925

(B) $3,085

(C) $3,575

(D) $3,735

580. An investor buys 100 shares of TUV at $40 and writes 1 TUV Jun 50 call for 6. What is this investor's maximum potential gain?

(A) $600

(B) $1,600

(C) $3,400

(D) Unlimited

581. Todd Goldflow purchases 100 shares of HLP at 25 and writes a 30 call at 3.25. If HLP stock increases to 40 and the call is exercised, Todd has a(n)

(A) $175 loss

(B) $175 gain

(C) $825 loss

(D) $825 gain

582. Mr. Hendricks owns 100 shares of TUF common stock. The price of TUF has been trading between 51 and 53 for the past year. Mr. Hendricks likes the stock but wants to generate some additional income. You should suggest that he

(A) write a TUF call

(B) buy a TUF put

(C) write a TUF put

(D) buy a TUF call

583. An investor shorts 100 shares of TUV at 44.50 and 1 TUV Aug 40 put at 3. What is the investor's break-even point?

(A) $37.00

(B) $41.50

(C) $43.00

(D) $47.50

584. The break-even point for covered call writers is

(A) the stock price plus the premium

(B) the stock price minus the premium

(C) the exercise price plus the premium

(D) the exercise price minus the premium

585. Mr. Steele purchased 100 shares of RST at $60 and wrote an RST May 80 call for 5. What is Mr. Steele's break-even point?

(A) 65

(B) 75

(C) 55

(D) 85

586. An investor purchases 400 shares of SSS Corp. at $32.50 per share and purchases 4 SSS Nov 30 puts at 4.5. What is the investor's break-even point?

(A) $25.50

(B) $28.00

(C) $34.50

(D) $37.00

587. An investor sold short 100 shares of DWN common stock at 47.50 and purchased 1 DWN Oct 50 call at 3.25. What is this investor's break-even point?

(A) $44.25

(B) $46.75

(C) $47.50

(D) $50.75

588. Buying a put option on a long stock position is an appropriate strategy when the market is expected to

(A) rise sharply

(B) fall sharply

(C) remain stable

(D) become volatile

589. Mr. Gold has shorted LMN common stock at 34. LMN common stock has recently dropped to 28, and Mr. Gold expects that the price will continue to decrease over the long term. If Mr. Gold wants to hedge against a possible increase in the price, he should

(A) buy an LMN call option

(B) sell an LMN call option

(C) buy an LMN put option

(D) buy an LMN straddle

590. Alyssa H. purchased 100 shares of DEF at 60 and wrote 1 DEF Oct 65 call at 3. Which of the following other positions would create a cashless collar?

(A) Long 1 DEF Oct 55 put at 2

(B) Long 1 DEF Oct 57 put at 3

(C) Short 1 DEF Oct 55 put at 2

(D) Short 1 DEF Oct 57 put at 3

591. An investor wrote ten uncovered puts on DWN common stock. What is the maximum potential loss?

(A) Unlimited

(B) The premium received

(C) (strike price − the premium) × 100 shares × 10 options

(D) (strike price + the premium) × 100 shares × 10 options

592. Sandy Silver purchased two GHI 35 calls and pays a premium of 4.5 for each option. Sandy also purchased two GHI 35 puts and pays a premium of 2 for each option. At the time of purchase, GHI was trading at $51.75. Just prior to expiration, GHI is trading at $36.25, and Sandy decides to close their options for their intrinsic value. Excluding commission, Sandy had a

(A) $525 loss

(B) $525 gain

(C) $1,050 loss

(D) $1,050 gain

593. Mike Mineshaft shorted three XYZ Oct 40 calls for a premium of $300 per option. Two months later, Mike closed their option positions for $260 per option. What was Mike's gain or loss?

(A) $40 loss

(B) $40 gain

(C) $120 loss

(D) $120 gain

594. An investor is long two HIJ Oct 40 calls at 6 each and short two HIJ Oct 50 calls at 2 each. What is the investor's maximum potential loss?

(A) $400

(B) $600

(C) $800

(D) $1,200

595. An investor purchased 400 shares of XYZ at 52 and 4 XYZ Aug 50 protective puts at 3.50 each. What is this investor's maximum potential gain?

(A) $600

(B) $800

(C) $1,400

(D) Unlimited

596. A client purchases 500 shares of ABC at 36 and buys 5 ABC Jun 35 puts at 4 each. What is your client's break-even point?

(A) 31

(B) 32

(C) 39

(D) 40

597. An investor purchases ten DEF Oct 40 call LEAPS at 4. The LEAPS expire in 30 months. If they are purchased on margin, what is the margin call?

(A) $2,000

(B) $3,000

(C) $4,000

(D) Options cannot be purchased on margin.

598. One of your clients purchases three LEAPS in the market with two years left until expiration. If the LEAPS expire out of the money, what is the investor tax consequence at expiration?

(A) Short-term capital gain

(B) Short-term capital loss

(C) Long-term capital gain

(D) Long-term capital loss

599. All of the following are TRUE about LEAPS EXCEPT

(A) they have a longer life than other listed options

(B) they are available only on index options

(C) they may be exercised at any time

(D) they have higher premiums than shorter-term options

600. LMN declares a stock dividend. What will happen to LMN option contracts as a result of the dividend?

(A) The number of contacts will increase, and the strike price will decrease.

(B) The number of shares per contract will increase, and the stock price will decrease.

(C) The number of contracts will decrease, and the strike price will increase.

(D) The number of shares per contract will decrease, and the strike price will increase.

601. If a 20% stock dividend is declared for HIJ stock, the owner of one HIJ Aug 30 call will own

(A) one HIJ contract for 100 shares with a strike price of 30

(B) one HIJ contract for 120 shares with a strike price of 25

(C) two HIJ contracts for 60 shares with a strike price of 30

(D) two HIJ contracts for 60 shares with a strike price of 25

602. When a corporation splits its stock evenly, what happens to holders of options on that stock?

- (A) The number of contracts will increase, and the strike price will decrease.
- (B) The number of shares per contract will increase, and the stock price will decrease.
- (C) The price of the stock will increase, and the number of contracts will decrease.
- (D) The price of the stock will increase, and the number of shares per contract will decrease.

603. An investor owns four HIJ Oct 40 calls. If HIJ announces a 5-for-2 split, what is the investor's new position after the split?

- (A) Ten HIJ Oct 40 calls, 250 shares each
- (B) Ten HIJ Oct 16 calls, 250 shares each
- (C) Four HIJ Oct 16 calls, 250 shares each
- (D) Four HIJ Oct 40 calls, 100 shares each

604. An investor owns four LMN Oct 60 calls. If LMN announces a 3-for-1 split, what is the investor's new position?

- (A) 4 LMN Oct 20 calls, 300 shares each
- (B) 4 LMN Oct 60 calls, 300 shares each
- (C) 12 LMN Oct 20 calls, 100 shares each
- (D) 12 LMN Oct 60 calls, 100 shares each

605–615 Non-equity Options

605. If a client is bullish on the S&P 500, which of the following option strategies would the client use?

- I.   Buy SPX calls.
- II. Buy SPX puts.
- III. Buy VIX calls.
- IV. Buy VIX puts.

- (A) I and III
- (B) I and IV
- (C) II and III
- (D) II and IV

606. An investor who buys SPX put options is

- (A) bearish on the market
- (B) bullish on the market
- (C) bearish on SPX common stock
- (D) bullish on SPX common stock

607. What is the maximum potential loss for an investor who is long an index put option?

- (A) The premium paid
- (B) The strike price minus the premium multiplied by 100 shares
- (C) The strike price plus the premium multiplied by 100 shares
- (D) The strike price multiplied by 100 shares

608. If an investor exercises an OEX call option, what form of delivery should they expect?

(A) 100 shares of OEX

(B) Cash equal to the intrinsic value of the option times 100 shares at the end of the exercise day

(C) Cash equal to 100 shares of OEX

(D) None of the above

609. If an investor exercises an OEX index call option, which of the following would be acceptable delivery from the seller of the call?

(A) 100 shares of the OEX index

(B) Cash equal to the market value of 100 shares of the OEX index

(C) Cash equal to the intrinsic value of the option at the end of the day of exercise

(D) Cash equal to the margin requirement for 100 shares of the OEX index

610. Yield-based options are based on yields of

(A) CDs

(B) Treasury securities

(C) General obligation bonds

(D) CMOs

611. If a client believes that interest rates will increase, which TWO of the following option positions are MOST appropriate?

I. Buy T-bond calls.

II. Buy T-bond puts.

III. Buy T-bond yield calls.

IV. Buy T-bond yield puts.

(A) I and III

(B) I and IV

(C) II and III

(D) II and IV

612. When can European-style options be exercised?

(A) Any time

(B) 1 business day prior to expiration

(C) 3 business days prior to expiration

(D) Any time during the expiration month

613. England has announced that there was an increase in the gross national product figures for another quarter. Japan just had an earthquake that was devastating to the economy. What would be the appropriate investment strategy for an investor who is aware of this news?

I. Buy British pound calls.

II. Buy British pound puts.

III. Buy Japanese yen calls.

IV. Buy Japanese yen puts.

(A) I and III

(B) I and IV

(C) II and III

(D) II and IV

614. World currency options trade on the

(A) NASDAQ OMX PHLX

(B) Chicago Board Options Exchange

(C) American Stock Exchange

(D) New York Stock Exchange

615. An investor buys one Japanese Yen 120 call at 3. What is the cost of this option?

(A) $300

(B) $3,000

(C) $30,000

(D) $300,000

616–636 Registered Options Principal (ROP), the OCC, the ODD, and the OAA

616. Place the following in order from first to last when a customer is opening a new options account.

I. Have a ROP approve the account.

II. Send out an ODD.

III. Have the customer sign and return the OAA.

IV. Execute the options trade.

(A) I, II, III, IV

(B) II, I, IV, III

(C) III, I, II, IV

(D) IV, III, II, I

617. The Option Clearing Corporation sets all of the following with regard to an option contract EXCEPT the

(A) premium

(B) contract size

(C) strike price

(D) expiration date

618. The individual responsible for approving all options accounts at a firm is

(A) a registered options principal

(B) a general securities principal

(C) an office manager

(D) the compliance officer

619. Prior to an initial option transaction, all investors must receive an

(A) OCC

(B) OAA

(C) OBO

(D) ODD

620. A special statement for uncovered option writers would be found in the

(A) OCC

(B) OAA

(C) OBO

(D) ODD

621. One of your clients wants to start trading options. Place the following option transactions in sequential order, from the first to last:

I. The registered options principal approves the account.

II. The client sends in a signed options account agreement.

III. An options risk disclosure document is sent to the client.

IV. The transaction is executed.

(A) III, I, IV, II

(B) II, I, III, IV

(C) I, III, II, IV

(D) I, IV, III, II

622. New options investors must sign an options account agreement

(A) at or prior to approval of the new account

(B) at or prior to the investor's first option transaction

(C) within 15 days after approval of the account

(D) whenever the investor sees fit

623. When is the last time that an investor can trade an options contract?

(A) 4:30 p.m. EST on the business day of expiration

(B) 4:30 p.m. CST on the business day of expiration

(C) 4:00 p.m. EST on the business day of expiration

(D) 11:59 p.m. EST on the business day of expiration

624. When is the last time a customer can exercise a stock option listed on the CBOE?

(A) 10:59 p.m. CST on the Saturday after the third Friday of the expiration month

(B) 3:02 p.m. CST on the third Friday of the expiration month

(C) 4:00 p.m. CST on the third Friday of the expiration month

(D) 4:30 p.m. CST on the third Friday of the expiration month

625. When do standard equity options expire?

(A) 4:30 p.m. EST on the business day of expiration

(B) 4:30 p.m. EST on the business day of expiration

(C) 4:00 p.m. EST on the business day of expiration

(D) 11:59 p.m. EST on the business day of expiration

626. Trades of listed options settle

(A) in 1 business day

(B) in 2 business days

(C) in 3 business days

(D) in 5 business days

627. The OCC uses which of the following methods when assigning exercise notices?

(A) First-in, first-out

(B) Random selection

(C) To the member firm holding the largest position

(D) Any of the above

628. When the firm chooses a customer to have an option exercised, the firm may use all of the following methods EXCEPT

(A) randomly

(B) FIFO

(C) based on size

(D) by any method fair and reasonable

629. All of the following can be used as collateral in a margin account EXCEPT

(A) listed stocks

(B) listed bonds

(C) call options

(D) mutual funds

630. An investor buys three HIJ Sep 40 calls for 3 each. When HIJ trades at 46, the investor exercises the three calls in order to buy 300 shares of HIJ for the margin account. How much must the investor deposit in the margin account for the stock purchase?

(A) $6,000

(B) $6,900

(C) $12,000

(D) $13,800

631. One of your clients owns ten HPPY Aug 30 calls, which were initially purchased for $3,000. HPPY increases to $40, and your client exercises the calls. The client tells you to sell the stock immediately after purchase. If all of these trades are executed in a margin account, how much must your client deposit?

(A) $2,000

(B) $15,000

(C) $20,000

(D) No deposit is required.

632. The profit on an option transaction will be taxed as

(A) a capital gain

(B) ordinary income

(C) investment income

(D) passive income

633. On the same day, an investor purchases 100 shares of LMN at 48 and 1 LMN Sep 45 put for 3. Nine months later, the put expires unexercised. What is the investor's tax consequence?

(A) owning stock with a cost basis of 45

(B) owning stock with a cost basis of 51

(C) a $300 capital loss

(D) a $300 ordinary loss

634. An investor purchased a standard option which expired out of the money. How would this transaction be categorized for tax purposes?

(A) A long-term capital loss

(B) A short-term capital loss

(C) An ordinary loss

(D) Ordinary income

635. You execute the following trades for one of your speculative investors:

> Buy one HIJ Oct 35 call at 7
>
> Write one HIJ Oct 40 call at 2

Would these trades be considered suitable?

(A) It is impossible to say.

(B) No, because it is impossible to profit from these option positions.

(C) Yes, because this investor is looking for risky positions.

(D) No, because these positions are too safe for a speculative investor.

636. Melissa R. purchased 100 shares of MKR common stock at $40 per share on February 1st of last year. On the same date, Melissa also purchased an MKR Aug 35 put for 3. On May 1st of the current year, Melissa sold the stock for $55 per share. What are the tax consequences as a result of these transactions?

(A) $1,200 short-term capital gain

(B) $1,200 long-term capital gain

(C) $1,500 short-term capital gain

(D) $1,500 long-term capital gain

637–640 Additional Option Rules

637. An investor is long 15,000 GHI calls. Which of the following additional positions may the investor have without violating position limits (position limit = 25,000)?

(A) Long 11,000 GHI calls

(B) Short 11,000 GHI puts

(C) Short 11,000 GHI calls

(D) None of the above

638. The exercise limits placed on option contracts is

(A) lower than the position limits

(B) the same as the position limits

(C) higher than the position limits

(D) either the same or lower than the position limits

639. What happens to open option orders on a particular security on the ex-date?

(A) The option strike price will be lowered to reflect the dividend.

(B) The option strike price will remain the same.

(C) The option strike price will be increased to reflect the dividend.

(D) The option strike price will remain the same unless the customer wishes the strike price to be changed.

640. Option confirmations must include

I. the option type

II. the option strike price

III. the number of contracts

IV. the premium

(A) I and III

(B) I, II, and III

(C) I, III, and IV

(D) I, II, III, and IV

Chapter 9

Portfolio and Securities Analysis

Instead of just randomly recommending securities to customers or potential customers, you're expected to know why you're recommending those securities. Typically, most brokerage firms have their own analysts who are responsible for doing the research and recommending which securities the registered reps should promote. The two main types are fundamental analysts, who examine the specifics of corporations, and technical analysts, who follow the market to determine the best time to buy or sell. As a registered rep, you'll also be responsible for examining your customers' portfolios to help them keep in line with their investment objectives.

The Problems You'll Work On

The questions in this chapter test your ability in the following areas:

>> Making appropriate recommendations based on your customers and their individual needs

>> Understanding a customer's investment objectives so you can accurately help manage his portfolio

>> Grasping the concepts of fiscal policy, money supply, the Fed, and how governmental intervention is likely to affect the market

>> Comprehending certain definitions and economic indicators

>> Recognizing the roles of fundamental analysts and technical analysts

>> Understanding the different types of issues and their risks and rewards

>> Remembering the different indexes and circuit breakers

What to Watch Out For

Simple things can trip you up; here's what you need to watch out for as you work through this chapter:

>> Really make sure you understand an investor's investment objectives and needs.

>> Always be aware of the key words, such as EXCEPT and NOT, that can change an answer.

>> Eliminate answers that you know are wrong to increase your chances of selecting the right one.

>> Perform math calculations carefully to avoid careless errors.

641–673 Portfolio Analysis

641. Which of the following is the MOST important consideration when making investment recommendations to a client?

(A) The client's age

(B) The client's marital status

(C) The client's financial needs

(D) The client's investment objectives

642. One of your new clients has a long-term investment objective of aggressive growth. However, they are planning on purchasing a fixer-upper home within the next year. Which of the following investments would you determine to be MOST suitable for her portfolio?

(A) Treasury bills

(B) High-yield bond fund

(C) Aggressive growth fund

(D) An oil and gas wildcatting program

643. A customer of yours has preservation of capital as their primary investment objective. Which of the following securities would you recommend to help them meet their objective?

I. AAA-rated corporate bonds

II. An exploratory direct participation program

III. Blue chip stocks

IV. U.S. government bonds

(A) I, II, and III

(B) I, III, and IV

(C) II and IV

(D) II, III, and IV

644. Which of the following investments would be proper for investors interested in capital growth?

(A) T-bonds

(B) Municipal bonds

(C) The stock of new corporations

(D) REITs

645. If a client is interested in investing in liquid securities, which TWO of the following would you NOT recommend?

I. Municipal bonds

II. Direct participation programs

III. Mutual funds

IV. Blue chip stocks

(A) I and II

(B) III and IV

(C) II and III

(D) I and IV

646. Your client has an investment objective of total return. They currently have 100% of their portfolio invested in common stocks and common stock mutual funds. What would you suggest they add to their portfolio to help them meet their investment objective?

(A) Blue chip stocks

(B) Preferred stocks

(C) Aggressive growth mutual funds

(D) Corporate bonds

647. Which of the following would be the BEST recommendations for an investor who has an investment objective of speculation?

I. Sector funds

II. Blue chip stocks

III. Zero-coupon bonds

IV. Technology stocks

(A) I and II

(B) II and III

(C) I and IV

(D) I, II, and IV

648. One of your wealthy clients is in the highest tax bracket and has a portfolio with a nice mixture of corporate bonds and stocks. What would be the BEST recommendation to help the client round out their portfolio?

(A) U.S. Treasury securities

(B) Municipal bonds

(C) REITs

(D) CMOs

649. A client would like to make sure their portfolio is diversified. Which of the following are ways that a portfolio can be diversified?

I. Buying different types of securities (equity, debt, options, DPPs, and packaged)

II. Buying securities from different industries

III. Buying bonds with different ratings

IV. Buying securities from different areas of the country or world

(A) I only

(B) I and III

(C) II, III, and IV

(D) I, II, III, and IV

650. A client new to investing has $10,000 to invest and wants to build a diversified portfolio. Which of the following is the BEST investment recommendation?

(A) Purchasing several different mutual funds

(B) Purchasing three different types of bonds and several different blue chip stocks

(C) Purchasing T-bonds and gradually adding stocks to the portfolio with the interest received

(D) Waiting until the client has more money to invest because you can't build a diversified portfolio with $10,000

651. Which of the following must occur before a registered representative makes an investment recommendation to his client?

(A) The registered representative must determine the client's suitability.

(B) The registered representative must receive written approval from a principal.

(C) The registered representative must obtain a written power of attorney from the client.

(D) All of the above.

652. A client's investment decisions should be based mostly on their

I. investment needs

II. registered representative's recommendations

III. risk tolerance

(A) I and II

(B) I and III

(C) II and III

(D) I, II, and III

653. A client's nonfinancial considerations are typically as important as their financial considerations. Nonfinancial considerations include

(A) the client's age

(B) the client's marital status

(C) the client's employment status

(D) all of the above

654. Changing which of the following nonfinancial information might change an investor's investment objectives?

I. The investor growing older

II. Getting married or divorced

III. Investment experience

IV. Family responsibilities

(A) II and IV

(B) I, II, and III

(C) I, II, and IV

(D) I, II, III, and IV

655. One of your 60-year-old clients has set up their account strategically so that it consists of 70% invested in stocks, 20% in bonds, and 10% in cash equivalents. One year later, they checked their account and because the stock market has been doing well, they now have 73% invested in stocks, 18% invested in bonds, and 9% invested in cash equivalents. What should this investor do?

(A) Sell some of their bonds and purchase more stocks and cash equivalents.

(B) Sell some of their stocks and purchase more bonds and cash equivalents.

(C) Sell their cash equivalents and purchase more stocks and bonds.

(D) Cannot be determined with the information given.

656. An investor believes the market is going to go on a run over the short term. Tactical asset allocation suggests that this investor should

(A) rebalance their portfolio to sell off some debt and equity securities and purchase more precious metals

(B) rebalance their portfolio to sell off some long-term debt securities and purchase more short-term debt securities

(C) rebalance their portfolio to sell off some equity securities and purchase more fixed-income securities

(D) rebalance their portfolio to sell off some fixed-income securities and purchase more equity securities

657. A pharmaceutical stock with negative alpha means that

(A) it is underperforming other stocks on the S&P 500

(B) it is underperforming other stocks on the S&P 100

(C) it is underperforming the return on the DJIA

(D) it is underperforming similar pharmaceutical stocks

658. One of your clients is interested in purchasing a stock with a beta of 1.6. You can tell them that

(A) the stock is equally volatile to the market

(B) the stock is less volatile than the market

(C) the stock is more volatile than the market

(D) cannot be determined

659. Joanie Johnson is pursuing an aggressive stock buying strategy. Which of the following investments would BEST suit Joanie's needs?

(A) ABC stock with a beta coefficient of 0.80

(B) LMN stock with a beta coefficient of 1.0

(C) XYZ stock with a beta coefficient of 1.20

(D) Blue-chip stock

660. A client wants to strengthen their portfolio by adding some defensive stocks. Which of the following stocks would be the defensive?

I. Appliance company

II. Automotive

III. Pharmaceutical

IV. Alcohol

(A) I and II

(B) III and IV

(C) I, III, and IV

(D) I and III

661. Which of the following could be part of an aggressive portfolio strategy?

(A) Selling uncovered call options

(B) Buying securities on margin

(C) Investing in high-yield bonds

(D) All of the above

662. Which of the following are systematic risks?

  I.   Currency risk
  II. Purchasing power risk
  III. Reinvestment risk

  (A) I and II
  (B) I and III
  (C) II and III
  (D) I, II, and III

663. Which of the following BEST describes systematic risk?

  (A) The risk that a security will decline due to negative market conditions
  (B) The likelihood of default by a particular issuer
  (C) The risk that a security won't keep pace with the inflation rate
  (D) The risk that the issuer won't perform to expectations

664. One of your clients is interested in purchasing the common stock from several companies based in Europe. As their registered representative, you should explain to them the risks of investing in these securities. The risks include

  I.   political risk
  II. market risk
  III. currency risk
  IV. interest rate risk

  (A) I and III
  (B) I, III, and IV
  (C) I, II, and III
  (D) I, II, III, and IV

665. If an investor is concerned about interest risk, which of the following bonds should a registered rep recommend?

  (A) Treasury bills
  (B) Treasury notes
  (C) Treasury bonds
  (D) Treasury strips

666. A client owns a large amount of Treasury bonds and long-term investment grade corporate bonds. Their main risk concern should be

  (A) credit risk
  (B) inflationary risk
  (C) systematic risk
  (D) timing risk

667. For an investor who is concerned about purchasing power risk, which TWO of the following would be the best recommendations?

  I.   Common stock
  II. Long-term investment grade corporate bonds
  III. Fixed annuities
  IV. Variable annuities

  (A) I and III
  (B) I and IV
  (C) II and III
  (D) II and IV

668. If the FDA increases pollution standards that are more costly for oil companies, investors who own shares of oil company stock would most likely see the value of their shares decline due to

  (A) purchasing power risk
  (B) reinvestment risk
  (C) credit risk
  (D) regulatory risk

669. Which TWO of the following statements are TRUE regarding portfolio diversification?

    I. Diversification reduces systematic risk.

    II. Diversification doesn't reduce systematic risk.

    III. Diversification reduces non-systematic risk.

    IV. Diversification doesn't reduce non-systematic risk.

    (A) I and III

    (B) I and IV

    (C) II and III

    (D) II and IV

670. An investor is interested in purchasing debt securities for the first time. If their biggest concern is credit risk, which of the following bonds should he NOT purchase?

    I. Income bonds

    II. High-yield bonds

    III. Investment grade bonds

    IV. AAA-rated industrial development revenue bonds

    (A) I only

    (B) I and II

    (C) II and III

    (D) II, III, and IV

671. Which of the following debt securities has no reinvestment risk?

    (A) Municipal GO bonds

    (B) Equipment trusts

    (C) Industrial development revenue bonds

    (D) Treasury STRIPS

672. All of the following securities have reinvestment risk EXCEPT

    (A) Treasury bills

    (B) Treasury notes

    (C) municipal revenue bonds

    (D) municipal GO bonds

673. Mr. Steele is a 55-year-old investor who has a couple hundred thousand invested in the market. He would like to add more securities to his portfolio that have a high degree of liquidity. All of the following would be acceptable recommendations EXCEPT

    (A) blue chip stocks

    (B) mutual funds

    (C) DPPs

    (D) Treasury bills

674–705 Fundamental Analysis

674. Which of the following WOULD NOT be examined by a fundamental analyst?

    (A) EPS

    (B) Balance sheets

    (C) Industry

    (D) Timing

675. When assessing ABC Corporation's stock, a technical analyst will consider all of the following EXCEPT

    (A) the market price

    (B) the trading volume

    (C) the earnings

    (D) market momentum

676. A fundamental analyst examines which of the following features of a corporation?

    (A) Earnings trends

    (B) Support and resistance

    (C) Breadth of the market

    (D) None of the above

677. All of the following are current assets EXCEPT

    (A) accounts receivable

    (B) securities

    (C) cash

    (D) machinery

678. All of the following are considered quick assets EXCEPT

(A) cash

(B) accounts receivable

(C) inventory

(D) marketable securities

679. All of the following are considered fixed assets EXCEPT

(A) inventory

(B) office furniture

(C) warehouse

(D) computers

680. A corporation's intangible assets include

I. inventory

II. patents

III. equipment

IV. goodwill

(A) I and III

(B) I, II, and III

(C) III and IV

(D) II and IV

681. Related to a corporation's balance sheet, which of the following are considered current liabilities?

I. Declared cash dividends

II. Wages

III. Taxes

IV. Accounts payable

(A) I, II, and III

(B) I, II, III, and IV

(C) III and IV

(D) II, III, and IV

682. The stockholder's equity portion of the balance sheet includes

I. the par value of the common stock

II. the par value of the preferred stock

III. Treasury stock

IV. retained earnings

(A) I, II, and III

(B) II, III, and IV

(C) III and IV

(D) I, II, III, and IV

683. To determine the net worth of a corporation, you would have to

(A) subtract the liabilities from the assets

(B) subtract the assets from the liabilities

(C) add the assets to the current liabilities

(D) subtract the stockholder's equity from the assets

684. Working capital equals

(A) assets – liabilities

(B) liabilities + stockholder's equity

(C) current assets – current liabilities

(D) net worth – liabilities

685. Use the following balance sheet to answer this question:

Income Statement for HIJ Corp.	
Net Sales	$10,000,000
Operating Expenses	$7,000,000
EBIT	$3,000,000
Bont Interest	$600,000
Taxable Income	$2,400,000
50% Tax	$1,200,000
Net Income	$1,200,000
Preferred Dividends	$600,000
	$600,000
Common Dividends	$300,000
Retained Earnings	$300,000

The market price of the common stock is - $12
1,000,000 common shares outstanding
$0.30 annual common dividend
Depreciation = $200,000

What is the current ratio?

(A) 1:1

(B) 2:1

(C) 3:1

(D) 4:1

686. Which of the following is NOT considered a quick asset?

(A) Inventory

(B) Accounts receivable

(C) Marketable securities

(D) Cash

687. Which of the following is NOT considered a quick asset?

I.   Working capital decreases

II. Working capital remains the same

III. Net worth decreases

IV. Net worth remains the same

(A) I and III

(B) I and IV

(C) II and III

(D) II and IV

688. MKR Corporation has announced a $0.50 dividend to holders of record of their common stock. At the time of the announcement and prior to the dividend being paid, what happens to MKR's working capital?

(A) It decreases.

(B) It remains the same.

(C) It increases.

(D) Cannot be determined.

689. When a corporation declares a cash dividend, which of the following is TRUE in relation to the corporation's balance sheet?

(A) Assets decrease.

(B) Liabilities increase.

(C) Working capital remains the same.

(D) The stockholder's equity increases.

690. What happens to the working capital of a corporation when they pay a previously announced dividend to their shareholders?

(A) It increases.

(B) It decreases.

(C) It first increases and then decreases.

(D) It remains the same.

691. What happens to a company's net worth when they issue common stock?

(A) It increases.

(B) It decreases.

(C) It remains the same.

(D) Cannot be determined.

692. ABC Corporation has recently issued $5,000,000 worth of bonds. Which of the following was NOT affected by the issuance of these bonds?

(A) Total assets

(B) Total liabilities

(C) Stockholder's equity

(D) Working capital

693. If ABCD Corporation issues new long-term bonds, all of the following would increase on its balance sheet EXCEPT

(A) assets

(B) liabilities

(C) net worth

(D) working capital

694. Which of the following ratios would help a fundamental analyst determine a corporation's risk of bankruptcy?

(A) Inventory turnover ratio

(B) Margin-of-profit ratio

(C) Net profit ratio

(D) Debt-to-equity ratio

695. All of the following ratios measure the liquidity of a company EXCEPT

(A) the current ratio

(B) the quick ratio

(C) the debt-to-equity ratio

(D) the ratio of cash and securities to current liabilities

696. Cash flow equals

(A) net income – depreciation

(B) gross income + depreciation + depletion

(C) net income + depreciation + depletion + amortization

(D) gross income – depletion + depreciation

697. Which of the following equations could NOT be determined by extracting numbers from an income statement?

(A) Book value per share

(B) Net profit margin

(C) Gross profit margin

(D) Bond interest coverage

698. A fundamental analyst can view or determine all of the following information from the balance sheet of a corporation EXCEPT

(A) long-term liabilities

(B) EPS

(C) shareholder's equity

(D) inventory

699. If LMN common stock has a $2.20 dividend, a current yield of 5.0%, and a PE ratio of 6 and is trading at $44, its approximate earnings per share is

(A) $0.44

(B) $2.73

(C) $7.33

(D) $8.80

700. ABC stock pays an annual dividend of $4, has an earnings per share of $8, and has a market price of $40. What is ABC's PE ratio?

(A) 2

(B) 5

(C) 10

(D) 20

701. PE ratio equals

(A) the market price divided by the earnings per share

(B) annual dividends per common share divided by the market price

(C) annual dividends per common share divided by earnings per share

(D) net income minus preferred dividends divided by the number of common shares outstanding

702. Use the following exhibit to answer this question:

Assets		Liabilities	
Cash	$10	Accts Payable	$10
Securities	$10	Bonds Due	
Accts Receivable	$20	This Year	$10
Inventory	$20	Bonds Due	
Machinery	$10	in 10 Years	$30
Land	$10		

What is the dividend payout ratio for HIJ Corp.?

(A) 10%

(B) 20%

(C) 50%

(D) 60%

703. MKR Corporation has 10 million common shares outstanding. If MKR's net income is $140 million, what are the earnings per share?

(A) $0.07

(B) $0.70

(C) $14.00

(D) Cannot be determined

704. A corporation is using a first-in-first-out (FIFO) accounting method to value its inventory. This information would most likely be found

(A) by examining the footnotes on the corporation's balance sheet

(B) by looking at the corporation's statement of additional information

(C) on a corporation's balance sheet

(D) on a customer's account statement

705. Which of the following may be found in footnotes of a corporation's income statements and balance sheets?

(A) The method of depreciation used by the corporation

(B) The names of the insiders of the corporation

(C) The number of outstanding shares

(D) The amount of treasury stock

706–720 Technical Analysis

706. A fundamental analyst examines all of the following EXCEPT

(A) earnings per share

(B) balance sheets

(C) income statements

(D) trend lines

707. Technical analysts would be MOST interested in which of the following?

(A) Corporate balance sheets

(B) The unemployment rate

(C) The trading volume on the NASDAQ OMX PHLX

(D) Corporate profits

708. Which of the following technical market theories is based on the belief that small investors usually buy and sell at the wrong time?

(A) Random walk theory

(B) Odd-lot theory

(C) Short interest theory

(D) Modern portfolio theory

709. According to a technical analyst, if short interest increases in the market, it is a

(A) bullish indicator

(B) bearish indicator

(C) volatility indicator

(D) none of the above

710. According to the Dow theory, the reversal of a bearish trend would be confirmed by

(A) advance/decline ratio

(B) the amount of short interest

(C) an increase in the DJIA and the DJTA

(D) an increase in investors buying call options

711. Which of the following would a technical analyst use to determine whether a security is a good investment?

(A) The price earnings ratio

(B) Balance sheets

(C) Income statements

(D) Trend lines

712. DEF Corporate stock's price has been very volatile over the past few years. However, over the past month, the stock has been trading between $40 and $41. DEF stock is

(A) consolidating

(B) saucering

(C) trend lining

(D) breaking out

713. A technical analyst notices that the market is generally consolidating. What does this mean?

(A) The trendline is moving upward.

(B) The trendline is moving downward.

(C) The trendline is moving sideways.

(D) All securities are trading within 10% of their trading range for the previous week.

714. The lower portion of a securities trading range is the

(A) support

(B) resistance

(C) breakout

(D) shoulder

715. When a stock is approaching its resistance line, it is generally considered a _____ sign.

(A) bullish

(B) bearish

(C) neutral

(D) none of the above

716. Which TWO of the following formations are considered bullish signs?

I. Saucer

II. Inverted saucer

III. Head and shoulders

IV. Inverted head and shoulders

(A) I and III

(B) I and IV

(C) II and III

(D) II and IV

717. A saucer formation is an indication that a security is

(A) consolidating

(B) breaking out

(C) reversing from a bullish trend

(D) reversing from a bearish trend

718. A head and shoulders top formation indicates the

(A) reversal of a bullish trend

(B) reversal of a bearish trend

(C) security is consolidating

(D) security is due for a breakout

719. Which of the following are considered bearish signs?

(A) Saucer and head and shoulders top formation

(B) Inverted saucer and head and shoulders top formation

(C) Saucer and inverted head and shoulders formation

(D) Inverted saucer and inverted head and shoulders formation

720. If the market is overbought, it would likely be a good time to

(A) buy securities

(B) buy index call options

(C) sell or sell short securities

(D) sell index put options

Chapter 10

Orders and Trades

A s a registered rep, you'll need to know the intricacies of orders and trades and, if needed, be able to explain them to customers or potential customers. This chapter covers questions about the different securities markets, primary and secondary markets, the roles of broker–dealers, types of orders, reporting systems, and so on.

The Problems You'll Work On

In this chapter, you should be prepared to answer questions on

>> The different securities markets

>> The difference between the primary and secondary markets

>> The roles of brokers and dealers

>> The different types of orders

>> The rules and reasons for short sales

>> What a market maker's book is

>> The different reporting systems and how to report trades

What to Watch Out For

As you work through the problems in this chapter, keep the following in mind:

>> Make sure you know the difference between the role of a broker and a dealer.

>> Read each question and answer choice completely before answering each question.

>> Watch out for key words, such as EXCEPT and NOT, that can change the answer you're looking for.

>> Focus on the last sentence of each question to make sure you know what's being asked.

721–726 Primary and Secondary Markets

721. All of the following trades occur in the secondary market EXCEPT

- (A) a syndicate selling new issues of municipal GO bonds to the public
- (B) a designated market maker purchasing common stock for their own account
- (C) a corporation selling its shares of treasury stock to the public using the services of a broker-dealer
- (D) a trade between an insurance company and a bank without using the services of a broker-dealer

722. Which of the following describe the secondary market?

- I. The trading for OTC issues
- II. The trading of listed securities
- III. The trading of outstanding issues
- IV. The underwriting of new issues
- (A) I and III
- (B) II and IV
- (C) I, II, and III
- (D) I, II, and IV

723. The first market is

- (A) listed securities trading OTC
- (B) listed securities trading on an exchange
- (C) institutional trading without using the services of a broker-dealer
- (D) unlisted securities trading OTC

724. The second market is

- (A) listed securities trading OTC
- (B) listed securities trading on an exchange
- (C) institutional trading without using the services of a broker-dealer
- (D) unlisted securities trading OTC

725. Which of the following BEST describes a third market trade?

- (A) Listed securities trading on an exchange
- (B) Unlisted securities trading OTC
- (C) Listed securities trading OTC
- (D) Institutional trading without using the services of a broker-dealer

726. A trade of securities between ABC Bank and DEF Insurance Company without using the services of a broker-dealer would be a

- (A) first market trade
- (B) second market trade
- (C) third market trade
- (D) fourth market trade

727–736 Exchanges and the OTC Market

727. Which of the following are considered "auction markets"?

- I. OTCBB
- II. NYSE Euronext
- III. Nasdaq PHLX
- IV. NYSE Arca
- (A) I, II, and III
- (B) II, III, and IV
- (C) I and IV
- (D) I, II, III, and IV

728. Which of the following are exchange markets?

- I. Nasdaq PHLX
- II. ECN
- III. NYSE Euronext
- IV. OTCBB
- (A) I and III
- (B) I, II, and III
- (C) II and IV
- (D) II, III, and IV

729. A client has entered a call option order with your broker-dealer. The order could be executed on the

I. CBOE
II. NYSE Arca
III. Nasdaq PHLX

(A) I only
(B) I and II
(C) I and III
(D) I, II, and III

730. The over-the-counter market is best described as

(A) an auction market
(B) a negotiated market
(C) unregulated market
(D) choices (A) and (C)

731. U.S. Treasury bonds and municipal bonds trade

(A) over the counter
(B) on the NYSE
(C) either over the counter or on the NYSE
(D) neither over the counter nor on the NYSE

732. Which of the following levels of NASDAQ includes subject quotes?

(A) Level I
(B) Level II
(C) Level III
(D) Level IV

733. Most brokerage firm traders trade using

(A) Level I
(B) Level II
(C) Level III
(D) Level IV

734. Market makers enter and change firm quotes on Nasdaq

(A) Level I
(B) Level II
(C) Level III
(D) Level IV

735. Non-Nasdaq securities are sold on

I. OTCBB
II. OTC Best
III. OTC Venture
IV. OTC Pink

(A) I and II
(B) II, III, and IV
(C) I and III
(D) I, II, III, and IV

736. The most speculative securities on the OTC Markets Group would be found on the

(A) Best Market
(B) Pink sheets
(C) Venture Market
(D) OTCBB

737–741 Broker-Dealer

737. Which of the following is TRUE?

(A) Brokers charge a commission, and dealers charge a markup or markdown.
(B) Dealers charge a commission, and brokers charge a markup or markdown.
(C) Brokers and dealers charge a commission.
(D) Dealers and brokers charge a markup or markdown.

738. When a broker-dealer makes a market in a particular security, they are acting as a(n)

(A) agent
(B) broker
(C) principal
(D) syndicate member

739. Which TWO of the following are TRUE relating to a firm that sells securities out of its own inventory?

    I.   It is acting as a broker.

    II. It is acting as a dealer.

    III. It charges a commission.

    IV. It charges a markup.

    (A) I and III

    (B) I and IV

    (C) II and III

    (D) II and IV

740. When a customer purchases a stock from a dealer, they pay a price that

    (A) includes a markup

    (B) includes a commission

    (C) includes a commission and a markup

    (D) any of the above

741. Which of the following is a responsibility of a municipal bond trader at a brokerage firm?

    (A) Positioning the clients of the firm

    (B) Rating the municipal bonds in the firm's inventory

    (C) Underwriting new issues

    (D) All of the above

742–771 Order Types and Features

742. A customer enters a market order to buy 100 shares of LMN. Which of the following is TRUE?

    (A) The trade will take place at the best available bid price.

    (B) The trade will take place at the best available ask price.

    (C) It is a GTC order, and the trade will take place at the best available bid price.

    (D) It is a GTC order, and the trade will take place at the best available ask price.

743. Short sellers are

    (A) bullish

    (B) bearish

    (C) bullish/neutral

    (D) bearish/neutral

744. Which of the following is TRUE regarding short sales?

    I.   They must be executed in margin accounts.

    II. OTCBB stocks may be sold short.

    III. Listed securities may be sold short.

    IV. They have unlimited risk.

    (A) I, III, and IV

    (B) II, III, and IV

    (C) I, II, and III

    (D) I, II, III, and IV

745. An investor sells short 1,000 shares of DWN at $35. If the investor buys back 1,000 shares of DWN at $30 five years later to cover the short position, what is the gain or loss?

    (A) $5,000 short-term gain

    (B) $5,000 short-term loss

    (C) $5,000 long-term gain

    (D) $5,000 long-term loss

746. All of the following securities are typically sold short EXCEPT

    (A) over-the-counter common stock

    (B) preferred stock

    (C) exchange-listed stock

    (D) municipal bonds

747. Regulation SHO covers

    (A) margin requirements for municipal and U.S. government securities

    (B) the short sale of securities

    (C) margin requirements for commodities

    (D) portfolio margining rules

748. Which of the following orders becomes a market order as soon as the underlying security passes a specific price?

(A) Limit

(B) Stop limit

(C) Market

(D) Stop

749. Why would an investor place a stop order?

I. To protect the profit on a long position

II. To protect the profit on a short position

III. To limit the loss on a long position

IV. To limit the loss on a short position

(A) I and II

(B) II and IV

(C) III and IV

(D) All of the above

750. One of your clients has an unrealized gain from selling short FFF common stock. If your client wants to protect his profit, you should recommend that they enter a

(A) buy stop order on FFF

(B) buy limit order on FFF

(C) sell stop order on FFF

(D) sell limit order on FFF

751. Sell stop orders are entered

(A) below the current market price

(B) at the current market price

(C) above the current market price

(D) either at or above the current market price

752. Darla Diamond purchases 1,000 STU at $42. After STU increases to $47, Darla would like to protect the profit on that investment. Out of the following choices, which of the following orders should you recommend?

(A) Sell limit at $50

(B) Sell limit at $45

(C) Sell stop at $46

(D) Sell stop at $48

753. Which of the following orders guarantee the order is executed at a specific price or better?

(A) Buy limits and sell stops

(B) Buy limits and sell limits

(C) Sell limits and buy stops

(D) Buy stops and sell stops

754. Sharlene W. placed an order to buy 1,000 shares of MKR at 22. This investor has placed a

(A) buy limit order

(B) buy stop order

(C) buy stop limit order

(D) market order

755. Which of the following are TRUE about short sales against the box?

I. They allow investors to defer taxes.

II. They hedge long positions.

III. They are executed in margin accounts.

IV. The securities being sold short are already owned by the investor.

(A) I and IV

(B) I, II, and IV

(C) II, III, and IV

(D) I, II, III, and IV

756. Which of the following orders stand a chance of not being executed?

(A) Stop orders

(B) Limit orders

(C) Stop limit orders

(D) All of the above

757. Which of the following orders would be placed at or below the market price of the security?

(A) Buy limit and sell limit orders

(B) Buy limit and sell stop orders

(C) Sell limit and buy stop orders

(D) Sell stop and buy stop orders

758. Which of the following orders would be placed at or above the market price of the security?

(A) Buy limit and sell limit orders

(B) Buy limit and sell stop orders

(C) Sell limit and buy stop orders

(D) Sell stop and buy stop orders

759. A customer enters a buy stop for ABC at $15. After the order is entered, trades occur as follows:

14.75, 14.88, 14.63, 15, 15.25,15.13

The order was

(A) triggered at 14.63, executed at 15

(B) triggered at 14.75, executed at 14.88

(C) triggered at 15, executed at 15.25

(D) triggered at 15, executed at 15.13

760. A client enters a sell stop order for LMN at $25.00. The ticker following entry of the order is as follows:

$25.25, $24.88, $25.25, $25.00

The order was

(A) triggered at $25.25, executed at $24.88

(B) triggered at $24.88, executed at $25.00

(C) triggered at $24.88, executed at $24.75

(D) triggered at $24.88, executed at $25.25

761. A customer enters a buy ABC at $25 stop $25.25 limit. The ticker following entry of the order is as follows:

24.13, 24.63, 24.88, 25.25, 25.38, 25.13

The order was

(A) triggered at 24.13, executed at 24.63

(B) triggered at 24.88, executed at 25.25

(C) triggered at 25.25, executed at 25.13

(D) triggered at 25.25, not executed

762. A client enters an order to sell HIJK at $20.50 stop $20.40 limit. The ticker following entry of the order is as follows:

$20.75, $20.60, $20.50, $20.30, $20.35, $20.40, $20.50

The order was

(A) triggered at $20.75, executed at $20.50

(B) triggered at $20.60, executed at $20.40

(C) triggered at $20.50, executed at $20.40

(D) triggered the first time it hit $20.50, executed the second time it hit $20.50

763. A customer places an order to buy 100 shares of RST at 50. Which TWO of the following are TRUE of this order?

I. It is a limit order.

II. It is a market order.

III. It is good for the day.

IV. It is good until canceled.

(A) I and III

(B) I and IV

(C) II and III

(D) II and IV

764. Which of the following orders can a designated market maker (DMM) NOT accept?

(A) NH

(B) FOK

(C) IOC

(D) AON

765. Which TWO of the following are TRUE of fill-or-kill orders?

I. They must be executed entirely.

II. They allow for partial execution.

III. They must be executed in one attempt immediately.

IV. They may be executed in several attempts.

(A) I and III

(B) I and IV

(C) II and III

(D) II and IV

766. Which TWO of the following are TRUE regarding immediate-or-cancel orders?

   I.   They must be executed entirely.

   II. They allow for partial execution.

   III. They must be executed in one attempt immediately.

   IV. They may be executed in several attempts.

   (A) I and III

   (B) I and IV

   (C) II and III

   (D) II and IV

767. All-or-none orders

   (A) must be executed in their entirety immediately or the order is canceled

   (B) must be executed in their entirety or the order is canceled

   (C) must be at least partially executed immediately or the order is canceled

   (D) must be at least partially executed or the order is canceled

768. Which TWO of the following are TRUE regarding market-on-open orders?

   I.   If they're not executed at the opening price, they're cancelled.

   II. If they're not executed at the opening price, they're executed on the next business day.

   III. They allow for partial execution.

   IV. They allow for full executions only.

   (A) I and III

   (B) I and IV

   (C) II and III

   (D) II and IV

769. Early in the afternoon, a customer gives a registered rep a market order to buy 200 shares of HIJ at the close of the market. What should be done in regard to the order?

   (A) The registered rep should refuse the order.

   (B) The registered rep should hold the order until ten minutes before the close of the market.

   (C) The order should be sent to the floor broker immediately.

   (D) The order should be held until after the market closes.

770. Mr. Smith owns 100 shares of HIJ common stock, which has a current market price of $43. Mr. Smith entered an order to sell 100 shares of HIJ at $38 stop or sell 100 shares of HIJ at $48. What type of order is this?

   (A) A sell stop limit order

   (B) A fill or kill order

   (C) A sell limit order

   (D) An alternative order

771. Which of the following is TRUE of a customer entering a buy minus order on ABC stock?

   (A) They want to buy ABC when the stock is below the previous sale price.

   (B) They want to buy ABC when the DJIA has declined from the previous day.

   (C) They want to buy ABC when the S&P 500 has declined from the previous day.

   (D) They want to buy ABC when the price is below their previous purchase price of ABC.

772–792 Designated Market Maker

772. Who is responsible for maintaining a fair and orderly market on the NYSE trading floor?

(A) Floor brokers

(B) Designated market makers

(C) Two-dollar brokers

(D) Order book officials

773. Which of the following are used by a designated market maker (DMM) in determining the order of trading?

I. Priority

II. Profit

III. Precedence

IV. Parity

(A) I, II, and III

(B) II, III, and IV

(C) I, III, and IV

(D) I, II, and IV

774. Which of the following is NOT TRUE about a DMM stopping stock?

(A) The DMM is guaranteeing a price.

(B) The DMM needs permission from an exchange official.

(C) This may be done only for public orders.

(D) All of the above.

775. If the inside market for an AAD common stock is 50.20–50.35, where can a Designated Market Maker enter an order to sell from their own inventory?

(A) 50.20

(B) 50.30

(C) 50.35

(D) 50.36 or higher

776. All of the following orders could be placed in a NYSE Display Book EXCEPT

(A) limit orders

(B) stop orders

(C) GTC orders

(D) market orders

777. All of the following are TRUE about SDBK EXCEPT

(A) it may be used to enter market, stop, or limit orders

(B) it is used for orders on the NYSE

(C) any order can be entered regardless of the quantity of shares traded

(D) orders bypass the floor broker and go directly to the DMM

778. Using the following table, what is the inside market of LMN?

BID	LMN	OFFER
5 Hurricane B/D	46.00	10 Firefly B/D (stop)
3 Tornado Sec	46.01	
9 Tide B/D 12 Lowland B/D	46.02	
	46.03	
	46.04	
	46.05	
	46.06	5 Mississippi Sec. 8 Tippy Top B/D 12 Overland Sec.
7 Highpoint Sec. (stop GTC)	46.07	7 Hudson B/D

(A) 46.00 to 46.07

(B) 46.02 to 46.06

(C) 46.00 to 46.06

(D) 46.02 to 46.07

779. The inside market is the

(A) lowest bid price and lowest ask price

(B) lowest bid price and highest ask price

(C) highest bid price and lowest ask price

(D) highest bid price and highest ask price

780. A NYSE Display Book indicates the following for TUV common stock:

BID	TUV	OFFER
4 Northwest B/D	30.00	
5 Northeast B/D	30.01	12 Pacific B/D (stop)
8 Southwest B/D 14 Southeast B/D	30.02	
	30.03	
	30.04	
	30.05	4 Atlantic Sec. 9 Gulf B/D (GTC)
9 Midland Sec. (stop GTC)	30.06	6 Mississippi Sec.

What is the size of the market?

(A) 14 × 4

(B) 22 × 13

(C) 31 × 19

(D) 40 × 31

781. Where can a designated market maker enter an order for their own inventory?

(A) In between the bid and offer prices

(B) At the bid and offer prices

(C) Higher than the current offer price or lower than the current bid price

(D) None of the above

782. Which TWO of the following open orders in a designated market maker's order display book would be adjusted on the ex-dividend date for a cash dividend?

I. Buy stop

II. Buy limit

III. Sell stop

IV. Sell limit

(A) I and III

(B) I and IV

(C) II and III

(D) II and IV

783. If a customer has entered an open order to sell 10,000 shares of LMN at $20 and LMN announced a 2-for-5 split that is allowed by stockholders, how will the order be adjusted by the designated market maker on the ex-split date?

(A) Sell 10,000 shares of LMN at $20.

(B) Sell 4,000 shares of LMN at $50.

(C) Sell 25,000 shares of LMN at $8.

(D) The order would be canceled.

784. The Order Audit Trail System tracks the

(A) execution of an order only

(B) cancellation of an order only

(C) entire life of an order from entry to execution

(D) none of the above

785. The computer system that broker-dealers use to keep track of the routing of over-the-counter orders is

(A) ACT

(B) SDBK

(C) ECN

(D) OATS

786. Which TWO of the following are TRUE regarding TRACE reports?

I. Only the buyer needs to report the transaction.

II. Both the buyer and seller need to report the transaction.

III. TRACE reports trades of corporate debt securities.

IV. TRACE reports trades of corporate stocks.

(A) I and III

(B) I and IV

(C) II and III

(D) II and IV

787. Where could a client find quotes for municipal bonds?

(A) Green sheets

(B) TRACE

(C) OTC Pink Market

(D) RTRS

788. A client wants to know the pricing information for several long-term bonds. Which of the following is a printed source of wholesale information on corporate bonds?

(A) OTC Pink Sheets

(B) TRACE

(C) the Magenta List

(D) EMMA

789. Which of the following is TRUE of FINRA's Trade Reporting Facility?

(A) It facilitates the reporting of trade data for NYSE-listed securities occurring on the floor of the NYSE.

(B) It facilitates the reporting of trade data for NASDAQ-listed securities and exchange-listed securities occurring off the exchange floor.

(C) It facilitates the reporting of trade data for municipal bonds traded on an exchange.

(D) It facilitates the reporting of trade data for U.S. government securities traded on an exchange.

790. Which of the following is TRUE regarding dark pools of liquidity?

I. They represent pools of institutional and large retail clients.

II. They reduce the amount of transparency of information relating to securities trading.

III. Firms trading for their own inventory may be included.

IV. Trades executed by the pools are reported as exchange transactions.

(A) I and IV

(B) I, III, and IV

(C) I, II, and III

(D) II and III

791. The NYSE will temporarily halt trading if the

(A) S&P 500 declines 7% or more from the previous day's close

(B) S&P 500 declines 5% or more from the previous day's close

(C) DJIA declines 7% or more from the previous day's close

(D) DJIA declines 5% or more from the previous day's close

792. If a _____ decline occurs any time during the trading day, the exchange will halt trading in all stocks until the next trading day.

(A) Level 1

(B) Level 2

(C) Level 3

(D) Level 4

Chapter 11

Taxes and Retirement Plans

Taxes are a part of life. Investors face additional taxes that aren't imposed on your average consumer, including capital gains and dividends. In addition, this chapter covers different retirement plans and how they're taxed. The Series 7 exam tests your ability to understand the tax categories, what happens when you purchase a bond at a discount or premium, qualified versus non-qualified retirement plans, health savings accounts (HSAs), and so on.

The Problems You'll Work On

The types of problems in this chapter require you to

>> Understand the different tax categories and types of income.

>> Calculate interest income and taxes on dividends.

>> Handle capital gains and losses.

>> Compute accretion and amortization.

>> Be familiar with wash sale rules, gift taxes, and estate taxes.

>> Recognize qualified and non-qualified plans.

>> Compare traditional IRAs and Roth IRAs.

What to Watch Out For

Don't let common mistakes trip you up; be careful that you

>> Read each question and answer choice completely before choosing an answer.

>> Eliminate false answers when the correct one doesn't reveal itself right away.

>> Watch out for key words such as EXCEPT and NOT that can change the answer choice you're looking for.

>> Remember the difference between progressive and regressive (flat) taxes.

793–830 Taxes on Investments

793. All of the following taxes are progressive EXCEPT

(A) personal income

(B) gift

(C) estate

(D) sales

794. Property tax is a

I.   flat tax

II. graduated tax

III. regressive tax

IV. progressive tax

(A) I and III

(B) I and IV

(C) II and III

(D) II and IV

795. Which of the following taxes are regressive?

I.   Income

II. Gas

III. Alcohol

IV. Sales

(A) I and III

(B) II and IV

(C) II, III, and IV

(D) I, II, and III

796. Earned income includes all of the following EXCEPT

(A) capital gains

(B) salary

(C) bonuses

(D) income received from active participation in a business

797. Portfolio income includes

I.   income from an oil and gas DPP

II. income from stock dividends

III. interest from corporate bonds

IV. capital gains from the sale of municipal bonds

(A) I, II, and III

(B) II, III, and IV

(C) II and III

(D) I, II, III, and IV

798. If a client is a resident of New Jersey, which of the following investment results would be subject to federal taxation?

I.   Cash dividends on stock

II. Interest on T-notes

III. Accretion of a zero-coupon debenture

IV. Capital gains on a New Jersey revenue bond

(A) I only

(B) I and II

(C) I, II, and III

(D) I, II, III, and IV

799. An investor receives interest from a corporate bond that they have held for more than one year. If the investor is in the 28% tax bracket, what tax rate will he be required to pay on the interest received?

(A) 0%

(B) 15%

(C) 20%

(D) 28%

800. One of your clients who lives in Florida purchased an Atlantic City, New Jersey, municipal revenue bond. The interest is

I. subject to state tax

II. exempt from state tax

III. subject to federal tax

IV. exempt from federal tax

(A) I and III

(B) I and IV

(C) II and III

(D) II and IV

801. Interest on U.S. government T-bonds is subject to

(A) state tax but not federal tax

(B) federal tax but not state tax

(C) neither state tax nor federal tax

(D) both state and federal tax

802. Items subject to alternative minimum tax (AMT) include

(A) certain depreciation expenses

(B) interest on IDRs

(C) certain items relating to owning an interest in a limited partnership

(D) all of the above

803. Which of the following are taxable to investors?

I. Stock splits

II. Cash dividends

III. Corporate bond interest

(A) I and II

(B) II and III

(C) I and III

(D) I, II, and III

804. Dirk Diamond purchased 100 shares of UPP preferred stock, paying a yearly dividend of $6 per share. Dirk originally purchased the stock one year ago. Exactly one year later to the day, Dirk sold the stock for a profit of $320. Which TWO of the following are TRUE relating to the tax treatment of Dirk's transactions?

I. The dividends will be taxed as ordinary income.

II. The dividends will be taxed as passive income.

III. The sale will be treated as a short-term capital gain.

IV. The sale will be treated as a long-term capital gain.

(A) I and III

(B) I and IV

(C) II and III

(D) II and IV

805. Cain Jones and his spouse Meisha received cash dividends in their brokerage accounts as follows:

Cain: $2,000

Meisha: $1,000

Joint: $1,500

How much of these dividends are subject to taxation if they file their taxes jointly?

(A) $0

(B) $1,500

(C) $3,000

(D) $4,500

806. What is the tax rate on qualified dividends for investors who are in the 39.6% federal tax rate?

(A) 0%

(B) 15%

(C) 20%

(D) 39.6%

807. Long-term capital gains are taxed at which of the following tax rates?

    I.   0%

    II.   15%

    III. 20%

    IV. The investor's tax bracket

    (A) II and III

    (B) I, II, and III

    (C) II, III, and IV

    (D) I, II, III, and IV

808. The short-term capital gains rate is

    (A) 0%

    (B) 15%

    (C) 20%

    (D) the investor's tax bracket

809. An investor buys 1,000 shares of a stock at $40. If the stock increases in value to $60, how would the result be categorized?

    (A) As a profit

    (B) Ordinary income

    (C) Appreciation

    (D) Capital gain

810. An investor purchases 1,000 shares of common stock at $23. If the stock increases in value to $25, how would the result be categorized?

    (A) Appreciation

    (B) Capital gain

    (C) Passive income

    (D) Ordinary income

811. An investor has made the following transactions in the current year:

    Jan. 4: Buy 100 TUV at 30

    Feb. 6: Buy 100 TUV at 40

    Feb. 13: Sell 100 TUV at 36

What is the investor's gain or loss?

    (A) $400 capital loss

    (B) $600 capital gain

    (C) $600 capital loss

    (D) $400 capital gain

812. An investor has been purchasing $500 worth of an ABC growth fund each month for the last six years. They need to sell off some shares to purchase a new car. The price of ABC has fluctuated over the last six years, and the investor wants to minimize his tax liability on the shares sold. When selling the shares, they should use which accounting method?

    (A) FIFO

    (B) LIFO

    (C) Average basis

    (D) Identified shares

813. An investor purchased 10 HIJ convertible bonds at an overall cost of $980 per bond including commission and fees. Several years later, the investor decides to convert their bonds into HIJ common stock. If the conversion price is $20, what is the investor's cost basis per share?

    (A) $19.00

    (B) $19.60

    (C) $20.00

    (D) $50.00

814. Ayla K. purchased 200 shares of LMN common stock with an overall cost of $12,400 including commission and fees. LMN declares a 2-for-1 split to shareholders of record on August 4. What is Ayla's cost basis per share after the split?

(A) $12.40

(B) $24.80

(C) $31.00

(D) $62.00

815. An investor purchased 100 shares of MKR common stock at 50. Two years later, the investor sold the stock when the price was $55 per share. What is the capital gains yield?

(A) 5%

(B) 10%

(C) 50%

(D) Cannot be determined

816. Mrs. Silver purchased 1,000 shares of LMN common stock at $20 per share. 1 year and 6 months later, Mrs. Silver sold the stock at $24 per share. If the long-term capital gain tax rate is 20%, what is the net yield after capital gains tax?

(A) 16%

(B) 8%

(C) 10%

(D) 20%

817. A client would like to sell short ABC common stock but is unfamiliar with the tax treatment of short sales. You should inform them that

(A) all gains are taxed as ordinary income

(B) all gains or losses are taxed as passive income or losses

(C) all gains or losses are considered short term

(D) all gains or losses are considered long term

818. A security purchased on September 30 would become long term on

(A) September 30 of the following year

(B) September 31 of the following year

(C) October 1 of the following year

(D) December 31 of the current year

819. One of your clients has the following investments for the current year:

Capital gains: $14,500

Capital losses: $21,000

What is the tax status for this investor?

(A) They have a $6,500 loss for the current year.

(B) They have a $3,000 loss for the current year and $3,000 carried over to the following year.

(C) They have a $3,000 loss for the current year and $3,500 carried over to the following year.

(D) They have a $6,500 loss for the current year and $3,000 carried over to the following year.

820. Uriah Florian sold GNP Corporation stock at a $6.50 loss per share and bought GNP call options 23 days later. Which of the following is TRUE?

(A) The $6.50 loss per share deduction is allowed.

(B) The $6.50 loss per share deduction is disallowed.

(C) The $6.50 loss per share deduction can be used to offset capital gains.

(D) The $6.50 loss per share deduction can be used to offset ordinary income.

821. An investor sold DEF common stock at a loss. Which of the following securities may the investor buy back immediately without violating the wash sale rule?

(A) DEF convertible bonds

(B) DEF call options

(C) DEF warrants

(D) DEF preferred stock

822. A return of capital is

(A) not taxed

(B) taxed as regular income

(C) taxed as a short-term capital gain

(D) taxed as a long-term capital gain

823. Mrs. Jones purchased a DEF corporate bond for 92 with ten years until maturity. If Mrs. Jones sells that bond at 94 in six years, what is the gain or loss?

(A) $28 loss

(B) $80 loss

(C) $20 gain

(D) $60 gain

824. A client purchased a 5% corporate bond at 95 with ten years until maturity. The bond is callable in five years at par value. How much taxable income does the investor have to claim each year?

(A) $0

(B) $5

(C) $50

(D) $55

825. Which TWO of the following are TRUE?

I. Corporate bonds purchased at a discount must be accreted.

II. Corporate bonds purchased at a discount may be accreted.

III. Corporate bonds purchased at a premium must be amortized.

IV. Corporate bonds purchased at a premium may be amortized.

(A) I and III

(B) I and IV

(C) II and III

(D) II and IV

826. An investor purchased a 7% DEF corporate bond at 80 with 10 years to maturity. Six years later, the investor sold the bond at 85. What is the gain or loss?

(A) $50 gain

(B) $70 loss

(C) $150 loss

(D) None of the above

827. Sally Silverhouse purchases a new municipal bond at a price of $970. Which TWO of the following are TRUE?

I. The discount on the bond must be accreted.

II. The discount on the bond would not be accreted.

III. Sally would be subject to a capital gain if she holds the bond until maturity.

IV. Sally would not be subject to a capital gain if she holds the bond until maturity.

(A) I and III

(B) I and IV

(C) II and III

(D) II and IV

828. One of your clients purchases ten 6% Albany municipal bonds in the secondary market at 110. If the bonds mature in eight years, what is the approximate amount of amortization after holding the bond for four years?

(A) $50

(B) $125

(C) $500

(D) $1,000

829. An investor buys an equipment trust bond in the secondary market for 106. The bond has 12 years until maturity. Four years later, the investor sells the bond for 104. What is the investor's gain or loss?

(A) $60 capital loss

(B) $20 capital gain

(C) $20 capital loss

(D) No gain or loss

830. An investor purchased a municipal bond at a premium. Which TWO of the following are TRUE regarding the amortization of the bond premium?

I. It increases the reported bond interest income.

II. It decreases the reported bond interest income.

III. It increases the cost basis.

IV. It decreases the cost basis.

(A) I and III

(B) I and IV

(C) II and III

(D) II and IV

831–836 Gift and Estate Tax Rules

831. What is the tax deduction limit for gifts between spouses?

(A) $100

(B) $17,000

(C) $78,000

(D) Unlimited

832. Mike Smith purchased 100 shares of TIP common stock for $42.50 per share. Several months later with TIP trading at $57, Mike gives the stock to his sister Michelle. Michelle eventually ended up selling the stock for $60 per share. Michelle would have to claim a capital gain of

(A) $0 because Mike would be responsible for paying taxes on the capital gain

(B) $300

(C) $1,450

(D) $1,750

833. Gary Goldman purchased 1,000 shares of GGG common stock four years ago at a cost of $42 per share. Gary gives the stock to his son Grant when the market value is $52 per share. Which TWO of the following are TRUE of this transaction?

I. Gary may be subject to a gift tax.

II. Grant may be subject to a gift tax.

III. Grant's cost basis is $42 per share.

IV. Grant's cost basis is $52 per share.

(A) I and III

(B) I and IV

(C) II and III

(D) II and IV

834. Declan K. purchased 1,000 shares of MKR Corp. common stock at $40 per share. MKR subsequently decreased in price to $30 per share, and Declan gave the securities to father-in-law, Fred. Three years later, Fred sold the stock for $37 per share. What is Fred's cost basis regarding the sale of the MKR stock?

(A) $30,000

(B) $35,000

(C) $37,000

(D) $40,000

835. Clay Rousey inherits stock valued at $52 from a grandfather, who purchased the stock at $32. If Clay sells the stock at $62, how much of a capital gain per share would Clay claim?

(A) $0

(B) $10

(C) $20

(D) $30

836. Which of the following have unified tax credits?

I. Estate tax

II. Gift tax

III. Sales tax

IV. Income tax

(A) I and II

(B) III and IV

(C) I, III, and IV

(D) I, II, and IV

837–864 Retirement Plans

837. Regarding qualified retirement plans, which of the following is TRUE?

(A) Money cannot be withdrawn until age 73.

(B) Distributions are taxed at 10%.

(C) Contributions are made with 100% pretax dollars.

(D) Contributions are made with 100% after-tax dollars.

838. Which of the following are NOT TRUE regarding qualified pension plans?

(A) They must adhere to anti-discrimination rules.

(B) They allow for tax-free growth.

(C) They must comply with IRS rules.

(D) They must cover all eligible employees.

839. Which of the following are qualified retirement plans under IRS rules?

I. ESOPs

II. 401(k)

III. Traditional IRA

IV. SEP IRA

(A) II only

(B) II and IV

(C) I and III

(D) I, II, III, and IV

840. ERISA regulations cover

(A) private pension plans

(B) public pension plans

(C) private and public pension plans

(D) none of the above

841. Which TWO of the following statements regarding qualified retirement plans are TRUE?

I. Distributions are 100% taxable at the holder's tax bracket.

II. Distributions are partially taxable at the holder's tax bracket.

III. Contributions are made with pretax dollars.

IV. Contributions are made with after-tax dollars.

(A) I and III

(B) I and IV

(C) II and III

(D) II and IV

842. All of the following business retirement plans are regulated by ERISA EXCEPT

(A) money purchase plans

(B) ESOPs

(C) payroll deduction plans

(D) 401(k)

843. Which of the following securities would be LEAST suitable for a pension fund to purchase?

(A) Common stocks

(B) Preferred stocks

(C) Corporate bonds

(D) Municipal bonds

844. This type of employer-sponsored retirement plan pays a specified benefit to their plan participants at retirement.

(A) 401(k)

(B) Defined benefit plan

(C) Profit sharing plan

(D) 457(b)

845. Which of the following is TRUE of corporate defined contribution plans?

I. The annual contribution percentage varies.

II. The annual contribution percentage is fixed.

III. Retirement benefits increase the longer the employee works for the corporation.

IV. In a bad year, the corporation may discontinue employee contributions.

(A) I and III

(B) I and IV

(C) II and III

(D) II, III, and IV

846. All of the following are non-qualified retirement plans EXCEPT

(A) deferred compensation plans

(B) payroll deduction plans

(C) 401(k) plans

(D) 457 plans

847. By what age may an individual begin withdrawing money from a Roth 401(k) without penalty?

(A) April 1 of the year after turning age 73

(B) April 15 of the year after turning age 59-1/2

(C) April 1 of the year after turning age 59-1/2

(D) 59-1/2

848. When an investor starts receiving payments at retirement from a 403(b) plan, they are

(A) not taxable

(B) 100% taxable at the investor's tax bracket

(C) partially taxable at the investor's tax bracket

(D) either fully taxable or partially taxable depending on the investor's tax bracket

849. Which TWO of the following are TRUE regarding deferred compensation programs?

I. They are qualified plans.

II. They are non-qualified plans.

III. The employer may discriminate and not offer the plan to all employees.

IV. The employer may not discriminate, and if there is a plan, it must be offered to all employees.

(A) I and III

(B) I and IV

(C) II and III

(D) II and IV

850. Which of the following is a deferred compensation plan established by states or local governments or 501(c)3 non-profit organizations?

(A) Stock purchase plans

(B) SEP IRAs

(C) 401(k) plans

(D) 457(b) plans

851. One of your 50-year-old clients does not have a job but earns all of their money from day trading. They are quite successful and consistently make more than $150,000 per year. They would like to open an IRA. Providing their income remains consistent, how much can they contribute to an IRA?

(A) $0

(B) $6,500

(C) $7,500

(D) $30,000

852. A 55-year-old self-employed massage therapist earns $95,000 per year and has no other retirement plan except a traditional IRA. If they deposit $4,500 into an IRA, which of the following is TRUE?

(A) It is partially tax deductible.

(B) It is not tax deductible.

(C) It is fully tax deductible.

(D) Because they are self-employed, they must open a Keogh.

853. If an investor makes an excess contribution to an IRA, they will be assessed a

(A) 6% penalty tax

(B) 10% penalty tax

(C) 15% penalty tax

(D) 50% penalty tax

854. Which of the following is TRUE regarding a 52-year-old investor who would like to withdraw money from her IRA?

(A) It will be taxed as ordinary income.

(B) It will be taxed as ordinary income plus a 10% penalty.

(C) It will be taxed as a capital gain.

(D) It will be taxed as a capital gain plus a 10% penalty.

855. What is the required beginning date for traditional IRAs?

(A) 59-1/2

(B) 70-1/2

(C) April 1 of the year after the holder turns age 73

(D) April 15 of the year after the holder turns age 73

856. What is the last day an investor can deposit money into a traditional IRA and be able to claim it as a write-off on the current year's taxes?

(A) December 31 of the current year

(B) January 31 of the following year

(C) April 1 of the following year

(D) April 15 of the following year

857. Which of the following are TRUE regarding Roth IRAs?

I. Distributions are partially taxable.

II. Distributions are not taxable providing the holding period and investor's age requirement are met.

III. Contributions are made with pretax dollars.

IV. Contributions are made with after-tax dollars.

(A) I and III

(B) I and IV

(C) II and III

(D) II and IV

858. As of 2023, what is the maximum yearly contribution allowed into a Roth IRA for a 51-year-old investor who earns $85,000 per year?

(A) $6,500 pretax

(B) $6,500 after tax

(C) $7,500 pretax

(D) $7,500 after tax

859. At what age must an investor begin withdrawals from a Roth IRA?

(A) 59-1/2

(B) 73

(C) April 1 of the year after turning age 73

(D) No requirement

860. Which TWO of the following is TRUE regarding SEP IRAs?

I. Contributions are made in pretax dollars.

II. Contributions are made in after-tax dollars.

III. SEP IRAs are designed for small business owners

IV. SEP IRAs are designed for employees of local governments

(A) I and III

(B) II and IV

(C) I and IV

(D) II and III

861. Mr. Smith has a 401(k) at his current job at ABC Corporation. Mr. Smith is going to leave his job at ABC and start working at DEF Corporation. Mr. Smith would like to transfer his 401(k) to DEF Corporation. Which of the following is TRUE of that transfer?

(A) Transfers are not allowed from one company's 401(k) to another company's 401(k).

(B) There is no limit on the amount he can transfer.

(C) Mr. Smith has to wait until he has been working for DEF for at least 6 months before any transfer can take place.

(D) Mr. Smith is limited to transferring $6,000 per year.

862. One of your clients has rolled over money from a pension fund into an IRA; how long must your client wait before executing another rollover?

(A) 30 days

(B) 60 days

(C) 90 days

(D) 1 year

863. Mrs. Jones is leaving her job and has $40,000 in a 401(k). After Mrs. Jones withdraws the money from the 401(k), how long does she have to roll over money into an IRA?

(A) 20 days

(B) 30 days

(C) 60 days

(D) 90 days

864. All of the following are TRUE about 529 plans and Coverdell ESAs EXCEPT

(A) deposits are made from after-tax dollars

(B) there are maximum annual contributions

(C) the beneficiary of the accounts must use the funds by age 30 for the funds not to be penalized

(D) money can be withdrawn tax-free if used for educational purposes

Chapter **12**

Rules and Regulations

T he Series 7 exam is riddled with rules and regulations. And believe it or not, they're not just in this chapter. Unfortunately, this chapter, more than any other one, requires you to remember specifics. But don't fear: A lot of the rules make sense, and the correct answer usually stands out like a sore thumb.

The number of questions in this category increased greatly when the USA Patriot Act was enacted. Due to the act, each firm must have and follow customer identification programs (CIPs) and anti-money laundering rules.

The Problems You'll Work On

In this chapter, you'll work on problems that deal with rules and regulations, including

>> Understanding the different self-regulatory organizations and agent registration

>> Opening and transferring customer accounts

>> Remembering the specifics for order tickets, trade confirmations, and account statements

>> Figuring out the payment and delivery dates for different trades

>> Handling customer complaints and the legal remedies

>> Recognizing violations

What to Watch Out For

The following tips can help you determine the correct answers for questions in this chapter:

>> Eliminate wrong answers when the correct one doesn't "pop out" at you right away.

>> Double-check that you're not confusing your rules before picking an answer.

>> Watch out for keywords such as EXCEPT and NOT that will change the answer

>> Focus on the last sentence of the question to help guide you to the correct answer.

865–870 Securities Regulatory Organizations

865. All of the following are SROs EXCEPT

(A) FINRA

(B) MSRB

(C) SEC

(D) NYSE

866. Which of the following investment advisers must register with the SEC?

(A) Advisers with at least $25 million under management

(B) Advisers with at least 100 clients

(C) None of them; they only have to register at the state level

(D) All of them

867. Which of the following are self-regulatory organizations?

I. FINRA

II. SEC

III. CBOE

IV. NYSE

(A) I, II, III, and IV

(B) I and II

(C) III and IV

(D) I, III, and IV

868. Which of the following entities is responsible for administering securities exams, such as the SIE and Series 7?

(A) NYSE

(B) SEC

(C) FINRA

(D) NASAA

869. Which of the following self-regulatory organizations does not enforce its own rules?

(A) CBOE

(B) FINRA

(C) NYSE

(D) MSRB

870. FINRA and the NYSE have the authority to do which of the following?

I. Incarcerate

II. Fine

III. Expel

IV. Censure

(A) II and III

(B) II, III, and IV

(C) I and II

(D) I and IV

871–919 Opening Accounts

871. Which of the following must be verified when opening an account for a new client?

I. Citizenship

II. Whether their name appears on the SDN list

III. Whether they work at another broker-dealer

IV. Whether they have any accounts at another broker-dealer

(A) I and IV

(B) II and III

(C) I, II, and III

(D) I, II, III, and IV

872. All of the following information must be obtained from a new individual customer EXCEPT

(A) the individual's Social Security number

(B) the individual's date of birth

(C) the individual's educational background

(D) the individual's residential address

873. You are in the process of opening a new customer account. Which of the following information do you need?

I. The customer's Social Security number or tax ID

II. The customer's investment experience

III. The customer's occupation and employer

IV. The customer's legal name and address

(A) I and IV

(B) I, II and IV

(C) I, III, and IV

(D) I, II, III, and IV

874. Which of the following needs to be filled out on a new account form?

I. The customer's name and address

II. The customer's date of birth

III. The type of account

IV. The customer's investment objectives

(A) I and II

(B) I, II and III

(C) I, II, and IV

(D) I, II, III and IV

875. Whose signature is required on a new account form?

I. The customer's

II. The registered rep's

III. A principal's

(A) I and II

(B) I and III

(C) II and III

(D) I, II, and III

876. If a customer wants to open a new account but refuses to provide some of the financial information requested, which of the following is TRUE?

(A) You may not open the account until the customer provides complete financial information.

(B) You may open the account and take unsolicited trades only.

(C) You may open the account if you can determine from other sources that the customer has the financial means to handle the account.

(D) You may open the account but refuse to do any trades until the customer provides complete financial information.

877. If a customer has not notified a brokerage firm about information on a new account form update, how often must a firm make sure the account information has not changed?

(A) Annually

(B) Once every 2 years

(C) Once every 3 years

(D) Once every 4 years

878. Chael Weidman wants to open an account at MMA Broker-Dealer. Chael does not want their name to appear on the account. How would MMA Broker-Dealer handle this request?

(A) MMA would open a numbered account for Chael.

(B) MMA would set up a street-named account for Chael if they are an accredited investor.

(C) MMA would refuse to open the account until Chael agrees to have the account in their name.

(D) MMA would provide a fictitious name for Chael from its book of approved names.

879. You have a new client who would like to open a numbered account. To open that account, what must occur?

- (A) The client must sign a written statement attesting to ownership of the account.
- (B) The client would need to receive permission from FINRA.
- (C) The client would need to receive permission from the SEC.
- (D) Choices (B) and (C)

880. A client of ABC Broker-Dealer owns 1,000 shares of DEF Corporation, which are held in street name. What procedure will ABC Broker-Dealer take in regard to a proxy sent from DEF Corporation?

- (A) ABC Broker-Dealer must forward the proxy to the client.
- (B) ABC Broker-Dealer will vote the proxy.
- (C) They must inform DEF Corporation to send the proxy directly to your client.
- (D) None of the above.

881. Under the USA Patriot Act, all banks and brokerage firms must maintain _____ to help prevent money laundering and the financing of terrorist operations.

- (A) CIPs
- (B) SDNs
- (C) OFACs
- (D) FinCEN

882. As part of the USA Patriot Act of 2001, all financial institutions must maintain

- (A) customer identification programs
- (B) a fidelity bond
- (C) SIPC coverage
- (D) all of the above

883. What is the minimum amount of equity required to be deposited by an investor with a day trading account?

- (A) $10,000
- (B) $15,000
- (C) $20,000
- (D) $25,000

884. What is the minimum amount of assets your client must have to establish a prime brokerage account?

- (A) $100,000
- (B) $500,000
- (C) $1,000,000
- (D) $5,000,000

885. Which of the following fee-based accounts charge a single fee for asset allocation, portfolio management, trade execution, and administration?

- (A) Wrap accounts
- (B) Joint accounts
- (C) Day trading accounts
- (D) All of the above

886. Mr. and Mrs. Faber opened a joint account several years ago as a JTWROS. Mr. Faber was involved in a sky-diving accident and didn't survive. Upon receiving confirmation of Mr. Faber's passing, what must be done with the account?

- (A) The entire account would be transferred to Mrs. Faber.
- (B) Mr. Faber's portion of the account would be transferred to the estate.
- (C) The account is divided up depending on percentage invested.
- (D) Any one of the above is acceptable.

887. Your clients, a husband and wife, open a joint account as tenants in common. If one spouse dies, what must be done with the account?

(A) The entire account is transferred to the survivor.

(B) The deceased party's portion of the account is transferred to their estate.

(C) The account is divided up on percentage invested.

(D) None of the above.

888. What type of joint account is typically set up for unrelated individuals in which the estate is the beneficiary?

(A) Joint tenants with rights of survivorship

(B) Tenancy in common

(C) Discretionary account

(D) Custodial account

889. If a married individual sets up an account in a state with community property laws, what happens to the account when they die?

(A) It is transferred equally to any children.

(B) It is transferred to a spouse.

(C) It becomes part of their estate.

(D) Any of the above.

890. All the following people may open a joint account EXCEPT

(A) three friends

(B) two cousins

(C) a parent and minor daughter

(D) a married couple

891. Which TWO of the following are TRUE regarding revocable trusts and irrevocable trusts?

I. With a revocable trust, the beneficiary can be changed.

II. With a revocable trust, the beneficiary cannot be changed.

III. With an irrevocable trust, the beneficiary can be changed.

IV. With an irrevocable trust, the beneficiary cannot be changed.

(A) I and III

(B) I and IV

(C) II and III

(D) II and IV

892. Which of the following people CANNOT open a joint account?

(A) A parent and a minor daughter

(B) Two close friends

(C) A husband and wife

(D) Three business partners

893. Which of the following accounts may a client open up without a written power of attorney?

(A) An account for a spouse

(B) An account for a minor daughter

(C) An account for a business partner

(D) None of the above

894. Pam Platinum would like to open an UGMA account for a 10-year-old daughter. Pam is also interested in being the custodian for the account. Which of the following governs investments purchased for UGMA accounts?

I. The legal list

II. The FINRA list of approved investments for minors' accounts

III. The prudent man rule

(A) I and II

(B) I and III

(C) II and III

(D) I, II, and III

895. You may open up a joint account for each of the following couples EXCEPT

(A) a parent and a minor daughter

(B) three unrelated individuals

(C) a husband and wife

(D) an individual and their 71-year-old mother

896. An UGMA account is a(n)

(A) joint account

(B) individual account

(C) custodial account

(D) trust account

897. All of the following are true about UGMA accounts EXCEPT

(A) the taxes are a responsibility of the minor

(B) the certificates are endorsed by the minor

(C) the custodian cannot give anyone else power of attorney over the account

(D) the custodian cannot be compensated for services

898. Which of the following occurs under the Uniform Gifts to Minors Act when a minor reaches the age of majority?

(A) The account must be changed to an UTMA account.

(B) The account is transferred to the donor.

(C) The account is closed, and the former minor receives a check from the broker-dealer equal to the market value of the securities in the account.

(D) The account is transferred to the former minor.

899. Trades executed in discretionary accounts must be approved by principals

(A) prior to execution

(B) by the completion of the transaction

(C) prior to order entry

(D) promptly after execution

900. Power of attorney is required for

I. discretionary accounts

II. custodial accounts

III. joint accounts

IV. fiduciary accounts

(A) I only

(B) I and II

(C) I, II, and IV

(D) I, II, III, and IV

901. A customer has given a registered rep limited power of attorney. All of the following are true EXCEPT

(A) the registered rep may not withdraw securities or cash from the account

(B) the registered rep may execute unsolicited orders in the account

(C) the registered rep must obtain approval of a principal prior to execution of each order

(D) the power of attorney is automatically canceled upon an investor's death

902. Which TWO of the following are TRUE regarding a power of attorney?

I. A durable power of attorney cancels upon mental incompetence or death of the investor.

II. A durable power of attorney only cancels upon death of the investor.

III. A regular power of attorney cancels upon mental incompetence or death of the investor.

IV. A regular power of attorney only cancels upon the death of the investor.

(A) I and III

(B) I and IV

(C) II and IIII

(D) II and IV

903. A corporate customer would like to open a cash account for their company. To open the account, you would need a copy of the

(A) Corporate Charter

(B) Corporate Resolution

(C) Corporate Charter and Corporate Resolution

(D) none of the above

904. A corporate customer would like to open a margin account for their company. To open the account, you would need a copy of the

(A) Corporate Charter

(B) Corporate Resolution

(C) Corporate Charter and Corporate Resolution

(D) none of the above

905. Banks, mutual funds, insurance companies and so on typically set up

(A) institutional accounts

(B) corporate accounts

(C) partnership accounts

(D) joint accounts

906. Anderson Tate is a registered representative who works for KO Securities. Anderson has just learned of the death of one of their clients. Which of the following actions should Anderson take regarding the deceased client's account?

(A) Mark the client's account as deceased.

(B) Cancel all open orders.

(C) Wait for the proper legal papers.

(D) All of the above.

907. If one of your clients dies, your brokerage firm should do all of the following EXCEPT

(A) cancel all open orders

(B) freeze the account

(C) transfer the money in the account to the executor of the estate

(D) cancel any written power of attorney

908. Which of the following statements could legally appear in advertisements or sales literature?

(A) "Our dedicated sales team is the best in the industry."

(B) "Our investment recommendations consistently outperform the market and will continue to do so."

(C) "We guarantee that we will earn each customer at least 7% on their investment each year."

(D) "Our dedicated sales team will work with you to help meet your investment goals."

909. A broker-dealer created a radio ad to try to attract new clients. This is considered

(A) correspondence

(B) retail communication

(C) institutional communication

(D) a violation of FINRA rules

910. According to FINRA Rule 2210, what is the maximum amount of retail persons a brokerage firm may send promotions to in a 30-day period for the promotions to be considered correspondence?

(A) 1

(B) 10

(C) 25

(D) There is no limit.

911. According to FINRA, institutional communication includes

(A) billboard advertisements

(B) magazine advertisements

(C) TV advertisements

(D) advertisements sent to banks

912. Rules for the financial exploitation of specified adults was designed for adults aged

(A) 60 and over

(B) 65 and over

(C) 70 and over

(D) 73 and over

913. FINRA has recently created rules to help curb or handle cases of financial exploitation of specified adults. According to FINRA, specified adults include which TWO of the following?

I. Seniors, or natural persons aged 65 or older

II. Seniors, or natural persons aged 70 or older

III. Natural persons aged 18 or older who have mental or physical impairments that render them unable to protect their own interests

IV. Natural persons aged 21 or older who have mental or physical impairments that render them unable to protect their own interests

(A) I and III

(B) I and IV

(C) II and III

(D) II and IV

914. A brokerage firm has a client who is a senior citizen. If the brokerage firm believes that the client has been or could be financially exploited, the firm may place a hold on distributions from the account for up to

(A) 5 business days

(B) 10 business days

(C) 15 business days

(D) 20 business days

915. All brokerage firms are required to have safeguards in place to protect customers' non-public information. The SEC regulation that outlines brokerage firm requirements to safeguard customers' information is

(A) Regulation T

(B) Regulation G

(C) Regulation S-P

(D) Regulation A

916. Under FINRA Rule 4530, member firms are required to report if an associated person of the firm

(A) is the subject of a written customer complaint involving allegations of theft or misappropriation of funds or securities.

(B) has been denied registration, suspended, expelled, or disciplined by a U.S. or foreign regulatory organization

(C) is indicted, convicted of, or pleads guilty to any felony or certain misdemeanors in or outside of the United States

(D) all of the above

917. While building their book, a newly registered representative would like to work weekends as a bartender for a local restaurant to earn a little extra income. They would be required to tell their

(A) broker-dealer

(B) broker-dealer and FINRA

(C) broker-dealer and the NYSE

(D) broker-dealer and the Fed

918. If a registered representative wants to open a new brokerage account at another firm, what must happen?

I. The account executive must obtain written permission from his firm.

II. The account executive must make sure that his firm receives duplicate copies of all confirmations for trades executed in the account.

III. The account executive must obtain permission to execute trades in the account.

(A) I only

(B) I and II

(C) II and III

(D) I, II, and III

919. An agent of a FINRA firm wants to open a new account at another brokerage firm. Which of the following are TRUE?

    I. The employing firm must be notified about the opening of the account.

    II. The employing firm must receive duplicate trade confirmations if requested.

    III. The employing firm must grant written permission to the agent to open the account.

    IV. The employing firm must grant permission to execute trades in the account.

    (A) I only

    (B) I and II

    (C) I, II, and III

    (D) I, II, III, and IV

920–973 Trading by the Book Once the Account Is Open

920. One of your clients places an order to purchase 100 shares of LMN at $35 per share, and the trade is executed. Prior to paying for the trade, your client sees that LMN has dropped in price significantly. Your client informs you that they no longer want the shares and is not going to pay for them. You should inform them that

    (A) you will cancel the order

    (B) they already purchased the shares, and they must submit the payment

    (C) you will immediately sell the stock in the market and cover the loss

    (D) your firm will purchase the securities for its own inventory

921. Which of the following information is required on an order ticket?

    I. The registered rep's identification number

    II. A description of the securities

    III. The time of the order

    IV. Whether the order was solicited or unsolicited

    (A) I and II

    (B) I, II, and III

    (C) I, II and IV

    (D) I, II, III, and IV

922. All of the following information would be found on an order ticket EXCEPT

    (A) the name of the brokerage firm

    (B) the customer's name

    (C) the quantity of securities

    (D) the investor's occupation

923. All of the following are required on an order ticket EXCEPT

    (A) the customer's signature

    (B) the registered rep's identification number

    (C) the number of securities being purchased

    (D) the customer's account number

924. Gina wants to buy 1,000 shares of Biff Spanky Corporation at $1.20 per share. As Gina's agent, you inform Gina that the investment doesn't fit into their investment profile and is probably too risky for them. If Gina still insists on buying Biff Spanky Corporation, you should

    (A) refuse the order

    (B) refuse the order unless Gina changes their investment profile

    (C) take the order but mark it as "unsolicited"

    (D) hand the phone to your principal to see if they can talk some sense into Gina

925. One of your clients is nearing retirement age, and their main investment objective is risk aversion. However, your client is dead set on purchasing a low-priced stock that you deem too risky considering their age and investment objectives. You should

(A) refuse the order

(B) take the order and mark it as "unsolicited"

(C) not take the order until the new account form is adjusted

(D) not take the order without a principal's approval

926. All order tickets must be signed by

(A) a principal

(B) the customer

(C) the state administrator

(D) a compliance officer

927. Principals must approve trades made by registered representatives

(A) at or prior to execution

(B) at or prior to completion of the transaction

(C) the same day as execution of the order

(D) none of the above

928. Corporate bonds settle in

(A) 1 business day, and payment is due in 3 business days

(B) 3 business days, and payment is due in 3 business days

(C) 2 business days, and payment is due in 4 business days

(D) 5 business days, and payment is due in 7 business days

929. A customer purchases 1,000 shares of XYZ common stock on Friday, October 3. What is the payment date?

(A) Monday, October 6

(B) Tuesday, October 7

(C) Wednesday, October 8

(D) Thursday, October 9

930. Municipal bonds settle

(A) 1 business day after the trade date, and payment is due in 2 business days after the trade date

(B) 1 business day after the trade date, and payment is due in 3 business days after the trade date

(C) 2 business days after the trade date, and payment is due in 2 business days after the trade date

(D) 2 business day after the trade date, and payment is due in 4 business days after the trade date

931. What is the settlement date for U.S. government bond transactions?

(A) 1 business day after the trade date

(B) 2 business days after the trade date

(C) 3 business days after the trade date

(D) The same day as the trade date

932. Option trades settle in _____ business day(s) after the trade date.

(A) one

(B) two

(C) three

(D) four

933. Melissa R. purchased 100 shares of MKR common stock at $33 per share on Friday, October 9. When does the trade settle?

(A) Friday, October 9, on a cash basis or Wednesday, October 14 regular way

(B) Friday, October 9, on a cash basis or Tuesday, October 13 regular way

(C) Monday, October 12, on a cash basis or Tuesday, October 13 regular way

(D) Monday, October 12, on a cash basis or Wednesday, October 14 regular way

934. Two broker-dealers trade a security, and there is some sort of discrepancy where one of the broker-dealers believes the trade was for a different number of shares. At least one of the broker-dealers would have to send out a

(A) DK notice

(B) rejection letter

(C) due bill

(D) none of the above

935. Which of the following regulatory organizations has the authority to grant an extension for the payment of a trade?

(A) The New York Stock Exchange

(B) The Pacific Stock Exchange

(C) FINRA

(D) All of the above

936. A client with a cash account buys stock. 5 business days later, the client calls and informs you that they cannot pay for the stock. What steps would the broker-dealer follow?

(A) Send an application to the FINRA to get an extension.

(B) Give the client a two-day extension.

(C) Sell out the stock and freeze the account for 90 days.

(D) Sell out the stock and if there are no losses, there is no penalty.

937. Mary Smith had their account frozen because they failed to pay for a trade. In order for Mary to purchase additional securities for their account, what must happen?

(A) They must deposit the full purchase price of the securities before the purchase order may be executed.

(B) They must get approval from a principal.

(C) They must wait until her account is no longer frozen.

(D) They must deposit the full purchase price of the securities before the settlement date.

938. The certificate sent out to customers at the completion of the trade, which supplies all the details of the trade, is called a(n)

(A) proxy

(B) order ticket

(C) confirmation

(D) account statement

939. Diamond Broker-Dealer sent a client a confirmation of their latest trade of Mineshaft Corp. common stock. Which of the following items should be on the confirmation?

I. The trade date and the settlement date

II. Whether Diamond Broker-Dealer acted as an agent or principal

III. The name of the security and how many shares were traded

IV. The amount of commission paid if Diamond Broker-Dealer acted as an agent

(A) I and III

(B) I, II, and III

(C) I, III, and IV

(D) I, II, III, and IV

940. For member-to-customer transactions, the member firm must send a trade confirmation

(A) at or prior to the completion of the transaction

(B) no later than 1 business day after the trade date

(C) no later than 2 business days after the trade date

(D) no later than 3 business days after the trade date

941. A client's confirmation must include

I. the markup or markdown for a principal transaction

II. the commission for an agency transaction

III. a description of the security

IV. the registered representative's identification number

(A) I and III

(B) I, II, and III

(C) II, III, and IV

(D) I, II, III, and IV

942. Under MSRB rules, a client's confirmation must include

(A) the markup or markdown

(B) the location of the bond resolution

(C) the settlement date

(D) whether the trade was executed on a dealer or agency basis

943. Which of the following would NOT be included on a trade confirmation?

(A) whether the trade was solicited or unsolicited

(B) the amount of commission charged on a broker transaction

(C) the trade date

(D) the address of the brokerage firm delivering the confirmation

944. According to SEC Rule 10b-10, confirmations of trades executed between firms must be sent no later than

(A) the trade date

(B) 1 business day following the trade date

(C) the completion of the transaction

(D) 3 business days following the trade date

945. All of the following can validate a mutilated certificate EXCEPT

(A) issuer

(B) broker-dealer

(C) registrar

(D) transfer agent

946. All of the following may be reasons to reject a delivery of municipal bond certificates EXCEPT

(A) the indenture is illegible

(B) a change in the market price

(C) a missing legal opinion

(D) a misspelling of the investor's name

947. All of the following are good delivery for a trade of 670 shares EXCEPT

(A) 4 certificates for 150 shares each and 14 certificates for 5 shares each

(B) 1 certificate for 600 shares each and 7 certificates for 10 shares each

(C) 335 certificates for 2 shares each

(D) 2 certificates for 300 shares each and 70 certificates for 1 share each

948. All of the following are good delivery for a trade of 640 shares EXCEPT

(A) 1 certificate for 600 shares and 20 certificates for 2 shares each

(B) 2 certificates for 300 shares each and 1 certificate for 40 shares

(C) 2 certificates for 200 shares each and 3 certificates for 80 shares each

(D) 3 certificates for 200 shares each and 4 certificates for 10 shares each

949. The return of securities previously accepted is called

(A) reclamation

(B) buy-in

(C) sell-out

(D) rejection

950. If a client sells securities they have in their possession and fails to deliver them, what is the buy-in date?

(A) 1 business day after the trade date

(B) 3 business days after the trade date

(C) 5 business days after the trade date

(D) 10 business days after the settlement date

951. In which of the following cases will the buyer of a stock receive a due bill from the seller to show proof of ownership for the purposes of receiving dividends?

I. The trade is executed before the ex-dividend date.

II. The trade is executed after the ex-dividend date.

III. The trade settles before the record date.

IV. The trade settles after the record date.

(A) I and III

(B) I and IV

(C) II and III

(D) II and IV

952. Investors are allowed to maintain stock or bond certificates in book entry form instead of receiving the actual certificates through

(A) DRS

(B) SIPC

(C) NAC

(D) DVP

953. All of the following are responsibilities of the transfer agent EXCEPT

(A) good delivery of certificates

(B) making sure that issued shares do not exceed authorized shares

(C) delivering proxies to investors

(D) canceling old certificates for each trade

954. For a customer who has an active account and trades several times a month, how often must account statements be sent?

(A) Monthly

(B) Quarterly

(C) Semiannually

(D) Annually

955. FINRA and SEC rules require that customer account statements be sent out at least

(A) monthly

(B) quarterly

(C) semiannually

(D) annually

956. How many times a year must a customer of a brokerage firm receive an account statement?

(A) 1

(B) 2

(C) 4

(D) 12

957. Mutual funds must send out account statements to investors at least

(A) monthly

(B) quarterly

(C) semi-annually

(D) annually

958. According to FINRA and SEC rules, account statements must be sent to clients

I. monthly for active accounts

II. quarterly for active accounts

III. quarterly for mutual funds

IV. semiannually for mutual funds

(A) I and III

(B) I and IV

(C) II and III

(D) II and IV

959. When is the ex-dividend date if a corporation announces a dividend payable to shareholders of record Thursday, September 17?

(A) Monday, September 14

(B) Tuesday, September 15

(C) Wednesday, September 16

(D) Monday, September 21

960. The ex-dividend date is

(A) 1 business day before the record date

(B) 2 business days before the record date

(C) 1 business day before the payment date

(D) 2 business days before the payment date

961. Place the following in order from first to last.

I.   Record date

II.   Ex-dividend date

III. Payment date

IV.   Declaration date

(A) I, II, III, IV

(B) II, III, I, IV

(C) IV, I, II, III

(D) IV, II, I, III

962. Armbar Corporation announces a dividend with record date Wednesday, October 17. When is the last day your client can buy the stock the "regular way" and receive the dividend?

(A) Monday, October 15

(B) Tuesday, October 16

(C) Wednesday, October 17

(D) Monday, October 22

963. A corporation announces a dividend with record date Thursday, August 15. If an investor wants to sell the stock and receive the dividend, when should the investor sell the stock?

I.   Tuesday, August 13

II.   Wednesday, August 14

III. Thursday, August 15 on a cash basis

IV.   Friday, August 16 on a cash basis

(A) I and III

(B) I and IV

(C) II and III

(D) II and IV

964. Miesha Silva has written a letter of complaint regarding their recent purchase of blue chip stocks to their broker-dealer. Upon receipt of the complaint, the broker-dealer must

(A) return the commission charged

(B) accept the complaint and write down any action taken

(C) guarantee to make Miesha whole

(D) repurchase the stocks at a price that is at or slightly above Miesha's purchase price

965. In disputes handled through code of procedure (COP), which of the following is TRUE?

(A) The customer decided to have it handled through COP, and any decision made by the court is appealable.

(B) The customer decided to have it handled through COP, and any decision made by the court is non-appealable.

(C) The brokerage firm decided to have it handled through COP, and any decision made by the court is appealable.

(D) The brokerage firm decided to have it handled through COP, and any decision made by the court is non-appealable.

966. Which TWO of the following are TRUE regarding arbitration?

I. Decisions are binding and non-appealable.

II. Decisions are not binding are appealable.

III. Members may take non-members to arbitration.

IV. Non-members may take members to arbitration.

(A) I and III

(B) I and IV

(C) II and III

(D) II and IV

967. All of the following is TRUE about arbitration EXCEPT

(A) members may take non-members to arbitration

(B) non-members may take members to arbitration

(C) members may take other members to arbitration

(D) decisions are binding and non-appealable

968. Simplified arbitration is used for member to non-member disputes not over

(A) $10,000

(B) $25,000

(C) $50,000

(D) $100,000

969. In the event of a loss, how long does a member have to comply with the terms of the arbitration decision?

(A) 15 days

(B) 30 days

(C) 45 days

(D) 60 days

970. Regarding arbitration and mediation, which TWO of the following are TRUE?

I. Arbitration decisions are binding and cannot be appealed.

II. Arbitration decisions are not binding and can be appealed.

III. Mediation decisions are binding and cannot be appealed.

IV. Mediation decisions are not binding and can be appealed.

(A) I and III

(B) I and IV

(C) II and III

(D) II and IV

971. To process an ACAT, a brokerage firm must be a member of the

(A) FINRA

(B) NSCC

(C) SIPC

(D) DRS

972. To process an ACAT, a brokerage firm must be a member of the

(A) FINRA

(B) NSCC

(C) DRS

(D) SIPC

973. According to FINRA rules, which of the following are true about ACATs?

I. When ACAT notices are received, firms have 1 business day to verify the customer's instructions.

II. When ACAT notices are received, firms have 3 business days to verify the customer's instructions.

III. Assets must be transferred within 3 business days after verification.

IV. Assets must be transferred within 4 business days after verification.

(A) I and III

(B) I and IV

(C) II and III

(D) II and IV

974–1001 Other Important Rules

974. According to MSRB Rule G-39, which of the following is TRUE of cold-calling?

(A) Calls must be made after 8:00 a.m. and before 9:00 p.m. local time of the customer.

(B) Calls must be made after 9:00 a.m. and before 8:00 p.m. local time of the customer.

(C) Calls must be made after 8:00 a.m. and before 9:00 p.m. local time of the caller.

(D) Calls must be made after 9:00 a.m. and before 8:00 p.m. local time of the caller.

975. Mr. Silva has asked to be placed on your firm's do not call list. How long must anyone at your firm wait before contacting Mr. Silva again?

(A) One year

(B) Two years

(C) Five years

(D) Life

976. Which of the following may NOT be a factor used in determining the markup charged to customers?

(A) The market price of the security sold

(B) The price the dealer paid to purchase the security

(C) The size of the trade

(D) Txpenses of executing the trade

977. The 5% markup policy applies to which of the following?

(A) IPOs

(B) The sale of mutual fund shares

(C) Regulation D offerings

(D) The over-the-counter sale of outstanding non-exempt securities

978. The 5% markup policy applies to which of the following types of secondary market transactions?

(A) Riskless or simultaneous transactions

(B) Common stock sold from a dealer's inventory

(C) Proceeds transactions on non-exempt securities

(D) All of the above

979. Which of the following trades is subject to the 5% markup policy?

(A) An agency transaction of municipal bonds

(B) The purchase of an IPO

(C) A dealer transaction of an OTC common stock

(D) The purchase of a mutual fund

980. All of the following are violations EXCEPT

(A) interpositioning

(B) freeriding

(C) hypothecation

(D) painting the tape

981. Commingling is

(A) combining fully paid and margined securities for use as collateral

(B) illegal manipulation of a security

(C) bringing in a third party to execute a trade

(D) buying securities with no intention of paying for the trade

982. Interpositioning is

(A) combining fully paid and margined securities for use as collateral

(B) illegal manipulation of a security

(C) bringing in a third party to execute a trade

(D) buying securities with no intention of paying for the trade

983. An investment adviser makes a political contribution to an elected government official. Under the Investment Advisers Act of 1940, that advisor may not provide investment advisory services for a fee to that government official for a period of

(A) six months after the contribution is made

(B) one year after the contribution is made

(C) two years after the contribution is made

(D) five years after the contribution is made or until the government official is out of office, whichever comes first

984. A client purchases a security and sells it shortly after without ever making a payment. This is a violation called

(A) matching orders

(B) freeriding

(C) commingling

(D) interpositioning

985. The failure of a dealer to honor a firm quote is a violation known as

(A) marking the open

(B) backing away

(C) commingling

(D) freeriding

986. When FINRA is considering the possibility that a brokerage account is being churned, all of the following are considered EXCEPT

(A) the profit or loss

(B) the amount of trades

(C) the client's investment objectives

(D) the amount of money in the client's account

987. Two dealers are trading securities back and forth without any essential change in ownership. The dealers are engaged in a violation known as

(A) matching orders

(B) freeriding

(C) commingling

(D) interpositioning

988. All of the following are violations EXCEPT

(A) painting the tape

(B) frontrunning

(C) paying for referrals

(D) entering an at the open order

989. SEC Regulation FD covers

(A) excessive trading in customer accounts

(B) political contributions

(C) markups charged to customers

(D) the releasing of material, nonpublic information

990. A broker-dealer must keep corporate or partnership documents for

(A) two years

(B) three years

(C) six years

(D) a lifetime

991. According to MSRB rules, which of the following records must be maintained by brokerage firms for 6 years?

I. Blotters

II. Confirmations

III. Complaints

IV. Public communications

(A) I and III

(B) I and IV

(C) II and III

(D) III and IV

992. According to FINRA rules, complaints must be maintained on records of brokerage firms for at least

(A) 2 years

(B) 3 years

(C) 4 years

(D) 6 years

993. According to MSRB rules, customer complaints must be kept on file by the brokerage firm for at least

(A) 1 year

(B) 2 years

(C) 4 years

(D) 6 years

994. All of the following records must be maintained by brokerage firms for 6 years EXCEPT

(A) closed accounts

(B) ledgers

(C) U-4 forms of terminated employees

(D) blotters

995. Customer powers of attorney must be kept by a broker-dealer for a minimum of

(A) 2 years

(B) 3 years

(C) 6 years

(D) lifetime of the firm

996. Under FINRA and MSRB rules, all required records must be kept easily accessible for

(A) 6 months

(B) 1 year

(C) 2 years

(D) 3 years

997. According to MSRB rules, when must a control relationship be disclosed to a potential purchaser of a security?

(A) At the time of the recommendation

(B) At the completion of the transaction

(C) Prior to the completion of the transaction

(D) At or prior to the completion of the transaction

998. According to the Customer Protection Rule (Rule 15c-3), which of the following is TRUE?

(A) A brokerage firm must integrate a customer's cash and securities with the brokerage firm's cash and securities.

(B) A brokerage firm must segregate a customer's cash from the brokerage firm's cash and integrate the customer's securities with the brokerage firm's securities.

(C) A brokerage firm must segregate a customer's securities from the brokerage firm's securities and integrate the customer's cash with the brokerage firm's cash.

(D) A brokerage firm must segregate a customer's cash and securities from the brokerage firm's cash and securities.

999. Which TWO of the following are TRUE?

I. The Rules of Fair Practice regulate trades between members.

II. The Rules of Fair Practice regulate trades between members and non-members.

III. The Uniform Practice Code regulates trades between members.

IV. The Uniform Practice Code regulates trades between members and non-members.

(A) I and III

(B) I and IV

(C) II and III

(D) II and IV

1000. Which of the following FINRA rules regulates transactions between FINRA members?

(A) Conduct rules

(B) Rules of Fair Practice

(C) Code of Procedure

(D) Uniform Practice Code

1001. Uniform Practice Code rules regarding account transfers state that

I. account transfers must be validated by the delivering firm within 1 business day after receiving an ACAT form

II. account transfers must be validated by the delivering firm within 3 business days after receiving an ACAT form

III. securities must be delivered within 3 business days after verification

IV. securities must be delivered within 4 business days after verification

(A) I and III

(B) I and IV

(C) II and III

(D) II and IV

2

Checking Your Answers

IN THIS PART . . .

Review your answers.

Study the explanations to help get ready for the Series 7.

Chapter 13
Answers and Explanations

Chapter 1 Answers

1. **C. corporate charter**

For an entity to become a corporation, the founders must file a document called a corporate charter (bylaws) in their home state of business.

2. **D. None of the above.**

Although *none of the above* is rarely the correct answer, in this case, it is. You should remember that until a company files a registration statement for a new issue with the Securities and Exchange Commission (SEC), you can't do anything. You can't accept money, accept indications of interest, or send a red herring (preliminary prospectus).

3. **D. I, II, III, and IV**

When a company files a registration statement with the Securities and Exchange Commission (SEC), it must include the issuer's name and description of its business, the names and addresses of all the company's control persons, what the proceeds will be used for, the company's capitalization, complete financial statements, any legal proceedings against the company, and so on.

4. **A. Shelf registration**

A *shelf registration* allows the issuer to sell securities registered with the Securities and Exchange Commission (SEC) for up to three years from the effective (release) date. A shelf registration allows an issuer to time the sale of its securities with market conditions.

5. B. shelf offerings

The Securities and Exchange Commission (SEC) Rule 415 outlines the rules for shelf offerings (shelf registration). Typically, a company isn't going to sell all of its shares in one shot; it may want to wait another six months, a year, or two years before selling all of its authorized shares. Under SEC Rule 415, an issuer has up to two years to sell its registered securities without having to file a new registration statement.

6. A. 20

The cooling-off period is when the Securities and Exchange Commission (SEC) is reviewing a company's registration statement before bringing new issues to market. The cooling-off period typically lasts about 20 days.

7. C. matching orders

Stabilization, due diligence, and cooling-off period are all terms that apply to a new issue of securities. However, *matching orders* is a violation that involves the illegal manipulation of securities prices by trying to make it look like the trading volume on security has increased.

8. B. II and III

Be careful, any time you see something about the Securities and Exchange Commission (SEC), or any self-regulatory organization for that matter, approving or guaranteeing an issue, it's a false answer. The SEC just clears the issue. During the cooling-off period, the SEC reviews registration statements and may issue stop orders.

9. D. Soliciting sales of the new security

The soliciting of sales during the cooling-off period is prohibited.

10. C. I and III

If a corporation wishes to sell securities publicly, they must file a registration statement with the SEC and issue a prospectus. However, tombstone advertisements are not required by issuers. If there is going to be a tombstone advertisement, it is usually handled by the syndicate manager.

11. A. selling group members

A tombstone ad is a print notice typically placed in newspapers or magazines. Companies use tombstone ads to make an announcement of a new issue of securities. Believe it or not, it got the name *tombstone ad* because the shape of the ad is typically in the shape of a headstone. The ad displays the names of the issuer, syndicate manager, and syndicate members but not selling group members.

12. B. the names of the selling groups

Tombstone ads are written advertisements placed in newspapers and financial magazines informing potential investors of the offering of a security. It's called a tombstone ad because the shape of the ad resembles the shape of a grave headstone. Tombstone ads provide limited information about the issue, including the name of the issuer, the name(s) of the syndicate manager(s), the names of the syndicate members, and where investors can get a prospectus. However, a tombstone ad doesn't disclose the names of the selling group members.

13. B. III and IV

Indications of interest for a new offering aren't binding on the customer or on the broker-dealer. For example, a customer may tell you that they want to buy 10,000 shares of Zamzow when it's available and then change their mind later. By the same token, the broker-dealer isn't obligated to have 10,000 shares available to sell to the customer when Zamzow becomes available.

14. A. I, III, and IV

Issuers can register securities on the state level by filing (notification), through coordination, or through qualification. The Series 63 and Series 66 exams explore this topic in much more detail. Communication was just thrown in there as a bogus answer choice because it looks something like the other words.

15. A. Notification

Notification is the simplest form of registration for established companies. Companies who have previously sold securities in a state can renew their previous application.

16. D. Qualification

Issues use this registration method for securities that are exempt from registration with the SEC but require registration on the state level.

17. C. the effective date

The managing underwriter (syndicate manager) may determine the public offering price for a new security, the takedown (profit made by syndicate members), and the allocation of orders (the way orders are filled). However, the effective date (the first day the securities can begin trading) is determined by the Securities and Exchange Commission (SEC).

18. B. the SEC has cleared the issue

Any statement that says that the SEC has approved or guarantees an issuer, issue, broker-dealer, or whatever, is false. When an issue becomes effective, it just means that the SEC has cleared the issue.

19. **A. Securities Act of 1933**

The Securities Act of 1933 covers the sale of new issues (primary market). The Securities Act of 1933 was designed to provide more transparency in financial statements and to curb fraudulent activities of issuers. The Securities Act of 1933 also goes by a myriad of other names, such as the Paper Act, New Issues Act, Full Disclosure Act, and Truth in Securities Act.

20. **D. I, III, and IV**

The Securities and Exchange Act of 1934 covers margin account rules, the issuing of proxies, short sale rules, and so on. However, trust indentures are covered under the Trust Indenture Act of 1939.

21. **C. $50 million**

Under the Trust Indenture Act of 1939, all corporate bond issued valued at greater than $50 million must be offered to investors with an indenture.

22. **D. all of the above**

An investment banking firm is a financial institution that provides a variety of services for issuers and sometimes high-net-worth investors. As related to new issues, investment bankers advise issuers how to raise money, help the issuers comply with securities laws, and often help the issuers raise money by selling securities.

23. **C. The syndicate agreement**

The syndicate agreement (agreement among underwriters or syndicate letter) must be signed by all members of the underwriting and outlines the liabilities and responsibilities of all parties involved.

24. **C. Syndicate agreement**

The allocation of orders establishes a priority for customer orders to be filled. The allocation of orders would be found in the syndicate agreement (agreement among underwriters). The typical priority of orders is presale, syndicate (group-net), designated, and then member orders. The allocation of orders is required to be in the syndicate agreement under Municipal Securities Rulemaking Board (MSRB) rules.

25. **B. Firm commitment**

A *firm commitment underwriting* is one in which any unsold securities are retained by the underwriters. *All-or-none (AON)* and *mini-max* are types of best-effort underwritings in which a certain amount of securities must be sold or the offering is canceled.

26. D. firm commitment underwriting

When an investment banking firm (underwriter) agrees to purchase the securities directly from the issuer, it has entered into a firm commitment underwriting. In this type of underwriting, the underwriters assume all the risk of the security being sold.

27. C. Standby

In this case, you're looking for the false answer. *All-or-none (AON)*, *best efforts*, and *mini-max* are all types of bond underwritings. However, a *standby underwriting* is only for common stockholders. A standby underwriter purchases shares that aren't purchased by existing shareholders during a rights offering.

28. B. All-or-none

An all-or-none offering is one in which the underwriter(s) is responsible for selling all the securities, or the offering is canceled. The securities and the money are held in an escrow account until the entire offering is sold. In the event that the offering is canceled, the money is returned to the purchasers, and securities are returned to the issuer. All-or-none and mini-max are types of best-efforts underwritings.

29. C. selling group agreement

Similar to a syndicate agreement, selling groups must sign a selling group agreement. Included are the quantity of shares they're responsible for selling, how much they will get paid, the offering price, the term of the agreement, and so on.

30. A. a price at or below the public offering price

Stabilizing bids must be entered at or slightly below the public offering price. Stabilizing bids can't be placed above the public offering price because they can't be used to help raise the market price of an issue.

31. B. The underwriting spread

The *underwriting spread* is the difference between what the issuer receives and the public offering price. The underwriting spread is equal to the takedown plus the manager's fee.

32. A. IV, I, III, II

Typically, the largest portion goes to the takedown, which is the syndicate's portion. Next would be the concession, followed by the reallowance, and then the manager's fee.

33.　B. The takedown

The takedown is the profit made by syndicate members when selling shares of a new issue.

34.　D. manager's fee

The manager's fee is typically the smallest portion of an underwriting spread.

35.　C. the additional takedown

The additional takedown is the profit syndicate member make on securities sold by the selling group.

36.　A. $0.45 per share

The additional takedown is the profit made by syndicate members on shares sold by the selling group. The syndicate members get the takedown, and the selling group gets the concession. To determine the takedown, take the spread (the difference between the public offering price and the amount that Armbar got per share) and then subtract the manager's fee:

$15.00 − $13.50 = $1.50 spread

$1.50 spread − $0.25 manager's fee = $1.25 takedown

Syndicate members get $1.25 per share if selling the shares themselves, but if the selling group helps sell the shares, they have to subtract the commission so the syndicate members get $0.45 per share:

$1.25 takedown − $0.80 concession = $0.45 additional takedown

37.　C. $450,000

The syndicate is responsible for paying the selling group when selling new shares. If the syndicate members sell the shares themselves, they receive $0.75 per share. However, if the selling group sells shares, they receive $0.30 per share out of the syndicate member's $0.75. Therefore, the syndicate members receive $0.45 ($0.75 − $0.30) per share on shares sold by the selling group. If the selling group sells its entire allotment, the syndicate will receive

(1 million shares)($0.45) = $450,000

The $450,000 is known as the additional takedown.

38.　D. $275,000

The selling group receives the concession. If the selling group sells all of its 500,000 shares, the total will be $275,000 ($0.55 × 500,000 shares).

39. B. 200,000

In a Western or divided account offering, each firm in a syndicate is responsible only for its original allocation. Because the firm has sold $1.8 million of the $2 million of bonds allocated to the firm, the firm is still responsible for selling the remaining $200,000 of its allocation.

40. A. I and IV

The easiest one for you to remember should be the Western (divided) account. Remember, in the wild, wild west, each man was for himself. That should help you remember that if the syndicate was set up on a Western account basis, each member is finished after its allotment is sold. Although you really don't need to do the math on this one because the answer choices give you only one choice for an Eastern (undivided) account where there were additional shares to sell, to find the answer, you'd multiply Liddell's original percentage by the offering size. Liddell Securities originally took 12.5% of the offering (1 million shares divided by 8 million shares); therefore, they're responsible for 12.5% of the shares left unsold by other members on an Eastern account basis:

$$(12.5\%)(800,000) = 100,000$$

41. C. 250,000

When a syndicate is formed on an Eastern (undivided) account basis, each syndicate member is responsible not only for their own allotment but also for a percentage of the shares left unsold by other syndicate members. This syndicate member was responsible for selling 2.5 million shares of a 10 million share offering, which is 25%. After selling its entire allotment, this firm is responsible for selling 25% of the 1 million shares left unsold:

$$(25\%)(1 \text{ million shares}) = 250,000 \text{ shares}$$

42. C. obtain indications of interest from investors

The correct answer is Choice (C). However, look closely at Choice (B). The Securities and Exchange Commission (SEC) (or any self-regulatory organization [SRO] for that matter) never approves or guarantees an issue of securities; the SEC just clears the issue for investment. The preliminary prospectus is released when the issue is in registration during the 20-day cooling-off period. The preliminary prospectus has no price and no effective date and may be used only to obtain indications of interest from investors.

43. D. I and III

Remember, you're looking for the exception in this question. The preliminary prospectus (red herring) would include such items as the financial history of the company (including financial statements) and what the company is going to do with the funds being raised. However, the preliminary prospectus doesn't include the effective (release) date or the public offering price. The effective date and the public offering price would be included in the final prospectus.

44. B. During the cooling-off period

A red herring (preliminary prospectus) will be available to potential investors during the cooling-off period. On the effective date (date that the security will be available for investors to purchase), the final prospectus will be available.

45. A. the offering price

The final prospectus includes the information contained in the preliminary prospectus plus the final offering price, when the securities will be available (the effective date), and the underwriter's spread.

46. D. 90 days after the effective date

If an initial public offering (IPO) will be traded initially on the Over-the-Counter Bulletin Board (OTCBB) or OTC Pink Market, brokerage firms that execute orders for customers to buy the stock must send a copy of the final prospectus with the confirmation (receipt of trade) within the first 90 days after the effective date. For any other unlisted offering, the prospectus needs to be available for 40 days. For an IPO trading immediately on the NASDAQ or exchange, the final prospectus is necessary for the first 25 days of trading. The final prospectus includes items such as the Securities and Exchange Commission's (SEC) "we don't guarantee or approve" disclaimer, the offering price, use of proceeds, description of the underwriting, stabilization bid procedure, business history, investor risk, information about the management, financial information about the issuer, and so on.

47. D. 90 days

Initial public offerings (IPOs) that aren't sold on an exchange have a 90-day prospectus requirement. All other new offerings have a 40-day prospectus requirement.

48. B. I and IV

Under the Securities Act of 1933, securities have to be an investment for profit and an investment risk. Variable annuities and oil and gas limited partnerships have those two elements, but fixed annuities and FDIC insured negotiable CDs don't. Fixed annuities provide guaranteed income, and FDIC-insured CDs don't have the element of risk.

49. **D. commercial paper**

Commercial paper is corporate debt securities that mature in 270 days or less. Debt securities with a maturity of 270 days or less are exempt from Securities and Exchange Commission (SEC) registration.

50. **C. III and IV**

Don't get confused by the terminology here. Exempt securities are exempt from the Securities and Exchange Commission (SEC) registration, but non-exempt securities must register with the SEC. Out of the choices listed, municipal bonds and treasury notes are exempt from SEC registration. However, blue chip stocks and variable annuities must register with the SEC. In the case of variable annuities, they must be registered with the SEC and state insurance commission in each state in which they're to be sold.

51. **A. Limited partnership public offerings**

This question is basically asking you which security must be registered with the Securities and Exchange Commission (SEC). Out of the choices given, the only one that isn't exempt and therefore must be registered is limited partnership public offerings.

52. **C. REITs**

Securities that are exempt from the registration requirements of the Securities Act of 1933 include U.S. government securities (Treasury bonds, Treasury bills, Treasury notes, and so on), municipal bonds, securities issued by banks, public utility stocks and bonds, and so on. However, real estate investment trusts (REITs) must register with the Securities and Exchange Commission (SEC).

53. **C. I and IV**

There is a difference between securities that are exempt because of whom the issuer is and transactions that are exempt. Exempt securities include U.S. government securities, municipal bonds, securities issued by banks, public utility stocks, securities issued by nonprofit organizations, and so on. Intrastate offerings, Regulation A offerings, Regulation D offerings (private placements), and so on are exempt transactions.

54. **D. II, III, and IV**

Rule 144 pertains to secondary market transactions involving restricted or control securities (securities owned by officers, directors, owners of 10% or more of the issuer's voting stock and their immediate family members) and, therefore, doesn't pertain to initial offerings.

55. **A. an offering of securities only within the issuer's home state**

A Rule 147 offering is an intrastate (not interstate) offering that's exempt from the Securities and Exchange Commission (SEC) registration provided the issuer conducts business only in one state and sells securities only to residents of the same state. This also includes the 80% rule that states that at least 80% of the issuer's assets are located within the state, and at least 80% of the offering proceeds are used within the same state.

56. **B. They are issued without using a prospectus.**

Regulation A+ Tier 1offerings are offerings of securities valued at $20 million or less within a one-year period. Regulation A+ Tier 1 and Tier 2 offerings are exempt from the full registration requirements of the Securities Act of 1933. Companies issuing securities through Regulation A+ offerings make an offering circular instead of a prospectus, which is available to all potential purchasers. An *offering circular* is somewhat of an abbreviated form of a prospectus.

57. **B. Regulation A+ Tier 2**

Regulation A+ Tier 2 offerings are offerings of securities valued at $75 million or less within a one-year period. Regulation A+ offerings are exempt transactions under the Securities Act of 1933.

58. **B. a U.S. issuer issuing new securities to non-U.S. investors**

A Regulation S registration exemption under the Securities Act of 1933 is given to U.S. issuers who are offering securities to non-U.S. investors.

59. **B. I and IV**

A Regulation S (Reg S) offering relates to U.S. companies offering securities outside of the United States to non-U.S. residents. The transaction is exempt, and the securities must be held for one year (12 months) before they can be resold in the United States.

60. **A. an offering of securities to no more than 35 unaccredited investors in a 12-month period**

A Regulation D (Reg D; private placement) offering is a provision in the Securities Act of 1933 that exempts offerings sold to no more than 35 unaccredited (small) investors each year. Even though Regulation D offerings are limited to the number of small investors, the amount of money they can raise isn't limited.

61. B. $300,000

Regulation D private placements allow up to only 35 unaccredited investors per year and an unlimited number of accredited investors. To be considered an accredited investor, an individual must have annual income of at least $200,000, and a couple with a joint account must have an annual income of at least $300,000.

62. B. I and IV

For an investor to be considered accredited, they must have a net worth that exceeds $1 million excluding the primary residence or an annual income exceeding $200,000 ($300,000 joint) in the most recent two years with an expectation of the same level in the current year. A Regulation D private placement may have up to only 35 unaccredited investors per year and an unlimited number of accredited investors.

63. A. At the time of sale

Insiders must file a Form 144 with the Securities and Exchange Commission (SEC) when ready to sell restricted or control stock. After notifying the SEC, the investor has 90 days to sell the stock registered with the SEC. The maximum amount of shares that the insider may sell in the 90-day period is 1% of the outstanding shares or the average weekly trading volume for the previous four weeks, whichever is greater.

64. D. 42,500

When the restricted stock is to be sold, a Form 144 must be filed with the Securities and Exchange Commission (SEC), which is good for 90 days. According to Rule 144, the most the investor can sell after holding the restricted stock for at least six months is the greater of 1% of the outstanding shares or the average weekly trading volume for the previous four weeks. You have to be careful to take just the previous four weeks, which in this case is the top four. Start by multiplying the 1% by the 4 million shares outstanding:

$$(1\%)(4 \text{ million}) = 40,000$$

Next, determine the average weekly trading volume for the previous four weeks by adding together the amount of shares sold and dividing by 4:

$$35,000 + 50,000 + 40,000 + 45,000 = 170,000$$

$$\frac{170,000}{4} = 42,500$$

This investor can sell a maximum of 42,500 shares.

Chapter 2 Answers

65. **A. I and III**

Both preferred stockholders and common stockholders have ownership of a corporation. Bondholders are creditors, not owners.

66. **A. Common stock**

Out of the choices listed, common stocks are considered the riskiest. The risk is that common stockholders are the last to be paid in the event of corporate bankruptcy. However, the trade-off is that common stockholders have the greatest potential reward because their prices can fluctuate more than any of the other investment choices listed. Remember: more risk = more reward.

67. **C. TUV common stock**

Common stockholders are the last to be paid in the event of corporate bankruptcy, so they're subject to the greatest risk. Common stock is a junior security. Out of the choices listed, the first to be paid would be the mortgage bondholders (secured creditors), subordinated debenture holders (unsecured creditors), preferred stockholders, and, last but not least, common stockholders.

68. **B. III and IV**

Common stockholders have a residual claim to the assets of the corporation at dissolution. Common stockholders are entitled to receive a report containing audited financial statements on a yearly — *not* monthly — basis. Stockholders do get to vote for stock splits but not dividends (whether cash or stock); the board of directors decides on dividends.

69. **C. I and II**

Stockholders can't vote for dividends. Stock and cash dividends are declared by the board of directors.

70. **C. 200 votes for each of the three positions**

If this was cumulative voting, any of the choices would be possible. Since this is statutory (regular) voting, an investor holding 200 shares can only vote 200 shares for each of the open positions.

71. **A. Cumulative**

Cumulative voting benefits minority shareholders because it provides them a better chance to gain representation on the board of directors.

72. **C. 3,000 votes each for three candidates**

This investor has a total of 8,000 votes (2,000 shares × 4 vacancies), which can be voted any which way because it's cumulative voting. The reason that Choice (C) doesn't work is because it would require 9,000 votes (3,000 votes × 3 candidates), and this investor has only 8,000.

73. **D. 4,000**

Cain has a total of 4,000 votes (1,000 shares × 4 vacancies). Because HIT allows cumulative voting, Cain can vote the shares in any way he sees fit, even if he votes them all for one candidate. Statutory or regular voting would allow Cain to vote only up to 1,000 shares for each candidate.

74. **C. 950,000**

Macrohard could have issued up to 2 million shares, but it issued only 1.1 million at this time. Macrohard repurchased 150,000 shares of its stock, which is called treasury stock. To determine the quantity of shares outstanding, use the following formula:

$$\begin{aligned} \text{Outstanding} &= \text{Issued} - \text{Treasury} \\ &= 1,100,000 - 150,000 \\ &= 950,000 \end{aligned}$$

75. **D. 8 million**

Remember, treasury stock is stock that was issued and repurchased by the company. In this case, MKR has issued 12 million of the 20 million shares they are authorized to issue. So, if it issued 12 million out of the 20 million, there are still 8 million shares that have been authorized but unissued.

76. **B. It is stock that was previously authorized but still unissued.**

Choices (B) and (C) oppose each other, so one of them has to be the answer to the question. Treasury stock is stock that was issued and subsequently repurchased by the company. Treasury stock has no voting rights and doesn't receive dividends.

77. D. repurchased stock

Choices (A) and (B) are wrong because stock represents ownership, and you can't own a percentage of the government. Treasury stock is stock that was outstanding in the market and subsequently repurchased by the issuer. Corporations repurchase their own stock sometimes to increase the demand for their outstanding shares or to avoid a takeover.

78. A. I and III

Unlike the par value of preferred stock and debt securities, the par value doesn't really matter too much to common stockholders. The par value of common stock is generally used for bookkeeping purposes of the issuer, and common stock is even sometimes issued with no par value. In the event of a stock split, the par value would be adjusted to reflect the split. And because stock is an equity security that represents ownership of the issuing corporation, there's no maturity date as there is with debt securities.

79. C. a stock split

Par value for a common stock is used for bookkeeping purposes for the issuer and isn't of much use to investors. However, when a company does split its stock (such as 2 for 1), the par value would be reduced.

80. A. I and III

The *ex-dividend date* is the first day a stock trades without a previously declared dividend. The ex-dividend date is 2 business days before the record date (except for mutual funds), and it's the date that the stock reduces by the amount of the dividend.

81. B. $24.65

You solve this question by simply subtracting the amount of the dividend from the previous day's closing price:

$24.95 − $0.30 = $24.65

82. C. II and III

When an investor receives a stock dividend, the amount of shares the investor owns increases, and the price decreases. The only answer that works is Choice (C). *Remember:* When an investor receives a stock dividend or stock split, the investor's overall value of investment doesn't change. You can also figure this out mathematically by multiplying the number of shares by the market price, like so:

(1,000 shares)($24 market price) = $24,000

This investor owns $24,000 worth of DIM stock, so they'll own $24,000 worth of DIM stock after the stock dividend. Your next step would be to figure out the new number of shares owned by the investor. The investor initially owned 1,000 shares and then received a stock dividend of 200 shares ($20\% \times 1{,}000$ shares):

$$1{,}000 \text{ shares} + 200 \text{ shares} = 1{,}200 \text{ shares}$$

$$\frac{\$24{,}000}{1200 \text{ shares}} = \$20 \text{ market price}$$

83. D. 525 shares valued at $52.38 per share

Your key here is that the overall investment value doesn't change. When investors receive a stock dividend, the number of shares has to increase, and the market price has to reduce. So out of the answer choices given, only one meets the criteria: Choice (D). First, you have to figure out the overall value of investment by multiplying the number of shares by the market price:

$$(500 \text{ shares})(\$55 \text{ per share}) = \$27{,}500$$

This investor had $27,500 worth of stock and will still have $27,500 worth of stock after the dividend. When this investor gets the 5% stock dividend, they'll get 5% more shares, which means that this investor now has 525 shares: 500 shares + 25 shares (5% stockdividend) = 525 shares. Divide the $27,500 by the new number of shares to find the new stock price.

$$\frac{\$27{,}500}{525 \text{ shares}} = \$52.38 \text{ per share}$$

84. D. Consolidations

Rule 145 applies to major changes to a company such as consolidations, mergers, acquisitions, and spin-offs. A consolidation happens when two or more companies combine to form a new company or entity.

85. B. a risk disclosure document

Unless otherwise exempt, all broker-dealers who trade penny stocks must provide a risk disclosure document (a penny stock disclosure document) to their penny stock customers. The penny stock disclosure document outlines the risks of investing in penny stocks (lack of liquidity, quick price changes, and so on).

86. D. II and IV

Penny stocks are non-Nasdaq securities, which trade under $5 per share. So, these stocks are ones too small to trade on an exchange or Nasdaq, so they trade over-the-counter typically on OTC Link or OTC Pink Market.

87. D. a customer who has purchased two different penny stocks previously through the broker–dealer of the rep

Under SEC Rule 15g–1, the following penny–stock transactions will be exempt:

» Transactions by a broker or dealer whose commissions, mark-ups, mark-downs, and commission equivalents from penny stock transactions did not exceed 5% of its total commissions in the preceding 3 months and during 11 or more of the preceding 12 months or the preceding 6 months and who hasn't been a market maker in that particular penny stock in the preceding 12 months

» Transactions that meet the requirements of Regulation D

» Transactions in which the client is an institutional accredited investor

» Transactions that are not recommended by the broker-dealer

» Transactions in which the customer is the issuer, officer, general partner, director, and so on of more than 5% of any class of equity security of the issuer of the penny stock

» Any other transaction deemed to be exempt by the SEC that it deems as consistent with the protection of investors and is in the public's interest

88. A. I and II

Common and preferred stock are considered equity securities because holders are owners of the issuing corporation. Dividends paid to both preferred and common stock are determined by the board of directors. However, only common stockholders have voting rights.

89. C. I and III

Straight preferred stock does receive a fixed dividend and has higher preference than common stock in the event of issuer bankruptcy. However, holders of preferred stock don't have voting rights unless they don't receive expected dividends. Also, unlike bonds, preferred stock has no maturity date.

90. A. I only

Unlike common stock, which can pay dividends in the form of cash, stock, or product, preferred dividends can be paid only in the form of cash.

91. C. II and III

Unlike holders of common stock, preferred stockholders typically don't have voting rights unless not receiving expected dividends. In the event of corporate bankruptcy, preferred stockholders are senior to common stockholders and would receive liquidation assets (if any) before common stockholders.

92. B. decrease

Preferred stocks, like bonds, are affected by interest rate changes. Rates and prices have an inverse relationship. Because interest rates have increased, straight preferred stock prices would decrease.

93. C. $7

If a company issues cumulative preferred stock, it's allowed to owe investors dividend payments. However, before the company pays a dividend to common stockholders, it must first make up any delinquent and current payments to the cumulative preferred shareholders. This company should be paying the preferred shareholders $4 per year (4% of $100 par). In the first three years, the company should have paid out $12 in dividends ($4 × 3 years). However, the company paid only $9, so it owes $3 from the first three years ($12 − $9) and $4 for the following year for a total of $7.

94. B. Convertible

Preferred stockholders are subject to inflation risk in the same way that most bondholders are. *Inflation risk* is the risk that the fixed interest or dividend payments will be worth less in terms of purchasing power over time. By purchasing convertible preferred stock, investors may convert their preferred stock into common stock of the same corporation at any time. Typically, common stock has a greater chance of keeping pace with inflation, which would reduce that risk.

95. D. convertible preferred stock

Typically, preferred stock trades somewhat close to its par value. Because it trades close to its par value, investors are subject to inflation risk. Inflation risk is the risk that the value of the security doesn't keep pace with the cost of living. Your client can minimize this risk by purchasing convertible preferred stock. Convertible preferred stock allows investors to convert their preferred stock into common stock of the same company at any time. Common stock is more likely to keep pace with inflation.

96. B. 5 shares

To determine the amount of common shares a convertible preferred stock is convertible into, use the following formula:

$$\text{Conversion ratio} = \frac{\text{Par}}{\text{Conversion price}}$$
$$= \frac{\$100}{\$20}$$
$$= 5 \text{ shares}$$

97. A. $21.50

Assume that the par value of convertible preferred stock is $100 unless stated differently in the question. As with other convertible problems, the first thing you must do is get the quantity of shares it's convertible into. You can use the following formula:

$$\text{Conversion ratio} = \frac{\text{Par}}{\text{Conversion price}}$$

$$= \frac{\$100}{\$25}$$

$$= 4 \text{ shares}$$

Next, you have to get the parity price by dividing the market price of the preferred stock by the conversion ratio:

$$\frac{\$90}{4 \text{ shares}} = \$22.50$$

DEF common stock should be trading at $22.50 to be at parity with the preferred stock. However, the question states that the common stock is trading one point ($1) below parity, so the common stock is trading at $21.50 ($22.50 − $1).

98. C. callable

This is another one of those investing situations where more risk = more reward. From an investor's standpoint, purchasing callable securities is riskier than non-callable securities because the issuer decides when the security is called. For example, the issuer may call the security after one year when you were hoping to hold it at least ten years. Because an investor is taking that additional risk, callable securities pay a higher dividend or higher interest (bonds) than non-callable.

99. C. It allows the issuer to issue preferred stock with a lower fixed dividend after the call date.

First, you should have crossed off Choice (D) right away because equity securities, such as preferred stock, don't have a maturity date. Callable preferred stock is issued with a higher fixed dividend rate than non-callable because it's riskier for investors (more risk = more reward) because they may not be able to hold the stock as long as they want. Issuers will typically call their callable preferred stock and/or callable bonds when interest rates decrease. If interest rates decrease, issuers would be able to issue preferred stock with a lower fixed dividend and/or bonds with a lower coupon rate.

100. D. the issuer can replace stock with a higher dividend with stock with a lower dividend

Although callable preferred stock would have a higher dividend than non-callable preferred stock, it's not an advantage to issuers. However, if interest rates drop, issuers of callable preferred stock can call in their high-dividend stock and issue stock with a lower dividend and save money.

101. A. minimum yearly dividend payment

The stated dividend for a participating preferred stock is the minimum dividend that an investor can receive. Participating preferred stock receives its own dividend and a portion of the dividend received by the common stockholders. In this case, the minimum the investor can receive is 5% if no common dividend was paid. If a common dividend was paid, the investor would receive greater than 5%.

102. B. Prior preferred shareholders

In the event of corporate bankruptcy, prior (senior) preferred shareholders would be the first owners to be paid.

103. A. Treasury bill rate

Adjustable-rate preferred stock (ARPS) has a dividend that typically varies with the Treasury bill (T-bill) rate. It's not typically set at the exact T-bill rate but at some predetermined formula tied to the T-bill rate (that is, a set percentage of the average T-bill rate for a given period of time).

104. C. ADR holders

ADRs (American Depositary Receipts) are receipts for foreign securities trading in the United States. If the issuer declares dividends, ADR holders will receive them. However, both rights and warrants give the holder the right, but not the obligation, to buy the underlying stock, so they aren't the stock. Therefore, they don't receive dividends.

105. A. a receipt for a foreign security trading in the United States

An ADR is an American depositary receipt. ADRs are receipts for foreign securities traded in the United States. Besides the normal risks of investing in securities, holders of ADRs also face currency risk.

106. C. it has low currency risk

American depositary receipts (ADRs) facilitate the trading of foreign securities in U.S. markets. ADRs carry currency risk because distributions on them must be converted from foreign currency to U.S. dollars on the date of distribution. The trading price of the ADR is actually quite affected by currency fluctuation, which can devalue any dividends and/or the value of the underlying security.

107. A. they help U.S. companies gain access to foreign dollars

American depositary receipts (ADRs) are receipts for foreign securities trading in the United States. Therefore, they help foreign companies gain access to U.S. dollars, not the other way around. Investors don't receive the actual stock certificates; they receive a receipt representing a certain number of shares of the issuer. Investors of ADRs don't have voting rights. Dividends (if any) are paid in U.S. dollars.

108. B. II, III, and IV

Holders of American depositary receipts (ADRs) face foreign currency risk, market risk, and political risk. However, because ADRs are actively traded, holders don't face liquidity risk.

109. B. a rights distribution to existing shareholders

Remember, the corporation is trying to raise money. Choices (A) and (C) would cost the corporation money, and Choice (D) would be a wash. However, having a rights distribution allows existing shareholders to purchase new stock at a discount and, thus, brings more money into the corporation.

110. D. rights are automatically received by preferred stockholders

Rights are automatically received by common stockholders, not preferred stockholders. Each share of outstanding common stock receives one right. Rights are short-term (usually 30 to 45 days), and rights offerings typically have a standby underwriter to purchase the shares not purchased by stockholders.

111. C. rights offering

Rights offering are offerings of additional shares of common stock to existing shareholders at a discount.

112. D. $2.00

The easiest way to determine the answer to this question is to set up the following equation for cum-rights (prior to ex-rights):

$$\frac{M-S}{N+1}$$

where M is the market price ($30), S is the subscription price (discount price – $24), and N is the number of rights needed to purchase one share (2).

$$\frac{\$30-\$24}{2+1}=\frac{\$6}{3}=\$2$$

After setting up the equation and plugging in the numbers, you see that the theoretical value of a right is $2.

## 113.	D. II and IV

Your client receives one right for each share of common stock owned. Because your client owns 80 shares of stock, the investor will receive 80 rights. Your client will need nine rights plus $10 for each share of stock purchased in the proposal. To determine the number of shares your client will be able to purchase in the rights offering, you need to divide the 80 rights by the 9 rights needed to purchase one share:

$$\frac{80 \text{ rights}}{9 \text{ rights}} = 8.3 \text{ shares}$$

However, the proposal allows fractional shares to become whole shares. Therefore, 8.3 shares changes to 9 shares. Your client is actually able to purchase 9 shares for $90 (9 × 10).

## 114.	C. $2.00

Each current shareholder receives one right for each share of common stock owned. To determine the value of a right (ex-rights), use the following equation.

$$\frac{M - S}{N}$$

where M is the market price ($45), S is the subscription price (discount price – $35), and N is the number of rights needed to purchase one share (5).

$$\frac{\$45 - \$35}{5} = \frac{\$10}{5} = \$2$$

After setting up the equation and plugging in the numbers, you see that the theoretical value of a right is $2.00.

## 115.	A. I and II

Be careful when answering questions that have words such as *except* or *not* so that you don't make a careless mistake. In this case, you're looking for the false answer(s). Warrants are sometimes issued with bond offerings in a unit to make a bond offering more attractive. Warrants give the holder the right to purchase the issuer's common stock at a fixed price. Warrants trade in the market independent of the bonds. Warrants trade at a price much lower than the company's common stock; holders have a leveraged position. This means that the true answers are statements III and V, so the correct answers for this question are statements I and II, or Choice (A). Holders of warrants don't receive dividends, because they're not holding equity securities until the warrants are exercised.

116. C. They have voting rights.

Warrants give investors a long-term and sometimes perpetual right to buy stock from the issuer at a fixed price. They are marketable, meaning that they may trade separately. Because warrants aren't the underlying security until the holder actually uses the warrants to purchase stock, they don't receive dividends. The answer that is *not true* is Choice (C). Warrant holders don't have voting rights.

117. B. they are non-marketable securities

Warrants *are* marketable securities, which means that they can be traded separately in the market. Warrants have longer maturities than rights because they typically have a maturity of up to ten years and sometimes longer. Rights typically have a maturity of only 30 to 45 days. When initially issued, warrants are usually combined in a unit with the issuer's bonds. The exercise price of the warrants would be at a price higher than the market price of the issuer's common stock.

118. B. I and III

Warrants are most often issued with a corporation's other securities, such as debt securities, to make an offering more attractive. Because of this, warrants are often called "sweeteners" because they're sweetening the deal. Statement II uses the word *perpetual,* which means never ending. Warrants typically provide a long-term and sometimes perpetual interest in the issuer's common stock. Holders of warrants have no voting rights until exercising their right to buy the common stock.

Chapter 3 Answers

119. C. I, II, and IV

The Trust Indenture Act of 1939 regulates all corporate bond issues exceeding $50 million. The only corporate bonds listed are equipment trust bonds. U.S. government T-bonds, municipal general obligation (GO) bonds, and municipal revenue bonds are exempt from the Trust Indenture Act of 1939.

120. B. $1,000 plus any outstanding interest

When holding a bond until maturity, an investor will receive par value plus any outstanding interest, which is usually the last interest payment. Assume par value is $1,000 unless stated differently in the question.

121.

B. $1,020

This question has a lot of information that you don't need to come up with an answer. All you need to know is that you're working with a 4% bond and that your client held it until maturity. The fact that it was yielding 5% and that it's a convertible bond aren't relevant to the question. When investors hold a bond until maturity, they receive par value (usually $1,000). However, if the bond is paying interest, holders also receive their last coupon payment at maturity. It's a 4% bond, so investors will receive $40 per year interest (4% of $1,000 par) broken down into two $20 semiannual payments. But you need to know what your client will receive, so you add the par value to the interest: $1,000 par value + $20 interest = $1,020.

122.

C. $10,137.50

The first thing you have to do is convert the fraction to a decimal. So, a bond trading at 101⅜ would convert to a bond trading at 101.375 (3/8 = 0.375). Next, you have to remember that these $1,000 par value bonds aren't actually trading at 101.375. The 101.375 is a percentage of par, so the bonds are actually trading at (101.375%)($1,000 par) = $1,013.75.

Next, because the investor is purchasing ten of these bonds, you have to multiply your answer by 10: ($1,013.75)(10 bonds) = $10,137.50.

123.

A. I and III

One point on a bond equals 1% ($10 on a $1,000 par bond). A basis point is 1/100 of a point, or 10 cents. In this case, because the bond increased by 50 basis points (1/2 a point), it increased by 0.50% or $5.

124.

B. $20.00

To determine the annual interest, you have to multiply the coupon rate (4%) by par value ($1,000): (4%)($1,000) = $40 annual interest.

Because bonds pay interest semiannually (twice a year), the investor will get paid $20 ($40/2) every six months.

125.

B. I and III

The indenture of a bond is a legal contract between the issuer and the bondholder. The indenture includes items such as the nominal yield (coupon rate), the maturity date, collateral backing the bond (if any), coupon payment dates, and callable and convertible features. The rating and the yield to maturity can't be included in the indenture because neither of them is static. The rating changes if the issuer's financial condition changes, and the yield to maturity changes when the market value changes.

126. D. nominal yield

The only yield that could be included on the indenture of a corporate bond is the nominal yield (coupon rate). None of the other choices could be placed on the indenture of a corporate bond because they don't remain fixed. The yield to maturity, yield to call, and current yield change over time and when the market price changes.

127. C. Mortgage bonds

First, eliminate the answer choices that won't work. *High-yield bonds* are also called "junk" bonds because of their high credit risk, and this investor is looking for only a moderate amount of risk, so that's not the best recommendation. *Convertible bonds* have a lower amount of income than comparable non-convertible bonds because of the conversion feature, so that won't work, either. *Mortgage bonds* may work because they provide income once every six months in the form of interest payments, and they're relatively safe because they're secured by property owned by the issuer. *Income (adjustment) bonds* are definitely out because they're issued by corporations in bankruptcy (reorganization) and are extremely risky. Therefore, out of the choices listed, *mortgage bonds* is the best recommendation.

128. D. a lien on property owned by HIJ Corp.

This is one of those questions that takes you on a ride full of superfluous information you don't need. All you need to know is what the bonds are secured by. In this case, you're dealing with mortgage bonds, which are secured by a lien on property owned by HIJ. In the event that HIJ failed to pay principal and/or interest to its bondholders, property owned by HIJ would be sold to generate the money to make the payments.

129. B. I and II

Corporations may issue unsecured bonds, such as debentures, subordinated debentures, and income bonds, or secured bonds, such as mortgage bonds, equipment trust bonds, income bonds, and guaranteed bonds. However, *double-barreled bonds* and *revenue bonds* are types of bonds issued by municipalities.

130. C. an equipment trust bond

Equipment trust bonds (or equipment trust certificates, ETCs) are typically issued by transportation companies, such as trucking companies, airlines, and railroads. These secured bonds are backed by rolling stock (assets on wheels). In the event of default, the rolling assets backing the bonds would be sold to pay off bondholders.

131. B. backed by stocks and bonds owned by the issuer

Collateral trust bonds are typically issued by holding companies that hold securities of other companies. In the event of default, the debt holders receive the securities held in trust. A trustee hired by the issuer is responsible for the safeguarding of the securities and transferring the assets in the event of default.

132. B. one that is backed by the assets of another company

A *guaranteed bond* is one that's backed by the assets of another company (typically a parent company).

133. D. Income bonds

Income (adjustment) bonds are issued by corporations in bankruptcy (reorganization). These bonds are typically sold at a deep discount, and holders won't receive interest unless the issuing corporation becomes popular. Therefore, income bonds typically trade flat (without accrued interest).

134. C. Debentures

Debentures are only backed by the issuer's good word and written agreement (the indenture) stating that they will pay interest when due and par value at maturity.

135. B. Income bonds

The one you need to stay away from is income (adjustment) bonds. Income bonds are typically issued by failing businesses (bankruptcy or reorganization). As such, the bondholders receive only the interest and principal if the issuer has enough money to pay it. Income bonds are extremely risky but if the company turns around, the reward can be high. Income bonds are typically issued at a deep discount. All of the other answer choices would be proper recommendations for an investor who is risk-averse.

136. A. Zero-coupon bonds

Out of the choices listed, the best answer is *zero-coupon bonds*. Mrs. Jones is planning for a future event (a child's college tuition). Zero-coupon bonds are purchased at a deep discount from par (for example, $600 per bond), and the bonds mature at $1,000 par and don't pay interest along the way. This type of bond allows investors to invest a smaller amount of money now in return for a larger amount of money at maturity.

137. A. II, III, and IV

Eurodollar bonds are denominated in U.S. dollars and issued by non-American companies outside of the United States and the issuer's home country. Because they're issued outside the United States by non-U.S. companies, they don't have to be registered with the Securities and Exchange Commission (SEC). All securities issued outside the United States are subject to currency risk.

138. B. sovereign bonds

Sovereign bonds are debt securities issued by foreign national governments. In the case of sovereign bonds, the interest and principal payments are paid in the foreign government's currency.

139. B. decrease

There is an inverse relationship between interest rates or yields and prices. If interest rates are being increased, the prices of outstanding bonds will decrease.

140. B. nominal yield

The nominal yield is the same as the coupon rate. As interest rates change, the nominal yield remains the same. So, a 7% bond would have a coupon rate of 7% and a nominal yield of 7%, regardless of the price of the bond.

141. C. 4.35%

To determine the current yield of a bond, you have to divide the annual interest by the market price. The annual interest is $40 (4% × $1,000 par), and the market price is $920 (92% × $1,000 par):

$$\text{Current yield} = \frac{\text{Annual interest}}{\text{Market price}}$$
$$= \frac{\$40}{\$920}$$
$$= 0.0435, \text{ or } 4.35\%$$

142. A. 4.19%

The coupon rate represents the annual rate of interest. In this case, the coupon rate is 4.25%, which means that the investor will receive $42.50 (4.25% of $1,000 par) per year broken down into two semiannual payments.

U.S. government bonds, such as Treasury bonds (T-bonds), are quoted in 32nds, not decimals, so pay close attention to the security in the question.

The market price of the bond is

$$101.16 = 101\frac{16}{32} = 101.50\% \text{ of } \$1,000 \text{ par} = \$1,015.00$$

Finally, to determine the current yield, use the following formula:

$$\text{Current yield on a bond} = \frac{\text{Annual interest}}{\text{Market price}}$$
$$= \frac{\$42.50}{\$1,015.00}$$
$$= 0.0419, \text{ or } 4.19\%$$

143. C. yield to maturity

Yield to maturity and basis mean the same thing. It's the yield an investor would expect if holding the bond to maturity regardless of the market price.

144. D. 7.0%

Determining the yield to call is somewhat similar to determining the yield to maturity. However, you need to use the call price rather than the maturity price. Use this formula to find the yield to call (YTC):

$$\frac{\text{Annual interest} + \text{Annual accretion to the call date}}{(\text{Purchase price} + \text{Call price}) / 2}$$

The annual interest is $50 because it has a 5% coupon rate, and par value is $1,000 (5% of $1,000 = $50). This bond was purchased at $950 (95% of $1,000 par) and was called at $1,050 in five years for a total accretion to the call date of $100. The bond price will increase from $950 to $1,050 in five years.

Take the $100 difference ($1,050 – $950) and divide it by five years to determine the yearly accretion:

$$\frac{\$100}{5 \text{ years}} = \$20 \text{ per year accretion until the call date}$$

Finally, add the $50 annual interest plus the $20 per year accretion and divide it by the average price to get the yield to call: $\frac{\$50 + \$20}{(\$950 + \$1,050) / 2} = \frac{\$70}{\$1,000} = 0.07$, or 7.0%.

145. D. Eurodollar bonds

The discount yield formula is used for debt securities that are issued at a discount and don't make interest payments. Treasury bills, Treasury strips, and zero-coupon bonds are all issued at a discount and don't make interest payments.

146. B. a premium

The easiest way for you to deal with questions like this is to set up a seesaw, like the following. The yields on the seesaw are always going to be in the same position. You just have to remember that higher numbers are raised up higher on the seesaw.

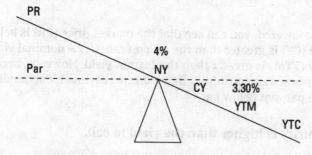

Note: PR = price of the bond, NY = nominal yield (coupon rate), CY = current yield, YTM = yield to maturity (basis), and YTC = yield to call.

The dashed line represents a bond trading at par value (normally $1,000). The NY is 4%, and the YTM is 3.30%. Because 3.30% is lower than 4%, you have to lower the right side of the seesaw. After you do this, the left side raises, and you can see that the bond would be trading at a premium to par value.

147. A. 4.76%

To find the yield, use this formula:

$$\frac{\text{Annual interest} + \text{Annual accretion or} - \text{Annual amortization}}{(\text{Purchase price} + \text{par}) / 2}$$

The annual interest is $60 because it has a 6% coupon rate, and par value is $1,000 (6% of $1,000 = $60). Because this bond was purchased at a premium, you have to determine the annual amortization by taking the difference between the purchase price and par value and dividing it by the ten years until maturity.

$$\frac{\$100}{10 \text{ years until maturity}} = \$10 \text{ per year amortization}$$

Now plug in the numbers to calculate the yield:

$$\frac{\$60 - \$10}{(\$1,100 + \$1,000) / 2} = \frac{\$50}{\$1,050} = 0.0476, \text{ or } 4.76\%$$

148. D. I, II, and IV

The best way to visualize a bond selling at a discount and how it affects the yields is by setting up a seesaw, like the following. Because the bond is selling at a discount, the price is below par value, so the left side of the seesaw has to be lowered.

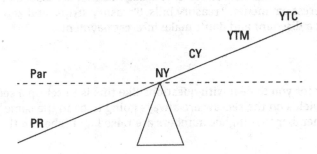

With the left side lowered, you can see that the market price (PR) is below par value, the current yield (CY) is greater than the coupon rate (NY = nominal yield), and the yield to maturity (YTM) is greater than the current yield. However, because rates and prices have an inverse relationship, if interest rates declined, outstanding bond prices would rise above par, not below par.

149. A. The yield to maturity is higher than the yield to call.

This investor purchased the bond at a premium, for a price of $1,020 (102% of $1,000 par). The best way for you to visualize a bond selling at a premium and how it affects the yields is to set up a seesaw, like the following. Because the bond is selling at a premium, the price is above par value, so the left side of the seesaw has to be raised.

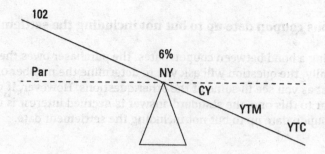

With a bond trading at a premium, the nominal yield (NY, or coupon rate) is the highest yield, the next highest is the current yield (CY), followed by the yield to maturity (YTM; basis), and the lowest is the yield to call (YTC). So, the only answer choice that's true is Choice (A), which says that the yield to maturity is higher than the yield to call.

150. C. the date on which a bond begins accruing interest

The dated date is the date on which bonds start accruing interest. When determining the number of days of accrued interest for new bonds, you start counting from the dated date because there's no previous coupon date.

151. D. 50 days

Because the question refers to a new municipal bond, no previous coupon date exists, so you need to use the dated date. The dated date is the first day a bond starts accruing interest. Municipal bonds settle in 3 business days. As such, this transaction settled on February 21 (2/21). So, subtract the previous dated date of January 1 (1/1) from that:

$$
\begin{array}{ccc}
 & 2 & / & 21 \\
- & 1 & / & 1 \\
\hline
\multicolumn{4}{c}{1\ \text{month and 20 days}}
\end{array}
$$

Corporate and municipal bonds assume 30-day months so you end up with $30 + 20 = 50$ days.

152. D. 88 days

Accrued interest is owed when a bond is purchased between coupon dates. Corporate bonds settle in 3 business days so the settlement date is Thursday, May 13 (5/13). From that, you need to subtract the previous coupon date of February 15 (2/15):

$$
\begin{array}{ccc}
 & 5 & / & 13 \\
- & 2 & / & 15 \\
\hline
\multicolumn{4}{c}{3\ \text{months and} -2\ \text{days}}
\end{array}
$$

Corporate and municipal bonds assume 30-day months, so you end up with 90 days (3 months × 30 days) less 2 days for a total of 88 days.

153. A. from the previous coupon date up to but not including the settlement date

When purchasing a bond between coupon dates, the purchaser owes the seller accrued interest. Typically, the question will ask you to determine the number of days of accrued interest as you see in some of the other questions. However, if you're asked a question similar to this one, the standard answer is Accrued interest is calculated from the previous coupon date up to but not including the settlement date.

154. B. I and IV

Corporate and municipal securities calculate accrued interest assuming 30-day months and a 360-day year. However, U.S. government securities calculate accrued interest using actual days per month and actual days per year (normally 365).

155. C. 97 days

This question is a little more difficult because you're calculating the days of accrued interest for a U.S. government bond and not a municipal or corporate bond. U.S. government bonds settle in 1 business day rather than 2 and calculate accrued interest, using actual days per month instead of 30-day months. So, the first thing you need to do is get the settlement date of Friday, October 20 (10/20), and subtract the previous coupon date of July 15 (7/15).

$$
\begin{array}{ccc}
10 & / & 20 \\
- \quad 7 & / & 15 \\
\hline
\end{array}
$$
3 months and 5 days

The best way to start is by assuming 30-day months and then adding additional days where needed. So, you have 90 days ($3\text{ months} \times 30\text{ days}$) plus 5 days for a total of 95 days. Next, because you're going through the end of July, August, and September, you have to add extra days for the months that have more than 30 days. In this case, July and August have 31 days, so you need to add 2 extra days:

$$90\text{ days} + 5\text{ days} + 2\text{ extra days (July and August)} = 97\text{ days}$$

156. C. long coupon

You can assume that bonds pay interest semiannually (once every six months) unless it's a zero-coupon bond. In this case, the first coupon date is 6½ months from the dated date, so the first payment is a long coupon. So, investors would receive a little more than their regular six-month coupon payment.

157. D. I, II, III, and IV

The liquidity (marketability) of a bond depends on many factors, including the rating (the higher, the more liquid), the coupon rate (the higher, the more liquid), the maturity (the shorter, the higher the liquidity), call features (non-callable bonds are more liquid), the current market value (the lower, the more liquid), and the issuer (the more well known, the more liquid).

158. A. Default risk

Moody's, Standard & Poor's, and Fitch rate the likelihood of default of bond issuers. The likelihood of default relates to the chances that investors won't receive their expected interest payments or par value at maturity.

159. C. I, II, and III

The top four Moody's ratings — Aaa, Aa, A, Baa — are considered investment grade, and everything Ba and below are considered speculative or "junk" bonds. Remember, S&P, Moody's, and Fitch rate the creditworthiness of debt securities.

160. C. Investment grade bonds

Out of the choices listed, the safest investment is *investment grade bonds.* For the most part, people who hold investment grade bonds receive par value at maturity, no matter whether the market is up or down. *Blue chip stocks* are stocks of well-established companies, but the stock is still subject to market fluctuation. *Warrants* and *call options* are the riskiest of the choices because investors have a higher likelihood of losing all money invested.

161. A. IV, III, II, I

The top four S&P (Standard & Poor's) investment ratings — AAA, AA, A, and BBB — are considered investment grade and have a relatively high degree of safety. Each rating can be broken down even further by adding plusses and minuses. For example, in the AA rating, you'd have from highest to lowest: AA+, AA, AA−. So, the first thing you need to look at is the letter rating and then whether it has any plusses or minuses. Out of the choices listed, AAA is the highest, AA is the next highest, AA− is the one after that, and A+ is the lowest. You can assume for test purposes that the lower the rating, the higher the yield (more risk = more reward).

162. C. BB

S&P ratings of BB and lower are considered high-yield (speculative or junk) bonds. The lower the rating, the higher the risk of default.

163. D. Little call protection

This is one of those questions where you have to look at things from a corporation's point of view rather than an investor's point of view. From a corporation's point of view, having to pay a high coupon rate, having a put feature, or having to pay a high call premium aren't desirable. However, having little call protection on callable bonds that it issued would be the best. Call protection has to do with the number of years an issuer has to wait before calling its bonds.

164. D. The amount that the issuer must pay to investors for calling its bonds early

A call premium is the amount that the issuer must pay to investors for calling its bonds early. When a corporation issues callable bonds, it typically has to pay a call premium (an amount over par value) as a disincentive for calling its bonds early. The issuer, not the investor, is the one that decides when the bonds are called.

165. B. the amount an issuer must pay above par value when calling its bonds early

A call premium is the amount over par value paid by an issuer if calling its bonds in the early years.

166. D. IV only

Looking at it from the issuer's point of view, the issuer will most likely refund the issue that will cost it the most money over the life of the issue. When selecting the correct answer, the first thing that an issuer would look at is the coupon rate (highest coupon first), next would be the call premium (lowest call premium first), after that, the call date (earliest call date first), and last, the maturity (longest maturity first). Out of the choices given, the one that the issuer would refund first would be option IV.

167. A. lower than

Put (puttable) bonds are better for investors. Put bonds allow the investors to "put" the bond back (redeem them) to the issuer at any time and price stated on the indenture. Since they give investors more flexibility, they are issued at a lower coupon rate. Put bonds are rarely issued.

168. A. If interest rates have decreased

An issuer would more likely call their bonds if interest rates have decreased. In this situation, they could call their bonds and issue new bonds with a lower coupon rate. This would save them money.

169. B. Convertible bonds

It's important for holders of convertible securities to have an anti-dilution clause (antidilutive covenant) to protect the conversion rights. For example, say that you have a bond that's convertible into 20 shares of common stock. If the issuer splits its stock 2 for 1, you wouldn't be happy having your bond convertible into 20 shares of stock worth half as much. So, with an anti-dilution clause, in this case, if the issuer splits its stock 2 for 1, you'd receive 40 shares of stock (2 for 1).

170. C. II and III

When a corporation declares a stock dividend, investors receive more shares at a lower market price.

When the corporation lowers the market price due to the stock dividend, it also lowers the conversion price. If the conversion price decreases, the conversion ratio (the amount of shares the bond is convertible into) increases.

171. C. $17.64

When dealing with convertible bond questions, you need to determine the amount of shares the bond is convertible into. In this case, the bond is convertible at $20, which gives you the following equation:

$$\text{Conversion ratio} = \frac{\text{Par}}{\text{Conversion price}}$$
$$= \frac{\$1,000}{\$20}$$
$$= 50 \text{ shares}$$

Next, to determine parity price, you have to divide the market price (98% of $1,000 par, or $980) of the bond by the conversion ratio:

$$\frac{\$980}{50 \text{ shares}} = \$19.60$$

So, if parity price of the stock is $19.60, the stock has to be at $17.64 ($19.60 − $1.96) to be at 10% below parity.

172. A. I and III

First, get the shares that the bond is convertible into, using the following formula:

$$\text{Conversion ratio} = \frac{\text{Par}}{\text{Conversion price}}$$
$$= \frac{\$1,000}{\$25}$$
$$= 20 \text{ shares}$$

To determine the parity price of the stock, multiply the number of shares by the market price of the stock: (20 shares)($42) = $840.

The bond is trading for $830 (83% of $1,000 par), and it's convertible into $840 worth of stock. This means that the bonds are trading below parity, and converting the bonds would be profitable.

173. A. Allow the bond to be called.

The best way to determine what's best for the investor is to determine the amount of money they'll receive for the call, for selling the bond in the market, and for converting the bond. Whichever is highest is the best for the investor.

Allowing the bond to be called: $1,020 (102% of $1,000 par)

Selling the bond in the market: $980 (98% of $1,000 par)

Converting the bond and selling the stock: $1,000 (25 shares × $40)

For an investor holding the convertible bond, the best alternative is to allow the bond to be called because the investor will receive $1,020, which is higher than the other two alternatives.

174. D. 25

As with some of the questions you'll see on the real Series 7 exam, this question includes information that isn't necessary to answer the question. Don't let the test writers take you on a ride that you don't need to be on. Just focus on the information you need to answer the question.

The conversion ratio is the amount of shares a convertible bond (or stock) is convertible into. You can use the following formula:

$$\text{Conversion ratio} = \frac{\text{Par}}{\text{Conversion price}}$$
$$= \frac{\$1,000}{\$40}$$
$$= 25 \text{ shares}$$

In this case, assuming that the par value for the bonds is $1,000, an investor would receive 25 shares of TUV's common stock if converting one of their bonds.

175. D. $1,120

The first step you have to take with convertible bond questions is to get the shares. To determine how many shares the bond is convertible into, use the following formula:

$$\text{Conversion ratio} = \frac{\text{Par}}{\text{Conversion price}}$$

$$= \frac{\$1,000}{\$25}$$

$$= 40 \text{ shares}$$

To determine the parity price of the stock, multiply the number of shares by the market price of the stock: (40 shares)($28) = $1,120.

176. A. a forced conversion

In this situation, you have to determine which would be most profitable for your client. The bond is being called at $1,040 (104% of $1,000 par) or is convertible into common stock valuing $1,140 ($28.50 × 40 shares). In this case, it'd make much more sense for investors to convert because they'd be losing $100 ($1,140 – $1,040) by accepting the call and not converting. Situations like this are called *forced conversions*. Corporations may also issue reverse convertible bonds that gives them the opportunity to convert the bonds at a predetermined date.

177. A. Book entry

The U.S. government has issued securities in book-entry form since the mid-1980s. Book-entry securities are sold without delivering a certificate. A central agency keeps the ownership records, and investors receive a receipt representing the securities owned.

178. B. I, II, and III

This is an *except* question, so you're looking for the false answer. Treasury bills (T-bills) are short-term U.S. government debt securities. T-bills have initial maturities of 4, 8, 13, 26, and 52 weeks and are sold in increments of $100. T-bills are sold at a discount and don't make semiannual interest payments. Because T-bills are short term, they're not callable. The one true statement is that they're traded on a discount yield basis because they're quoted in yields, not prices.

179. B. Treasury bill

Typically, when you're looking at the bid and ask prices, the number on the left is smaller than the number on the right. However, in this case, the number on the left is larger. That means that this has to be the quote for a Treasury bill (T-bill). T-bills are quoted on a discount yield basis where the bid is higher than the ask. If the yields were converted to prices, you'd see that the number on the left would be lower than the one on the right, just like other securities.

180. B. I, II, and IV

This question is a little tricky. The keyword to this question is *earn*. Although holders of Treasury bills and Treasury STRIPS don't receive interest payments, they do receive interest. Treasury bills and Treasury STRIPS are issued at a discount and mature at par value, and that difference is considered interest. Treasury bondholders receive interest payments once every six months. However, Treasury stock is stock that was issued and subsequently repurchased by issuing corporation. Stockholders never receive interest but sometimes receive dividends.

181. C. III, I, II

Treasury bills are issued with maturities of 4, 8, 13, 26, and 52 weeks. Treasury notes are issued with maturities of 2, 3, 5, 7, and 10 years. Treasury bonds are issued with maturities of 20 years or 30 years.

182. C. II and III

Treasury STRIPS (T-STRIPS) are purchased at a discount and mature at par value. As such, the principal and interest aren't received until maturity. However, holders must pay taxes on the accretion (the difference between the previous year's cost basis and current year's cost basis) every year.

183. A. a guaranteed profit

Treasury inflation-protected securities (TIPS) are marketable U.S. government securities with 5-, 10-, and 30-year maturities. TIPs pay interest semiannually at a fixed rate tied to the principal. Because the principal of the bond is tied to the Consumer Price Index (CPI), the interest payments may rise or fall depending on whether the economy is in a period of inflation or deflation. At maturity, holders receive the greater of the original face value or the adjusted principal. Even though these are low-risk securities, investors aren't guaranteed a profit because they may end up being sold at a lower price than the investor's cost basis.

184. C. either 20 or 30 years

Treasury bonds (T-bonds) have the longest maturity and have an initial maturity of 20 or 30 years.

185. D. ten years

Treasury securities have the following maximum maturities:

T-bills: 1 year

T-notes: 10 years

T-bonds: 30 years

T-STRIPS: 30 years

186. A. I and II

Ginnie Maes (GNMAs) are mortgage-backed securities issued by the U.S. government and are considered safer investments than Freddie Macs (FHLMCs). GNMAs pay interest monthly, and the interest is taxed on all levels (federal, state, and local). GNMAs are issued with a face value of $25,000 but can be purchased in denominations as low as $1,000.

187. B. GNMA

GNMAs (Government National Mortgage Association) are the only agency securities backed by the full faith and credit of the U.S. government. GNMAs support the Department of Housing and Urban Development (HUD). The interest earned is taxed on all levels.

188. C. They pay interest semiannually.

Unlike a majority of other debt securities, interest on Ginnie Maes (GNMAs) is paid monthly just like people pay their mortgages. Interest is not paid semiannually.

189. A. II, III, and IV

The keyword to this question is *farm*. The Federal Farm Credit System is comprised of the Federal Intermediate Credit Banks (FICB), Bank for Cooperatives (COOPs), and Federal Land Banks (FLBs). These institutions give loans to farmers, not to homeowners, as in Statement I.

190. A. I and II

Because collateralized mortgage obligations (CMOs) are backed by U.S. government and U.S. government agency mortgages, they typically have a Standard & Poor's (S&P) rating of AAA or AA.

191. C. SLMA

Collateralized mortgage obligations (CMOs) diversify their investments in mortgages issued by Ginnie Mae (GNMA), Fannie Mae (FNMA), and Freddie Mac (FNMA). Sallie Mae (SLMA) is an agency that issues bonds to fund student loans and can't be part of a CMO.

192. C. II and III

The average maturity on collateralized mortgage obligations (CMOs) depends highly on mortgage interest rates. If interest rates fall, more homeowners will refinance to take advantage of the lower rates, and the amount of prepayments will increase. If interest rates rise, homeowners won't refinance, and the amount of prepayments will decrease.

193. D. they are subject to prepayment and extension risk

Collateralized mortgage obligations (CMOs) are subject to prepayment and extension risk depending on the amount of people refinancing or moving. Prepayment risk and extension risk are highly tied to prevailing mortgage interest rates. CMOs aren't guaranteed by the U.S. government; they carry varying amounts of risk; and they're taxable on all levels.

194. A. PAC

Planned amortization class (PAC) and targeted amortization class (TAC) tranches are supported by companion tranches. Companion tranches absorb the prepayment risk associated with collateralized mortgage obligations (CMOs).

195. D. PAC

The planned amortization class (PAC) tranche is considered the safest because a large portion of the prepayment risk and extension risk associated with collateralized mortgage obligations (CMOs) is absorbed by a companion tranche. The targeted amortization class (TAC) tranche isn't quite as safe as the PAC tranche because it's more subject to prepayment and extension risk. A companion tranche absorbs the prepayment and extension risk associated with PAC and TAC tranches and is risky because the average life varies greatly with interest rate changes. A Z-tranche is the most volatile of the CMO tranches because investors receive no payments until all the CMO tranches are retired.

196. C. II and III

Companion tranches absorb the prepayment risk associated with CMOs. All PAC and TAC tranches are supported by a companion tranche.

197. A. Certificates of deposit

Because collateralized mortgage obligations (CMOs) are such unique investments, they may be compared only to other CMOs.

198. B. they are always backed by mortgages

Collateralized debt obligations (CDOs) are asset-backed securities secured by loans, such as credit cards, auto loans, and rarely mortgages. The assets backing the CDOs aren't very liquid on their own, so they have been pooled together and repackaged to make them available to investors. As with CMOs, CDOs are broken down into tranches with varying degrees of risk and varying maturities.

199.

D. II, III, and IV

Collateralized debt obligations (CDOs) are asset-backed securities similar to collateralized mortgage obligations (CMOs). However, the main difference is that CMOs are backed by mortgages, and CDOs are backed by other debt, such as credit cards and auto loans. CDOs add liquidity to the loan market. However, the individual loans aren't liquid because they include loans of small amounts. Therefore, CDOs are more liquid than the individual loans on their own.

200.

C. $100,000

Negotiable certificates of deposit (CDs) aren't appropriate investments for smaller investors. The minimum denomination is $100,000, and they're often traded in blocks of $1 million. Because of the high minimum denomination, negotiable CDs are typically purchased and traded only by institutional investors.

201.

A. short-term debt

Money market instruments are short-term debt securities that typically have maturities of one year or less.

202.

B. The interest rate is determined from the discount rate set by the Federal Reserve Board (FRB).

Eurodollar deposits are dollar-denominated deposits held in banks outside of the United States; thus, the risk and interest paid is higher, but the rate has nothing to do with the Federal Reserve Board (FRB). Investors making Eurodollar deposits are attempting to take advantage of the higher interest rates.

203.

D. 270 days

Corporate commercial paper is a money market instrument. To be exempt from the Securities and Exchange Commission (SEC) registration, commercial paper has a maximum expiration of 270 days.

204.

C. Jumbo CDs

The only money market instrument (short-term debt security) that trades with accrued interest is certificates of deposit (CDs). All the other money market instruments are issued at a discount and mature at par value. Holders of CDs receive interest payments; therefore, investors purchasing CDs are required to pay the seller any accrued interest due.

205. **A. I, III, and IV**

> Corporate commercial paper matures in 270 days or less and is exempt from the Securities and Exchange Commission (SEC) registration. It's issued at a discount and matures at par value and, therefore, trades without accrued interest. Unlike some other corporate debt securities, commercial paper isn't backed by the issuer's assets.

206. **B. Bankers' acceptance**

> Bankers' acceptances (BAs) are money market instruments used to provide short-term financing for importers and exporters. BAs trade at a discount and mature at face value.

207. **D. ETN**

> ETNs (Exchange Traded Notes) are unsecured debt securities issued by a bank or financial institution. Their return is usually linked to a particular market index or in some cases commodities or currency.

208. **D. II and IV**

> Unlike exchange traded note, equity linked notes are not traded on an exchange. Equity linked notes are most often created as bonds. However, instead of having fixed interest payments, the interest payments are variable depending on the return of the underlying equity securities. The return on equity linked notes may be based off of the return of a single stock, basket of stock, or equity index (sometimes referred to as equity index linked notes).

Chapter 4 Answers

209. **D. I, II, III, and IV**

> Actually, all of the choices given are important. The higher your client's tax bracket, the bigger the advantage for buying municipal bonds. If a client purchases municipal bonds issued from within his home state, they'll have the advantage of them being triple tax-free. The bond's rating and maturity are important depending on the risk tolerance of your client.

210. **B. II, III, and IV**

> General obligation (GO) bonds are issued to fund non-revenue-producing facilities and are backed by the taxing power of the municipality. Because the people living in the municipality will be paying additional taxes to back the bonds, they do need voter approval. Also, GO bonds are subject to a debt ceiling, which is the maximum amount of money that a municipality may borrow to meet its needs.

211. B. I and III

Municipal general obligation (GO) bonds and double-barreled bonds are backed by the full faith and credit and taxing power of the municipal issuer. Double-barreled bonds are backed by a revenue-producing facility, and, if the revenues are insufficient to be able to pay the principal and interest on the bonds, they're backed by the municipality.

212. B. flow of funds

The flow of funds is important to purchasers of revenue bonds, not general obligation bonds.

213. B. the dated date

The dated date is the first day that a bond starts accruing interest and isn't a factor in the marketability of a bond. However, the credit rating, the maturity date, and the issuer's name are all important and would affect the marketability of a bond.

214. C. I, II, and III

If you take a quick glance at the answer choices, you'll notice that they all include Statements II and III, which means that you don't have to look closely at those answers. So, you have a choice of Statement I or IV being correct. When determining the marketability of municipal bonds, the maturity is important because bonds with short-term maturities are more marketable. The dated date (the first day that bonds start accruing interest) doesn't affect a bond's marketability.

215. A. I and II

When analyzing municipal general obligation (GO) bonds, investors should be concerned with the tax base, efficiency of the government, existing debt, debt per capita, and so on. If investing in municipal revenue bonds, an investor should be concerned about covenants and flow of funds.

216. C. the call feature makes the bonds more marketable

Looking at Choices (A) and (C), you'll notice that they directly oppose each other, so the chances are extremely high that one of those is the correct answer. You're looking for the answer that's the exception in this case, so it has to be Choice (C). The call feature of a bond doesn't make the bond more marketable; it makes it less marketable. Therefore, the issuers would have to pay higher coupon rates to attract investors.

217. C. default risk

Municipal bond insurance is a credit enhancer that insures municipal bonds against default risk. Default risk is the risk that interest and principal payments won't be received. In the event that the issuer fails to make expected payments, the insurance company will make them. Insured municipal bonds are typically rated AAA.

218. B. it increases the credit rating and marketability of the bonds

Municipal bond insurance is called a *credit enhancer* because it increases the credit rating of the bonds. Insured municipal bonds typically have a Standard & Poor's credit rating of AAA. The higher the credit rating, the more marketable the bonds.

219. D. I, II, III, and IV

All of the choices listed are important. General obligation (GO) bonds are backed by the full faith, credit, and taxing power of the municipality. Although the largest backing for GO bonds is property (ad valorem) taxes, they're also backed by items such as license fee and fines. The issuer's home state is important because if purchasing a tax-free municipal bond within your own home state, the interest will be triple tax-free. You'd also want to see a growing population trend because that means that more people will be backing the bonds. Obviously, bonds being backed by a wealthy community are better than ones backed by a poor community. You'd also want to see a diversity of industry within the tax base because that would help a community grow.

220. D. a state

Overlapping (coterminous) debt is important to not only taxpayers but also purchasers of municipal general obligation (GO) bonds. Overlapping debt has to do with debt being shared by more than one municipality. An example would be a town that's responsible for a portion of the county's debt. People who live in a county are also responsible for a portion of the state's debt. However, states can't be overlapped because one state isn't responsible for a portion of another state's debt.

221. B. overlapping debt

Coterminous debt is the same as overlapping debt. Overlapping debt occurs when several authorities in a geographic area have the ability to tax the same residents.

222. A. $769.23

Direct debt is the debt owed by a municipality that doesn't include overlapping debt. The question states that Fort Myers has $50 million in debt. To calculate debt per capita, divide the debt by the population:

$$\frac{\$50,000,000}{65,000} = \$769.23$$

223.   B. I and II

General obligation (GO) bonds require voter approval prior to being issued because they're mostly backed by taxes on people living in the municipality. GO bonds are issued to fund non-revenue-producing facilities, such as schools and jails. A municipality would issue revenue bonds to fund revenue-producing projects, such as toll roads and airports. Revenue bonds are backed by users, not taxes.

224.   C. State governments

States don't collect property taxes. Local governments, such as school districts, counties, and towns, collect property taxes.

225.   A. property tax

The largest backing for municipal general obligation (GO) bonds is property taxes. The credit rating of GO bonds is highly dependent on the municipality's tax collection record, the number of people living in the municipality, property values, whether it's a limited tax GO bond or unlimited tax GO bond, and so on. Unlike revenue bonds, GO bonds typically require voter approval prior to being issued.

226.   C. $3,290

Ad valorem (property) taxes are the largest source of backing for general obligation (GO) bonds. They're based on the assessed property value, not the market value. These taxes are based on mills (0.001). To determine the ad valorem tax, multiply the assessed property value by 0.001 and then multiply by the tax rate in mills (14):

$$(\$235,000)(0.001)(14) = \$3,290$$

227.   D. Banks may claim an 80% tax deduction of the amount of interest charges for purchases in margin accounts.

Bank-qualified municipal bonds are municipal bonds that banks may purchase on margin and deduct 80% of interest charges of the brokerage firm on the debit balances of the margin accounts.

228.   C. Property taxes

Property taxes (ad valorem taxes) are the largest source of funding for municipal general obligation (GO) bonds, not revenue bonds.

229. D. I, II, and IV

Revenue bonds are backed by the revenue-producing facility and are supposed to be self-sustaining. Raising money by issuing revenue bonds to build toll roads, airports, and sports stadiums all make sense because the revenues from these projects would be used to pay off bondholders. However, if a municipality wanted to build a new library, it would issue GO bonds because libraries don't make enough money to be self-sustaining.

230. B. Property taxes

Property taxes are the largest source of backing for general obligation (GO) bonds, not revenue bonds. What's important to revenue bond investors is the *feasibility study* (how much sense the income producing project makes), *the flow of funds* (priority of payments from revenues), and *rate covenants* (a promise to adequately charge users of the facility).

231. A. I and III

With revenue bonds, a feasibility report (engineering report) is required to estimate the costs and revenues of the facility paying off the debt. In addition, the flow of funds must be included on the indenture of the revenue bonds to indicate how the money raised from the facility is spent by the municipality. Debt limitation and debt per capita are related to general obligation bonds rather than revenue bonds.

232. A. the maturity date of the issue will typically exceed the useful life of the facility backing the bonds

In this case, you need to find the exception. The maturity of revenue bonds may be 25 to 30 years, but the facility being built by the income received from the revenue bond issue is usually expected to last a long time, if not a lifetime. Revenue bonds may be issued by interstate authorities, such as tolls, and the interest and principal on the bonds are paid from revenue received from the facility backing the bonds. In addition, revenue bonds aren't subject to a debt ceiling (maximum tax that can be imposed on people living in the municipality); general obligation bonds are.

233. C. the tax base of the municipality

The tax base of the municipality is important when analyzing general obligation bonds, not revenue bonds. Revenue bonds are backed by a revenue producing facility, not taxes.

234. A. higher

Typically, general obligation bonds are considered safer than revenue bonds because general obligation bonds are backed by the taxing power of the municipal issuer. Therefore, since revenue bonds are considered somewhat riskier, they typically have yields that are higher than revenue bonds.

235. A. trustee acting for the bondholders

The bond resolution (indenture) outlines the characteristics of the offering (interest payment dates, covenants, coupon rate, maturity date, and so on) and the obligations that the issuer has to holders of the issue. In the event of issuer default, the trustee will act to protect the bondholders.

236. C. insurance covenants

You're looking for the exception in this question. Covenants are promises placed on the indenture of revenue bonds, not general obligation bonds. However, general obligation (GO) bonds are subject to a debt ceiling and are backed by items such as property taxes and traffic fines.

237. D. covenants

Covenants are promises stated on the indenture and are important for investors of revenue bonds, not general obligation bonds. An example is an insurance covenant in which the issuer promises to adequately insure the income-producing facility backing the bonds.

238. A. Rate covenants

A rate covenant would be on the indenture of a revenue bond, not a general obligation (GO) bond. However, per capita debt (debt per person), assessed property values, and the tax collection history of the municipality would all certainly affect the credit rating of a GO bond.

239. D. revenue bonds

The flow of funds is used for municipal revenue bonds. The indenture specifies whether the municipal bond principal and interest is paid using net or gross revenues.

240. B. operation and maintenance

You'll find that most revenue bonds and industrial development revenue bonds have a net revenue pledge. This means that the first priority of revenue goes to pay operation and maintenance on the facility, which makes sense. If they don't keep the facility running, they'll never be able to pay off bondholders. Next is the debt service (principal and interest on bonds), followed by a debt service reserve fund, a reserve maintenance fund, a renewal and replacement fund, and, finally, a surplus fund.

241. A. bond principal and interest

Under a gross revenue pledge, the issuer will pay principal and interest (debt service) prior to any other expenses. Most municipalities issue revenue bonds under a net revenue pledge in which the net revenues (after operation and maintenance are paid) are used to cover the debt service.

242. B. III and IV

What's nice about this question is that if you know you can eliminate Statement I, you can quickly come up with the correct answer of Choice (B). *Direct debt per capita* and *net debt per assessed valuation* are important to purchasers of general obligation bonds, not revenue bonds. Items that are important to purchasers of revenue bonds include the *debt service coverage ratio* (how much money is netted as compared to how much is owed in principal and interest) and *flow of funds* (whether bondholders are paid first or operating and maintenance is paid first).

243. B. 3 to 1

Because these bonds were issued under a net revenue pledge (which almost all are), bondholders are paid from net revenues after operation and maintenance are paid. To calculate this question, remember that net revenue equals gross revenue minus operating and maintenance expenses. Here, net revenue is $76 million − $40 million = $36 million. You also need to calculate debt service, which is the combination of interest and principal repayment. Here, debt service is $10 million + $2 million = $12 million. Finally, to compute the debt service ratio, you divide the net revenue by the debt service:

$$\text{Debt service coverage ratio} = \frac{\text{Net revenues}}{\text{Debt service}}$$
$$= \frac{\$36,000,000}{\$12,000,000}$$
$$= 3$$

This means that the debt service coverage ratio is 3 to 1 (3:1).

244. A. 4 to 1

The question didn't state whether it was a net revenue pledge or gross revenue pledge, so you can assume net. To get the net revenues, subtract the operating and maintenance expenses from the gross revenues.

Net revenues = $30,000,000 − $12,000,000 = $18,000,000

Next, to determine the debt service coverage ratio, divide the net revenues by the combined principal and interest ($1,500,000 interest + $3,0000,000 principal = $4,500,000):

$$\text{Debt service coverage ratio} = \frac{\text{Net revenues}}{\text{Principal and interest}}$$
$$= \frac{\$18,000,000}{\$4,500,000}$$
$$= 4$$

That means that the debt service coverage ratio is 4 to 1 (4:1).

245.   B. I and IV

Since GO bonds are backed by taxes, they are usually issued on a competitive basis to find the lowest cost to the municipality and taxpayers. Revenue bonds are not backed by taxes, so revenue bonds are more likely issued on a negotiated basis, where the underwriter is chosen directly.

246.   B. I and III

In a negotiated offering, the spread must always be disclosed on the customer confirmation. In addition, municipal confirmations must show yield to maturity or yield to call, whichever is lower. In a premium bond, the yield to call is lower than the yield to maturity.

247.   B. Negotiated

A competitive offering is the choosing of an underwriter through an auction. If the issuer chooses an underwriter directly, this is a negotiated offering.

248.   C. The proposal with the lowest interest cost

When a municipality, such as Suffolk County, New York, is issuing bonds through a competitive offering, it means that it's allowing syndicates to bid on the issue. Suffolk County will accept the bid with the lowest interest cost to the taxpayer. For example, if Syndicate A said that it could sell the bonds with a 5% coupon and Syndicate B said that it could sell the bonds with a 4.75% coupon, Syndicate B would be the winner.

249.   A. the bond rating

The official notice of sale is an official invitation from a municipality, asking for broker-dealers to bid on a new issue of municipal bonds. The official notice of sale includes the date, time and place of sale, the bond maturity date, interest payment dates, any call provisions, the amount of good faith deposit, a description of the issue, and so on. The rating of the bond issue comes from ratings companies, such as Moody's and Standard & Poor's, and isn't determined until the bond is issued.

250.   C. Notice of sale

When a municipality wants to inform potential underwriters that it's taking bids for a new issue, it would post an official notice of sale in *The Bond Buyer*.

251. D. I, II, III, and IV

The official notice of sale is published in *The Bond Buyer* and is designed to solicit bids from underwriters for a new issue of municipal bonds. Included in the official notice of sale is all the information needed by underwriters to come up with a bid for the new issue, such as the name of the issuer, a description of the issuer, type of bond (GO, revenue, double-barreled), any bidding restrictions, required interest payment dates, the dated date, any call provisions, maturity structure (long term, short term), denomination of certificates, the name of the bond counsel, the name of the trustee, and so on.

252. C. A syndicate that could sell the issue with the lowest cost to the municipality

The issuer will determine the winning bid on the lowest cost. The issuer will take into consideration the coupon rate (the lower, the better) and the selling price (the higher, the better).

253. B. True interest cost

The two methods of interest evaluation are true interest cost (TIC) and net interest cost (NIC). In this case, the issuer is taking into consideration the timing of interest payments or the time value of money. That means that the issuer is determining the bids based on the true interest cost because it's discounting future interest payments to arrive at a present value.

254. D. refunding

Refunding is when an issuer issues new bonds and uses the proceeds to call outstanding bonds. *Pre-refunding* or *advance refunding* is when an issuer issues new bonds for a time prior to the call date (at least 90 days) of existing bonds to take advantage of low interest rates. The money received is held in an escrow account and invested in U.S. government securities until the existing bonds can be called. Because the money is there to pay off the bond holders, pre-refunded bonds are typically rated AAA.

255. B. *The Bond Buyer*

The Bond Buyer provides the best source of information about municipal bonds in the primary market. *The Bond Buyer* includes the 40-Bond Index, 20-Bond index, 11-Bond Index, Revenue Bond Index (RevDex), the visible supply, and the placement ratio.

256. C. a lump sum payment that includes the par value of the bond plus the net present value of future coupon payments that will not be paid as a result of the call

A make whole call provision allows the issuer to pay off the debt securities early but at a higher expense. In the case of make whole calls, the issuer must make a lump-sum payment based on the net present value of future interest payments that would be due on the bonds that will not be paid because the bonds are being called. Because of the high cost to the municipality, bonds with make whole call provisions are rarely issued.

257. **A. the bonds can be issued with a lower coupon rate**

A sinking fund is often set up for callable bonds. A sinking fund means that the issuer is putting aside money to pay off the bonds at some future date. Having a sinking fund adds a degree of safety so they can issue the bonds with a lower coupon rate. Having a sinking fund also allows the issuer to call the bonds ahead of the maturity date if it works to their benefit.

258. **D. Mandatory**

Mandatory redemptions occur either on a scheduled basis (in specified amounts or in amounts then on deposit in the sinking fund) or based on when a certain amount of money is available in the sinking fund (sinking fund call).

259. **C. Optional**

An optional call provision gives the issuer the option to redeem bonds on or after a specified date at the call price plus any accrued interest. Typically, that date is at least 10 years from the issue date.

260. **B. The facility backing the bond has been condemned due to a hurricane.**

An extraordinary (catastrophe or calamity) call is just what it sounds like. It means that something catastrophic has happened to the revenue-producing facility backing the bonds. In this event, the outstanding bonds would be called, and investors would be paid par value and any accrued interest (typically by an insurance company).

261. **B. backed by excise taxes**

Special tax bonds are a type of municipal bond that's funded (backed) by taxes on certain items (excise taxes). Excise taxes are taxes on nonessential goods, such as gasoline, alcohol, and tobacco.

262. **A. They are backed by charges on the benefitted property.**

Special assessment bonds are types of municipal bonds that are backed by taxes on the properties that benefit. For example, say that people who live a few blocks from you got all new streetlights and sidewalks. Why should you pay additional taxes to pay for their streetlights and sidewalks? The answer is, you shouldn't, and that's where special assessment bonds come into play. In this case, just the properties that benefit will be taxed at a higher level, while yours stays the same.

263. D. double-barreled bonds

Double-barreled bonds are kind of a combination of revenue and general obligation bonds. Revenue bonds are typically 100% supported by revenues generated by the revenue-producing facility. If it's a double-barreled bond and if the revenues aren't high enough to pay interest and/or principal on the bonds, the revenues are supplemented with municipal taxes.

264. C. They are backed by a corporation.

An industrial development revenue (IDR) bond is a municipal bond that's backed by a private company. The municipality uses the lease payments that the private company makes to pay principal and interest on the bonds. Therefore, IDRs are the riskiest municipal bonds.

265. D. I and IV

A double-barreled bond is a combination of revenue and general obligation (GO) bonds. If the revenues from the revenue-producing facility fall short, the bonds will be backed by the full faith and credit (taxing power) of the municipality.

266. C. II and III

Certificates of participation (COPs) are revenue bonds. As such, COPs don't require voter approval to be issued. The holders of COPs receive interest backed by lease or loan payments received from land or facilities owned by the municipality. In the event of issuer default, COP holders could actually foreclose on the asset associated with the bond certificate.

267. B. The type of tax that can be used to back the bond issue

A limited tax general obligation bond (LTGO) is typically backed by a specific tax. As an example, an LTGO may be backed by revenue only from sales taxes and not necessarily property taxes. Therefore, LTGOs are riskier investments and would likely have a higher coupon rate than a regular GO bond.

268. B. Public housing authority bonds

Public housing authority (PHA) bonds are municipal bonds issued to finance the repair or construction of low-income housing. These bonds are extra safe because even though they're technically municipal bonds, they're guaranteed by the federal government. As with most other municipal bonds, their interest is exempt from federal taxation.

269. **B. backed by a private user**

An industrial development bond is issued for the construction of a facility for the benefit of a private corporation. The lease payments are used by the issuing municipality to pay the debt service (principal and interest).

270. **A. they are backed by U.S. government subsidies**

New housing authority (NHA) bonds are also known as public housing authority (PHA) bonds or simply housing authority bonds. NHA bonds are issued to build or repair low-income housing. Besides the rental income, these bonds are considered quite safe because they're backed by a subsidy from the U.S. government and are typically rated AAA.

271. **A. A moral obligation bond**

A moral obligation bond is a revenue bond in which the state legislature has the authority, but no legal obligation, to provide financial backing for the issuer in the event of default.

272. **D. a bond that requires legislative approval**

A moral obligation bond requires legislative approval to be issued. These bonds are issued by a municipality but backed by a pledge from the state government to pay off the debt if the municipality can't.

273. **C. Long-term**

Because Uriah believes that interest rates are going to drop over the next 20 to 30 years, they should lock in at a high interest rate right now. Buying long-term bonds makes sense for Uriah because they believe that the rates are high right now, and if interest rates drop like they expect them to, Uriah would be locking in a high rate for a long period of time. Additionally, if interest rates drop, the price of the bonds will increase, because interest rates and outstanding bond prices have an inverse relationship.

274. **D. term and serial**

Municipalities issue both term and bonds with serial maturity. Term bonds have one issue date and one maturity date. Serial bonds have one issue date but have serial maturity (an equal portion of the bond issue matures in successive years).

275. **D. Term**

Term bonds have one issue date and one maturity date.

276. B. Serial

Serial bonds have one issue date but equal portions of the issue maturing in successive years (i.e., 10% in year 21, 10% in year 22, ... the final 10% in year 30).

277. B. $900 return of capital and $500 federally tax-free interest over the life of the bond

Because this municipal bond is an original issue discount (OID), the annual accretion is treated as part of the investor's federally tax-free income. This investor originally purchased the bond for $900 (90% of $1,000 par), so when they receive $1,000 at maturity, $900 of that is a return of capital. The other $100 had to be accreted over the life of the bond, which added an extra $10 ($100/10 years) of federally tax-free interest each year.

278. C. No tax liability

If an investor purchases a zero-coupon municipal bond at the original offering, the accretion is considered tax-free interest. Holders of zero-coupon bonds receive no interest payments, because the bonds are issued at a discount and mature at par value.

279. D. Auction-rate securities

Auction-rate securities are municipal bonds in which the interest rate is reset periodically based on a Dutch auction. A Dutch auction is a process by which new securities are sold at the best bid price, which translates to the lowest yield to the issuer.

280. B. the bond price should remain stable

Variable rate bonds have no fixed coupon rate. The rate on these bonds is tied to a particular market rate, such as the yield to T-bonds, and is subject to regular change. Because the coupon rate varies, the bond price remains close to its par value.

281. C. II, III, and IV

The coupon on a variable rate municipal bond is adjusted periodically to keep pace with the current interest rates. Because the coupon rate keeps pace with interest rates, the bond price stays relatively stable. Therefore, variable rate municipal bonds aren't subject to interest rate risk (the risk that a securities value will decline due to rising interest rates). However, variable rate municipal bonds are still subject to market risk, default risk, and liquidity risk.

282. **A. BABs**

BABs (build America bonds) are taxable municipal bonds issued to raise money for infrastructure projects, such as bridges, tunnels, and roads. There are two types of BABs: *tax credit BABs,* in which holders receive tax credits from the U.S. Treasury equal to 35% of the coupon rate, and *direct payment BABs,* in which the issuer receives tax credits from the U.S. Treasury equal to 35% of the coupon rate. Direct payment BABs are more commonly issued than tax credit BABs. Therefore, investors would likely receive a higher coupon rate than tax credit BABs.

283. **C. Tax-credit BABs**

BABs (build America bonds) are taxable municipal bonds issued to raise money for infrastructure projects, such as bridges, tunnels, and roads. *Tax credit BABs* allow holders to receive tax credits from the U.S. Treasury equal to 35% of the coupon rate.

284. **B. Direct payment BABs**

Direct payment BABs (build America bonds) are bonds issued to fund infrastructure projects, such as bridges, roads, and tunnels, where municipalities receive tax credits from the U.S. government of 35% of interest paid to investors. Because municipality is receiving a tax credit, it can issue the bonds with higher coupon rates than comparable bonds.

285. **D. I, II, III, and IV**

All of the choices listed are municipal notes. Municipal notes are issued to provide short-term financing. The maturity of municipal notes is one year or less.

286. **A. provide short-term financing**

Municipalities issue short-term notes, such as RANs (revenue anticipation notes), BANs (bond anticipation notes), TANs (tax anticipation notes), and CLNs (construction loan notes), to provide interim financing until a permanent long-term bond issue is floated, until tax receipts increase, or until revenue flows in.

287. **B. AONs**

Municipal notes are short-term debt securities issued by municipalities to provide interim financing while waiting for other revenues to come in. Municipal notes include TANs, RANs, TRANs, BANs, CLNs, PNs, and GANs. AON (all-or-none) is an order qualifier, not a type of municipal note.

288. B. Tax anticipation notes

The key phrase in this question is *temporary cash flow shortage*, which tells you that the municipality needs to issue short-term debt securities. So, you can cross off Choices (C) and (D) because revenue bonds and general obligation (GO) bonds are long term. That leaves you with the *construction loan notes* or *tax anticipation notes*. Because construction wasn't mentioned anywhere in the question, the best answer is *tax anticipation notes* because a municipality is always collecting taxes.

289. D. GAN

GANs (Grant Anticipation Notes) provide interim financing for the municipality while waiting for a grant from the U.S. government.

290. D. Bond anticipation notes

Market risk is the risk that the price of a security will decline due to negative market conditions. Because bond anticipation notes (BANs) are short term, they're not in the market as long and, therefore, are less subject to market risk.

291. C. MIG1

A bond anticipation note (BAN) issued by municipalities is backed by bonds that will be issued. Municipal notes are short term and are rated by Moody's, using the Moody's investment grade (MIG) scale. MIG1 is the best rating available for a municipal note.

292. D. GOs

Moody's investment grade (MIG) determines the creditworthiness of municipal notes (short-term municipal bonds). PNs (project notes), TRANs (tax and revenue anticipation notes), and CLNs (construction loan notes) are all types of municipal notes. However, GOs are general obligation bonds issued to provide long-term financing for a municipality and can't have an MIG rating.

293. B. municipal notes

Moody's investment grade (MIG) ratings are applied to municipal notes, such as BANs, RANs, TANs, CLNs, and so on.

294. C. amount

When looking at a client's portfolio of securities, you should make sure that they're diversified. A client shouldn't have too many of their eggs in one basket, so to say. Relating to municipal bonds, diversification could be buying bonds of different types (revenue, GO, notes), buying bonds with different credit ratings (AAA, A, BBB), buying bonds from different geographical locations (New York, California, Guam), buying bonds with different maturities (short term, intermediate term, long term), and so on. However, buying a different amount of one security doesn't figure into the diversified portfolio mix.

295.
C. II and IV

Geographical diversification is purchasing municipal bonds from different areas of the country. Geographical diversification would protect investors against economic and business risks that may affect only certain areas or regions of the country. Geographical diversification wouldn't protect against purchasing power risk because municipal bonds have long-term maturities. In addition, diversification can't eliminate interest risk because if interest rates increase, outstanding bond prices fall.

296.
D. Geographical

Mr. Mullahy has purchased bonds from municipal bonds from different geographical locations. Other types of municipal diversification include buying bonds with different ratings, different maturities, different types (such as revenue, GO, IDRs), and so on. All investors should have a diversified portfolio.

297.
D. municipal fund securities

Qualified tuition plans (Section 529 plans), ABLE (Achieving a Better Life Experience) accounts, and local government investment pools (LGIPs) are all types of municipal fund securities. Municipal fund securities are similar to investment companies, but are exempt from the definition under the Investment Company Act of 1940. Municipal fund securities are established by municipal governments, municipal agencies, or educational institutions but do not represent loans to the government.

298.
A. Contributions are tax-deductible on the state level.

529 plans only allow for after-tax contributions on the state and federal level.

299.
C. ABLE accounts

ABLE (Achieving a Better Life Experience) accounts are designed for individuals with provable disabilities and their families. ABLE accounts allow individuals to invest after-tax money into the account and any distributions (including earnings) are tax-free as long as they're used for the qualified expenses for the beneficiary.

300.
B. I and IV

LGIPs are established by states to provide other government entities (cities, counties, school districts, and so on) with a short-term investment vehicle for investing their funds. Since they are set up by state governments for state entities, they are exempt from SEC registration and prospectus requirements.

301.   A. The discount is accreted annually and not taxed on the federal level.

The interest received from municipal bonds is federally tax-free. When investors purchase municipal bonds that were issued at a discount, the difference between the purchase price and par value is also treated as part of the tax-free income. The discount would be accreted over the 30 years until maturity and wouldn't be taxed on the federal level. An investor of these bonds wouldn't be subject to a capital gain or loss unless the bond(s) is sold.

302.   A. I only

Interest on municipal bonds is federally tax-free, but capital gains on all securities are fully taxed. Interest on U.S. government bonds is state tax-free but is taxed at the federal level. Cash dividends on stock are always taxable.

303.   B. GO bonds

For Series 7 purposes, you can assume that municipal bonds have the lowest yields of all bonds. You may have chosen T-bonds (Treasury bonds) because they would be the safest, but then you didn't take into consideration the tax advantage of investing in municipal bonds. Municipal GO (general obligation) and municipal revenue bonds have lower yields because the interest investors receive is federally tax-free. Therefore, municipalities are able to offer lower pre-tax yields to investors than with other debt security investments.

304.   B. Municipal GO bonds

Because your client is in a high income tax bracket, municipal bonds are ideal. Remember, the higher the customer's tax bracket, the better benefit they get out of buying municipal bonds. Therefore, you can cross off Choices (C) and (D). Because your client is looking for income, you wouldn't recommend a zero-coupon bond because your client wouldn't receive any income until maturity. The best answer is *municipal GO bonds.*

305.   B. Tito's tax bracket

To determine the best investment for Tito, you must do a taxable equivalent yield (TEY) calculation. To accomplish this, you need to know Tito's tax bracket. Remember, the interest received from municipal bond investments is federally tax-free, and investors in higher tax brackets will save more money by investing in municipal bonds when compared to other debt securities. The formula for TEY is as follows:

$$TEY = \frac{Municipal\ yield}{100\% - Investor's\ tax\ bracket}$$

306. C. 4% GO bond

To determine the best after-tax investment for an individual investor, look for municipal bonds. A general obligation (GO) bond is a municipal bond in which the interest received is exempt from federal taxation. To compare all the listed bonds equally, you need to determine the GO bond's taxable equivalent yield (TEY), using this formula:

$$TEY = \frac{\text{Municipal yield}}{100\% - \text{Investor's tax bracket}}$$
$$= \frac{4\%}{100\% - 28\%}$$
$$= \frac{4\%}{72\%}$$
$$= 5.56\%$$

For this investor, the taxable equivalent yield is 5.56%, which is higher than all the other bonds listed. The 5.56% represents the coupon rate needed on a taxable bond to be equal to the 4% that they'd be receiving on the federally tax-free bond.

307. A. The general obligation bond has a higher after-tax yield.

Because the interest on municipal general obligation bonds is federally tax-free, you have to work out the taxable equivalent yield (TEY) by using the following formula:

$$TEY = \frac{\text{Municipal yield}}{100\% - \text{Investor's tax bracket}}$$
$$= \frac{5\%}{100\% - 28\%}$$
$$= \frac{5\%}{72\%}$$
$$= 6.94\%$$

For this investor in the 28% tax bracket, purchasing a 5% municipal bond is equivalent to purchasing a 6.94% corporate bond. This means that the 5% municipal bond has a higher after-tax yield than the 6% corporate bond.

308. B. 4.14%

As compared to starting with a municipal yield and trying to find the taxable equivalent yield (TEY), in this case, you're starting with a corporate bond and trying to find the municipal equivalent yield (MEY). You can use the following formula to determine the MEY:

$$MEY = (\text{Taxable bond yield})(100\% - \text{Investor's tax bracket})$$
$$= (6\%)(100\% - 31\%)$$
$$= (6\%)(69\%)$$
$$= 4.14\%$$

The MEY is 4.14%, which means that for an investor in the 31% tax bracket, purchasing a 4.14% municipal bond is equivalent to purchasing a 6% taxable bond.

309. C. I, II, and III

Interest received from municipal bonds issued by the U.S. territories Guam, Puerto Rico, and U.S. Virgin Islands is triple tax-free (exempt from federal, state, and local taxes). You'd probably also want to let your client know that purchasing municipal bonds issued by their own state would also be triple tax-free.

310. D. It is exempt from federal, state, and local taxes.

When purchasing a municipal bond issued within your home state, the interest received is triple tax-free and is exempt from federal, state, and local taxes. Additionally, if you purchase a bond issued by a U.S. territory (such as Puerto Rico, U.S. Virgin Islands, Guam, Samoa, and Washington, D.C.), the interest is also triple tax-free. If you purchase a bond issued by another state, the interest is exempt from federal taxes only.

311. C. Yield to call

Because it's a pre-refunded (advance-refunded) municipal bond that's going to be called in two years, the yield shown must be yield to call. For municipal bonds that aren't pre-refunded, the confirmation must show yield to maturity or yield to call, whichever is lower.

312. B. $0.10

One point on a bond is 1/100th of $1,000 par or $10. One basis point is 1/100th of a point or $0.10.

313. C. $4,950

If the bond is trading at 99, it is trading at 99% of $5,000 par. $5,000 × 99% = $4,950.

314. C. 2 business days after the trade date

Regular way settlement for municipal bonds is 2 business days after the trade date.

315. A. the bond rating

The bond rating would not be found on the customer's confirmation (receipt of trade).

316. C. 5% bond trading at 4.5% basis maturing in 2035

Municipal bond confirmations must disclose the yield to maturity (YTM, or basis) or yield to call (YTC), whichever is lower. The best way to visualize the bond price and yields is to set up a seesaw. Remember, the higher the number, the higher it goes on the seesaw. Choices (A) and (B) would make a seesaw that has the left side down and right side up, so those would have to be quoted yield to maturity. Choice (D) would be flat, so it would trade on its coupon rate. However, by plugging in the numbers from Choice (C), you get the following situation:

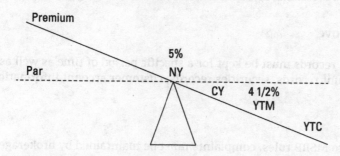

In this case, the NY (coupon rate) is 5%, and the YTM (basis) is 4.5%, so the right side has to be lowered. Therefore, this bond would have to be quoted YTC because it's lower than the YTM. Also, as you can see from the seesaw, municipal bonds trading at a premium and callable at par must show YTC on the confirmation, which means that municipal bond trading at a discount and callable at par must show YTM on the confirmation.

Note: Zero-coupon bonds (bonds making no interest payments), variable rate bonds, and bonds in default would trade on the bond price.

317. D. I, II, III, and IV

Under MSRB Rule G-15, the confirmation (receipt of trade) must include the customer's name, the capacity of the broker-dealer (agency or principal trade), the par value of the securities, trade date, execution price, whether it was a purchase or sale, the settlement date, yield or dollar price, CUSIP number (if there is one), and so on.

318. D. a municipal securities principal

All advertisements relating to municipal securities must be approved by a municipal securities principal (manager) or general securities principal prior to being sent to customers or potential customers. All advertising sent out by a firm (municipal or otherwise) must be approved by a principal.

319. A. issuers

The Municipal Securities Rulemaking Board (MSRB) establishes rules that broker-dealers, bank-dealers, and municipal advisors must follow when engaging in transactions of municipal securities. Issuers aren't subject to MSRB rules.

320. A. arbitration

According to MSRB rules, disputes must be settled through arbitration.

321. D. All of the above

All of those records must be kept for a specific period of time as well as records of entry, account records, securities records, customer account information, and so on.

322. C. 6 years

According to MSRB rules, complaints must be maintained by brokerage firms for 6 years.

323. C. a bona fide quote

You should have been able to cross out Choices (A) and (D) right away because nominal and subject quotes mean the same thing. When a municipal dealer gives or publishes a quote for a municipal security, it must be a bona fide (firm) quote. Because it's a bona fide quote, the dealer must be prepared to trade the security at that price.

324. A. I, II, III, and IV

Certainly, all of the choices fit for this question. When recommending a security to a customer, you should have a reasonable basis to believe that the recommendation is appropriate for that customer.

325. C. Buying a client season passes to the Yankees

According to MSRB rules, no municipal securities brokers or dealers shall give (directly or indirectly) a gift in excess of $100 per year to any person other than a partner or employee of the dealer. However, normal business expenses, such as business meals, airline tickets, and hotel expenses, are exempt. So, sending a client a picture of yourself in an $80 frame may be inappropriate (or not), but it's not a violation. However, buying season tickets for the Yankees would go way and beyond the $100 limit and wouldn't be deemed a business expense.

326. **A. I and IV**

A municipal dealer must notify the employing firm in writing before opening an account for an employee of another firm. In addition to notifying the employing firm, the municipal dealer must also send duplicate confirmations of each trade to the firm.

327. **C. fair and reasonable**

There is no hard and fast rule about the amount of markup or commission charged but it must be fair and reasonable based on the circumstances of the trade.

328. **A. the spread**

If the municipal underwriting was done on a negotiated basis (where the issuer chose the underwriter directly), the municipal firm must disclose the initial offering price, the spread, and any fee received as a result of the transaction.

329. **C. under no circumstances**

MSRB Rule G-38 deals with the solicitation of municipal securities business. Brokers, dealers, or municipal securities dealers may not provide or agree to provide payment for solicitation of municipal securities business to any person who is not affiliated with the broker, dealer, or municipal securities dealer.

330. **B. $250 per election**

According to MSRB Rule G-37, the maximum contribution allowed for a municipal finance professional (MFP) to a candidate running for a local government office is $250 per election. If a particular candidate is running in a primary and a general election, the MFP may contribute a total of $500 ($250 for the primary election and $250 for the general election).

331. **C. An employee of a broker-dealer holds a position of authority over the municipal issuer.**

According to MSRB rules, a control relationship exists when a firm or employee of a firm has a position of authority over the issuer of the securities being recommended (such as an employee of a firm is on the school board in the municipality of the municipal securities being recommended).

All control relationships must be disclosed prior to the execution of the trade verbally or in writing. If the first disclosure is verbal, written disclosure is required no later than the completion of the transaction. The same rule applies if the brokerage firm is a syndicate member or investment adviser of the issuer.

332. B. I, III, and IV

The indenture of a revenue bond would include items such as the maturity date, interest payment dates, the coupon rate, the legal opinion, covenants, the flow of funds, and so on. However, anything that's subject to change, such as the rating, wouldn't be placed on the indenture of a bond.

333. D. bond counsel

The legal opinion is a statement by a bond counsel (attorney) affirming that the interest received from a bond issue meets the requirements to be exempt from federal taxation. All municipal bonds must be accompanied by a legal opinion unless the issue is marked as ex-legal (a municipal bond that trades without a legal opinion).

334. B. rating the bonds

Ratings of bonds are only found in Moody's, S&P, Fitch's, and White's, which rates the marketability of municipal issues.

335. D. the issuer meets all conditions without restrictions

As funny as it sounds, an unqualified legal opinion as related to municipal bonds is actually a good thing. It's not saying that the bond counsel is unqualified but that the bond counsel found no problems with issue. Remember, the bond counsel (attorney) has to examine the issue and make sure that the issue is legally binding on the issuer and that it meets the tax laws to provide federally tax-free income. By contrast, a qualified legal opinion may mean that the issuer may not have clear title to a property, the issuer may have liens or judgments against property he owns, and so on.

336. A. official statement

Municipal bonds don't have a prospectus, but they do have an official statement. The official statement gives investors the most information about the issuer and the bond issue.

337. D. The official statement

The official statement is similar to a prospectus but for a municipality, not a corporation. In the official statement, investors would be able to find out what the bond funds will be used for, the tax base, tax collection history, interest payment dates, the maturity date, insurance backing the bonds, and so on.

338. D. guaranteeing timely payment of interest

A municipal bond counsel prepares the legal opinion for new municipal bonds. The main function of a municipal bond counsel is to make sure that it's valid and binding on the issuer and meets the laws that will make it federally tax-free. However, municipal bond counsels don't guarantee timely payment of principal and interest.

339.

D. the preliminary official statement

Because a municipal issuer prepares the preliminary and official statements, they don't need to be approved by a municipal securities principal. However, most of the things that happen within your firm, such as opening accounts, transactions in accounts, and advertisements sent out by your firm, do need to be approved by a principal (manager) of the firm.

340.

D. The total dollar amount of municipal bonds expected to reach the market in the next 30 days

The visible supply is published in the Friday edition of *The Bond Buyer* and is the total dollar amount of municipal bonds expected to reach the market in the next 30 days. If the visible supply is much larger than normal, interest rates are likely to rise to entice investors to buy.

341.

A. *The Bond Buyer*

The 30-day visible supply is published in the Friday edition of *The Bond Buyer*. The visible supply is the dollar volume of municipal bonds expected to reach the market within the next 30 days.

342.

A. the placement ratio

The Bond Buyer's placement ratio indicates the demand for new issues by disclosing the number of new municipal issues that have sold within the last week as compared to the amount available. You can set this up mathematically as

$$\text{Placement ratio} = \frac{\text{New issue municipal bonds sold during the week}}{\text{New issue municipal bonds available during the week}}$$

343.

D. Notice of sale

Municipalities looking to accept underwriting bids for new issues of municipal bonds publish the official notice of sale in *The Bond Buyer*.

344.

A. NIC or TIC

Because GO bonds are backed by taxes paid by people living in the municipality, issuers are more likely to take bids by underwriters for GO bonds than for revenue bonds. The winning bid has the lowest NIC (net interest cost) or TIC (true interest cost) to the issuer (the lowest interest rate and/or the highest purchase price).

345.

C. the rating of the bonds being auctioned

The ratings of the bonds of a new issue haven't been established yet, and when they are, they are subject to change. Therefore, the bond rating would not be included in the official notice of sale.

346. C. 20, 20-year GO bonds in the investment grade category

The Bond Buyer's Index (20-bond index) measures the average yield of 20 municipal GO (general obligation) bonds with 20 years to maturity. These bonds have a rating of A or better.

347. B. I and II

The Bond Buyer's 11-Bond Index uses a select group of general obligation bonds taken from the 20-Bond Index rated AAA or AA. The average rating is AA+ (Standard & Poor's) or Aa1 (Moody's).

348. B. I and II

The Bond Buyer's 11-Bond Index is made up of a select group of municipal general obligation (GO) bonds found in the 20-Bond Index. The 11 bonds have an average Standard & Poor's rating of AA+ and are made up of bonds rated AAA and AA.

349. C. the RevDex

Credit ratings from ratings agencies, such as Moody's and Standard & Poor's, the placement ratio, and the visible supply, are all important in helping determine the marketability of municipal general obligation (GO) bonds. However, the RevDex (Revenue Bond Index) discloses the average yield of 25 revenue bonds with 30-year maturities and has nothing to do with GO bonds.

350. B. 20 years

The Bond Buyer's Municipal Bond Index (40-Bond Index) provides the average dollar price of 40 highly traded revenue and general obligation (GO) bonds with an average maturity of 20 years and a rating of A or better.

351. A. EMMA

EMMA (electronic municipal market access) is a centralized online site that provides information about municipal securities to retail, non-professional investors. The site gives access to official statements for most new municipal bond offerings and provides real-time access to prices.

352. D. MSRB RTRS

The Real-Time Reporting System (MSRB RTRS) gets information from services that execute municipal trades to the public within 15 minutes of execution. The MSRB RTRS is open from 7:30 a.m. to 6:00 p.m. every business day.

Chapter 5 Answers

353. **D. All of the above**

U.S. government bonds (T-bills, T-notes, T-bonds, and so on), U.S. government agency securities, and municipal securities can be purchased on margin but are exempt from the Regulation T (50%) margin requirement. The margin requirement for these securities is much lower than for other securities.

354. **B. The FRB**

The FRB (Federal Reserve Board) determines which securities are marginable.

355. **D. Risk disclosure document**

Because of the additional risk involved when purchasing securities on margin, all margin customers must receive a risk disclosure document prior to opening the account. The risk disclosure document covers some of the broker-dealer's rules and outlines the risks like "investors may lose more money than initially deposited." Because of the additional risk involved, not all investors are good candidates for margin accounts. As far as the other answers go, the credit agreement, the hypothecation agreement, and the loan consent form are all part of the margin agreement.

356. **D. I, II, and IV**

Margin accounts are always held in street name (in the name of the broker-dealer for the benefit of the customer). Because the customer borrowed money from the broker-dealer to purchase the securities, the customer would be required to pay interest on the money borrowed (the debit balance; DR). In addition, a portion of the securities (140% of the DR) may be pledged as collateral for a bank loan by way of rehypothecation. However, a decrease or increase in the market value of the securities doesn't affect the debit balance.

357. **C. I, III, and IV**

Because of the additional risk taken in margin accounts, customers must sign a margin agreement before executing any trades. The margin agreement is broken down into the credit agreement, a hypothecation agreement, and a loan consent form. A risk disclosure document needs to be sent out prior to opening an options account.

358. **A. The credit agreement**

The credit agreement discloses the terms for borrowing, which includes the interest rate to be charged on the debit balance, the broker-dealer's method of computation, and how and when the interest rate may change. There's no such thing as a *margin interest rate form*, so Choice (D) is obviously wrong.

359. B. allows the broker-dealer to loan a customer's margined securities to other investors

A loan consent form is required only for margin accounts, not cash accounts. Although technically it isn't required, almost all firms require that customers sign it prior to opening a margin account. The loan consent form allows the broker-dealer to loan a margin customer's securities to other investors or broker-dealers, typically for the short sale of securities.

360. A. I and II

Securities that are marginable include stock and bonds listed on an exchange, NASDAQ stocks, non-NASDAQ stocks approved by the Fed, and warrants. However, mutual funds and IPOs (initial public offerings) can't be purchased on margin because they're new issues. New issues can't be purchased on margin for at least 30 days. However, after you've held mutual fund shares for more than 30 days, they can be transferred to a margin account.

361. D. 5 business days after the trade date

The deadline for customers meeting margin calls is 5 business days after the trade date. The customer must deposit 50% of the purchase (or short) amount or deposit fully paid securities worth twice the amount of the margin call. If needed, the broker-dealer may request an extension from a designated examining authority. In the event that the customer is less than $1,000 short, the broker-dealer isn't required to take action.

362. D. $3,000

Even though Regulation T may be set at 50% and minimum maintenance at 25% for long accounts, the broker-dealer (house) can increase those percentages if they choose not to take as much risk. Because the house margin requirement is 60%, the investor must come up with 60% of the $5,000 purchase: $(60\%)(\$5,000) = \$3,000$.

363. C. $25,000

A day trader is an individual who purchases and sells the same security within the same day in an attempt to take advantage of price fluctuations. Pattern day traders are individuals who execute four or five more day trades within 5 business days. The minimum equity for a pattern day trader is $25,000.

364. D. $100,000

Portfolio margin accounts can be set up for individuals who have at least $100,000 invested in marginable securities. Portfolio margin looks at the actual risk of the securities held as a whole and adjusts the margin requirement accordingly. So, investors who purchase safer securities would have a lower margin requirement.

365. B. $1,800

Because this is the initial transaction in a margin account, different rules apply. After the margin account is open, the customer would just have to deposit Regulation T (Reg T; 50%) of the purchase. However, in an opening transaction for a long margin account, the investor must pay in full, deposit $2,000, or pay the Reg T amount. If the customer is purchasing less than $2,000 worth of securities, they'd have to pay in full. If the amount of securities purchased is greater than $2,000 but Reg T is less than $2,000, the customer would have to deposit $2,000. If the amount of securities being purchased is greater than $2,000 and Reg T is greater than $2,000, the customer would pay the Reg T amount.

The best way to deal with this situation is to take the three numbers — the value of the securities, Reg T, and $2,000 — and then choose the number in the middle. This will always work for an initial transaction in a margin account. For this question, you have $1,800 in securities, $900 Reg T amount, and $2,000. The middle number is $1,800, so that's the answer.

366. C. $2,000

You have to pay particular attention to whether it's an initial transaction because different rules apply. Because this customer is opening the margin account, it's an initial transaction. This customer is selling short as an initial transaction, so they must deposit a minimum of $2,000. If the customer had an existing margin account, they'd have had to deposit 50% (Regulation T) of the $1,500 short sale, or $750.

367. C. $2,500

In an initial transaction for a short margin account, the investor has to deposit Regulation T (Reg T; 50%) of the amount of securities shorted, or $2,000, whichever is more. Because this investor is shorting $5,000 worth of securities, they have to deposit ($5,000)(50%) = $2,500.

368. C. $2,000

In an initial transaction for a short margin account, the investor has to deposit Regulation T (Reg T; 50%) of the quantity of securities shorted, or $2,000, whichever is more. Because this investor is shorting $3,000 worth of securities, Regulation T would be $1,500 ($3,000 × 50%). Since $2,000 is more, that is what the investor has to deposit.

369.   C. $8,000

You can tell that this is a long margin account because it has a debit balance (DR), not a credit balance (CR). In this particular equation, you have to ignore the SMA (special memorandum account) because it doesn't help you get the answer you need. Use the following equation to help you get your answer:

$$LMV - DR = EQ$$
$$\$30,000 - \$22,000 = \$8,000$$

Here, LMV is the long market value of the securities, DR is the debit balance (the amount owed to the broker–dealer), and EQ is the equity (the owner's portion of the account).

370.   A. $5,400

You have to start by getting the long market value (LMV) of all the securities held in the account. Mr. Flanagan has $6,000 of CSA (100 × $60 per share), $4,800 of TUV (200 × $24 per share), and $1,800 of LMN (100 × $18 per share) for a total of $12,600. Next, pop it into the equation to see where he stands:

$$LMV - DR = EQ$$
$$\$12,600 - \$7,200 = \$5,400$$

Mr. Flanagan has $5,400 in equity (EQ) with the long market value (LMV) at $12,600 and the debit balance (DR) at $7,200.

371.   C. $45,000

The short selling of securities must always be executed in a margin account. Set up the equation as follows, where SMV is the short market value, EQ is the equity, and CR is the credit balance:

$$SMV + EQ = CR$$
$$\$30,000 + \$15,000 = \$45,000$$

The investor sold short 1,000 shares of LMN at $30, so you have to place $30,000 (1,000 × $30) under the SMV. You can assume that Regulation T is 50%, so the investor had to come up with $15,000 (50% of $30,000). Place the $15,000 under the EQ (the investor's portion of the account), and you can see that the credit balance (CR) has to be $45,000 ($30,000 + $15,000).

372. B. $27,000

Your client has a combined long and short margin account. You can either take each equation for each account and plug the numbers in separately to determine the equity or use the following formula:

$$\text{Combined equity} = \text{LMV} + \text{CR} - \text{DR} - \text{SMV}$$
$$= \$30{,}000 + \$40{,}000 - \$18{,}000 - \$25{,}000$$
$$= \$27{,}000$$

Note that the SMA (special memorandum account) has no effect on the combined equity.

373. C. $5,000 increase in equity

When you purchase securities, you want the price to increase, and when you short securities, you want the price to decrease. In this case, both things happened, which is great for this investor. A direct correlation exists between the market value of the stock and the equity (1 to 1). Therefore, because the long account went up by $3,000 ($35,000 to $38,000) and the short account went down by $2,000 ($28,000 to $26,000), the combined equity increased by $3,000 + $2,000 = $5,000.

374. B. $10,000

Loan value is the complement of Regulation T. So, with Regulation T at 50%, the loan value is also 50%. If Regulation T was set at 60%, the loan value would be 40%. So, the investor purchased $20,000 worth of securities (1,000 shares × $20,000) so, they would have to deposit 50% of that amount, and the loan value would be 50%. 50% of $20,000 is $10,000, which is the amount the firm would lend to them (loan value) as a result of the transaction.

375. A. a cash withdrawal

When withdrawing cash from a margin account, the SMA (special memorandum account) decreases by the full amount of the cash withdrawal.

376. D. $2,000

The full amount of cash dividends received in a margin account will go to the special memorandum account (SMA).

377. D. $30,000

The first thing that you have to do is set up the short margin account equation. The short market value (SMV) is $80,000 (1,000 × $80), and the investor had to deposit 50% (Reg T) of that amount, which gives them an equity (EQ) of $40,000. Plugging these values into the equation, you can see that their credit balance (CR) is $120,000.

$$SMV + EQ = CR$$
$$\$80{,}000 + \$40{,}000 = \$120{,}000$$

Next, the market value drops to $70,000 (1,000 × $70), and the credit balance (CR) stays the same, so that means that the EQ had to increase to $50,000. At this point, you can cross off the top set of numbers because you don't need them anymore.

$$SMV + EQ = CR$$
$$\cancel{\$80{,}000 + \$40{,}000 = \$120{,}000}$$
$$\$70{,}000 + \$50{,}000 = \$120{,}000$$

Next, multiply Reg T (50%) by the new short market value of $70,000 to get $35,000. Compare the $35,000 needed to be at 50% with the $50,000 in equity, and you see that this investor has $50,000 – $35,000 = $15,000 more than needed in equity. With Regulation T being set at 50%, Mrs. Diamond can purchase (or short) $30,000 worth of securities with having excess equity of $15,000.

378. B. $7,000

Normally, an investor purchasing $30,000 worth of stock on margin would have to deposit $15,000 to meet the margin call (you can assume Regulation T is 50% of the purchase). First, you have to find out whether Mr. Jones has any excess equity in the margin account to help offset the $15,000 payment. Use the following equation:

$$LMV - DR = EQ$$

After setting up the equation, enter the $60,000 market value of the securities under the long market value (LMV). Next, enter the $22,000 under the debit record (DR), also known as the debit balance.

$$LMV - DR = EQ$$
$$\$60{,}000 - \$22{,}000 = \$38{,}000$$

Multiply Regulation T (50%) by the LMV to get the amount of equity the customer should have in the account to be at 50%: (50%)($60,000) = $30,000. This investor needs only $30,000 in equity to reach 50%, and this investor has $38,000, which is $8,000 more than necessary.

The $8,000 is excess equity (SMA; special memorandum account), which they can use to help offset the margin call for the $30,000 worth of stock they want to buy:

$15,000 margin call – $8,000 excess equity = $7,000 to deposit

379. A. increase

The excess equity (SMA) in a margin account is built in to the equity. If your client removes equity from a margin account, they're borrowing more money from the account, and the debit balance (the amount owed to the broker–dealer) will increase.

380. A. $5,500

Normally, an investor purchasing $25,000 worth of stock on margin would have to deposit $12,500 to meet the margin call (you can assume Regulation T is 50% of the purchase). First, you have to find out whether this investor has any excess equity in their margin account to help offset the $12,500 payment by using the following equation:

$$LMV - DR = EQ$$

Here, you use the market value of the securities for the long market value (LMV) and the $18,000 debit balance for the debit record (DR).

$$LMV - DR = EQ$$
$$\$50,0000 - \$18,000 = \$32,000$$

You come up with an equity (EQ) of $32,000. Now, multiply Regulation T (50%) by the LMV to get the amount of equity the customer should have in the account to be at 50%: (50%)($50,000) = $25,000. This investor needs only $25,000 in equity to reach 50%, and this investor has $32,000, which is $32,000 − $25,000 = $7,000 more than necessary.

The $7,000 is excess equity (also known as special memorandum account, SMA), which they can use to help offset the margin call for the $25,000 worth of stock they want to buy. To determine how much the investor needs to deposit, use the following formula:

$$\$12,500 \text{ margin call} - \$7,000 \text{ excess equity} = \$5,500 \text{ to deposit}$$

381. B. $7,000

Buying power is the amount of additional securities that you can purchase on margin with the SMA (excess equity) in the account. You must first set up the equation so you can determine the SMA.

There is a debit balance (DR); therefore, you know that it has to be a long margin account. The long market value minus the debit balance (the amount borrowed from the broker–dealer) equals the equity (the investor's portion of the account).

$$LMV - DR = EQ$$
$$\$46,000 - \$19,500 = \$26,500$$
$$\text{Reg Tx LMV} \quad \underline{- \$23,000}$$
$$\$3,500$$

Next, you have to multiply the LMV by the Regulation T margin requirement (50%) to determine the amount of equity the investor should have in the account to be at 50% margin: (50%)($46,000) = $23,000. Because the investor has $26,500 in equity, the investor has an excess equity (SMA) of $26,500 – $23,000 = $3,500. This $3,500 is additional money that the investor can use (if he chooses to) to purchase additional securities. Assuming Regulation T is at 50%, the investor can purchase $7,000 worth of securities on margin with $3,500 SMA.

382.   A. I only

If a customer's margin account is restricted, the equity (EQ) has fallen below the 50% Regulation T requirement, so Statement I is true. Therefore, you know that Statement II is false. They may borrow additional money by depositing Regulation T (50%) of any new purchases. They don't have to take the account out of restricted status, and the only time they have to deposit money immediately is if the account falls below minimum maintenance (25% of the LMV).

383.   D. $3,750

Whenever an investor sells securities short, the sale has to be executed in a margin account. Short sellers are bearish and want the price of their securities to decrease. Mr. Steyne will end up with a restricted account because the value of the securities increased. To determine how much the account is restricted, use the following equation:

$$SMV + EQ = CR$$

Here, SMV (short market value) = $42,000, EQ (equity) = $21,000 (the Regulation T amount, or 50% of the SMV, because that's how much the investor has to deposit into the account).

$$\$42,000 + \$21,000 = \$63,000$$

Now, change the SMV to $44,500 to adjust for the change in the market price and then calculate the new equity. Bring the CR down because that number doesn't change as the SMV goes up or down. Now that the SMV is $44,500 and the CR is $63,000, the EQ has to be $18,500 ($63,000 – $44,500). You can draw a line through the top numbers because you don't need them from this point on.

$$SMV + EQ = CR$$
$$\cancel{\$42,000 + \$21,000 = \$63,000}$$
$$\$44,500 + \$18,500 = \$63,000$$

Multiply Regulation T (you can assume 50%) by the new SMV to find the amount of equity (EQ) the investor should have to be at 50%: (50%)($44,500) = $22,250.

This investor needs $22,500 to be at 50% of the SMV. They have only $18,500; therefore, the account is restricted by $22,250 – $18,500 = $3,750.

384.   C. 5,000

The standard equation for long margin accounts is

$$LMV - DR = EQ$$

Here, LMV is the long market value of the securities, DR is the debit balance (the amount owed to the broker-dealer), and EQ is the equity (the owner's portion of the account). In this case, the long market value is $50,000 ($50 × 1,000 shares). Then, you find the EQ by multiplying the LMV by 50% (Reg T requirement), which equals $25,000. So, the DR also must be $25,000.

$$LMV - DR = EQ$$
$$\$50,0000 - \$18,000 = \$32,000$$

Now, change the long market value to $40,000 ($40 × 1,000 shares). The DR remains the same because the customer didn't borrow any additional money from the broker-dealer. This means that the EQ reduces to $15,000. Place all of those numbers in the equation and cross off the initial numbers because you don't need them anymore.

$$LMV - DR = EQ$$
$$\cancel{\$50,000} - \cancel{\$25,000} = \cancel{\$25,000}$$
$$\$40,000 - \$25,000 = \$15,000$$

Next, you have to multiply Reg T (50%) by the new LMV ($40,000) to determine how much the investor should have in EQ to be at 50%: (50%)($40,000) = $20,000. This investor should have at least $20,000 in equity in order not to have a restricted account. They have only $15,000 in equity, so the account is restricted by $5,000.

385.   A. $2,400

First, you have to figure out the credit balance. Mr. Jones sold short $16,000 worth of securities (400 shares × $40 per share), so enter $16,000 under the SMV (short market value). Then Mr. Jones had to deposit the Reg T amount (50%) of the purchase, so enter $8,000 (50% × $16,000) under the EQ (the investor's portion of the account). You find that the credit balance (CR) is $24,000:

$$SMV + EQ = CR$$
$$\$16,000 + \$8,000 = CR$$
$$CR = \$24,000$$

Next, find Mr. Jones' current equity. The SMV changes to $17,600 ($44 × 400 shares), so you need to put that under the SMV in a new equation. In a short account, the CR remains the same as the market price changes, so you need to bring the $24,000 straight down from the preceding equation. You can see that the EQ has decreased to $6,400 (the difference between $17,600 and $24,000):

$$SMV + EQ = CR$$
$$\cancel{\$16,000 + \$8,000 = \$24,000}$$
$$\$17,600 + \$6,400 = \$24,000$$
$$(50\% \times 17,600) = \underline{\$8,800}$$
$$(\$2,400) \text{ restricted}$$

Finally, multiply the SMV by Regulation T to get the amount Mr. Jones should have in equity to be at 50%. Take the $8,800 ($17,600 × 50%) and compare it to the EQ. Because Mr. Jones has only $6,400 in equity ($2,400 less than the Reg T requirement), the account is restricted by $2,400:

386. A. on demand

If a margin account falls below minimum maintenance (25% for a long account and 30% for a short account), payment must be made right away. If the payment isn't made, the broker-dealer has the right to sell securities in the account to bring it out of restricted status. The customer can deposit fully paid marginable securities or cash to meet the maintenance call.

387. B. $5,000

Minimum maintenance is the minimum percentage an investor must have in equity in a margin account. You have to start by adding the market value of all the investments together. This investor has $1,500 (100 × $15) of TUV, $6,000 (200 × $30) of XYZ, and $12,500 (500 × $25) of LMN, so you get $1,500 + $6,000 + $12,500 = $20,000.

The minimum maintenance for a long margin account is 25% of the long market value (LMV): (25%)($20,000) = $5,000.

388. B. $8,000

Minimum maintenance on a long margin account is 25% of the current market value (CMV). The best way to determine how low the market value can drop before the investor receives a maintenance call is to divide the $6,000 debit balance by 0.75. For this investor, if the current market value drops below $8,000 ($6,000 divided by 0.75) before receiving a maintenance call. If you forget the equation, you can always plug the answers in one at a time to see which one works.

389. A. 50% initial and 25% maintenance

Under Regulation T, the initial margin requirement for long accounts is 50% of the market value, and minimum maintenance is 25%. For short accounts, the initial margin requirement is 50% of the market value, and minimum maintenance is 30%. However, broker-dealers may increase the initial margin requirement and minimum maintenance through house rules.

390.   B. $7,500

Minimum maintenance on short accounts is 30% of the short market value. So simply multiply $25,000 by 30%:

$$(\$25,000)(30\%) = \$7,500$$

391.   C. $3,000

First, you need to set up the equation. Since Ayla sold short $50,000 worth of securities ($50 × 1,000 shares), that is the short market value (SMV). So, Ayla had to deposit $25,000 (50% of $50,000), which is the equity. This means that the credit balance (CR) is $75,000.

$$SMV + EQ = CR$$
$$\$50,000 + \$25,000 = CR$$
$$CR = \$75,000$$

Next, find Ayla's current equity. The SMV changed to $60,000 ($60 × 1,000 shares), so you need to put that value under the SMV. In a short account, the CR remains the same as the market price changes, so the CR is $75,000. Therefore, the equity has decreased to $15,000:

$$SMV + EQ = CR$$
$$\cancel{\$50,000} + \cancel{\$25,000} = \cancel{\$75,000}$$
$$\$60,000 + \$15,000 = \$75,000$$
$$(30\% \times \$60,000) = \underline{\$18,000}$$
$$(\$3,000) \text{ maintenance call}$$

Now multiply the SMV by 30% to get the amount Ayla should have in equity to be at minimum maintenance. Take the $18,000 ($60,000 × 30%) and compare it to the equity. Because Ayla has only $15,000 in equity, they'll receive a maintenance call of $3,000.

392.   D. 130% or 1.3

Minimum maintenance on short margin accounts is 30% of the short market value. To determine how high the short market value can rise before the investor receives a maintenance call, you can divide the credit balance by 1.3 (130%).

Chapter 6 Answers

393.   **C. The next computed bid price**

When investors redeem shares of a mutual fund, they're essentially selling shares back to the issuer. When investors sell, they sell at the bid price. The bid price for a mutual fund is the net asset value (NAV). Because mutual funds hold so many different securities, there's no current bid or ask price. Mutual funds use *forward pricing* so investors selling shares are selling them at the next computed bid price, which is typically at the end of the trading day.

394.   **A. II and III**

Closed-end funds are typically listed on an exchange and have a fixed number of shares outstanding. Closed-end funds must be sold to another investor and aren't redeemable. In addition, closed-end funds may issue common stock, preferred stock, and bonds.

395.   **B. Closed-end**

In both open- and closed-end funds, the NAV indicates the performance of the fund's portfolio. If the NAV (net asset value) and POP (public offering price) move in opposite directions, the fund must be a closed-end fund. The price of a closed-end fund depends not only on the performance of the securities held but also on supply and demand. In an open-end fund, the NAV and POP must move in the same direction because the price depends solely on the performance of the securities held by the fund.

396.   **A. next computed NAV**

Mutual fund redemptions and purchases take place at the next computed NAV (net asset value) and next computed POP (public offering price) respectively. There is no current NAV or POP price so purchases and redemptions typically take place at the end of the day. This is known as forward pricing.

397.   **C. They charge commissions to customers who purchase shares.**

Open-end investment companies (mutual funds) don't charge a commission; they charge a sales charge added to the NAV.

398.   **D. II, III, and IV**

Closed-end investment companies make a one-time offering of new shares and then trade in the market like other equity securities. Also, closed-end investment companies may issue preferred stock and bonds in addition to common stock.

399. A. mutual funds can't be purchased on margin

New securities can't be purchased on margin for at least 30 days. Because mutual funds are new securities, they're not marginable. However, investors who have held onto mutual fund shares for more than 31 days can place them in margin accounts and borrow money against them.

400. C. $27.52 plus a commission

Closed-end funds charge a commission added to the POP (public offering price). Open-end funds charge a sales charge, which is built into the POP, except for no-load funds, which don't charge a sales charge.

401. A. I and III

Open-end (mutual) funds allow for exchanges of mutual fund shares within the same family of funds (closed-end funds do not). In addition, open-end funds allow for investors to automatically reinvest capital gains and dividends (closed-end funds do not).

402. D. shares over a fixed period of time, a fixed number of shares periodically, or a fixed dollar amount periodically

As an extra service, many, but not all, mutual funds offer systematic withdrawal plans as a way of redeeming shares. This type of plan is ideal for someone who's at the retirement age and is looking for a little extra cash each month while still keeping the balance invested. Systematic withdrawal plans can be set up as a fixed dollar amount periodically, a fixed share amount redeemed periodically, or a fixed amount of time (for example, redeeming all the shares over a 10-year period).

403. D. 95

For an investment company to be considered regulated (regulated investment company, RIC) under Subchapter M and avoid being taxed as a corporation, it must distribute (pass-through) at least 90% of their net investment income to shareholders.

404. A. the 75-5-10 test

For an investment company to be considered diversified, it must meet the 75-5-10 test. (The 75, 5, and 10 represent percentages.) So for an investment company to claim it's diversified, no more than 5% of the 75% can be invested in one company. In addition, out of the 75% portion, the investment company cannot own more than 10% of the outstanding shares of any company. The remaining 25% can be invested in any way.

405. **B. investors are prohibited from redeeming the money market fund for a year**

Money market funds are types of mutual funds that hold short-term debt securities. The NAV of the fund is set at $1. They do offer a check-writing feature; they're no-load (no sales charge); and they compute dividends daily and credit them monthly. However, investors aren't prohibited from redeeming their funds for a year; they can redeem at any time.

406. **D. investment objectives**

Although all of the choices listed are important, investors should start at a fund's investment objectives. For example, is the customer looking for growth, income, growth and income, a tax-advantaged investment (municipal bond fund), and so on? After the client determines the type of fund, they can then start comparing the performance and expenses of those types of funds from several issuers prior to making a decision.

407. **D. income fund**

Although hedge funds, growth funds, and aggressive growth funds have capital appreciation potential, they don't provide current income. Income funds invest in stocks paying dividends and bonds paying interest. Therefore, the best choice for this investor would be an income fund or some sort of bond fund.

408. **C. Growth funds**

In this case, you aren't told what the couple's investment objectives are. However, because they've already invested the maximum for the year into their IRAs and are young, growth funds would be ideal. Younger investors can afford to take more risk than older investors. Growth funds invest in a diversified portfolio of stocks that have capital appreciation potential.

409. **A. Specialized**

If an investor is looking for capital appreciation, you should recommend some type of stock fund. Out of the choices listed, a specialized (sector) fund would be the best fit for this customer. Specialized funds invest in stocks of a particular industry or region with a main objective of capital appreciation.

410. **B. A sector fund investing in high-tech stocks**

Investors interested in current income would purchase some sort of bond or income fund. They wouldn't purchase a fund that invests in high-tech stocks because they're growth companies. Growth companies usually don't pay dividends but invest their earnings back into the company to expand or purchase new equipment.

411. C. special situation fund

Funds that hold stocks of corporations that are releasing new products, have new management, have patents pending, and so forth are called *special situation funds*.

412. C. An international fund

If an investor is concerned about the U.S. economy, an investor could invest in international funds that buy investments of foreign issuers. Global funds invest in U.S. and foreign companies.

413. B. I, III, and IV

Mutual fund performance statistics must show results for one, five, and ten years, or the life of the fund, whichever is less.

414. B. life-cycle fund

Life-cycle funds are pretty interesting and would meet this client's needs perfectly. As investors grow older, they typically don't have the ability to assume as much risk as younger investors. In most cases, investors adjust their portfolio every so often to move a larger percentage into fixed-income securities as they get older to minimize risk. Life-cycle (target-date) funds adjust the portfolio of securities held on their own. The investment adviser for the fund will rebalance the securities held by the fund every so often by selling off equity securities held by the fund and purchasing more fixed-income securities. Clients interested in investing in life-cycle funds should choose one with a target retirement date in line with their own needs.

415. C. Hedge funds

ETFs (exchange-traded funds) and inverse ETFs are easily tradable, and money market funds are easily redeemable, so they all have a high degree of liquidity. Hedge funds are the least liquid because they're unregulated and require a minimum holding period (lock-up provision) before investors can make withdrawals. Hedge funds are speculative and employ strategies unavailable to regulated investment companies. Hedge funds may purchase securities on margin, sell securities short, purchase or sell options, and so on.

416. A. An insured municipal bond fund

Out of the choices listed, the only fund that provides tax-free interest is a municipal bond fund. The interest received on the municipal bonds held by the fund is passed through to investors by way of federally tax-free dividends. The fact that the municipal bonds held by the fund are insured adds another level of safety.

417. B. a municipal bond fund

The interest received on municipal bonds is federally tax-free. Therefore, they're of a bigger advantage to investors in higher income tax brackets. When purchasing municipal bond funds, the dividends received by investors that represent the flow-through of interest received from the municipal bonds held by the fund aren't taxable.

418. B. Fixed share averaging

Fixed share averaging is buying the same amount of shares periodically. Dollar cost averaging is buying the same dollar amount of securities periodically. A constant dollar plan is keeping the same amount of money invested in a security at all times. Market timing has to do with switching between different types of funds to take advantage of bullish or bearish markets.

419. C. 90 days

By signing a letter of intent, an investor is able to take advantage of a breakpoint (reduced sales charge) right away, even though not purchasing enough to receive a breakpoint. A letter of intent allows an investor up to 13 months to purchase enough to receive the breakpoint. Letters of intent can be backdated for up to 90 days (3 months) so they can apply to previous purchases.

420. C. You should remind your client that they have another month to invest an additional $5,000 into ABC.

Your client signed a letter of intent (LOI) to receive a breakpoint (a discounted sales charge for large dollar purchases). A letter of intent is good for 13 months, which means that your client has 13 months to purchase $20,000 worth of ABC. The fact that ABC has appreciated to more than $20,000 doesn't come into play. This means that your client has one more month to deposit the additional $5,000, or ABC will sell shares held in escrow to make up for the money it lost in sales charges by providing the discount.

421. A. $32.26

This question isn't quite as easy as it looks. Most people take the numbers, add them together, and then divide by 5. Unfortunately, that may give you the average price per share but not average cost per share. What your client has set up here is dollar cost averaging. Dollar cost averaging is depositing the same amount periodically into the same security. By sticking with this plan, it allows investors to purchase more when the price is low and less when the price is high. The benefit of dollar cost averaging can be demonstrated by seeing what happens with this client by looking at how many shares they were able to purchase each month.

Month 1: 50 shares ($1,000/$20)

Month 2: 40 shares ($1,000/$25)

Month 3: 25 shares ($1,000/$40)

Month 4: 20 shares ($1,000/$50)

Month 5: 20 shares ($1,000/$50)

So, this investor deposited a total of $5,000 over the past five months and was able to purchase 155 shares (50 + 40 + 25 + 20 + 20). To determine the average cost per share, just divide $5,000 by 155 shares:

$$\frac{\$5,000}{155 \text{ shares}} = \$32.26 \text{ per share}$$

422. D. 8.5% of the amount invested

The maximum sales charge for a mutual (open-end) fund is 8.5% of the amount invested.

423. B. 5.7%

To determine the sales charge percent, use the following formula:

$$\text{Sales charge \%} = \frac{POP - NAV}{POP}$$

where POP is the public offering price, and NAV is the net asset value per share. In this case, the POP is $14.00, and the NAV is $13.20, so you get

$$\text{Sales charge \%} = \frac{\$14.00 - \$13.20}{\$14.00}$$

$$= \frac{\$0.80}{\$14.00}$$

$$= 5.7\%$$

424. A. the net asset value + the sales charge

The public offering price (POP) of a mutual fund is the net asset value (NAV) plus the sales charge, so the answer is Choice (A). If the mutual fund is no-load, the net asset value and the public offering price are the same.

425. B. 1,298.701 shares

Notice that the answer choices include a decimal point because mutual funds can sell fractions of shares. This investor is going to receive a breakpoint for purchasing more than $20,000 worth of the fund, so they won't be paying the public offering price (POP) of $31.40 per share. To determine how much they'll be paying per share, use the following formula:

$$POP = \frac{NAV}{100\% - \text{Sales charge \%}}$$

POP equals the Public Offering Price and NAV equals the Net Asset Value. In this case, the NAV is $29.26. To whittle down to this investor's public offering price, plug in the numbers:

$$POP = \frac{\$29.26}{100\% - 5\%}$$
$$= \frac{\$29.26}{95\%}$$
$$= \$30.80$$

So, this investor will be paying $30.80 per share instead of $31.40. Now, you need to determine how many shares they can purchase when depositing $40,000 and paying $30.80 per share. You can figure that out by simply dividing the deposit amount by the price per share, like so:

$$\frac{\$40,000 \text{ invested}}{\$30.80 \text{ per share}} = 1,298.701 \text{ shares}$$

Because this investor received a breakpoint, they were able to purchase 1,298.701 shares. Without the breakpoint, they would have been able to purchase only 1,273.885 shares.

426. A. Class A

Class A shares are front-end loads, where the investor is charged a sales charge when purchasing the fund shares. Class A shares will work out to be better for most long-term investors.

427. C. Class C

With Class C class shares are ones in which investors do not pay a front-end sales charge but pay an annual asset-based sales charge. If shares are held for a long period of time, Class C shares end up costing investors more.

428. D. Face-amount certificate company

A face-amount certificate is a type of packaged security that's similar to a zero-coupon bond; investors make either a lump sum payment or periodic payments in return for a larger future payment. The issuer of a face-amount certificate guarantees payment of the face amount (a fixed sum) to the investor at a preset date. Very few face-amount certificate companies are around today.

429. A. UIT

UITs (unit investment trusts) invest in a fixed portfolio of securities. Because the trust is a fixed portfolio, the trust wouldn't need a manager to supervise the money invested. Therefore, UITs don't charge a management fee.

430. D. they offer redeemable securities

ETFs (Exchange Traded Funds) are closed end index funds and are not redeemable. Shares of ETFs must be sold to other investors. Since ETFs are closed end funds, they may be purchased on margin and sold short. They may be traded on exchanges or the OTC market.

431. B. An inverse exchange-traded fund

Exchange-traded funds (ETFs) are funds that track a basket of securities or an index, such as the S&P 500, NASDAQ 100, Russell 2000, or even specific sectors. Inverse ETFs (short funds) are constructed to take advantage of a declining market. Inverse ETFs are often purchased by investors to hedge their portfolios against falling prices. Choices (A) and (D) are out because mutual funds can't be sold short.

432. D. I, II, and IV

In this question, you're looking for the differences between exchange-traded funds (ETFs) and mutual funds. Unlike mutual funds, ETFs can be sold short, they can be purchased on margin, and provide real-time pricing, not forward pricing like mutual funds. What is similar is that both ETFs and mutual funds represent a basket or portfolio of securities.

433. C. REITs

REITs (real estate investment trusts) are actively traded in the secondary market. However, open-end funds and unit investment trusts (UITs) must be redeemed with the issuer and don't trade in the secondary market.

434. C. double-barreled

Double-barreled bonds are ones issued by municipalities and aren't types of REITs (real estate investment trusts). The three basic types of REITs are

>> Equity REIT: Purchases properties

>> Mortgage REIT: Invests in construction and/or mortgage loans

>> Hybrid REIT: A combination of equity and mortgage REITs

435. **A. The REIT must generate at least 75% of income from construction and mortgage loans.**

A mortgage REIT must generate at least 75% of gross income from construction and mortgage loans and doesn't invest in ownership of properties. An equity REIT invests in ownership of properties. A Hybrid REIT invests in a combination of loans and properties. Because a REIT must generate at least 75% of gross income from real estate investments, dividends, and interest, 25% of income may be earned from securities, such as stocks and bonds.

436. **C. 90%**

A REIT (real estate investment trust) must distribute at least 90% of its income to shareholders to avoid taxation as a corporation.

437. **A. I only**

REITs (real estate investment trusts) raise money from investors to invest in real estate–related projects. At least 75% of the trust's gross income must be earned from real estate–related projects. They may invest a small portion of their assets in non–real estate investments, such as stocks and other securities. They do have to register with the SEC, and they don't issue redeemable securities.

438. **C. I and III**

This one is a little tricky. Most of the securities you will be dealing with only have to be registered with the SEC (Securities and Exchange Commission). However, variable annuities are a security that has to be registered with the SEC and an insurance product that must be registered with the State Insurance Commission.

439. **B. fixed annuities**

The payout on a fixed annuity is guaranteed, so fixed annuities aren't regulated by the Investment Company Act of 1940. Fixed annuities are exempt from SEC registration, and the payouts are made out of the insurance company's general account, not a separate account. Because fixed annuities have a fixed payout, they're subject to purchasing power risk. You need an insurance license but not a securities license like a Series 7 to sell fixed annuities.

440. **A. the holder of the policy**

Annuities are retirement plans issued by insurance companies. The big difference with fixed and variable annuities is that in variable annuities, the investment risk is on the policyholder. In a fixed annuity, the insurance company holds the investment risk. Variable annuities are riskier but more likely to keep pace with inflation.

441. C. investors are protected against capital loss

Variable annuities have a separate account that's professionally managed and often contains mutual funds. Variable annuities are much more likely to keep pace with inflation than fixed annuities. However, variable annuity investors aren't protected against capital loss the way that holders of fixed annuities are.

442. B. It will be higher.

If the return in the separate account is higher than the AIR (assumed interest rate) for a particular month, the payout for the following month would be higher. Conversely, if the return is lower than the AIR, the payout would be lower than the AIR for the following month.

443. A. II only

Accumulation units are similar to shares of a mutual fund. A variable annuity holder purchases accumulation units during the pay-in phase. During the pay-out phase, the accumulation units are converted into annuity units. So, for a variable annuity to have accumulation units, there had to be a pay-in phase. Out of the choices listed, the only one that had a pay-in phase was the *periodic payment deferred annuity*.

444. D. Single payment deferred annuity

This investor has a large amount of money right now, so they'll likely make a single (lump-sum) payment. Because they're only 25 years old, they'll defer payments until they retire. Single payment deferred annuity would work best for this investor. As a side note, Choice (A) is bogus because the insurance company won't pay out without an investor depositing money first.

445. D. a fixed number of annuity units based on the value of his accumulation units

When a variable annuity is annuitized during the payout phase, investors receive a fixed number of annuity units based on the value of the accumulation units. The part that's variable with a variable annuity is that the payouts vary based on the value of the securities held.

446. A. Life income annuity

Because the life income annuity (life annuity) payments cease at the death of the annuitant, they have the highest monthly payments. Joint and last survivor annuities have the lowest monthly payments.

447.   A. Straight life annuity

Annuities are retirement plans issued by insurance companies. Straight-life annuities are annuities with no beneficiaries and, therefore, provide the largest monthly payout. After the investor dies, the insurance company isn't required to pay a beneficiary. Life annuity with period certain, joint and survivor annuities, and unit-refund annuities have named beneficiaries to be paid if the policyholder dies early.

448.   B. mortality guarantee

Actually, the only answer that wasn't made up was Choice (B). Holders of variable annuities receive payments for life even if they live beyond their life expectancy. The insurance company assumes the mortality guarantee.

449.   D. the designated beneficiary

If the owner of a variable annuity dies during the accumulation (pay-in) phase, the death benefit will be paid to the designated beneficiary. The death benefit is typically the total of all investments plus any earnings. It's typically paid in a lump sum, and the beneficiary would be responsible for paying taxes on the earnings (amount received over the deceased's cost basis) at the beneficiary's tax rate.

450.   D. I, II, and III

Persons selling variable annuities, variable life insurance, and variable universal life insurance must have not only an appropriate securities license but also an insurance license. Prior to recommending any of the previously mentioned products, you should do an analysis of the client's needs and make appropriate recommendations.

451.   C. I and IV

In variable life insurance policies, the minimum death benefit is guaranteed, but the cash value isn't. Based on the performance of the securities held in the separate account, the death benefit may increase but may never decrease below the minimum. The cash value (surrender value) varies depending on the performance of the separate account and isn't guaranteed.

452.   D. II and IV

Unlike variable life policies, variable universal life policies do not have fixed premiums. As such, they are sometimes called *flexible premium* variable life policies. As with variable life policies, the investors can pick the securities held in the separate account. In this case, since the premium is not fixed and the securities held in the separate account may perform poorly, the minimum death benefit and cash value are not guaranteed.

453. A. variable annuity to variable life insurance

Money cannot be switched from annuities to life insurance tax free. The first money withdrawn from annuities is taxable while life insurance allows a death benefit to be inherited tax free to the beneficiary.

454. D. no more than 60% insiders

The board of director of an investment company must be made up of no more than 60% insiders (those who have affiliation with the company that issued the fund). Having this rule allows investors to gain some representation on the board of directors through voting. Although up to 60% is the rule, many investment companies have a board of directors that is made up of around 25% insiders.

455. A. If voted for by a majority of its outstanding voting securities

Unless voted on by a majority of its outstanding voting securities, registered investment companies may not change its classification from a diversified to a non-diversified company.

456. C. semiannually

Under the Investment Company Act of 1940, mutual (open-end) funds must send out account statements at least semiannually. Regarding account statements and how often they must be sent out, remember AIM:

Active accounts: monthly

Inactive accounts: quarterly

Mutual funds: semiannually

Chapter 7 Answers

457. B. an oil and gas limited partnership

If Marge is looking to add some liquidity (ease of trading) to their portfolio, an oil and gas limited partnership wouldn't make sense. Limited partnerships (direct participation programs, DPPs) are some of the most difficult investments to get in and out of. Limited partnerships require approval not only of the registered rep but also of the general partner of the limited partnership. Limited partnership investors need a certain minimum deposit and need to have liquidity in other investments in case the limited partnership needs additional funds to meet its goal.

458. B. I and IV

In order for a partnership to not be taxed as a corporation, it must avoid at least two corporate characteristics. The easiest corporate characteristic for a partnership to avoid is having a perpetual life (partnerships are set up for a finite period of time) and having free transferability to partnership interest. Because of the approval process, limited partnerships are some of the most difficult investments to get in and out of.

459. D. All of the above

All of the choices listed are benefits of investing in a limited partnership. Investors are certainly getting (or hoping for) professional management by way of a general partner. Also, since a partnership is not taxed as a corporation, the gains and losses are passed through to investors. In addition, limited partners' losses are limited to the amount invested plus any recourse loans (for real estate DPPs only).

460. B. It could jeopardize the status of the limited partner.

The role of a limited partner is supposed to be limited. If a limited partner gets involved in business activity that is supposed to be handled by a general partner, they could lose their limited liability status.

461. C. providing a bulk of the capital for the partnership

The general partner is responsible for running and making decisions for the partnership. However, the limited partners provide the bulk of the capital.

462. B. general partners

The risk assumed by a limited partner is limited to the amount invested plus any additional loans. However, because general partners can be sued as a result of the partnership, they assume unlimited risk.

463. A. an active role and unlimited liability

A general partner has an active role in managing the partnership and has unlimited liability. A limited partner has an inactive role and limited liability.

464. D. Real estate

Non-recourse debt is available to limited partners in real estate direct participation programs (DPPs) only. Non-recourse debt involves pledging partnerships assets as collateral for a loan, and the limited partners aren't held personally responsible.

465. A. I, II, and III

Limited partners can't make management decisions for the partnership; that is the job of the general partner(s). However, limited partners may inspect the books, compete with the partnership (invest in another competing partnership), and vote to terminate the partnership.

466. C. I, II, and IV

Limited partnerships require a subscription agreement to accept new limited partners, a certificate of limited partnership to be filed with the Securities and Exchange Commission (SEC) and states, and a partnership agreement (agreement of limited partnership) that outlines the rights and responsibilities of the general and limited partners.

467. B. Partnership agreement

The partnership agreement is a document that includes the rights and responsibilities of the limited and general partners.

468. D. I, II, and III

The certificate of limited partnership must be filed with the Securities and Exchange Commission (SEC) and states. Included would be things such as the partnership's name, type of business, amount of time the partnership expects to be in business, the amount of contribution made by the limited and general partners, and so on.

469. A. Certificate of limited partnership

A limited partnership (DPP) must file a certificate of limited partnership with the SEC (Securities and Exchange Commission) prior to a public offering. The subscription agreement is the paperwork a general partner must sign prior to accepting a new limited partner. The agreement of limited partnership states the rights and responsibilities of the limited and general partners.

470. D. An oil and gas limited partnership

Limited partnerships require written proof of the customer's financial background. Both the broker-dealer and the general partners must verify that the customer has a high enough net worth, enough money to invest now, and more money to invest in the future if necessary.

471. D. A subscription agreement

A general partner would sign a subscription agreement to accept a new limited partner.

472. B. It is considered an exempt offering under Regulation D

DPPs being sold as private placements are exempt under Regulation D. As with other private placements, the number of accredited investors is not limited, but the amount of unaccredited investors is limited to 35 per year. Many DPPs are sold as private placements.

473. D. All of the above

All of the choices listed are true regarding DPP public offerings.

474. A. I only

Direct participation program (DPP) losses are deemed to be passive losses under IRS rules. Passive losses can be used to offset only passive gains from another direct participation program (partnership).

475. C. The partnership is fully taxed by the IRS.

Remember, you're looking for a false answer for this question. If you look at Choices (C) and (D), you can see that they're opposing answers, so it has to be one of them. One of the advantages of being a partner in a limited partnership is that all gains, losses, expenses, and income flows through to the limited and general partners. Remember that partnership passive gains and passive income can be written off only against passive losses.

476. D. income from a real estate DPP

Losses could be used to offset income. DPP losses and income are termed passive losses and passive income. Passive losses can be used only to offset passive income.

477. D. I, II, III, and IV

All of the choices listed would be important when evaluating a direct participation program.

478. C. Section 8

Although your client may be limiting the upside potential, investing in a partnership specializing in Section 8 housing would provide stability of income. Section 8 housing is backed by U.S. government subsidies and is, therefore, considered quite safe.

479. D. depletion

Depletion is using up a natural resource such as oil in an oil and gas DPP. Depletion has no relation to real estate DPPs.

480. **C. appreciation**

The main concern of investors of undeveloped (raw) land limited partnerships is appreciation potential. Their hope is that land purchased by the partnership can be purchased cheaply and sold sometime in the future at a much higher price.

481. **B. At least 25% of the partnerships properties are not specified.**

A blind pool DPP gives the general partner wide discretion as to the types of investments that the DPP makes. A blind pool may have a stated goal of growth, income, and so on. However, at least 25% of the properties are not specified.

482. **A. Raw land**

DPPs that invest in raw land are buying property and sitting on it with the hope that it'll be worth more in the future. Because the DPP isn't spending money on improving the property and land can't be depreciated, raw land DPPs have the fewest write-offs.

483. **B. oil well drill heads**

Equipment leasing partnerships generate revenue by leasing out equipment purchased by the partnership. Oil well drill heads are used by oil and gas drilling programs and aren't leased out by equipment leasing programs.

484. **C. Capital appreciation potential**

You're looking for the false answer in this question. Equipment leasing limited partnerships make money by leasing out equipment. The equipment leased out gets worn out or outdated, so capital appreciation potential makes no sense. However, a steady stream of income, depreciation deductions, and operating expenses to offset revenues are all advantages of investing in an equipment leasing program.

485. **A. An operating lease is riskier than a full payout lease and allows for depreciation write-offs.**

Operating leases are riskier than full payout leases because the equipment being leased out isn't leased out for its full useful life. Each time it's leased out, it is older and in many cases becoming more obsolete. Whether the lease is set up as an operating lease or full payout lease, depreciation deductions are allowed.

486. **A. I, III, and IV**

IDCs are write-offs for drilling expenses. IDCs are on items that have no salvage value and include items such as wages, fuel, insurance, permits, and so on. IDCs are current write offs, while tangible drilling costs are on items that have salvage value and can be depreciated over several years. Tangible drilling costs include items such as trucks, storage tanks, drilling equipment, and so on.

487. D. Well equipment

Tangible drilling costs are costs on equipment, which can be depreciated over several years. These include items such as well equipment, trucks, storage tanks, bulldozers, and so on.

488. B. II only

Out of the choices given, the only partnership that could claim depletion deductions is oil and gas. Depletion deductions can be claimed only on a natural resource that has been used up (depleted). However, all three of the types of partnerships listed can claim depreciation deductions.

489. D. sold

Depletion has to do with reducing the amount of a mineral resource, such as oil and gas. Depletion deductions are based on the amount of oil and gas sold, not extracted from the ground and put in storage.

490. C. depletion deductions

Depletion deductions can be claimed only on natural resources that can be used up. Because real estate can't be used up, real estate partnerships can't claim depletion deductions.

491. A. Exploratory

IDCs are intangible drilling costs and are associated only with oil and gas partnerships. IDCs are highest in the first year of operation; therefore, exploratory (wildcatting) is the best answer. IDCs are usually completely deductible in the first year, and they include expenses, such as fuel costs, insurance, wages, and supplies.

492. A. Oil and gas exploratory program

You should direct John to invest in a partnership that produces immediate write-off to offset the gains from the real estate DPP. Oil and gas exploratory (wildcatting) programs have immediate write-offs as they're searching and/or drilling for oil. Oil and gas exploratory programs drill in unproven areas. Write-offs include things such as payroll, equipment, fuel, and leasing or purchasing land. Exploratory programs are the riskiest oil and gas DPPs but have the highest return if oil or gas is reached.

493. A. I, II, III

Income programs have the least risk because they purchase income-producing wells and sell what comes out of the ground. And exploratory (wildcatting) programs are the riskiest because they purchase land in unproven areas, hoping they find oil.

494. B. developmental program

Oil and gas exploratory programs drill in unproven areas. Oil and gas developmental programs drill in proven areas. Oil and gas income programs take over existing, productive areas. Oil and gas combination programs are a combination of all three.

495. A. depletion deductions

Oil and gas income programs are ones that are already generating income. So, there are no drilling costs needed to find and drill for the oil. Although there may be some depreciation costs on equipment owned by the partnership, the main tax benefit is depletion write-offs on the amount of oil sold. Depletion deductions have to do with depleting (using up) natural resources.

496. C. A combination program

Oil and gas combination programs offer diversification between exploratory, developmental, and income producing areas.

Chapter 8 Answers

497. B. I and II

The purchase of call options and the sale of covered call options may be executed in cash accounts. Because of the additional risk, short sales, the sale of naked options, and spreads must be executed in margin accounts.

498. C. 100 shares of the underlying security

Most option contracts represent 100 shares of the underlying security.

499. B. 9 months

Standard option contracts are issued with nine-month expirations. Long-term equity anticipation securities (LEAPS) have expirations of up to 39 months.

500. C. 12.25

An options premium (P) is made up of intrinsic value (I) and time value (T). This option has an intrinsic value (an in-the-money amount) of 12 because it's a 40 call option, and the stock is at 52. Call options go in the money when the price of the stock goes above the strike price. So, the premium has to be at least 12. Because the option is only 2 days away from expiration, the time value has to be really small. The only answer that works is Choice (C).

501. C. $65.00

This is a fairly easy question if you remember that options are for 100 shares, unless otherwise stated in the question. It's as simple as taking the premium increase and multiplying it by 100:

$$0.65 \times 100 = \$65.00$$

502. B. I and IV

Buying calls is a bullish strategy because the investor wants the price of the underlying security to increase. For example, if an investor purchased an ABC 30 call option, the investor would want the price of the stock to go above 30. If the price of ABC increases above 30, the investor could exercise the option to buy the stock at 30 and sell it in the market for a higher price. In addition, selling in-the-money put options is also a bullish strategy because the seller wants the price of the underlying security to increase. When selling a naked option, the most an investor can hope to make is the premium received. Therefore, the seller wouldn't want the put option to go into the money more; they'd want the underlying stock to increase in value.

503. B. Buying a DWN put option

You should have knocked out Choice (A) right away because buying a call option is a bullish strategy used when you believe the price of the security is going to increase. Choices (C) and (D) would work, but they aren't the cheapest options. Buying a straddle is ideal when you aren't sure which direction the stock is going because you're buying a put and buying a call. When shorting a stock, an investor has to come up with 50% of the market value. Buying a put is the best answer because it's a bearish strategy, and investors can have an interest in a large quantity of securities for a small outlay of money.

504. A. above the strike price

Call options are in the money when the market price of the security is above the strike price. Put options are in the money when the market price of the security is below the strike price.

505. A. I, III, and IV

Call options go in the money when the market price is greater than the strike (exercise) price. Put options go in the money whenever the market price is lower than the strike price. Therefore, the only option that isn't in the money when UPP is trading at 43.50 is short a 40 put.

506. C. ABC May 50 call

The phrase *call up and put down* will help you remember that call options go in the money when the price of the stock goes above the strike price, and put options go in the money when the price of the stock goes below the strike price. Choice (A) is in the money because the price of the stock is below the put price of 45. Choice (B) is in the money because the price of the stock is above the 35 call strike price. Choice (D) is in the money because the price of the stock is below the 55 put strike price. However, Choice (C) is out of the money because the price of the stock is below the 50 call strike price.

507. D. I, II, and III

All of the choices listed are important factors in an option's premium. If the underlying security is subject to wide price swings, the option has more of a chance of going in the money, and sellers would expect a higher premium for taking more risk. Also, when comparing two options with everything equal except the expiration month, the one with the longer time until maturity would have a higher price because it has more of a chance of going in the money. *Remember:* An option's premium is made up of intrinsic value (how much the option is in the money) and time value. If the intrinsic value goes up, the premium goes up.

508. B. 4

To determine the time value of an option, you can use the following equation:

$$P = I + T$$

where P is the premium of the option, I is the intrinsic value of the option (how much it's in the money), and T is the time value of the option. In this case, you're looking for the time value, so plug in the numbers for the premium and intrinsic value and then solve for time. The premium is 9, and the intrinsic value is 5 because call options go in the money when the stock price goes above the strike price. To determine the intrinsic value, just subtract the 50 strike price from the market price of $55, which equals 5.

$$9 = 5 + T$$
$$T = 9 - 5$$
$$T = 4$$

509. D. 3.5

The premium of an option is made of intrinsic value (how much the option is in the money) and time value (the longer the maturity, the higher the premium). In this case, the option isn't in the money because put options go in the money when the price of the stock goes below the strike price. That means that the price of the stock would have to be below $45, which it isn't. So, because there's no intrinsic value, the premium is made up entirely of time value, which is 3.5.

510. C. II and III

You have to remember that sellers (writers or shorters) of options always face more risk than the buyers. The buyers' risk is limited to the amount they invest. However, sellers of put options don't face a maximum loss potential that's unlimited because put options go in the money when the price of the stock drops below the strike price, and it can go down only to 0.

Sellers of uncovered calls face an unlimited maximum loss potential because call options go in the money when the price of the stock increases above the strike price, and the seller would have to purchase the stock at a price that could keep going higher. Additionally, investors who short stock (Statement II) face an unlimited maximum loss potential because they're bearish and lose money when the price of the security increases, and nothing tops the price from increasing. Investors who have sold covered calls don't face an unlimited maximum loss potential because they already have the stock to deliver if exercised.

511. C. Selling uncovered calls

When purchasing an option, the most you can lose is the premium. Therefore, option sellers always face more risk than option buyers. When selling uncovered call options, the maximum loss potential is unlimited because call options go in the money when the price goes above the strike price. In theory, the price of the stock can keep going up. Put options go in the money when the price of the stock goes below the strike price. Because the price can go only to zero, the maximum loss potential when selling an uncovered put isn't unlimited.

512. A. above the exercise price plus the premium paid

In order for an investor to profit from a long call position, they'd have to exercise the option when the market price is above the exercise (strike) price plus the premium paid.

513. D. $41.75

When you're determining the break-even point for an individual option, the current market value doesn't fit into the equation. You just have to look at what the investor paid for the option and the strike price. Call options go in the money when the price of the stock goes above the strike price. In this case, Mr. Couture paid 1.75 for the option, so the break-even point would be $40 + 1.75 = \$41.75$.

514. A. $700

This question is relatively easy. You can use an options chart, but it's probably not really necessary. The question doesn't mention anything about this investor having any other stock or option positions, so you're just dealing with the individual option. Because this investor sold the option, the most they can hope to make is the premium received. The premium received is $700 (7 premium × 100 shares per option).

515. C. obligation to buy stock at a fixed price if exercised

The purchasers of options always have the right, and the writers (sellers) have the obligation to live up to the terms of the contract if exercised. Here it is in a nutshell:

>> *Buy a call* is the right to buy stock.

>> *Buy a put* is the right to sell stock.

>> *Sell a call* is the obligation to sell stock.

>> *Sell a put* is the obligation to buy stock.

516. D. the option is exercised when the price of the underlying stock is below the strike price minus the premium

When selling an uncovered put option, an investor takes a bullish position. The maximum potential gain is the premium received. In other words, the investor doesn't want the option to be exercised because they'll start losing money and possibly even end up taking a loss. Therefore, Choice (D) is the correct answer.

517. B. $415

When selling an individual option, the maximum potential gain is the premium. When looking at the exhibit, the first column is the market price of RST, the second column is the strike prices, and everything to the right of that column is the premiums. To find the premium for a Dec 50 put, find where the *Dec* column (the last one) and the *50p* row (the bottom one) intersect. In this case, it's 4.15, which represents a price of $415 because options are for 100 shares.

518. A. Strike price minus the premium

When writing (selling) a naked (uncovered) call option, the maximum loss is unlimited. However, when writing a naked put option, the maximum loss is the strike (exercise) price minus the premium. Put options go in the money when the price of the stock drops below the strike price. This means that a put option can go only so far in the money because the price of the underlying stock can drop only to zero. Therefore, the maximum loss per share is the strike price less whatever Mr. Drudge received per share when they sold the option.

519.   A. 34

The easiest way to determine the break-even point for an individual option is to remember *call up* and *put down:*

>> Call up: Add the premium to the call strike price.

>> Put down: Subtract the premium to the put strike price.

In this case, you must *put down:* $40 - 6 = 34$.

520.   A. 31.5

Put options go in the money when the price of the stock goes below the strike price. Therefore, this stock has to go 3.5 points below the strike price of 35 for this investor to break even.

$$35 - 3.5 = 31.5 \text{ break-even point}$$

521.   C. 68.38

This question includes a lot of information that isn't needed to get the answer. Put options go in the money when the price of the stock goes below the strike (exercise) price. To get the answer, all you need to do is "put down" (subtract the premium from the strike price). In this case, you need to subtract 6.62 from 75.

$$75 - 6.62 = 68.38$$

522.   C. the strike price minus the premium

The best way to determine a break-even point for an investor who has only an option position is to remember *call up* and *put down.* Because this is a put option, you need to put down by subtracting the premium from the strike price. This answer would apply whether the investor was long the put or short the put.

523.   C. Long a put or short a call

Investors who are long a put or short a call deliver a stock when the option is exercised. Here's the breakdown:

>> *Long a call* is the right to buy the stock.

>> *Long a put* is the right to sell the stock.

>> *Short a call* is the obligation to sell the stock.

>> *Short a put* is the obligation to buy the stock.

524. **B. opening sale**

Since it is the first time the investor purchased or sold an option, it is an opening transaction. The investor wrote (sold) the option, so it is an opening sale.

525. **D. $300 loss**

Start by setting up an options chart. In the *Money Out* side, place the $600 (6 × 100 shares per option) and the $200 (2 × 100 shares per option) that the customer paid to purchase the two options. To *close* means to do the opposite. Because the customer originally purchased the two options, to close, they have to sell the two options. Place the closing transactions in the *Money In* side of the chart. They sold the call for $100 and the put for $400.

Money Out	Money In
$600	$100
$200	$400
$800	$500

The customer has $300 more out than in, so that is their loss.

526. **D. Closing sale**

Break this question down into two parts. First, look at whether it's an initial purchase or sale or whether the customer is getting rid of an option position. In this case, the customer is getting rid of (closing) an option position. Next, is the customer buying (purchasing) or selling themself out of the position? This customer owns the option, so they have to sell themself out of the position. This means that you'd mark the option order ticket as a *closing sale*.

527. **B. $100 loss**

Start by setting up an options chart. This investor purchased the 70 put for 4, so you need to put $400 (4 × 100 shares per option) in the *Money Out* side of the chart. Next, the investor wrote (sold) the 90 put for 12, so you need to put $1,200 (12 × 100 shares per option) in the *Money In* side of the chart. This investor closed the 70 put by selling it at 6, so you need to put $600 in the *Money In* side of the chart. Finally, they closed the 90 put by purchasing it for 15, so you need to put $1,500 in the *Money Out* side of the chart. Total up the two sides, and you see that this investor had a $100 loss.

Money Out	Money In
$400	$1200
$1500	$600
$1900	$1800

Remember, for an investor to close themself out of a position, they have to do the opposite of what they did initially. If they originally bought an option, to close, they'd have to sell the option. If they originally sold the option, to close, they'd have to buy the option.

528.   B. $75 gain

The easiest way for you to see what's going on is to set up an options chart. This investor wrote (sold) the RST put for a premium of 3.25, so you have to put $325 ($3.25 × 100 shares per option) in the *Money In* side of the chart because the investor received the money for selling the option. Next, the option was exercised, so you have to put $4,000 (the $40 strike price × 100 shares per option) in the *Money Out* side of the chart because "puts switch," meaning that the exercised option has to go on the opposite side of the chart from the premium. After that, the investor sold the 100 shares of stock in the market for $37.50 per share for a total of $3,750, which goes in the *Money In* side of the chart because the investor received money for selling the stock. Total up the two sides, and you'll see that the investor had received $4,075 and spent $4,000 for a miniscule profit of $75.

Money Out	Money In
$4000	$325
	$3750
$4000	$4075

529.   B. $495

The easiest way for you to see what's going on is to set up an options chart. Your customer purchased 100 shares of DEFG at 45.10, so you have to put $4,510 (45.10 × 100 shares) in the *Money Out* side of the chart. Next, your customer purchased an OEX put for 4.50, so you have to put $450 (4.50 × 100 shares per option) in the *Money Out* side of the chart. If your customer closes the stock position (to close means do the opposite — so, if they originally bought, to close, they have to sell) for 43.55, you have to put $4,355 (43.55 stock price × 100 shares) in the *Money In* side of the chart. Then, because you're dealing with an option that settles in cash instead of delivery of the underlying security, you need to put the profit of $1,100 in the *Money In* side of the chart. To get to the $1,100, you have to remember that put options go in the money when the price of the stock goes below the strike price, which it is by 11 (790 − 779), and options are for 100 shares. Total up the two sides, and you see that your customer had a profit of $5,455 − $4,960 = $495.

Money Out	Money In
$4510	$4355
$450	$1100
$4960	$5455

530. D. Buying a call and buying a put

You should remember that "long" means to buy. Therefore, you can cross off answers (A), (B), and (C) right away because they all have the investor selling something. To create a long straddle, you're buying a call and buying a put with the same underlying stock, the same expiration, and the same strike price.

531. C. Long straddle

Beta tells you how volatile a stock is in relation to the market. A stock with a high beta is a volatile stock. Holders of long straddles and long combinations are looking for volatility of the underlying security.

532. C. volatile

Remember, investors who are long straddles or long combinations are buying a call in case the price of the underlying stock increases in value and buying a put in case the underlying stock decreases in value. So, looking at that, these investors don't care if the underlying security increases in value or decreases in value; they just want it to move enough in either direction for them to have a profit. Therefore, they are looking for volatility.

533. A. $44.70

This investor has established a long straddle. The investor purchased the call for 6.5 and the put for 3.2 for a combined premium per share of 9.7 (6.5 + 3.2). To find the points where the investor breaks even, you have to add the 9.7 to the call strike price and subtract the 9.7 from the put strike price:

$$55 + 9.7 = 64.7$$
$$55 - 9.7 = 45.3$$

The break-even points for this investor are 64.7 and 45.3. For this investor to see a profit, the stock would have to be trading below 45.3 or above 64.7. The only answer that works is $44.70.

534. C. I and III

When you're holding a straddle, you're holding a call and holding a put on the same security. This means that you're neither bullish nor bearish, but you want the underlying security to move enough in either direction for you to make a profit. Therefore, you're looking for volatility.

535. B. long combination

Because the investor purchased both options, it has to be long because *long* means to buy. Therefore, you can knock out Choices (C) and (D) right away. Next, you have to determine whether it's a combination or a straddle. To be a straddle, the call and put purchased would have to have the same stock, same expiration month, and same strike price. Because the strike prices are different, it's a combination.

536. A. $200 gain

You can best work out this question in an options chart. Look at the following setup:

Money Out	Money In
$400	$3500
$700	
$2200	
$3300	$3500

This investor bought the CDE Nov 35 call for 4, so you enter $400 (4 × 100 shares per option) on the *Money Out* side of the options chart. The investor also bought the CDE Nov 35 put for 7, so enter $700 (7 × 100 shares per option), again on the *Money Out* side.

Next, the investor bought the stock in the market at the market price of $22 per share for a total of $2,200 ($22 per share × 100 shares) to cover the put option. The investor spent $2,200 for the stock; therefore, that amount also goes on the *Money Out* side of the options chart. After that, you exercise the put. You have to exercise the put at its strike price of 35. Calculating 35 × 100 shares per option gives you a price of $3,500, which you enter on the *Money In* side of the chart because "puts switch" (go on the opposite side of the options chart from its premium). Add up each side, and you see that this investor had a gain of $200 ($3,500 in and $3,300 out).

537. D. Unlimited

This question is a lot easier than the answer choices suggest. When purchasing a straddle, you're buying a call and buying a put. The maximum potential gain is unlimited on the call side. Purchasing a put along with a call doesn't change that fact.

538. A. $400 gain

Start by setting up an options chart. Look at the following setup:

Money Out	Money In
$900	$5,800
$500	
$4,000	
$5,400	$5,800

This investor bought the ABC May 40 call for 9, so you enter $900 (9 × 100 shares per option) on the *Money Out* side of the options chart. The investor also bought the ABC May 40 for 5, so enter $500 (5 × 100 shares per option), again on the *Money Out* side. Next, the investor exercised the call, so you have to put $4,000 (40 strike price × 100 shares per option) on the same side as its premium because "calls same" (the exercised option goes on the same side of the options chart as its premium). Next, the investor received $5,800 ($58 × 100 shares) for selling the stock in the market, so you have to put $5,800 on the *Money In* side of the chart. Total up, and you see that the investor had a $400 gain ($5,800 − $5,400).

539. C. neutral on DEF

When an investor sells an at-the-money straddle, the investor has already maximized their profit. If the price of the underlying stock moves in either direction, one of the options will go in the money, and the seller will start losing money. Therefore, this investor wants the stock to stay at the same price and is neutral on DEF.

540. D. II and IV

Sellers of straddles and combinations maximize their profits when the underlying security doesn't go in the money. They make their profit on the premium received and start to lose it if the underlying security goes in the money.

541. B. Write a DUD straddle.

To generate income, your client has to sell something. The only answer choice that has your client selling something is Choice (B). Writing (selling) a straddle would allow your client to generate income on a stock that's remaining stable because they'd receive the premiums for selling the straddle. Your client would be able to profit if neither the call option nor put option that are part of the straddle go too much in the money.

542. D. short one TUV Sep 40 put

First, to create a *short* anything, you can't have a *long* in it. Therefore, you can eliminate Choices (A) and (B) right away. A short combination is selling (shorting) a call and selling a put on the same stock, with the same strike price, and the same expiration month. The only answer choice that fits that description is Choice (D).

543. C. remain stable

Selling a straddle is selling a call and selling a put on the same stock, same strike price, and same expiration month. When selling a straddle, the most you can hope to make is the premiums that you received. In this case, the investor would hope that the stock price of XYZ stays right at the strike price of 35 so that neither option will be exercised. If that happens, they get to keep the premiums they received for selling the options. Remember, the buyer and the seller want opposite things to happen — the seller wants stability, and the buyer wants volatility.

544.　B. Short combination

Sellers always face more risk than buyers. When shorting (selling) a combination, a straddle, or uncovered call option, the seller faces an unlimited maximum loss potential. There's no unlimited maximum gain or loss potential, whether long or short a spread.

545.　C. 25 and 50

This investor sold the two options for a combined premium of $10 per share (7 + 3). Therefore, this investor would break even when either the call option goes 10 in the money or the put goes 10 in the money. Call options go in the money when the price of the stock goes above the strike price, and put options go in the money when the price of the stock goes below the strike price.

40 call + 10 = 50

35 put − 10 = 25

546.　A. I or II

With straddles, you must add the premiums and use "call up" (add the combined premiums to the strike price) and "put down" (subtract the combined premiums from the strike price) to figure out the break-even points. An investor who is long a straddle has a loss, unless the price of the underlying security goes below the put break-even point or above the call break-even point.

547.　B. 51 and 64

This strategy is a long combination (buy a call and buy a put on the same securities but with different expiration dates and/or strike prices). For straddles and combinations, there are two different break-even points: one on the way up and one on the way down. The first thing you have to do is add the two premiums and then call up (add the combined premiums to the call strike price) and then put down (subtract the combined premiums from the put strike price). Because this investor paid 9 (7 + 2) per share for the premiums, the break-even points are 64 (55 + 9) and 51 (60 − 9).

548.　A. I and III

To create a spread, you have to have one long and one short option. Therefore, you can eliminate Statement II, which leaves you with Choice (A). Statement IV is also out because you need either two calls or two puts.

549. D. II and IV

This question is a bit more difficult because you aren't given the premiums. However, because the options are on the same stock and have the same expiration month, the one that goes in the money first would have to have a higher premium. Call options go in the money when the price of the underlying stock goes up, so the 50 call has to have a higher premium than the 60 call. That means that it has to be a credit spread because the investor received more money for the option sold than they paid for the option purchased. The easiest way to tell whether it's a bullish position or a bearish position is to look at the strike prices. If the investor is buying the low one and selling the higher one (like they did in this case), they are bullish. If they're buying the higher one and selling the lower one, they are bearish. Whether you're dealing with a put spread or call spread doesn't make a difference here.

550. D. $325

You can cross out the GHI Sep 40 put and the GHI Sep 50 put right away because you can't create a call spread with puts. To create a debit call spread, the investor has to pay more for the option purchased than they received for the one they sold. Investors always buy at the offer (ask) price and sell at the bid price. Having this knowledge, the only thing that makes sense is the investor's buying the GHI Sep 40 call for 5.25 and selling the GHI Sep 50 call for 2. Place these values in the options chart to get your answer:

Money Out	Money In
$525	$200

The investor bought the GHI Sep 40 call for $525 (5.25 premium × 100 shares per option), so that goes on the *Money Out* side of the options chart. Next, enter the $200 (2 premium × 100 shares per option) on the *Money In* side of the options chart, because the investor received $200 for selling that option. The investor paid $325 more for the option purchased than he received for the option sold.

551. B. bearish call spread

This customer bought one option and sold the other on the same stock, so it's a spread position. Because the customer bought the option with the higher strike price and sold the one with the lower strike price, they created a bearish spread.

552. C. bullish/neutral on LMN

Your client received more money for the option sold than they paid for the one pur-chased, so they have a short (credit) spread. At this point, neither option is in the money, and they have the maximum profit that they can make. If the options start going in the money, they'll start losing money, which wouldn't be good. Because put options go in the money when the price of the stock goes down, they're okay with the stock sitting at the price it is now (neutral position) and with the stock price going up (bullish).

553. B. Bearish

A debit put spread is purchasing a put with a higher strike price and selling a put with a lower strike price. Debit means that the investor paid more for the option purchased than they received for the option sold. The investor would need their put option to go in the money to have any chance of making money. Because put options go in the money when the market price of the security goes down, holders of debit put spreads are bearish.

554. D. Buying a put at a low strike price and selling a put at a high strike price

To create a spread, you're buying an option and selling an option on the same security. To create a short (credit) spread, you have to have received more money for the option sold than the money you paid for the option purchased. This question is particularly tough because you weren't given the premiums. However, using a little bit of logic, you can get the answer. When comparing two options where everything is the same except the strike (exercise) price, the one that's in the money first will have a higher pre-mium. So, Choice (D) is correct. Put options go in the money when the price of the stock goes down. Therefore, the one with the higher strike price will be in the money first and, therefore, have a higher premium. Because you're buying the one with the lower premium and selling the one with the higher premium, you have created a credit spread.

555. C. Long 1 JKL Sep 40 call/short 1 JKL Sep 30 call

To create a credit spread, you have to sell the option that has the higher premium and purchase the option with the lower premium. Choice (C) is a credit spread because you're short the 30 call and long the 40 call. Call options go in the money when the price of the stock increases and it has to hit 30 before 40. This means that the 30 call option sold has to have a higher premium.

556. C. $1,300

Using an options chart to answer the question, you first need to put the premiums in the chart. The investor bought the 40 call for 9, so you need to put $900 (9 premium × 100 shares per option) on the *Money Out* side of the chart. Next, they wrote (sold) the 60 call for 2, so you have to place $200 ($2 premium × 100 shares per option) in the

Money In side of the chart. Stop and take a look at the chart to see whether you have more money in than out. At this point, you have $700 more out than in, so that is the investor's maximum potential loss.

To get the maximum potential gain, you need to exercise both options. First, exercise the 40 put option and place the $4,000 (40 strike price × 100 shares per option) on the same side as its premium because "calls same" (the exercised option goes on the same side of the chart from its premium). Then, place the $6,000 (60 strike price × 100 shares per option) in the chart on the same side as its premium for the same reason.

Money Out	Money In
$900	$200
$4000	$6000
$4900	$6200

Total up the two sides, and you see that you have $1,300 more money in than money out, so that is the investor's maximum potential gain.

---

557. **B. $900**

Using an options chart to answer the question, you first need to put the premiums in the chart. Mr. Levin wrote (sold) the 60 put for 6, so you need to put $600 (6 premium × 100 shares per option) on the *Money In* side of the chart. Next, they bought the 75 put for 12, so you have to place $1,200 ($12 premium × 100 shares per option) in the *Money Out* side of the chart. Stop and take a look at the chart to see whether you have more money in than out. At this point, you see that you have $600 more out than in, so that is Mr. Levin's maximum potential loss.

To get the maximum potential gain, you need to exercise both options. First, exercise the 60 put option and place the $6,000 (60 strike price × 100 shares per option) on the opposite side of its premium because "puts switch" (the exercised option goes on the opposite side of the chart from its premium). Then, place the $7,500 (75 strike price × 100 shares per option) in the chart across from its premium for the same reason.

Money Out	Money In
$1,200	$600
$6,000	$7,500
$7,200	$8,100

Total up the two sides, and you see that you have $900 more money in than money out, so that is Mr. Levin's maximum potential gain.

558. D. $425

You can cross out the ZAM Dec 45 put and the ZAM Dec 50 put right away because you can't create a call spread with puts. To create a debit call spread, the investor has to pay more for the option purchased than they receive for the one they sold. Investors always buy at the offer (ask) price and sell at the bid price. Having this knowledge, the only thing that makes sense is the investor's buying the ZAM Dec 45 call for 5.25 and selling the ZAM Dec 50 call for 1. Place these values in the options chart to get your answer:

Money Out	Money In
$525	$100

Because the investor purchased the Dec 45 call for 5.25, place $525 (5.25 × 100 shares per option) in the *Money Out* side of the chart. Then the investor sold the Dec 50 call for 1, so you need to place $100 (1 × 100 shares per option) in the *Money In* side of the chart. Total up, and you see that the investor had an out-of-pocket expense of $425 ($525 − $100).

559. C. $46

To determine the break-even point for spreads, you have to subtract the premiums and then call up (add the adjusted premium to the lower call price) or put down (subtract the adjusted premium from the higher strike price). Your client purchased the one option at 8 ($800) and sold the other one at 2 ($200) for a net cost of $6 per share (8 − 2). That means that the option that your client owns has to go in the money by $6 for them to break even. The one they purchased was the $40 call, so you just need to call up from the $40 strike price by adding $6 to it: $40 + $6 = $46.

560. B. $62

To determine the break-even point for spreads, you have to subtract the premiums and then call up (add the adjusted premium to the lower call price) or put down (subtract the adjusted premium from the higher strike price). Stan sold the one option at 5 ($500) and purchased the other one at 2 ($200) for a net profit of $3 per share (5 − 2). To determine the break-even point, you need to subtract the $3 from the higher strike price of $65: $65 − $3 = $62.

561. C. 56

When determining the break-even point for spreads, you have to start by subtracting the premiums. In this case, they shorted (sold) the one option for 6 and longed (purchased) the other one for 2 for a net gain of 4 (6 − 2). Next, because it's a put spread, you have to subtract that 4 from the higher strike price (60) to get the break-even point: 60 − 4 = 56.

562. C. diagonal spread

To create a spread, an investor has to buy a call and sell a call or buy a put and sell a put on the same security. In this case, Mrs. Jones has indeed created a spread. To determine whether it's a vertical, horizontal, or diagonal spread, you need to look at the strike prices and expiration months. If just the strike prices are different, it's a vertical spread. If just the expiration months are different, it's a horizontal spread. If both the strike prices and the expiration months are different, as in this case, it's a diagonal spread.

563. D. Long one HIJ Dec 80 call/short one HIJ Nov 70 call

To create a spread, you need to buy a call and sell a call or buy a put and sell a put with the same stock. To create a bearish spread, you have to buy the option with the higher strike price and sell the option with the lower strike price.

Remember: Buy low, sell high is bullish, and buy high, sell low is bearish.

You may have inadvertently picked Choice (C), but if you look closely, you'll notice that you're dealing with two different stocks, so it's not a spread.

564. A. vertical spread

Because Mrs. Smith has spent more money for the option they purchased than they received for the option sold, they have a long (debit) spread. To tell whether it's vertical, horizontal, or diagonal, you have to look at the strike prices and expiration months of the options. If just the strike prices are different, it's a vertical (price) spread. If just the expiration months are different, it's a horizontal (calendar) spread. If both are different, it's a diagonal spread. In this case, just the strike prices are different, so it's a vertical spread.

565. B. I and IV

A vertical spread means that the strike prices of the two options used to create the spread are different. When creating a long (debit) call spread, an investor is buying the call option that's going to be in the money first and selling the one that's going to be in the money second. Therefore, creating a vertical long call spread is bullish. When shorting a put spread, the investor is selling the option that's going to be in the money first if the price of the stock goes down and buying the one that's going to be in the money second. This means that the investor already has a profit and doesn't want the price of the stock to go down. Investors of vertical short put spreads are bullish or neutral.

566. A. different expiration months

A horizontal spread is also known as a calendar spread because the two options that make up the spread have different expiration months.

567. D. II and IV

Because both the expiration months and the strike prices are different, it's a diagonal spread. This investor paid more for the option purchased (13) than they received for the option sold (9), so it's also a debit spread.

568. A. I or III

To answer this question, you need to determine whether you're dealing with a credit or debit spread. Start out by placing the premiums in an options chart, like the following:

Money Out	Money In
$200	$700

This investor bought the STU Sep 30 put for a premium of $200 (2 × 100 shares per option). Because the investor bought for $200, place this amount in the *Money Out* portion of the options chart. Next, the investor sold the STU Sep 40 put for a premium of $700 (7 × 100 shares per option). Put that premium in the *Money In* portion of the options chart, because the investor received money for selling that option. This investor has a credit spread, because they have more money in than money out. When an investor has a credit spread, they want the premium difference to narrow (premiums narrow as the options get closer to expiration or move further away from being in the money), and they want the options to expire so they can keep the profit.

569. A. The difference between the exercised strike prices minus the difference between the premiums

The easiest way to see this is to set up an options chart, using made-up numbers. To create a debit call spread, you have to purchase a call option with a higher premium and sell an option with a lower premium. Call options go in the money when the price of the stock goes above the strike price, so to create a debit spread, you have to purchase the one with the lower strike price because it will be in the money first. Here's an example:

Buy 1 ABC Oct 40 call for 8

Sell 1 ABC Oct 50 call for 2

Now set up an options chart.

Money Out	Money In
$800	$200

The option was purchased for $800 (8 premium × 100 shares per option), so you have to place $800 in the *Money Out* side of the chart. Next, the 50 call option was sold for $200 (2 premium × 100 shares per option), so you have to place $200 in the *Money Out* side of the chart. At this point, you have established a maximum loss of $600 ($800 – $200). So, to get the maximum potential gain, you have to exercise both options.

Money Out	Money In
$800	$200
$4000	$5000
$4800	$5200

Exercise the 40 call option by placing $4,000 (40 strike price × 100 shares per option) under its premium because "calls same" (the exercised strike price goes on the same side of the chart as its premium). Then, put $5,000 under its premium of $200 for the same reason. Total up, and you come up with a maximum potential gain of $400 ($5,200 – $4,800).

The only answer choice that works is Choice (A). Here's the proof: The difference between the exercised strike prices is $1,000 ($5,000 – $4,000). The difference between the premiums is $600 ($800 – $200). And $1,000 – $600 = $400.

570. C. II and III

If an investor creates a spread, it means that they're long a call and short a call or long a put and short a put. When creating a debit spread, when just looking at the premiums, the investor already has a loss. So, they'd want the options to be exercised. Also, if the premium difference widens, they could sell themself out of the position for more money than they paid for creating the debit spread to begin with.

571. A. debit bull spread

Because the 40 call that the individual purchased will go in the money first, it would be more expensive. Therefore, this individual has a debit spread (more money out than in). In addition, this investor would need their option to go in the money; otherwise, they will have a loss. Their option will go in the money when the price of DEF goes above the strike price, so they're bullish.

572. B. The premium decreases the cost basis.

Selling covered calls reduces the cost basis. The best way to see this is to use sample numbers. Say that an investor purchased stock for $50 per share and then sold a covered call for $3. They originally spent $50 per share and then got $3 back, so their cost basis was reduced from $50 to $47 ($50 – $3).

573. D. Long 1 XYZ Aug 70 put

To be covered for the sale of an XYZ Aug 60 put, the investor would either have to be short 100 shares of XYZ stock or own an XYZ put with the same or longer expiration and the same or higher strike price. In this case, Choice (D) works because put options go in the money when the price of the stock goes down, and a 70 put would go in the money before a 60 put.

574. D. 100 shares of DLQ stock

When looking at whether an investor is covered or uncovered (naked), you're looking to see whether the investor has the security to deliver if exercised. An investor who sells a DEF call option would be considered covered if the investor owns 100 shares DEF stock or owns anything convertible into 100 shares of DEF stock. An escrow receipt for DEF stock is proof of ownership. An investor may also sell a covered call option if owning a call option with the same strike price or lower on the same stock with the same expiration or later because the investor may buy the stock at the same price or less for just as long as the other investor. Obviously, owning the stock of another company, such as DLQ, wouldn't cover the seller of a DEF call option.

575. B. The investor is bullish on MKR, and their upside is limited.

To tell what direction an investor wants the price of their stock to go, look at whether they're long or short the stock. This investor purchased the stock, so they're bullish. However, since they sold the call against it (covered call), they have limited their upside potential but lowered their cost basis from 50 to 47 (50 stock price minus the premium of 3 they received).

576. B. $4,425

The first thing you should do is put the stock and the option in an options chart. Because Mr. Goldshack purchased the stock for $4,750 ($47.50 × 100 shares), you need to put that in the *Money Out* side of the chart. And they sold the option for $325 ($3.25 × 100 shares per option), so you need to put that in the *Money In* side of the chart.

Money Out	Money In
$4750	$325

At this point, you stop to take a look to see whether you have your answer. Because the question is asking for the maximum potential loss, you don't need to go any further because you already have more money out than in. Subtract the two numbers to get the answer: $4,750 − $325 = $4,425.

577.   A. $25 gain

The easiest way for you to see what's going on in this question is to set up an options chart. Zeb bought the put for $275 (2.75 × 100 shares per option) and the stock for $5,100 (51 × 100 shares), so you need to put $275 and $5,100 in the *Money Out* side of the chart. Next, Zeb sold the stock for $5,350 (53.50 × 100 shares) and closed the option — that is, they sold (remember to close, you have to do the opposite) — for $50 (0.50 × 100 shares per option), so you put $5,350 and $50 in the *Money In* side of the chart. Total up the two sides, and you see that they had a $25 gain.

Money Out	Money In
$275	$50
$5100	$5350
$5375	$5400

578.   B. $1,100

When you get a question like this, look for the action words, such as *buys, purchases, writes, exercises,* and *sells.* Every time you see an action word, you need to enter something into the options chart. Your client *purchased* 100 shares of DEF at 54, so you have to put $5,400 into the chart on the *Money Out* side. Next, your client *wrote* a call for 5, so you have to place the $500 (5 × 100 shares per option) on the *Money In* side of the chart. After that, the call was *exercised,* so you have to put $6,000 (the call strike price) below its premium because "calls same," meaning the exercised call has to go on the same side as its premium. Total up the two sides, and you see that your client had a gain of $1,100 ($6,500 in − $5,400 out).

Money Out	Money In
$5400	$500
	$6000
$5400	$6500

A mistake people often make in questions like this is that they want to put the stock price (73 in this case) in the chart. You have to remember that by your client selling the call at a 60 strike price, they sold the right to someone else to purchase the stock at 60. The stock price could have gone to $150 per share, and it wouldn't have changed the outcome of this equation.

579.   A. $2,925

To determine your client's maximum potential loss, set up the equation in an options chart, like the following:

Money Out	Money In
$3250	$325

Your client purchased 100 shares for $32.50 per share, totaling $3,250. Because they paid $3,250, enter $3,250 in the *Money Out* portion of the options chart. Next, enter the $325 ($3.25 premium × 100 shares per option) that your client received for selling the WIZ Jun 35 call in the *Money In* side of the options chart. Stop at this point to see whether the chart lets you answer the question. Because you're looking for the maximum potential loss and you have more money out than money in, you have your answer. The totals are on opposite sides of the chart, so subtract the two numbers to get the maximum potential loss: .$3,250 − $325 = $2,925.

580.   B. $1,600

To make this question easier, use an options chart. Because the investor purchased 100 shares of TUV at $40, you need to put $4,000 on the *Money Out* side of the chart because that's how much the investor spent. Next, the investor wrote (sold) a 50 call for $600 (6 premium × 100 shares per option), so you need to put that in the *Money In* side of the chart because the investor received $600 for selling the option. Before going any further, stop to see if that answered your question. At this point, you have $3,400 more money out than in so that is the maximum potential loss, not maximum potential gain. This tells you that you need to exercise the option to get the answer you need. Take $5,000 (50 strike price × 100 shares per option) and put it in the *Money In* side of the options chart because calls same, meaning that the exercised strike price goes on the same side of the chart as its premium. Total up the sides to get your answer.

Money Out	Money In
$4000	$600
	$5000
$4000	$5600

After totaling the two sides, you see that you have $1,600 more money in than money out, so that is the investor's maximum potential gain.

581. D. $825 gain

The easiest way for you to see what's going on is to set up an options chart. Todd purchased 100 shares of HLP at 25, so you have to put $2,500 (25 × 100 shares) in the *Money Out* side of the chart. Next, Todd wrote (sold) an HLP call for 3.25, so you have to put $325 (3.25 × 100 shares per option) in the *Money In* side of the chart. After the stock increased, the call was exercised, so you have to put the exercised strike price of $3,000 (30 strike price × 100 shares per option) under its premium of $325 because "calls same," meaning that for call options, the premium and the exercised strike price go on the same side of the chart. Total up the two sides, and you see that Todd had a gain of $825 ($3,325 in − $2,500 out).

Money Out	Money In
$2500	$325
	$3000
$2500	$3325

582. A. write a TUF call

The key to this question is that Mr. Hendricks is trying to generate some additional income. This means that he has to sell something because buying something costs him money. Because Mr. Hendricks has the stock to deliver if the option is exercised, his best option is to write a covered call on TUF.

583. D. $47.50

When shorting a stock, an investor makes money when the price of that stock decreases and loses money when the price increases. In this case, the investor received $44.50 per share for shorting the stock and another $3 per share for selling the covered put. That means that the investor's break-even point is $44.50 + $3 = $47.50.

584. B. the stock price minus the premium

For this question, use some logic. A *covered call* means that the investor has the stock to deliver if exercised. Say that the investor purchased the stock at $50 per share and then sold the call for $4 per share. Now, the investor's cost basis or break-even point is $46 ($50 − $4). In essence, the price of the stock could go down to $46 per share before the investor starts losing money. You get that answer by taking the stock price minus the premium.

585. C. 55

Mr. Steele purchased the stock for $60 per share and then received $5 per share for selling the option, so his break-even point is $55 ($60 − $5). Mr. Steele is bullish on the stock because he owns it, and he sold the covered call against it to generate additional income.

586. D. $37.00

The easiest way to calculate the break-even point for stock/option problems is to take a look at what's happening. This investor purchased the stock for $32.50 per share and then purchased the options for $4.50 per share. This investor paid $37 ($32.50 + $4.50) per share out of pocket and would need the stock to be at $37 per share to break even.

587. A. $44.25

This investor sold short DWN at $47.50 per share. When an investor sells short, they stand to make a profit when the security decreases in price. Because this investor purchased the protective call for 3.25, the stock that he shorted would have to decrease by that amount for them to break even: $47.50 – $3.25 = $44.25.

588. B. fall sharply

Buying a protective put on a stock owned protects the investor if the market falls quickly. Even though the investor will be losing money on the stock owned, the put will be gaining in value to offset some of the loss.

589. A. buy an LMN call option

To *hedge* means to protect. If Mr. Gold wants to hedge his position, he should buy a call on LMN above the market price. Remember that Mr. Gold is short the stock and must buy LMN back at some point to close his short position. Buying an LMN call gives him the right to buy back LMN at a fixed price, which would allow him to protect the position and not face an unlimited maximum loss potential.

590. B. Long 1 DEF Oct 57 put at 3

A collar is when an individual who owns stock buys a protective put and sells a covered call on that stock. In order for it to be considered a *cashless* collar, the premium of the option sold has to equal the premium of the option purchased as it is in answer Choice (B).

591. C. (strike price – the premium) × 100 shares × 10 options

When selling an uncovered (naked) put option, the most the seller could lose is the strike price minus the premium multiplied by 100 shares and then by 10 options. Put options go in the money when the price of the stock goes down below the strike (exercise) price. Because the stock can go down only to zero, the seller can lose money from the strike price down to zero less the premium received. However, because options are for 100 shares, you have to multiply that answer by 100 shares and then by the 10 options the customer sold.

592.   C. $1,050 loss

The easiest way for you to see what's going on in this question is to set up an options chart. Sandy purchased two calls and two puts, so the first thing that you should do is put the multiplier of × 2 on the outside of the chart, as if you're dealing with single options. Because Sandy bought the calls for 450 each (4.5 × 100 shares per option) and the puts for 200 each (2 × 100 shares per option), you need to put 450 and 200 in the *Money Out* side of the chart. Next, Sandy closed their options for their intrinsic value (the in-the-money amount). Because call options go in the money when the price of the stock goes above the strike price, only the call option is in the money, not the put option. With the stock price at $36.25 and the strike price at 35, the call is 1.25 in the money ($36.25 − $35.00), so you need to put $125 (1.25 × 100 shares per option) in the *Money In* side of the chart because Sandy is closing the option (to *close* means to do the opposite — so if you originally bought, to close, you have to sell). Total up the two sides, and you see that Sandy had a loss of $525 per option. Because Sandy bought two options, they had a total loss of $1,050.

(x2)	Money Out	Money In
	$450	$125
	$200	
	$650	$125

593.   D. $120 gain

Set up an options chart so you're less likely to make a mistake. First, because Mike shorted (sold) and subsequently closed three options, move the multiplier × 3 to the side of the chart, as if you're dealing with one option. Mike sold the options, so you have to put $300 in the *Money In* side of the chart. Next, they closed (in this case, purchased) the options for $260 per option, so you have to place that number in the *Money Out* side of the chart. At this point, you see that Mike had a $40 gain ($300 − $260).

(x3)	Money Out	Money In
	$260	$3

Now, you can go back to the multiplier to figure out the final answer. Because Mike sold three options, you have to multiply the $40 gain by 3: $40 × 3 = $120.

594. C. $800

Set up an options chart to get this answer quickly. Because the investor purchased two options and shorted (sold) two options, move the multiplier (× 2) to the outside of the chart, as if it's one option on each side. The investor purchased the 40 call for 6, so put $600 (6 × 100 shares per option) in the *Money Out* side of the chart. They sold the 50 call at 2 so put $200 (2 × 100 shares per option) in the *Money In* side of the chart.

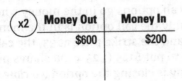

x2	Money Out	Money In
	$600	$200

At this point, you can see that the investor has a maximum loss of $400 ($600 − $200) per option. Now you have to multiply that by 2 to get the answer: $400 × 2 = $800.

595. D. Unlimited

This investor has an unlimited maximum potential gain on the stock they own. The fact that the investor purchased puts to protect themself in the event that the stock drops in value doesn't affect the maximum gain potential.

596. D. 40

When determining the break-even point, it doesn't matter that the client purchased more than one option and more than 100 shares. The client purchased the ABC stock for $36 per share and purchased the options for $4 per share. This means that the client has $40 ($36 + $4) out of their pocket, so the stock would have to go to $40 for them to break even.

597. B. $3,000

Most options can't be purchased on margin. However, LEAPS (Long–Term Equity Anticipation Securities), which have more than nine months until maturity, can be purchased on margin by coming up with 75% of the premium. The premium for each option is $400 (4 × 100 shares per option), and this investor purchased 10 of them for $4,000, so the margin call is 75% × $4,000 = $3,000.

598. D. Long-term capital loss

Options are always taxed as capital gains or capital losses. This investor purchased an option that expired worthless, and therefore their lost money. The investor held the LEAPS for over one year, so they would be taxed as a long-term capital loss.

599. **B. they are available only on index options**

LEAPS (Long-Term Equity Anticipation Securities) are long-term options. They may be exercised at any time; they have a longer life than other options; and they have higher premiums because holders have a longer time to use the options. However, LEAPS are available on both individual stocks and indexes.

600. **B. The number of shares per contract will increase, and the stock price will decrease.**

As with stock splits, when a company provides a stock dividend, option contracts are adjusted. Stock dividends are treated like uneven splits; the number of shares per contract is increased, and the strike price is decreased.

601. **B. one HIJ contract for 120 shares with a strike price of 25**

An option contract doesn't change for cash dividends, but it does change for stock dividends. Because options are normally for 100 shares, it would have to be increased for a stock dividend. In this case, there'd be 120 shares after the dividend (20% more shares). If the number of shares per option contract is increased, the strike price would have to be reduced to make up for it. The only answer that works is Choice (B).

602. **A. The number of contracts will increase, and the strike price will decrease.**

When a corporation splits its stock evenly (2 for 1, 3 for 1, 4 for 1, and so on), the number of contacts will increase, and the strike price will decrease.

603. **C. Four HIJ Oct 16 calls, 250 shares each**

This one is a little bit tougher than a regular something-for-1 split. This is an uneven split, so the rules are a little different. First, show what the options looked like prior to the split:

four HIJ Oct 40 calls (100 shares per option)

Because this is an uneven split, you change the number of shares per option instead of the amount of options. So, because it's a 5-for-2 split, you have 5 shares for every 2 you had before.

$$\frac{5 \times 100 \text{ shares}}{2} = 250 \text{ shares}$$

Next, you have to take the strike price of 40 and multiply it by 2/5 (the reciprocal of 5/2).

$$\frac{40 \text{ call} \times 2}{5} = 16 \text{ new strike price}$$

Now, the option will read as follows:

four HIJ Oct 16 calls (250 shares per option)

604. C. 12 LMN Oct 20 calls, 100 shares each

First, list the options prior to the split:

four LMN Oct 60 calls (100 shares per option)

Because this is an even split, you change only the number of options and the strike price. You don't need to change the number of shares per option. And because it's a 3-for-1 split, you have 3 options for every 1 you had before, which means that the investor is now going to have 12 options (3×4). Next, because you multiplied the number of options by 3, you have to divide the strike price by 3.

$$\frac{60}{3} = 20 \text{ strike price}$$

After the 3-for-1 split, the investor will have

12 LMN Oct 20 calls (100 shares per options)

605. B. I and IV

SPX options are based on the S&P 500, and VIX options are based on the S&P 500 volatility index. Because your client is bullish on the market, they'd buy SPX calls. However, the VIX is the fear index and usually moves the opposite way of the S&P 500. When investors are bullish on the market, they're more confident, and market volatility is reduced. Therefore, because the VIX would probably decrease, the client would buy VIX puts.

606. A. bearish on the market

SPX options are options on the S&P 500 index rather than an individual security. Index options are always settled in cash. As with other securities, an investor who buys a put option is bearish. In this case, the investor is bearish on the market.

607. A. The premium paid

Whenever an investor purchases an individual option, the maximum potential loss is the premium paid.

608. B. cash equal to the intrinsic value of the option times 100 shares at the end of the exercise day

OEX is an index option on the S&P 100. The rule for index options is that exercises are settled in cash instead of delivering, in this case, 1 share of each of the securities that are part of the index. The holder of the index option being exercised is expected to deliver cash equal to the intrinsic value (the in-the-money amount) of the option multiplied by 100 shares per option based on the closing price of the index at the end of the exercise day.

609. C. Cash equal to the intrinsic value of the option at the end of the day of exercise

OEX index options are based on the movement of the S&P 100 index. Index options may be exercised only in cash. The money received by the owner must be equal to the intrinsic value of the option at the end of the day of exercise.

610. B. Treasury securities

Yield-based options are based on the yields of U.S. Treasury securities, such as T-bonds, T-notes, and T-bills. An investor who purchases a yield-based call is expecting yields to increase. As with index options, yield-based options are also settled in cash.

611. C. II and III

If your client believes that interest rates are going to increase, they're bullish on yields (rates), so they'd buy yield calls. Now, you have to remember that yields and outstanding bond prices have an inverse relationship. If an investor is bullish on yields, they're bearish on outstanding bond prices. Therefore, this investor may also be interested in purchasing T-bond puts.

612. B. 1 business day prior to expiration

Unlike American-style options, which can be exercised at any time, European-style options can be exercised only 1 business day prior to expiration. Almost all options are American-style but world-currency options may be either American-style or European-style.

613. B. I and IV

The easiest way to think about this is that good news is bullish and bad news is bearish. And when bullish, you buy calls and sell puts; when bearish, you buy puts and sell calls.

Because England had good news, an investor would buy calls or sell puts on the British pound. Japan had bad news, so an investor would buy puts or sell calls on the Japanese yen.

614. A. NASDAQ OMX PHLX

The NASDAQ OMX PHLX (Philadelphia Exchange) is the exchange where world currency (foreign currency) options trade. The NASDAQ OMX PHLX offers options settled in U.S. dollars on the euro, Canadian dollar, Australian dollar, British pound, Mexican peso, New Zealand dollar, Norwegian krone, South African rand, Swedish krona, Japanese yen, and the Swiss franc.

615. A. $300

Prices of Japanese yen options are quoted in units of 0.0001 and have a contract size of 1,000,000 yen. Because $1{,}000{,}000 \times 0.0001 = \$100$, the premium and strike price may be multiplied by 100 to calculate the full cost of the strike price or premium. The cost of the option is the premium, so $3 \times 100 = \$300$.

616. B. II, I, IV, III

When a customer is interested in purchasing or selling options, you must first send them an ODD (options risk disclosure document). The ODD isn't an advertisement but lets the customer know the risks of investing in options. Next, a ROP (registered options principal) must approve the account. Then, the trade can be executed. Finally, within 15 days of the approval of the account, the customer must sign and return the OAA (options account agreement). The OAA basically states that the customer understands the risks and rules regarding option transactions.

617. A. premium

The Option Clearing Corporation (OCC) sets the strike price, contract size, and expiration date for each listed option. The premium of an option is based on the market price of the security, the expiration date, and market sentiment.

618. A. a registered options principal

A registered options principal (ROP) is responsible for approving all options accounts. In addition, he must approve all options transactions and approve all options advertising. To become a ROP, you must pass a Series 4 exam.

619. D. ODD

Because options have a risk that is greater than almost any other investment, all investors must receive an options risk disclosure document (options disclosure document or ODD) and a copy of amendments (if any) prior to their first options transaction (at the time of or before the account is approved). This ODD explains to investors option terminology, strategies, potential rewards, and risks involved in investing in options, such as the chance of losing all money invested or, if selling call options, facing an unlimited maximum loss potential. In addition to the risks, the ODD must also explain tax rules related to options, transaction costs, margin requirements, a special statement for uncovered option writers, and so on.

620. D. ODD

Selling uncovered options is the riskiest option strategy. Particularly, selling uncovered call options is the riskiest because the maximum potential loss is unlimited. The statement for uncovered option writers is found in the ODD (options disclosure document or options risk disclosure document). This statement goes into the additional risks associated with selling uncovered options.

621.   A. III, I, IV, II

Prior to opening an options account for a client, the client must first receive an options risk disclosure document (ODD), which outlines the risks of investing in options. Next, the registered options principal (ROP) would have to approve the account. After that, you can finally execute the trade for the client. The last thing that has to happen is that the client must send in a signed options account agreement (OAA) within 15 days after approval of the account.

622.   C. within 15 days after approval of the account

Investors must receive an options risk disclosure document (ODD) at or prior to the approval of the account. However, investors must sign and return an options account agreement within 15 days after approval of the account.

623.   C. 4:00 p.m. EST on the business day of expiration

The last time an investor can trade an option is 4:00 p.m. EST (3:00 p.m. CST) on the business day of expiration of the option.

624.   D. 4:30 p.m. CST on the third Friday of the expiration month

Stock options expire on the Saturday following the third Friday of the expiration month. The last time a customer can exercise an option is 4:30 p.m. CST (5:30 p.m. EST) on the business day prior to expiration.

625.   D. 11:59 p.m. EST on the business day of expiration

Standard equity options expire 11:59 p.m. EST on the third Friday of the expiration month.

626.   A. in 1 business day

Listed option trades settle in 1 business day after the trade date.

627.   B. Random selection

The OCC (Options Clearing Corporation) chooses which firm to receive the exercise notice randomly only. When the firm receives the exercise notice, it chooses which customer's options to exercise randomly, first-in, first-out, or any other method fair and reasonable.

628.   C. based on size

When exercising an option, the firm can choose a customer by any method except based on size (the number of contracts that each investor sold).

629. C. call options

Options aren't marginable except for LEAPS, which have more than nine months until maturity. LEAPS can be purchased on margin by coming up with 75% of the premium. All other options must be paid for in full.

630. A. $6,000

The original purchase of the three HIJ Sep 40 calls for 3 had to be paid for in full. When the investor exercises the calls, the stock is purchased at the strike price of $40. The investor is purchasing 300 shares (3 options at 100 shares each) for a total of $12,000 ($300 × $40). Assuming that the Regulation T margin requirement is 50%, the investor would have to deposit $6,000 ($12,000 × 50%).

631. D. No deposit is required.

Your client owns the calls that he's exercising. Your client is exercising at a profit of $10 per share (less the premium) and is selling the stock immediately, so no deposit is required. It wouldn't make much sense to have your client pay $30 per share when exercising the options and then have your firm send him a check for $40 per share. The key here is that your client exercised the option and sold the stock on the same day.

632. A. a capital gain

All option transactions will result in a capital gain, a capital loss, or a break-even position.

633. B. owning stock with a cost basis of 51

Because the investor purchased the stock and bought the protective put on the same day, it's a *married put*. As a result of the two transactions being married together, the investor won't experience a capital loss by the option expiring worthless. However, his cost basis was adjusted for purchasing the put. They spent $48 per share for the stock and $3 per share for the put for a cost basis of $51.

634. B. A short-term capital loss

Options are always taxed as capital gains or capital losses. Because this investor paid for an option that expired out of the money, they had a loss. In order to be a long-term loss, they needed to have purchased a LEAP option with over one year until expiration. So, this was a short-term capital loss.

635.

B. No, because it is impossible to profit from these option positions.

These trades aren't suitable for any investor because it's impossible for the investor to make a profit. You can see this by setting up an options chart. First, put the premiums for the options in the chart. Because the investor bought the Oct 35 call option at 7, you have to put $700 (7 premium × 100 shares per option) in the *Money Out* side of the chart. Next, put $200 (2 premium × 100 shares per option) in the *Money In* side of the chart because the investor sold that option. Because the investor has $700 out and $200 in, it tells you that the investor's maximum loss potential is $500 ($700 − $200). To get the maximum gain, you have to exercise both options. Because "calls same," you have to put the exercised strike prices below their respective premiums in the chart. Place $3,500 (35 strike price × 100 shares per option) under its premium of $700, and place $4,000 (40 strike price × 100 shares per option) under its premium of $200. After that, you have to total the sides to see that because the *Money In* side and the *Money Out* side of the chart each equal $4,200, the investor can't make a profit.

Money Out	Money In
$700	$200
$3500	$4000
$4200	$4200

636.

B. $1,200 long-term capital gain

When an investor buys a stock and a protective put option on that same stock on the same day, it is considered a married put. Since they were purchased on the same day, you have to add the purchase price of the stock and the purchase price of the put to determine the cost basis. In this case, the cost basis is $43 ($40 stock price plus the $3 premium for the put). Melissa sold the stock for $55 per share, so the profit is $12 per share ($55 minus $43). Since 100 shares were purchased, it is a gain of $1,200. Married puts do not affect the holding period of the stock. So, since Melissa sold the stock after holding it for over one year, it is a long-term gain.

637.

C. Short 11,000 GHI calls

Options have certain position limits, meaning there can't be more than a certain number of options on the same security on the same side of the market (bullish or bearish). (Currently, the option position limits are 25,000, 50,000, 75,000, 200,000, and 250,000.) In this case, the investor can't have more than 25,000 bullish option positions or 25,000 bearish option positions.

Remember: *Bullish* means buying calls and selling puts, and *bearish* means selling calls and buying puts.

This investor is already long 15,000 GHI calls, so they can't purchase more than 10,000 more calls on GHI or sell more than 10,000 puts on GHI without violating position limits. Therefore, the only answer choice that works is Choice (C) because shorting calls is bearish.

638. B. the same as the position limits

The exercise limits is a number placed on the amount of option contracts that a person can exercise on the same side of the market (bullish or bearish) within 5 consecutive business days. The exercise limit is exactly the same as the position limit, which is currently 25,000, 50,000, 75,000, 200,000, and 250,000.

639. A. The option strike price will be lowered to reflect the dividend.

Since the underlying stock price will be lowered to reflect the dividend, the OCC will adjust option contracts accordingly, unless otherwise instructed by the customer.

640. D. I, II, III, and IV

All option confirmations must include the option type, the underlying security, the strike price, the number of contracts, the premium, and commission.

Chapter 9 Answers

641. D. The client's investment objectives

The most important consideration is the client's investment objectives. You'd hope that the client's age, marital status, and financial needs should help your client determine their investment objectives. Investment objectives include current income, capital growth, tax-advantaged investments, preservation of capital, diversification, liquidity, and speculation.

642. A. Treasury bills

Although your client has a main investment objective of aggressive growth, they may have to put that on hold for a short while because they're purchasing a home. Actually, Choices (B), (C), and (D) are ideal for an aggressive growth strategy; they're too risky for someone purchasing a home in the near term. In this case, you should let your client know that purchasing Treasury bills is a safe investment, which ensures that they have the funds available when needed to purchase the new home.

643. B. I, III, and IV

If one of your customers has a primary investment objective of *preservation of capital*, you wouldn't recommend speculative investments, such as an exploratory direct participation program. However, AAA-rated corporate bonds, blue chip stocks (such as IBM, Ford, and GE), and U.S. government bonds are all proper recommendations.

644. C. The stock of new corporations

Investors looking for capital growth are more speculative investors. These investors are looking to invest money now, hoping that the investment will grow at a rapid rate. To meet that objective, the investor should invest in stock of new corporations.

645. A. I and II

Liquidity has to do with ease of trading. The more liquid a security is, the easier it is to trade. To get the answer for this question, you have to find the two answers that aren't liquid. Municipal bonds usually aren't very liquid because they're usually thinly traded. Direct participation programs are some of the most difficult investments to get in and out of, so they're not liquid.

646. D. Corporate bonds

Your client is looking for total return, which is growth and income. At the current time, 100% of his portfolio is invested in stocks, which provide only growth potential. They also need to invest in fixed-income securities, like corporate bonds, which provide income to meet their investment objective.

647. C. I and IV

An investor who has an investment objective of speculation (aggressive growth) would purchase securities that have a potential for growth, such as sector funds or technology stocks. The risk of investing in sector funds and technology stocks is high, but if the investments become profitable, the reward can be quite high. Speculative investors are looking to purchase securities at a low price and sell them at a much higher price.

648. B. Municipal bonds

Because your client is in the highest tax bracket, they should have some tax-advantaged investments, like municipal bonds or municipal bond funds, in their portfolio. Because the interest received from municipal bonds is federally tax-free, high income tax bracket investors save more tax money by investing in them.

649. D. I, II, III, and IV

You'd do well to advise all your clients to have a well-diversified portfolio. Smaller investors can build a well-diversified portfolio by purchasing mutual funds. Diversification happens in many ways, such as buying different types of securities, buying securities from different industries, buying debt securities with different maturity dates, buying securities with different ratings, and buying securities from different areas of the country or world. Most investors diversify in several ways to limit their risk.

650. A. Purchasing several different mutual funds

Because this investor has no other investments and has only $10,000 to invest, it's impossible to build a diversified portfolio without mutual funds. Mutual funds are designed for investors who don't have enough money and/or expertise to build a diversified portfolio. Each mutual fund in itself is diversified because the fund invests in several different securities.

651. A. The registered representative must determine the client's suitability.

The registered representative should get the customer's investment objectives and suitability prior to making a recommendation. A principal's approval isn't required for a registered representative to make an investment recommendation to a client.

652. B. I and III

Clients' investment decisions should be based on their own risk tolerance and investment needs. However, registered representatives should take a client's needs and risk tolerance into consideration before making a recommendation.

653. D. all of the above

When opening an account for a client, you should help determine the risk tolerance and investment goals. Part of that includes looking at the client's financial and nonfinancial considerations. Some of the nonfinancial considerations are the customer's age, marital status, number of dependents, employment status, and employment of other family members.

654. D. I, II, III, and IV

All of the choices listed would likely change the investor's investment objectives. Typically, as investors grow older, they want to take less risk. By the same token, investing for one person or two people, as in someone getting married or divorced, would change the investment objectives. Also, as people gain investment experience, they're likely open to more speculative investments. And you can assume that as investors acquire more family responsibilities, they'll want to take less risk.

655. B. Sell some of their stocks and purchase more bonds and cash equivalents.

Since this investor set up their account strategically (strategic asset allocation) to have 70% in stocks, 20% in bonds, and 10% in cash equivalents, they should rebalance their portfolio to bring things back in line to match their initial percentages. Investors employing strategic asset allocation should rebalance their portfolio every so often to make sure it's in line with their original strategy.

656.

D. rebalance their portfolio to sell off some fixed-income securities and purchase more equity securities

Tactical asset allocation refers to rebalancing a portfolio due to market conditions. For example, if the stock market is expected to do well in the short-term, you put a higher percentage into stocks. If the stock market is expected to do poorly over the short-term, you lower the percentage of stocks and purchase more fixed-income securities (bonds).

657.

D. it is underperforming similar pharmaceutical stocks

Alpha is how a security performs as compared to a certain benchmark. Let's say that a particular mutual fund somewhat mirrors the S&P 500. Now, let's say that the S&P 500 increased 10% over a period of time but that fund only increased 7% over that same period of time. Your mutual fund would have a negative alpha, which would be bad. If the fund increased more than the S&P 500 over that same period of time, the fund would have a positive alpha, which is good. Alpha can also be used for individual company stocks, such as pharmaceutical stocks. In this case, you could compare how a particular pharmaceutical stock is doing compared to all similar pharmaceutical stocks.

658.

C. the stock is more volatile than the market

Beta is a measure of how volatile a stock is compared to the market. A stock with a beta of 1 is equally volatile to the market, meaning that if the market increased 5% over a given period of time, you'd expect the price of your stock to increase 5%. If the market declines by 5%, you'd expect the price of your stock to decline by 5%. If you're purchasing a stock with a beta greater than 1, it's more volatile than the market. In this case, you're dealing with a stock with a beta of 1.6, meaning that if the market increased or decreased by 10% over a given period of time, you'd expect the price of your stock to increase 16% or decrease 16%. A stock with a beta less than 1 is less volatile than the market.

659.

C. XYZ stock with a beta coefficient of 1.20

Securities with a beta coefficient of 1.0 are as volatile as the market (if the market goes up 5% over a given period of time, you'd expect the price of the stock to go up 5%). Someone like Joanie, who's pursuing an aggressive stock-buying strategy, would be looking for stocks with a beta coefficient greater than 1.0 because they're more volatile than the market. Therefore, the security that would best meet their needs is the XYZ stock, with a beta coefficient of 1.20. You'd expect this stock to move more than the market — if the market goes up 10% over a given period of time, you'd expect the price of the stock to go up 12%. This all sounds great, but if the market goes down 5% over a given period of time, you'd expect the price of the stock to fall 6%. Stocks with a beta coefficient of less than 1.0 are more defensive securities that don't move as much as the market. Blue chip stocks are securities issued by well-established, stable companies and wouldn't be part of an aggressive stock portfolio.

660. B. III and IV

Defensive stocks are ones that perform consistently no matter how the economy's doing. Companies that sell goods such as alcohol, food, tobacco, and pharmaceutical supplies, issue defensive stocks. Automotive and appliance company stocks aren't defensive because when the economy is doing poorly, investors wait a little longer to purchase these items.

661. D. All of the above

An investor who adopts an aggressive investment strategy is attempting to maximize gains by investing in securities with higher risk and purchasing securities on margin. An aggressive portfolio strategy includes all of the choices listed.

662. A. I and II

Both currency risk and purchasing power risk are systematic risks while reinvestment risk is a non-systematic risk.

663. A. The risk that a security will decline due to negative market conditions

Systematic risk is the same as market risk. All securities are subject to systematic risk, which is the risk that securities will decline due to negative market conditions. The risk that a security won't keep pace with the inflation rate, Choice (C), is called purchasing power risk or inflation risk.

664. C. I, II, and III

Your client would face political risk, market risk, and currency risk but not interest rate risk because they aren't buying fixed income securities. *Political (legislative) risk* is the risk that laws may change that may adversely affect the securities purchased. *Market risk* is the risk that the securities might decline due to negative market conditions. *Currency risk* is the risk that the security declines in value due to an unfavorable exchange rate between the U.S. dollar and foreign currencies.

665. A. Treasury bills

Interest risk is the risk of rising interest rates causing bond prices to decrease. Long-term bonds decrease in price more than short-term bonds. Therefore, short-term bonds, such as T-bills, have low price volatility and low interest risk.

666. B. inflationary risk

All long-term bonds have inflationary (purchasing power) risk. Inflationary risk is the risk that the return on the investment doesn't keep pace with inflation. To limit inflationary risk, investors should purchase stocks. Over the long haul, stocks have more than kept pace with inflation.

667.   B. I and IV

Purchasing power risk is also known as inflation risk. So, investors who are concerned about purchasing power risk are concerned that their investment won't keep up with the rate of inflation. Out of the choices given, common stock and variable annuities have a much better chance of keeping up with and hopefully beating the rate of inflation than long-term corporate bonds and fixed annuities.

668.   D. regulatory risk

Regulatory risk is the risk that the price of a security declines due to new regulations placed on specific corporations.

669.   C. II and III

Portfolio diversification doesn't reduce systematic (market) risk because a bearish market can affect all securities. However, portfolio diversification does reduce non-systematic (business) risk because some companies may perform better than expected, even though others may not be performing as well.

670.   B. I and II

Investment grade bonds and AAA-rated industrial development bonds are both considered safe investments. However, income bonds are issued by corporations in bankruptcy, and high-yield bonds are also known as junk bonds. This investor should definitely stay away from purchasing income bonds and high-yield bonds.

671.   D. Treasury STRIPS

Reinvestment risk is the additional risk taken with interest and dividends received each year. All securities making interest or dividend payments have reinvestment risk. Treasury STRIPS have no reinvestment risk because they're issued at a discount and mature at par value without making interest payments along the way.

672.   A. Treasury bills

Reinvestment risk is the additional investment risk taken with interest or dividends received. Treasury notes, revenue bonds, and GO (general obligation) bonds all have reinvestment risk because they pay interest. However, Treasury bills (T-bills) don't have reinvestment risk because they're issued at a discount and mature at par value. Therefore, there are no interest payments made along the way to reinvest.

673. C. DPPs

DPPs (direct participation programs; limited partnerships) wouldn't be a proper recommendation because of the difficulty of buying and selling them. Not only do you have to prequalify a DPP investor, but also the investor has to be accepted by a general partner. All of the other choices would be considered quite liquid and would meet Mr. Steele's needs.

674. D. Timing

The main function of a fundamental analyst is to help investors determine what to buy or sell based on examining items such as income statements, balance sheets, industries, management, and so on. It is the job of a technical analyst who study the market to determine when to buy or sell.

675. C. the earnings

Technical analysts look at the market and price movements. Corporate earnings are something that a fundamental analyst would examine.

676. A. Earnings trends

Fundamental analysts compare companies to help determine what to buy. Technical analysts examine the market to try to determine when to buy. Knowing that, fundamental analysts are definitely interested in earnings trends. Technical analysts are interested in such things as support and resistance and the breadth of the market.

677. D. machinery

Current assets are items that are easily converted into cash within the next 12 months; included in current assets are cash, securities, accounts receivable, inventory, and any prepaid expenses (like rent or advertising). Machinery is a fixed asset.

678. C. inventory

Quick assets are assets that someone can convert into cash within a 3- to 5-month period. Cash, accounts receivable, and marketable securities that the company owns are all quick assets. Inventory is a current asset but not a quick asset, because you can assume that a company will take up to a year to sell its entire inventory.

679. A. inventory

Inventory is a current asset, which is convertible into cash within a one-year period. All of the other choices are considered fixed assets.

680. D. II and IV

Intangible assets are listed on a corporation's balance sheet and don't have any physical properties, such as trademarks, patents, formulas, and goodwill (based on the reputation of the corporation). Inventory is part of a corporation's current assets, and equipment is part of a corporation's fixed assets.

681. B. I, II, III, and IV

Debt obligations that are due to be paid within the next 12 months; included in current liabilities are accounts payable (what a company owes in bills), wages, debt securities due to mature, notes payable (the balance due on money borrowed), declared cash dividends, and taxes.

682. D. I, II, III, and IV

The stockholder's equity (net worth) is the difference between the assets and liabilities. This includes the par value of the common stock, the par value of the preferred stock, the additional paid-in capital, Treasury stock, and retained earnings.

683. A. subtract the liabilities from the assets

The net worth of a company is pretty self-explanatory. It is determined the same way you would determine your net worth: by subtracting everything you owe from everything you own.

684. C. current assets − current liabilities

You can calculate working capital by working with the numbers on a corporation's balance sheet. Working capital is the amount of money that a corporation has to work with, and the basic formula is

Working capital = current assets − current liabilites

Current assets are items convertible into cash in a one-year period (such as cash, securities owned, and accounts receivable). Current liabilities are expenses due in a one-year period (such as accounts payable, debt securities due to mature, cash dividends, and taxes).

685.   C. 3:1

To determine the current ratio, you have to divide the current assets (all assets convertible into cash within a one-year period) by the current liabilities (everything that must be paid within a one-year period). When looking at the exhibit, the current assets are cash, securities, accounts receivable, and inventory. Machinery and land are fixed assets. The current liabilities are accounts payable and bonds due this year. Bonds due in ten years are a long-term liability. The equation sets up like this:

$$\text{Current ratio} = \frac{\text{Current assets}}{\text{Current liabilities}}$$
$$= \frac{\$60,000,000}{\$20,000,000}$$
$$= 3:1$$

686.   A. Inventory

Current assets (assets convertible into cash within a one-year period) include inventory, marketable securities held by the corporation, cash, and so on. However, when dealing with quick assets, you have to take inventory out of the equation. Quick assets are convertible into cash within a three- to five-month period. In most cases, inventory takes longer to sell than three to five months.

687.   B. I and IV

When converting bonds into stock, investors do not have to spend any money for the conversion. Therefore, the assets of the company remain the same. Since the bonds are converted, the company's liabilities are reduced. Since the company has the same amount of assets and less debt, the net worth of the company increases.

688.   A. It decreases.

The formula for working capital is as follows:

working capital = current assets – current liabilities

Working capital is the amount of money that a corporation has to work with. Current assets are assets a company has that are easily convertible into cash within a one-year period. Current liabilities are what a company owes within a one-year period. So, if a company declares a cash dividend, it becomes a current liability. If the current liabilities increase and the current assets remain the same, the working capital decreases.

working capital $\downarrow$ = current assets – current liabilities $\uparrow$

689. **B. Liabilities increase.**

When a corporation declares a cash dividend, its liabilities increase. Liabilities are something that is owed. When a corporation declares a dividend, it must pay it. The assets will remain the same until it pays the dividend, and then the assets will decrease. The working capital and stockholder's equity decrease when a corporation declares a cash dividend.

690. **D. It remains the same.**

When the company initially declares the cash dividend, the current liabilities increase, but when the company pays that dividend, the current liabilities fall. However, the current assets also decrease because the company has to use cash to pay the dividend. If the current assets (and overall assets) decrease and the current liabilities (and overall liabilities) decrease by the same amount, the working capital remain the same.

691. **A. It increases.**

When a company issues stock, it receives cash, which is a current asset (and part of the overall assets). The company doesn't owe anything to investors, so the overall liabilities (and current liabilities) remain the same. Therefore, the net worth and working capital both increase.

692. **C. Stockholder's equity**

When a company issues bonds, the total assets increase because the cash that the company brought in by selling the bonds is an asset. Also, the total liabilities increase by the same amount as the total assets because the company has to pay investors back at maturity of the bonds. Additionally, the working capital (the amount of money a company has to work with right now) increases because the cash that the company brought in is a current asset, but the bonds are a long-term liability, so the company has many years in which to use the cash. However, the stockholder's equity (net worth) of the company did not change, because the stockholder's equity is total assets minus total liabilities. If the total assets increase by the same amount as the total liabilities, the stockholder's equity remains the same.

693. **C. net worth**

When a company issues bonds, net worth doesn't change. The assets and the liabilities increase by the same amount when a company borrows money. Therefore, the net worth would have to remain the same.

Because the bonds are a long-term liability, the working capital (the amount of money the corporation has to work with) increases.

694. D. Debt-to-equity ratio

The debt-to-equity ratio and the bond ratio help fundamental analysts determine a corporation's risk of bankruptcy.

695. C. the debt-to-equity ratio

The debt-to-equity ratio doesn't measure the liquidity of the issuer; it just measures the percentage of debt securities issued as compared to the amount of equity securities issued.

696. C. net income + depreciation + depletion + amortization

Cash flow helps measure the financial health of a company. Cash flow is determined by taking the net income (after-tax income) and adding back in the depreciation, depletion deductions (if any), plus amortization. You need to add depreciation and depletion back in because they're write-offs for a company but aren't out-of-pocket expenses. So, the equation looks like this:

$$\text{Cash flow} = \text{net income} + \text{depreciation} + \text{depletion} + \text{amortization}$$

697. A. Book value per share

To determine the book value per share, you need to use numbers from a balance sheet, not an income statement. Book value per share is based on the net worth of the company. The book value per share formula is

$$\text{Book value per share} = \frac{\text{Net worth} - \text{intangible assets} - \text{par value of preferred stock}}{\text{Number of common shares outstanding}}$$

698. B. EPS

When determining the EPS (earnings per share) of a company, a fundamental analyst looks at the income statement, not the balance sheet.

699. C. $7.33

To determine a stock's earnings per share (EPS), you can divide the stock's price by the PE (price earnings) ratio.

$$\begin{aligned} \text{EPS} &= \frac{\text{Stock price}}{\text{PE ratio}} \\ &= \frac{\$44}{\$6} \\ &= \$7.33 \end{aligned}$$

700. B. 5

The *P* in PE ratio stands for market price, the *E* stands for earnings per share, and the word *ratio* lets you know that you need to divide. So set up the equation like so:

$$\text{PE Ratio} = \frac{\text{Market Price}}{\text{EPS}}$$

The market price is $40, and the earnings per share is $8, so that means that the PE ratio is 5:

$$\text{PE Ratio} = \frac{\$40}{\$8}$$
$$= 5$$

701. A. the market price divided by the earnings per share

The PE ratio is a tool that technical analysts use to help determine whether a stock is overpriced or underpriced. Typically, they'll compare the PE ratios of several different companies within the same industry to see whether there's a good investment opportunity. Actually, the lower the PE ratio, the better. A company with a low PE ratio means that the earnings per share (EPS) are high compared to its price. The equation for PE ratio is

$$\text{PE ratio} = \frac{\text{Market price}}{\text{EPS}}$$

702. C. 50%

To determine the dividend payout ratio (DPR), use the following formula and then just plug in the numbers from the question:

$$\text{DPR} = \frac{\text{Annual dividends per common share}}{\text{Earnings per share (EPS)}}$$
$$= \frac{\$0.30}{\$0.60}$$
$$= 50\%$$

703. C. $14.00

Use the following formula to determine the earnings per share (EPS) for MKR Corporation:

$$\text{EPS} = \frac{\text{net income} - \text{preferred dividends}}{\text{no. of common shares outstanding}} = \frac{\$140,000,000 - 0}{10,000,000} = \$14.00$$

Since the question doesn't mention anything about preferred dividends, you can't assume that the company issued preferred stock. Therefore, the preferred dividends are zero. So, for this company the earnings per share, is $14.00.

704. **A. by examining the footnotes on the corporation's balance sheet**

Footnotes on balance sheets, income statements, cash flow statements, and so on provide investors with a greater understanding of an issuer's accounting methods.

705. **A. The method of depreciation used by the corporation**

Financial statements such as income statements and balance sheets also contain footnotes. Footnotes are added so that investors and analysts will more clearly understand how a corporation came up with its numbers. Included are the methods of depreciation, the inventory valuation used, fully diluted earnings per share (EPS), the market price of the securities, and so on.

706. **D. trend lines**

Fundamental analysts decide what to buy, and technical analysts decide when to buy. A fundamental analyst compares the earnings per share (EPS) of different companies as well as balance sheets and income statements. However, trend lines are something that a technical analyst examines.

707. **C. The trading volume on the NASDAQ OMX PHLX**

Technical analysts follow the market to determine when to buy or sell securities. One of the things that they look at is trading volumes.

708. **B. Odd-lot theory**

Smaller investors are more likely to engage in odd-lot trading (trading for less than 100 shares). Investors who subscribe to the odd-lot theory believe that by the time smaller investors get their information and execute trades, it's too late. Therefore, believers in the odd-lot theory buy when smaller investors are selling and sell when smaller investors are buying.

709. **A. bullish indicator**

Short sellers are bearish, meaning that they want the price of a security to decrease. However, looking at it from a technical analyst's point of view, if short interest increases, it's a bullish sign. Remember, short sellers must eventually cover their short positions by buying stock. When the market starts to increase, short sellers will be buying stock at a rapid rate, thus accelerating a bullish market.

710. **C. an increase in the DJIA and the DJTA**

According to the Dow theory, trends must be confirmed by the DJIA (Dow Jones Industrial Average) and the DJTA (Dow Jones Transportation Average). For it to be a real trend, both need to be going the same direction. This makes sense because it isn't enough that industries are selling and producing goods unless they're also being shipped.

711. D. Trend lines

Technical analysts look at the market and decide when to buy. Technical analysts look at things like trend lines, trading volume, and short interest. Fundamental analysts look at things like the price earnings ratio, income statements, and balance sheets.

712. A. consolidating

When a stock stays within a narrow trading range (trading channel), it's consolidating. A breakout occurs when a stock breaks out of its normal trading range.

713. C. The trendline is moving sideways.

A trendline is the line on a price chart for a security that indicates the price's direction: up, down, or sideways. A trendline that's consolidating is moving sideways (staying within a certain trading range or trading channel).

714. A. support

The lower portion of a securities trading range is called the support. The upper portion of a securities trading range is called the resistance. A breakout occurs when a security breaks out of its normal trading range.

715. B. bearish

The support line is the upper portion of a stock's trading range. When a stock hits the support line, it will often decrease in price. Therefore, it is a bearish sign.

716. B. I and IV

Both saucer and inverted head and shoulders formations are signs that a security has hit a low and is starting to reverse.

717. D. reversing from a bearish trend

A saucer formation is similar to an inverted head and shoulders pattern in that it's a reversal of a bearish trend. However, a saucer formation is a more gradual change in direction. A saucer formation is a bullish sign, and an inverted saucer formation is a bearish sign.

718.   A. reversal of a bullish trend

A head and shoulders top formation pattern indicates that the stock has possibly hit a high and is reversing. A head and shoulders top formation pattern is a bearish sign because it's the reversal of a bullish trend. Check out the following figure to see what a head and shoulders top formation looks like.

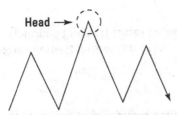

Head →

Head and shoulders top formation

The highest peak is the head, and the two shorter peaks are the shoulders.

719.   B. Inverted saucer and head and shoulders top formation

Both inverted saucer and head and shoulders top formations are signs that a security has hit a high and is starting to reverse.

720.   C. sell or sell short securities

If the market is overbought (the market is increasing but fewer stocks are advancing than declining), it's typically a good time to sell securities or sell securities short.

Chapter 10 Answers

721.   A. a syndicate selling new issues of municipal GO bonds to the public

Remember, new issues are always sold in the primary market regardless of whether they're municipal GO bonds or any other security. By contrast, sales of outstanding securities or previously outstanding securities (treasury stock) always take place in the secondary market. The secondary market is broken down into the following:

>> **First market:** Listed securities trading on an exchange

>> **Second market:** Unlisted securities trading over-the-counter

>> **Third market:** Listed securities trading over-the-counter

>> **Fourth market:** Institutional trading without using the services of a broker-dealer

722.

C. I, II, and III

The secondary market is the trading of outstanding securities whether OTC (over-the-counter) or securities listed on an exchange. The underwriting of new issues is executed in the primary market.

723.

B. listed securities trading on an exchange

The first market is the trading of listed securities on the exchange floor, such as the New York Stock Exchange (NYSE).

724.

D. unlisted securities trading OTC

The second market, not to be confused with the secondary market, is unlisted securities trading OTC (over-the-counter). The secondary market is broken down into the first market, the second market, the third market, and the fourth market. The first market is listed securities trading on an exchange; the third market is listed securities trading OTC; and the fourth market is institutional trading without using the services of a broker–dealer.

725.

C. Listed securities trading OTC

A third market trade is listed securities trading OTC (over-the-counter).

726.

D. fourth market trade

A trade between institutions without using the services of a broker–dealer is considered a fourth market trade. Fourth market trades usually take place using ECNs (electronic communications networks).

727.

B. II, III, and IV

The OTCBB (over-the-counter bulletin board) is a negotiated market where buyers and sellers negotiate on price. Unlisted securities typically trade on the OTCBB or the OTC Pink Market. NYSE Euronext, Nasdaq PHLX, and NYSE Arca are all examples of auction markets, where buyers and sellers bid or offer securities. Auction markets have a centralized trading floor, and all trades are executed at the same location.

728.

B. I, II, and III

Nasdaq PHLX, ECN (electronic communications network), and NYSE Euronext are all exchange markets. However, the OTCBB (over-the-counter bulletin board) is an over-the-counter negotiated market.

729. **D. I, II, and III**

Options orders can be executed on the CBOE (Chicago Board Options Exchange), the NYSE, and the Nasdaq PHLX.

730. **B. a negotiated market**

The over-the-counter (OTC) market is a negotiated market where buyers and sellers negotiate the trading price of a security. Exchanges are considered auction markets where prices and trading volumes are shouted out on the exchange floor.

731. **A. over the counter**

U.S. government securities and municipal bonds trade over the counter (OTC).

732. **A. Level I**

As a registered rep, you likely have a computer with Level I access on your desk. NASDAQ Level I includes the inside market (highest bid and lowest ask) prices. These are subject quotes because they're subject to change. Levels I and II include all firm quotes. Level II displays all market maker quotes, while Level III is where market makers enter their firm quotes. The NASDAQ market doesn't include Level IV.

733. **B. Level II**

Leve II is the second level of Nasdaq, which provides up-to-the-minute firm bid and ask (offer) prices of each market maker (dealers or principals) and quote sizes for the security.

734. **C. Level III**

Level III is the most complete level of NASDAQ; this level not only shows the bid and ask prices of all market makers and their firm quotes, but also allows a market maker to enter and change quotes. Once a market maker enters a quote, they will appear on the system right away.

735. **D. I, II, III, and IV**

Non-NASDAQ securities are OTC equity securities that don't meet the listing requirements of national securities exchanges such as NYSE or NASDAQ. Non-NASDAQ securities include warrants, ADRs, equity stocks (foreign and domestic), and DPPs. Non-NASDAQ securities can be purchased on the OTCBB or OTC Pink Market (OTC Best, OTC Venture, and OTC Pink). As you can imagine, non-NASDAQ securities are among the riskiest securities available and certainly aren't suitable for all investors.

736. **B. Pink sheets**

The OTC Pink (Pink Sheets) is the riskiest of all the markets and should only be considered for sophisticated investors with a high risk tolerance. There are no financial standards or disclosure requirements for companies to be listed on the OTC Pink. Companies whose securities trade on the OTC Pink include certain foreign companies with limited disclosure information, companies issuing U.S. penny stocks, distressed companies, delinquent companies, and companies not willing to provide information to investors.

737. **A. Brokers charge a commission, and dealers charge a markup or markdown.**

Brokers charge a commission for trades and dealers charge a markup or markdown on securities sold from or purchased for their inventory.

738. **C. principal**

When broker-dealers make a market in a particular security, they're acting as a principal or market maker. This means that they're willing to buy securities for their own inventory or sell securities from their own inventory. Broker-dealers not acting from their own account are acting as a broker or agent.

739. **D. II and IV**

When a securities firm buys securities for or sells securities from its own inventory, it's acting as a dealer (principal or market maker). When a dealer sells securities from their own inventory, they charge a price that includes a markup.

740. **A. includes a markup**

Dealers (principals) sell securities out of their own inventory and buy securities for their own inventory. Dealers charge a markup when selling securities from their own inventory and a markdown when purchasing securities for their own inventory. Brokers act as middlemen and charge a commission.

741. **A. Positioning the clients of the firm**

A firm's trading department works on positioning (buying and selling securities). Traders handle the brokerage firm's inventory and execute all customer's orders.

742. **B. The trade will take place at the best available ask price.**

A market order to buy will take place at the best available ask price. GTC (good till cancelled) is used for stop and limit orders, not market orders.

743. B. bearish

Short sellers borrow securities for immediate sale in the market. Their hope is that the price of the security drops, and they can repurchase it in the market at a lower price and return it to the lender. Therefore, short sellers are definitely bearish because they want the price of the security to decrease. If they were neutral, they would want the price of the security to stay the same. If this were the case, they wouldn't make money, and they'd still have to pay a commission, which is a losing proposition.

744. A. I, III, and IV

Short sellers face unlimited risk; the trades must be executed in margin accounts; and listed securities may be sold short. However, because OTCBB (over-the-counter bulletin board) stocks aren't marginable, they can't be sold short.

745. A. $5,000 short-term gain

When you're looking at whether something is long term or short term, you have to look at the holding period. When selling securities held for more than one year (at least a year and a day) the gain or loss is long term. When selling securities held for one year or less, the gain or loss is short term. However, relating to this question, the investor had a short position and never held the stock. When buying back securities to cover a short sale, the gain or loss is always short term. Because the investor sold the stock initially for $35,000 ($35 × 1,000 shares) and then purchased it for $30,000 ($30 × 1,000 shares), the investor had a $5,000 short-term gain.

746. D. municipal bonds

Although municipal bonds may be sold short, they typically aren't. The reason is that the security must be borrowed and later found to cover the short position. Because municipal bonds are usually thin issues, they're not very liquid and, therefore, not good candidates for selling short.

747. B. the short sale of securities

Regulation SHO covers the rules for short sales. Under SHO rules, all order tickets must be marked as short sale as compared to long sale, which is when an investor is selling securities that are owned. In addition, all brokerage firms must establish rules to locate, borrow, and deliver securities that are to be sold short. All brokerage firms must make sure that the security can be located and delivered by the delivery date prior to executing a short sale.

748. D. Stop

Stop (stop loss) orders become market orders for immediate execution as soon as the underlying security passes the stop price. Stop orders are used for protection.

749. D. All of the above

Stop orders are used to help protect investors from losing too much money when holding either long or short positions. For argument's sake, say that you purchased stock for $30 per share, so you could enter a sell stop order at $28. If the market price touched or passed through the $28 per share, your stock would be sold at the next price. By the same token, if you purchased the stock at $30 per share and the stock subsequently rose to $37 per share, you could enter a sell stop order below that price to protect your profit. Buy stop orders are used to limit the loss on a short position or protect the profit on a short position. Unlike sell stop orders, which are entered below the market price, buy stop orders are entered above the market price. Investors who sell securities short lose money when the price of security increases.

750. A. buy stop order on FFF

Remember that stop orders are used for protection, so you can cross off Choices (B) and (D) right away. Because your client has a short position on FFF, they'd have to buy themself out of the short position. Therefore, the answer is Choice (A), buy stop order on FFF. Your client would enter a buy stop order above the current market price.

751. A. below the current market price

Investors who own a security use sell stop orders for protection. Because these investors are concerned about the price dropping, they enter sell stop orders below the current market price of the security. If the market price of the security hits or passes the sell stop order price, the sell stop order becomes a market order for immediate execution.

752. C. Sell stop at $46

Stop orders (not limit orders) are used for protection. Therefore, none of the answer choices that include the word *limit* would fit. A sell stop order would be entered below the market price of the security, so the correct answer is Choice (C).

753. B. Buy limits and sell limits

By placing a limit order, an investor guarantees that the order will be executed at a specific price or better if it ever hits that price. Stop orders are triggered when hitting the stop order price or better but may be executed at a price at, above, or below the stop price.

754. A. buy limit order

Sharlene has placed a buy limit order because she is price specific. If it was a stop order, it would have to say stop as part of the order. In this case, Sharlene wants to purchase 1,000 shares of MKR at a price of 22 or lower.

755.   C. II, III, and IV

Although short sales against the box used to be used as a tax deferral, IRS rules have changed, and investors would be responsible for any capital gains due on the long position at the time they go short against the box. All of the other answer choices are true.

756.   D. All of the above

Stop orders, limit orders, and stop limit orders may or may not be executed because they are price specific and the price of the security may or may not touch or pass the price on the order.

757.   B. Buy limit and sell stop orders

Buy limit and sell stop orders are placed at or below the market price of the security.

758.   C. Sell limit and buy stop orders

Sell limit and buy stop orders are place at or above the market price of the security.

759.   C. triggered at 15, executed at 15.25

SLoBS (sell limit, buy stop) orders are triggered at or above the order price. So, the order is triggered (elected) at or above $15. And executed at the next price, which is $15.25.

760.   D. triggered at $24.88, executed at $25.25

BLiSS (buy limit, sell stop) orders are triggered at or below the order price. The order is triggered (elected) at or below $25.00 ($24.88) and is executed at the next price ($25.25).

761.   C. triggered at 25.25, executed at 25.13

This customer has entered a buy stop limit order. You must first take care of the buy stop portion of the order. Buy stop orders are SLoBS (sell limit, buy stop) orders that are triggered at or above the order price. Follow the ticker from left to right and look for the first transaction at or above $25. The first transaction at or above $25 is $25.25, so that's where the order is triggered. From that point forward, you need to take care of the buy limit portion. Buy limit orders are BLiSS (buy limit, sell stop) orders that are executed at or below the order price. From where the order was triggered, the first transaction that was at or below $25.25 was $25.13.

762.

C. triggered at $20.50, executed at $20.40

This client has entered a sell stop limit order. You must first take care of the sell stop portion of the order. Sell stop orders are BLiSS (buy limit, sell stop) orders that are triggered at or below the order price. Follow the ticker from left to right and look for the first transaction at or below $20.50. The first transaction at or below $20.50 is $20.50, so that's where the order is triggered. From that point forward, you need to take care of the sell limit portion. Sell limit orders are SLoBS (sell limit, buy stop) orders that are executed at or above the order price. From where the order was triggered, the first transaction that was at or above $20.40 was $20.40.

763.

A. I and III

The customer specified a price, so it's a limit order. In this case, it would be a limit order to buy 100 shares at a price of 50 or lower. Market orders aren't price specific; they're used to buy or sell at the best price available. All stop and limit orders are good for the day unless the customer specifies that they want the order in place for a longer time. If the day order isn't executed that day, the order is canceled.

764.

A. NH

A designated market maker can't hold NH (not held) orders. NH orders are ones in which your client gives you (the registered rep) authority over the price and time that the order is placed. These are used in the case where you believe that you can get a client a better price later in the day. NH orders aren't discretionary orders and don't require a written power of attorney.

765.

A. I and III

Fill-or-kill (FOK) orders must be executed immediately in their entirety, or the order must be canceled.

766.

C. II and III

An immediate-or-cancel (IOC) order must be attempted to be filled immediately by the firm handling the order but may be filled partially. It's a one-time order and doesn't allow the order to be executed in several attempts.

767.

B. must be executed in their entirety or the order is canceled

Unlike fill-or-kill (FOK) orders and immediate-or-cancel (IOC) orders, all-or-none (AON) orders don't have to be executed immediately. However, like FOK orders, they must be filled entirely or the order is canceled. AON orders remain active until they're executed or canceled.

768. **A. I and III**

Market-on-open (MOO or at-the-open) orders are to be executed at the security's opening price. At-the-open orders can be market or limit orders, but if they aren't executed at the opening price, they're cancelled. These orders allow for partial execution.

769. **C. The order should be sent to the floor broker immediately.**

This is an at-the-close order (or market on close, MOC, order). The registered rep should take the order and mark the order ticket at close. The firm will then transfer the order to its floor broker who will make sure that the order is executed properly.

770. **D. An alternative order**

An alternative order is also known at a one cancels the other (OCO) or either/or order. In this case, if either the stop or limit order is executed, the other portion of the order is cancelled because the investor wouldn't own the stock anymore.

771. **A. They want to buy ABC when the stock is below the previous sale price.**

When a customer enters a buy minus order, it means that they only want to buy the stock below the previous sale price.

772. **B. Designated market makers**

Designated market makers (DMMs) are responsible for maintaining a fair and orderly market on the NYSE floor and helping to keep trading as active as possible.

773. **C. I, III, and IV**

A designated market maker (DMM) uses priority, parity, and precedence to determine which orders get executed first.

>> **Priority:** Orders at the best price will be executed first.

>> **Parity:** If more than one order comes in at the best price, the one that came in first will be executed first.

>> **Precedence:** If more than one order came in at the best price and at the same time, the largest order will be executed first.

774. **B. The DMM needs permission from an exchange official.**

When a DMM (designated market maker specialist) stops stock, they're guaranteeing a trading price to a floor broker for a public order while the floor broker attempts to get a better price. DMMs have the ability to trade out of their own accounts, so they don't need permission to stop stock.

775. **B. 50.30**

Remember, it is the designated market maker's (DMM) job to keep trading as active as possible. If the bid and ask prices are too far apart and trading slows down, a DMM may enter an order to buy or sell securities out of their inventory in between the bid and ask prices to narrow the spread. At no point can a DMM enter a quote at the same price as a customer's order because a DMM is not allowed to compete with public orders.

776. **D. market orders**

A display book keeps track of stop orders, limit orders, and GTC orders but not market orders. Remember, market orders aren't price specific but are for immediate execution at the best price available. Therefore, they wouldn't need to be kept in a book for later execution.

777. **C. any order can be entered regardless of the quantity of shares traded**

The SDBK (Super Display Book) is a computerized routing and trading system used on the NYSE (New York Stock Exchange). The SDBK will automatically pair orders that it can, and the rest will be left for the DMM (designated market maker) to keep in the display book for later execution. The SDBK is used only for orders of 6.5 million shares or less.

778. **B. 46.02 to 46.06**

When you're looking at an exhibit such as this, you must ignore the stop orders. Then find the highest bid, which is 46.02, and the lowest offer (ask), which is 46.06, to get the inside market.

779. **C. highest bid price and lowest ask price**

The inside market of a security is the highest bid price (the most an entity is willing to pay for a security) and the lowest ask (offer) price, which is the least an entity will accept for selling the security. So, when investors purchase a security, they would be buying at the lowest ask price or selling at the highest bid price.

780. B. 22 × 13

When you're looking at the NYSE Display Book, the first thing you have to do is ignore the stop orders. Then, you need to look for the highest bid price and the lowest ask (offer) price. The highest bid price is 30.02, and the lowest ask price is 30.05. That's the inside market. Next, add up the numbers at each price to get 22 (8 Southwest B/D + 18 Southeast B/D) × 13 (4 Atlantic Sec. + 9 Gulf B/D). This is the number of round lots (100 shares); therefore, another acceptable answer would be 2,200 × 1,300.

781. A. In between the bid and offer prices

A designated market maker (DMM) would enter an order for their own inventory in between the bid and offer (ask) prices to help keep trading as active as possible. A DMM cannot place an order for their own inventory anywhere other than in between the bid and offer prices because they cannot compete with public orders.

782. C. II and III

On the ex-dividend date (ex-date), buy limit and sell stop orders are reduced to reflect the cash dividend unless marked DNR (do not reduce). Sell limit and buy stop orders remain the same.

783. D. The order would be canceled.

Unlike forward splits, reverse splits cancel all stop and limit orders on the ex-split date. *Open order* is just another way of saying good-till-canceled (GTC).

784. C. entire life of an order from entry to execution

The Order Audit Trail System (OATS) is an automated computer system that tracks the life of an over-the-counter (OTC) order from entry to execution or cancellation. OATS tracks all OTC securities including OTCBB (over-the-counter bulletin board) stocks and OTC Pink Market stocks.

785. D. OATS

OATS (Order Audit Trail System) tracks the life of an order entered OTC from entry to execution or cancellation. OATS tracks orders of all listed and unlisted stocks in which the order is negotiated by brokerage firms without the use of an exchange.

786. C. II and III

TRACE (Trade Reporting and Compliance Engine) reports trades of all long-term corporate bonds and U.S. government agency bonds but not convertible bonds. All trades must be reported by the buyer and seller within 15 minutes of execution. TRACE displays the trade date, time of execution, amount of the trade, price of the trade, yield of the bond, and so on. However, TRACE doesn't provide the names of the brokerage firms who executed the order.

787. D. RTRS

RTRS (Real-Rime Transaction Reporting System) provides up-to-the-minute pricing information regarding municipal bond transactions. The information is made available within 15 minutes of the trade.

788. B. TRACE

TRACE (Trade Reporting and Compliance Engine) is the FINRA-approved trade reporting system for OTC long-term corporate bonds, CMOs, CDOs, and U.S. government agency bonds.

789. B. It facilitates the reporting of trade data for NASDAQ-listed securities and exchange-listed securities occurring off the exchange floor.

The Trade Reporting Facility (TRF) is an automated system that expedites the reporting of trade data for NASDAQ-listed securities and exchange-listed securities occurring off the exchange floor.

790. C. I, II, and III

If dark pools of liquidity execute trades, the trades are reported as over-the-counter (OTC) transactions, not exchange transactions. Dark pools of liquidity represent pools of institutions, large retail clients, and firms trading for their own inventory. Because the clients and sizes of accounts remain anonymous, dark pools reduce transparency of the markets.

791. A. S&P 500 declines 7% or more from the previous day's close

To keep investors from panicking when things are going the wrong way, the NYSE has put in place a way to halt trading temporarily if the market drops severely too quickly. A level 1 halt will occur if the S&P 500 Index declines 7% or more from the previous day's close.

792. C. Level 3

A Level 3 halt will occur on the New York Stock Exchange if the S&P 500 index declines 20% or more from the previous day's close. If a Level 3 halt occurs, the exchange will halt stock trading until the next trading day.

Chapter 11 Answers

793. D. sales

Progressive taxes are taxes that increase depending on an individual's tax bracket. Progressive taxes affect individuals with high incomes more than individuals with low incomes. Personal income, gift, and estate taxes are progressive taxes. Sales tax and excise taxes (gas, alcohol, tobacco, and so on) are regressive taxes because everyone is taxed at the same rate.

794. A. I and III

Property tax is a flat or regressive tax in which taxes are levied equally regardless of the individual's income level. Flat taxes include sales, gasoline, excise, payroll, and property tax.

795. C. II, III, and IV

Regressive taxes are ones in which all individuals are taxed at the same rate regardless of income level. Regressive taxes include sales, gas, and alcohol. Progressive taxes, where individuals with higher income pay a higher rate, include income, gift, and estate taxes.

796. A. capital gains

Earned (active) income includes salaries, bonuses, and any income received from active participation in a business. Capital gains are considered portfolio income.

797. B. II, III, and IV

Portfolio income includes net capital gains from the sale of securities (including municipal bonds), dividends, and interest. Income, gains, and losses from a DPP (direct participation program) are passive.

798. D. I, II, III, and IV

All cash dividends are subject to federal taxation. Interest on T-notes is state tax-free but not federally tax-free. In addition, investors must pay taxes on accretion unless purchasing a municipal bond in the primary market at a discount. All capital gains are subject to state and federal taxation.

799. D. 28%

When dealing with bond interest, the holding period doesn't come into play. Unlike qualified dividends and long-term capital gains, corporate bond interest is taxed at the investor's tax bracket.

800. B. I and IV

Municipal bond interest is exempt from federal tax. However, unless purchasing a municipal bond within your home state or from a U.S. protectorate (such as Guam, U.S. Virgin Islands, or Puerto Rico), the interest is subject to state tax.

801. B. federal tax but not state tax

Interest on U.S. government T-bonds (Treasury bonds) is subject to federal tax but not state tax.

802. D. all of the above

Congress created the alternative minimum tax (AMT) so that certain taxpayers with high income must pay a minimum tax on certain tax-preference items that taxpayers with lower income may not have to pay or may pay a lower amount. Items subject to AMT include interest on certain municipal bonds such as IDRs, certain depreciation expenses, and certain items related to owning an interest in a limited partnership.

Individuals subject to AMT must calculate (or have someone calculate for them) their taxes using the standard method and then again using AMT calculations. After the calculations are done, the individual is responsible for paying the higher of the two.

803. B. II and III

Stock splits aren't taxable events. However, cash dividends and interest payments on corporate bonds are taxable.

804. A. I and III

Dividends received from stock and interest received from bonds are always taxed as ordinary income. Passive income is income that an investor receives from limited partnerships only. Long-term capital gains are for securities held for longer than one year. Because this investor held the stock for exactly one year, it's taxed as a short-term capital gain.

805. D. $4,500

Cash dividends are always fully taxable for the year in which they were received.

806. C. 20%

Unless qualified, dividends are taxed at the holder's tax bracket. Qualified dividends are ones on stock that has been held for more than 60 days during the 121-day period, which begins 60 days prior to the ex-dividend date. The tax rate on qualified dividends is as follows:

>> Zero percent for investors who are in the 10 or 15% tax bracket

>> Fifteen percent for investors who are taxed at a rate higher than 15% but below 39.6%

>> Twenty percent for investors who are taxed at 39.6%

807. B. I, II, and III

Short-term capital gains are taxed at the investor's tax bracket. Long-term capital gains are ones realized after holding a security for more than a year. Long-term capital gains are taxed at the same rate as qualified dividends:

>> Zero percent for investors who are in the 10 or 15% tax bracket

>> Fifteen percent for investors who are taxed at a rate higher than 15% but below 39.6%

>> Twenty percent for investors who are taxed at 39.6%

808. D. the investor's tax bracket

Short-term capital gains or losses occur when an investor sells a security after holding it for one year or less. Short-term capital gains are taxed at the investor's tax bracket.

809. C. Appreciation

At this point, the investor just has appreciation of securities. You don't know whether the investor is going to have a profit or loss until the securities are sold. Capital gains or losses take place when a security is sold, and ordinary income would be from interest or dividends received.

810. A. Appreciation

In this case, the shares just appreciated in value. The investor wouldn't have a capital gain or loss unless selling the securities at a price other than their cost basis. Passive income is income received from limited partnerships, and ordinary income is interest received from bonds or dividends received from stock.

811.

B. $600 capital gain

When an investor buys and sells the same security several times, gains and losses are figured out by FIFO (first in, first out) unless specified otherwise by the investor. Therefore, the first stock purchased is the first stock sold, and the stock sold in February is the stock purchased in January.

812.

D. Identified shares

Because the price has been fluctuating, this investor would be best to identify which shares are to be sold. To minimize the tax burden, they'd choose to sell the shares with the highest purchase price. Unless specified, it's assumed that the first shares purchased are the ones that are going to be sold (FIFO — first in, first out).

813.

B. $19.60

Assuming that the par value of the bond is $1,000, you have to get the conversion ratio:

$$\text{Conversion ratio} = \frac{\text{par}}{\text{conversion price}} = \frac{\$1,000}{\$20} = 50 \text{ shares}$$

Next, divide the overall cost by the conversion ratio to get the cost basis per share:

$$\text{Cost basis per share} = \frac{\$980}{50 \text{ shares}} = \$19.60$$

814.

C. $31.00

The best way to handle this one is to determine the original cost basis per share prior to doing the split first:

$$\text{Cost basis per share} = \frac{\$12,400}{200 \text{ shares}} = \$62.00$$

The overall cost basis for the initial transaction is not going to change, but, since the company is calling for a 2-for-1 stock split, this investor is now going to have 2 shares for every 1 that they had previously. So, if the amount of shares gets doubled, the cost basis per share has to get cut in half:

$$\text{Cost basis per share after the split} = \frac{\$62}{2} = \$31.00$$

815.

B. 10%

Remember, capital gains on any security (including municipal securities) is taxed. To determine the capital gains yield, use the following formula:

$$\text{Capital gains yield} = \frac{\text{selling price} - \text{purchase price}}{\text{purchase price}} = \frac{\$55 - \$50}{\$50} = \frac{\$5}{\$50} = 10\%$$

816.

A. 16%

Capital gains on any security is taxed. To determine the net yield after capital gains tax, you have to start by determining the capital gains yield. Use the following equation:

$$\text{Capital gains yield} = \frac{\text{selling price} - \text{purchase price}}{\text{purchase price}} = \frac{\$24 - \$20}{\$20} = \frac{\$4}{\$20} = 20\%$$

The investor held the security for over one year, so it's a long-term capital gain. If the long-term capital gain was taxed at 20%, what would be the net yield after capital gains tax?

Net yield after capital gains tax = capital gains yield × (100 − capital gains tax rate)
Net yield after capital gains tax = 20 × (100 − 20%) = 20% × 80 = 16%

For this investor, even though they had a capital gains yield of 20%, after paying capital gains tax, the net yield was only 16%.

817.

C. all gains or losses are considered short term

Short selling is selling a borrowed security. Investors are hoping that the price of the security drops so that they can purchase the securities in that market at a lower price and return the securities to the lender. Short selling is a bearish strategy because investors want the price of the security to decrease. Because the investor isn't actually holding the securities, all gains and losses from selling short are considered short term, and the investor is taxed at his tax bracket.

818.

C. October 1 of the following year

This is somewhat of a trick question. Securities become long term after holding them for more than a year. In this case, you may think that September 31 would be the answer. However, September has only 30 days, so there's no September 31; the correct answer is October 1 of the following year.

819.

C. They have a $3,000 loss for the current year and $3,500 carried over to the following year.

Capital losses can be used to offset capital gains. In this case, your client had losses exceeding their gains by $6,500 ($21,000 losses − $14,500 gains). Out of the $6,500, the client can write a total of $3,000 against their ordinary income each year. This means that your client would be carrying a $3,500 loss ($6,500 − $3,000) into the following year.

820.

B. The $6.50 loss per share deduction is disallowed.

According to the wash sale rule, if an investor sells a security at a loss, the investor can't buy or sell the same security or anything convertible into the same security for 30 days (prior and after) and be able to claim the loss. Because Uriah sold GNP Corporation stock at a loss, they can't buy GNP call options within 30 days because GNP call options give him the right to buy GNP stock. In this case, the loss would be disallowed, and the cost basis of GNP stock would be adjusted for the $6.50 per share loss.

821. D. DEF preferred stock

The IRS wash sale rule states that investors can't sell a security at a loss and buy back the same security or anything convertible into the same security for 30 days (before or after). If an investor violates the wash sale rule, they wouldn't be able to claim the loss on their taxes (it would increase the cost basis of the securities repurchased). In this case, DEF convertible bonds are convertible into DEF common stock; DEF call options give the holder the right to buy DEF common stock; and DEF warrants give the holder the right to purchase DEF common stock at a fixed price. DEF preferred stock is allowable because it's a different security and isn't convertible into DEF common stock.

822. A. not taxed

A return of capital is not considered a dividend. This is a situation in which an investor receives a portion of their money back, so they don't have as much at risk. A return of capital is not a taxable event because the investor is just receiving some of their invested money back that was taxed already. A return of capital will lower the investor's cost basis. A good example of return of capital is when an investor invests in mortgage-backed securities in which monthly mortgage payments are passed through to the investor. A portion of the money passed through will be taxable interest and the other portion will be nontaxable return of capital.

823. A. $28 loss

Because Mrs. Jones purchased the bond at a discount, you're going to accrete the bond. Accretion is the act of adjusting the cost basis of the bond and bringing it closer to par over the number of years until maturity. Accretion is taxable yearly in addition to whatever interest Mrs. Jones receives. The first thing you must do is take the purchase price of $920 (92% of $1,000 par) and adjust it toward par over the ten years until maturity.

$$\frac{\$80}{10 \text{ years}} = \$8 \text{ per year accretion}$$

After doing the math, you see that there's an $8 per year accretion. Take that $8 and multiply it by the number of years Mrs. Jones held the bond before selling it: $8 × 6 years = $48.

Next, you must get the new cost basis by adding the $48 to Mrs. Jones' purchase price of $920.

$920 + $48 = $968 new cost basis

As the final step, you have to compare the new cost basis to the selling price to determine the amount of gain or loss.

$968 cost basis − $940 selling price = $28 loss

824. D. $55

You should be able to eliminate Choices (A) and (B) right away. Because it's a 5% bond purchased at a discount, this investor has to claim at least $50 (5% × $1,000 par). The next thing you have to do is accrete the bond by spreading the discount over the number of years until maturity. The bond was purchased at $950 (95% of $1,000 par) and matures at $1,000 in ten years.

Take the $50 discount ($1,000 − $950) and divide it by the number of years until maturity.

$$\frac{\$50}{10 \text{ years}} = \$5 \text{ per year accretion}$$

Accretion is a taxable event, so you need to add the $5 accretion to the $50 interest to see how much this client will have to claim each year:

$$\$50 + \$5 = \$55$$

825. B. I and IV

All corporate bonds purchased at a discount, either in the secondary market or as an OID (original issue discount), *must* be accreted. However, if a corporate bond is purchased at a premium as a new issue or in the secondary market, it doesn't have to be amortized. In this case, the investor *may* amortize or elect to take a capital loss at maturity.

826. B. $70 loss

First, adjust the cost basis of the bond in the time the bond matures:

10 years
$800 → $1,000

The bond was purchased at $800 (80% of $1,000 par) and matures at $1,000 par in ten years. Next, take that $200 difference and divide it by the ten years to maturity:

$$\text{annual accretion} = \frac{\$200}{10 \text{ years}} = \$20$$

Then take the $20 per year accretion and multiply it by the number of years that the investor held the bond: $20 per year × 6 years = $120 total accretion

Next, add the total accretion to the purchase price of the bond to determine the investor's adjusted cost basis:

$800 original cost + $120 total accretion = $920 (adjusted cost basis)

After that, compare the adjusted cost basis to the selling price to determine the gain or loss:

$920 adjusted cost basis − $850 selling price = $70 capital loss

The investor incurred a $70 capital loss on the sale of the DEF bond, which can be used to offset capital gains on other investments (see the earlier section).

827. **B. I and IV**

All new municipal bonds purchased at a discount must be accreted. The accretion would be part of Sally's tax-free interest. If she holds the bond until maturity, the difference won't be taxed as a capital gain or loss. To have a capital gain or loss, Sally would have had to sell the security at a price that differs from her cost basis.

828. **C. $500**

Amortization reduces the cost basis of bonds purchased at a premium (over $1,000 par) over several years.

Your client purchased the bonds for a price of $11,000 (110% of $1,000 par × 10 bonds), and they mature in eight years at $10,000.

Divide the $1,000 difference ($11,000 purchase price − $10,000) by eight years until maturity.

$$\frac{\$1,000}{8 \text{ years}} = \$125 \text{ per year amortization}$$

Your client is losing $125 per year on the value of their bonds (at least as far as the IRS is concerned); they'll lose $500 ($125 × 4 years) over the course of four years.

829. **D. No gain or loss**

You use amortization for premium bonds (bonds purchased at a price greater than $1,000 par) to reduce the cost basis over several years. This investor purchased the bond for a price of $1,060 (106% of $1,000 par), and it matures in 12 years at $1,000 par.

Take the $60 difference ($1,060 purchase price − $1,000 par) and divide it by the 12 years until maturity.

$$\frac{\$60}{12 \text{ years}} = \$5 \text{ per year amortization}$$

If this investor is losing $5 per year on the value of the bond (at least as far as the IRS is concerned), they'll lose $20 ($5 × 4 years) over the course of four years. Next, subtract the $20 from the purchase price of the bond to determine the investor's cost basis after six years: $1,060 − $20 = $1,040. This investor's cost basis is $1,040, and they sold the bond at $1,040 (104% of $1,000 par); therefore, they saw no gain or loss.

830. **D. II and IV**

Under IRS rules, all municipal bonds purchased at a premium must be amortized. Amortization of a bond decreases its cost basis and decreases the reported bond interest income.

831. D. Unlimited

There is no gift tax between spouses, so the tax deduction limit is unlimited.

832. D. $1,750

Michelle received a gift of securities that has increased in value since purchase, so she'd assume the original purchase price of the securities. Because the securities were purchased at $4,250 ($42.50 × 100 shares) and sold at $6,000 ($60 × 100 shares), she'd have a capital gain of $1,750 ($6,000 − $4,250).

833. A. I and III

Each person may give an individual a gift of up to $14,000 per year that's exempt from gift tax. This gift is for $52,000 worth of securities; therefore, Gary (the donor) is subject to paying a gift tax. When receiving a gift of securities, the recipient assumes the donor's original cost basis (in this case, $42).

834. A. $30,000

Because DIM decreased from the original purchase price, Fred assumes the cost basis of the DIM stock on the date of the gift, which was $30,000 (1,000 shares × $30).

835. B. $10

Because the securities are inherited, the cost basis to the beneficiary (Clay) is the closing price on the day of the grandfather's death. Therefore, the cost of the stock is $52, and the stock is sold at $62. Clay realizes a $10 capital gain per share.

836. A. I and II

An IRS unified tax credit is one that's allowed for every man, woman, and child in America. This credit allows each person to gift a certain amount of their assets to other parties without having to pay gift or estate taxes.

837. C. Contributions are made with 100% pretax dollars.

Under IRS laws, qualified retirement plans allow investors to invest money for retirement with pretax dollars. This means that investors can write it off. In addition, earnings accumulate on a tax-deferred basis (the investor isn't taxed until withdrawal). However, distributions (tax-deferred earnings and contributions) for which the participant received a tax deduction are 100% taxable at the investor's tax bracket.

838. B. They allow for tax-free growth.

Growth in a qualified retirement plans is not tax free; it is tax-deferred. This means that any money taken at retirement is fully taxable.

839. **D. I, II, III, and IV**

All of the choices listed meet the IRS requirements to be considered qualified retirement plans. Qualified plans allow investors to contribute pretax money and the retirement account to grow on a tax-deferred basis.

840. **A. private pension plans**

ERISA (Employee Retirement Income Security Act) regulations cover private pension plans only.

841. **A. I and III**

Contributions to IRS qualified retirement plans are made with pretax dollars, and the distributions are 100% taxed at the holder's tax bracket.

842. **C. payroll deduction plans**

Payroll deduction plans are non-qualified plans that aren't required to include all full-time employees. ERISA (Employee Retirement Income Security Act) regulates only qualified plans that are available to all full-time employees of a company.

843. **D. Municipal bonds**

Because pension funds and other retirement plans are tax-deferred, it wouldn't make much sense to purchase municipal bonds because of their low yield. Remember, because the interest in municipal bonds is federally tax-free, they typically have the lowest yields of all bonds.

844. **B. Defined benefit plan**

As the name implies, defined benefit plans pay a specified benefit to plan participants at retirement.

845. **C. II and III**

In a defined contribution plan, the annual contribution percentage remains fixed. Certainly, the longer the employee stays with the corporation, the more money is contributed into the retirement plan and the more money the employee will receive at retirement. Contributions will continue even in bad years.

846. **C. 401(k) plans**

Deferred compensation plans, payroll deduction plans, and 457 plans are all non-qualified retirement plans. 401(k)s are qualified salary reduction plans that allow investors to deposit pretax money.

847. D. 59-1/2

Individuals may begin withdrawing money from a Roth 401(k) without penalty at age 59-1/2. As with other qualified retirement plans, the penalty may be waived under certain circumstances.

848. B. 100% taxable at the investor's tax bracket

403(b) plans are also known as tax-sheltered annuities (TSAs). TSAs are available to school employees, tax-exempt organizations, and religious organizations. These are salary reduction plans in which the contributions are made on a pretax basis. Because the investor didn't pay any taxes on the contributions, the distributions are 100% taxable at the investor's tax bracket.

849. C. II and III

With deferred compensation programs, the employee agrees to delay receiving a portion of their salary until they retire, are terminated, are disabled, or die. Theoretically, when they retire, they would be at a lower tax bracket and would pay less in taxes later than if receiving money currently. The employer only receives a tax deduction once the employee is paid. Because these are non-qualified plans, the employer may discriminate and not offer the plan to all employees.

850. D. 457(b) plans

457(b) are also deferred compensation plans established by state or local governments or 501(c)3 non-profit organizations. However, if a 457(b) plan is established for municipal employees, the plan must be qualified. In both cases, a person having a 457(b) plan could also have another retirement plan and make the maximum contribution into both plans. Employees may defer up to 100% of their compensation up to a rate determined by the IRS (indexed for inflation). Because investors have not paid tax on the money initially deposited or on the earnings, withdrawals from qualified plans are fully taxed at the rate determined by the investor's tax bracket.

851. A. $0

For an investor to open an IRA, they must have earned income. In this case, the investor is making income only from trading and doesn't have a job. Therefore, they can't contribute money into an IRA.

852. C. It is fully tax deductible.

Because the therapist has no other retirement plan, the IRA contributions are fully tax deductible. Because this investor is over age 50, as of 2023, they may deposit up to $7,500 per year and be able to write it off on their taxes. If they had another retirement plan, they could still contribute to the IRA, but the contribution may or may not be tax deductible depending on the amount of earned income.

853. **A. 6% penalty tax**

If an investor makes an excess contribution to an IRA, the excess contribution is subject to a 6% penalty tax.

854. **B. It will be taxed as ordinary income plus a 10% penalty**

Withdrawals before age 59-1/2 will be taxed as ordinary income plus a 10% penalty.

855. **C. April 1 of the year after the holder turns age 73**

Payouts for traditional IRAs must begin no later than April 1 of the year after the holder turns age 73 (required beginning date, RBD). In the event that the holder doesn't withdraw the required minimum distribution (RMD) by April 1 of the year after turning age 73, they will be hit with a 50% tax penalty on the amount that should have been withdrawn.

856. **D. April 15 of the following year.**

Investors can deposit money into a traditional IRA up to April 15 (tax day) of the following year and claim it as a write-off on the previous year's taxes.

857. **D. II and IV**

Unlike traditional IRAs, contributions made to Roth IRAs are made with after-tax dollars. Providing the investor has held the Roth IRA for at least five years and is at least 59-1/2 years old, distributions are 100% tax-free.

858. **D. $7,500 after tax**

Normally, the maximum contribution to a Roth IRA per year is $6,500. However, because this investor is over 50 years old, there's $1,000 additional catch-up contribution allowed. Unlike traditional IRAs, all contributions are after tax, but all withdrawals after age 59-1/2 and holding the account for at least five years are tax-free.

859. **D. No requirement**

A Roth IRA is different than a traditional IRA because the money deposited into a Roth IRA is not tax deductible. However, all of the money withdrawn from a Roth IRA after age 59-1/2 is tax-free, including the gains in the account. Therefore, because the IRS won't be taxing the money withdrawn, there's no requirement as to when the money has to be withdrawn.

860. A. I and III

An SEP-IRA is a retirement vehicle designed for small business owners, self-employed individuals, and their employees. SEP-IRAs allow participants to invest money for retirement on a tax-deferred basis. Employers can make tax-deductible contributions directly to their employees' SEP-IRAs. As of 2023, the maximum employer contribution to each employee's SEP-IRA is 25% of the employee's compensation (salary, bonuses, and overtime) or $66,000 (subject to cost-of-living increases in the following years), whichever is less. Employees who are part of the plan may still make annual contributions to a traditional or Roth IRA.

861. B. There is no limit on the amount he can transfer.

Since he is not taking possession of the funds, it is considered a transfer. There is no limit placed on the amount of transfer that can take place in one year.

862. D. 1 year

Your client would have to wait at least one more year before executing another rollover.

863. C. 60 days

After withdrawing money from a pension plan, individuals have 60 days to roll over the money into an IRA without being taxed as a withdrawal.

864. C. the beneficiary of the accounts must use the funds by age 30 for the funds not to be penalized

Coverdell ESAs (educational savings accounts) and 529 plans (qualified tuition plans) are non-qualified plans designed to provide money for higher education. All of the answer choices given are true except for Choice (C). In a Coverdell ESA, the funds must be used by age 30 or transferred to another candidate. In a 529 plan, there are no age requirements.

Chapter 12 Answers

865. C. SEC

SROs are self-regulatory organizations that are unaffiliated with the federal government. The SEC (Securities and Exchange Commission) is a government agency.

866. **A. Advisers with at least $25 million under management**

Any investment adviser with at least $25 million of assets under management or anyone who advises an investment company must register with the SEC. All other investment advisers have to register on the state level.

867. **D. I, III, and IV**

Besides having their own rules, self-regulatory organizations help to implement and oversee SEC rules. The self-regulatory organizations (SROs) you're likely to see on the Series 7 exam are FINRA, MSRB, NYSE, and CBOE.

868. **C. FINRA**

FINRA (Financial Industry Regulatory Authority) administers exams such as the SIE, Series 7, Series 6, Series 24, and so on.

869. **D. MSRB**

The MSRB (Municipal Securities Rulemaking Board) makes its own rules but does not enforce them.

870. **B. II, III, and IV**

As self-regulatory organizations (SROs), FINRA and the NYSE can fine, expel, and/or censure members. However, because FINRA and the NYSE aren't affiliated with the government, they can't imprison members.

871. **C. I, II, and III**

Although it may be helpful, you're not required to know whether a new customer has an account at another brokerage firm. However, you do need to know the customer's citizenship, whether his name appears on the SDN (Specially Designated Nationals) list, and whether he works for another broker-dealer.

872. **C. the individual's educational background**

The individual's Social Security number, date of birth, and residential address are all required from a customer when opening an account. Although the individual's educational background would be helpful to have, it's not required.

873. **C. I, III, and IV**

Statements I and IV were probably a given. But you also need the type of account that the customer is opening (cash, margin, corporate, and so on), the customer's age and marital status, and the customer's occupation and employer. You don't need the customer's educational background.

874. D. I, II, III, and IV

All of the information listed needs to be on the new account form. In addition, you also need the Social Security number (or tax ID if a business), the occupation and type of business, bank references, net worth, annual income, if the customer is an insider of a company, and the signature of the registered rep and a principal.

875. C. II and III

Yes, believe it or not, a customer's signature isn't required on a new account form. However, if you're opening a new account for a customer, you'd have to fill out and sign the new account form and have it signed by a principal (manager) of the firm.

876. C. You may open the account if you can determine from other sources that the customer has the financial means to handle the account.

Unfortunately, this situation isn't unusual. When you're opening an account for a new customer, they may not feel comfortable sharing all of his financial information. However, you can still make recommendations and do trades for the customer if you can determine financial information from other sources, such as Dun & Bradstreet (D&B) cards.

For argument's sake, say that the D&B card says that your new customer is the owner of a company that made $500 million last year. In this case, you can assume that the customer has a lot of money. Recommendations made to customers should be suitable to their investment objectives and financial situation. If you can't determine the information from other sources, you can still make trades and recommendations that would be suitable for all investors, such as U.S. government securities and mutual funds.

877. C. Once every 3 years

Brokerage firms must make sure customer account information is correct at least once every 3 years.

878. A. MMA would open a numbered account for Chael.

Numbered (street-named) accounts are very common at broker-dealers. If Chael wants to remain anonymous, they can have the broker-dealer set up their account as a numbered account. All order tickets would contain a number or code; however, the broker-dealer must have a signed document on file by Chael, stating that they are the owner of the account.

879. A. The client must sign a written statement attesting to ownership of the account.

Numbered accounts are also known as street-name accounts. To open an account for a client in street name, the customer must sign paperwork attesting to responsibility for the account. Because accounts of different investors can't be commingled (combined), the firm must keep this client's account segregated from other clients' accounts held in street name.

880. **A. ABC Broker-Dealer must forward the proxy to the client.**

Street-name accounts are numbered accounts held in the name of the broker-dealer for the benefit of the client. In this case, DEF Corporation would send the proxy to ABC Broker-Dealer who must in turn forward the proxy to its client.

881. **A. CIPs**

The USA Patriot Act requires financial institutions, such as broker-dealers and banks, to maintain CIPs (customer identification programs) to help prevent money laundering and the financing of terrorist organizations. Financial institutions are required to look at the Specially Designated Nationals (SDNs) list published by the Office of Foreign Asset Control (OFAC) to see whether any of their new customers are on the list. If a new customer is on the list, their assets will be frozen, and your firm must cease doing business with him.

882. **A. customer identification programs**

Under the USA Patriot Act, all financial institutions must maintain customer identification programs (CIPs). It's up to the financial institution to verify the identity of any new customers, maintain records of how they verified the identity, and determine whether the new customer appears on any suspected terrorist list or terrorist organization. As part of the identification program, they must obtain the customer's name, date of birth, address (no P.O. boxes), and Social Security number.

883. **D. $25,000**

The minimum deposit required to open a day trading account is $25,000. A pattern day trader is an investor who executes at least 4 day trades every 5 business days.

884. **B. $500,000**

Your client must have at least $500,000 in assets available for investments to establish a prime brokerage account. Prime brokerage firms consolidate information from all brokerage accounts the client has to provide one statement for the customer.

885. **A. Wrap accounts**

Wrap accounts include charges for advisory fees, commissions, and any other services provided by an adviser to clients.

886. **A. The entire account would be transferred to Mrs. Faber.**

This account was set up as joint tenants with rights of survivorship (JTWROS). When an investor with a JTWROS account dies, the investor's portion of the account is transferred to the remaining survivors of the account (in this case, Mrs. Faber). Most married couples set up their joint accounts this way to avoid probate issues.

887. **B. The deceased party's portion of the account is transferred to their estate.**

In a joint account with tenants in common (TIC), if one investor dies, the deceased party's portion of the account is transferred to their estate. In a joint account with rights of survivorship, the entire account is transferred to the survivors of the account.

888. **B. Tenancy in common**

In a joint tenancy in common (TIC) account, if one investor dies, that investor's portion of the account is transferred into the investor's estate while the remainder of the assets are transferred to the survivors. Persons may or may not have equal ownership of the account. The account may be divided based on percentage of money contributed.

889. **B. It is transferred to a spouse.**

Community property accounts are similar to JTWROS accounts but are only for legally married couples. Certain states have community property laws that require the account to be transferred to the surviving spouse in the event of death of one of the account holders.

890. **C. A parent and minor daughter**

A joint account is an account in the name of more than one adult. Choices (A), (B), and (D) are all possible for joint accounts; however, an account opened for a minor must be a custodial account.

891. **B. I and IV**

As the name implies, a revocable (living) trust is one that can be revoked or changed by the trustee. An irrevocable trust is one that can't be changed. So, the beneficiary can't change, the terms can't change, and it can't be canceled.

892. **A. A parent and a minor daughter**

A joint account is one in the name of more than one adult. An account for an adult and a minor would be an UGMA (Uniform Gifts to Minors Act) or UTMA (Uniform Transfer to Minors Act) account. Both UGMA and UTMA accounts are custodial accounts in the name of the adult for the benefit of the minor.

893. **B. An account for a minor daughter**

An individual may open an account and trade the account for a minor without a written power of attorney. However, if a client wants to open and trade an account for a wife or for a partner, they'd need them to sign a power of attorney, giving the client the authorization to open the account and execute trades.

894. B. I and III

Fiduciary accounts, such as UGMA and UTMA accounts, are required to follow the prudent man rule or legal list of the state in which the account is set up. The prudent man rule or legal list establishes a guideline of appropriate investments for fiduciary accounts. There isn't a FINRA list of approved investments for minors' accounts.

895. A. a parent and a minor daughter

A joint account is an account in the name of more than one adult. That means that Choice (A) doesn't work. UGMA accounts are designed for situations in which you have one minor and one adult.

896. C. custodial account

UGMA (Uniform Gift to Minors Act) accounts are custodial accounts. These accounts are managed by a custodian for the benefit of the minor. The custodian has full control over the account and has the right to buy or sell securities, exercise rights or warrants, hold securities, and so on. The custodian must do what is in the best interest of the minor. Once the minor reaches the age of majority, which varies from state to state, the account is transferred to the former minor. A UGMA account can have only one custodian and one minor.

897. B. the certificates are endorsed by the minor

In an UGMA account, all certificates are endorsed by the custodian.

898. D. The account is transferred to the former minor.

Under the terms of the Uniform Gifts to Minors Act (UGMA), the account must be handed over to the former minor when they reach the age of majority. You won't be expected to know the age of majority because it varies from state to state, but it's typically between the ages of 18 and 21.

899. D. promptly after execution

Whether orders are executed for discretionary accounts or non-discretionary accounts, trades must be approved by principals promptly after execution. FINRA does not require orders to be approved prior to execution since that may delay an order from being executed and cause an order to be executed at a worse price.

900. A. I only

A power of attorney or trading authorization is required for discretionary accounts. In this case, an individual is giving trading authorization to their registered rep or broker-dealer. All discretionary orders must be marked as such at the time they're entered for execution. These types of accounts must be monitored closely by a principal to make sure that there's no excessive trading for the purpose of generating commission (churning).

901.
C. the registered rep must obtain approval of a principal prior to execution of each order

With a limited power of attorney, the registered rep does not need to obtain permission from a principal prior to execution of each trade. With a limited power of attorney, the authorized party cannot withdraw securities or cash without permission of the customer. The authorized party may not transfer securities or cash from the account without verbal approval of the customer. However, the authorized party may still execute trades without verbal approval of the customer.

902.
C. II and III

A durable power of attorney only cancels upon the death of an investor. A regular power of attorney cancels upon the death or mental incompetence of the investor.

903.
B. Corporate Resolution

For a corporation to open a cash account, you or your firm would need to receive a copy of the Corporate Resolution. The Corporate Resolution tells you who has trading authority for the account. If the corporation was opening a margin account, you'd need a copy of the Corporate Resolution and the Corporate Charter. The Corporate Charter (by-laws) lets you know that the corporation is allowed to purchase securities on margin according to their own by-laws.

904.
C. Corporate Charter and Corporate Resolution

When a corporation opens a margin account, you need a copy of the corporate charter (bylaws), which would state that they are allowed to purchase on margin, and a corporate resolution, which would state which individual(s) has/have trading authority.

905.
A. institutional accounts

Institutional accounts are set up by institutions such as banks, mutual funds, insurance companies, pension funds, hedge funds, and investment advisers are considered institutional accounts. Their role is to act as specialized investors on behalf of others.

906.
D. All of the above

When learning of the death of a client, you should mark the account as deceased, freeze the account (don't do any trading), cancel all open orders (GTC), cancel all written powers of attorney, and await the proper legal papers for instructions about what to do with the account.

907.
C. transfer the money in the account to the executor of the estate

If a client dies, all open orders should be canceled, the account should be frozen (no trading), and any written power of attorney needs to be canceled. No assets should be transferred until receiving instructions from the executor of the estate.

908.
D. "Our dedicated sales team will work with you to help meet your investment goals."

Choices (B) and (C) aren't legal because they're guarantees, and a firm can't guarantee that its investment recommendations will outperform the market, even if they did for the last ten years. Also, a firm can't guarantee customers that it will earn them at least 7% on their investments each year. Additionally, there's no way to prove that this broker-dealer's "dedicated sales team" is the best in the industry. However, stating that its sales team will help investors meet their investment goals is fine and is what every broker-dealer should be doing.

909.
B. retail communication

TV ads, radio ads, magazine ads, newspaper ads, billboards, and so on are considered retail communication. Retail investors are those investors other than institutional investors. Retail communication is any written or electronic communication that is made available or distributed to more than 25 retail investors within any 30 calendar-day period.

910.
C. 25

Correspondence is like retail communication but is sent (written or electronically) to 25 or fewer retail investors within any 30 calendar-day period.

911.
D. advertisements sent to banks

Communication is any written (including electronic) communication that is made available or distributed. However, institutional communication is only to be made available or distributed to institutional clients such as banks, savings and loan associations, registered investment companies, insurance companies, registered investment advisers, government entities, employee benefit plans, FINRA member firms, persons or entities with assets of at least $50 million, and so on.

912.
B. 65 and over

Rules for the financial exploitation of specified adults includes adults aged 65 and over and natural persons aged 18 or older who have mental or physical impairments that render them unable to protect their own interest.

913. A. I and III

Rules for financial exploitation of specified adults include seniors, or natural persons aged 65 and over, and natural persons aged 18 or older who have physical or mental impairments that render them unable to protect their own interests.

914. C. 15 business days

If a brokerage firm believes that a customer who is a specified adult (a client who is age 65 or older or a mentally incompetent adult) has been or could be exploited, the firm can place a hold on withdrawals from the account for up to 15 business days.

915. C. Regulation S-P

All brokerage firms must have safeguards to protect customer records from unauthorized use (Gramm-Leach-Bliley Act). The safeguards must be disclosed in writing to all new customers at the time of the opening of the account and to all existing customers annually. Non-public information includes customers' Social Security number, transaction history, account balance, and so on.

916. D. all of the above

Even though you may not remember any of the problems listed, you can see why they would all be reportable offenses.

917. A. broker-dealer

When a registered representative takes a job outside of his firm, they are moonlighting. Moonlighting rules for registered representatives require the individual to disclose this information to their employing broker-dealer only.

918. B. I and II

If an employee of a brokerage firm or immediate family wants to open a new account at another brokerage firm, the employee must obtain written permission from their firm of employment. In addition, the employing firm must receive duplicate confirmations of all trades. Approval is not necessary for executing trades in the account.

919. C. I, II, and III

Because the agent works for a FINRA firm, the agent needs to notify their firm about the opening of the account. The agent needs written permission to open the account but not to trade once the account is open. Duplicate confirmations and statements must be sent to the employing firm if requested.

920. **B. they already purchased the shares, and they must submit the payment**

As soon as the purchase order is executed, your client owns the securities and must pay for them no matter what happens to the market price of the securities.

921. **D. I, II, III, and IV**

When you become a registered rep, you receive your own unique identification number. This number has to be placed on any order ticket you fill out along with a description of the securities (such as ABC common stock), the time the order was placed, and whether the order was solicited or unsolicited. An unsolicited order is when a client tells you the securities they want to purchase or sell without your input.

922. **D. the investor's occupation**

The investor's occupation is something that's on the new account form, not the order ticket.

923. **A. the customer's signature**

The customer's signature is not required on an order ticket. You have to remember that most customer orders take place over the phone, so it would be next to impossible to get the customer's signature in a timely fashion.

924. **C. take the order but mark it as "unsolicited"**

Even though the shares of Biff Spanky Corporation may not fit into Gina's investment objectives, you can still accept the order. However, to protect yourself, you need to mark the order ticket as "unsolicited." The only unsolicited orders that you wouldn't be able to accept are on options (unless their options account was approved) and DPPs (direct participation programs).

925. **B. take the order and mark it as "unsolicited"**

You probably want to let your client know about the risks of investing in low-priced stocks and let them know that it doesn't fit their investment objectives. However, you should definitely take the order and mark the order ticket as "unsolicited." By marking the order ticket as "unsolicited," you're putting the responsibility for the order on your client's shoulders.

926. **A. a principal**

New account forms and order tickets must be signed by a principal (manager) of the firm. Order tickets don't have to be signed prior to placing the order for trade but must be signed by the end of the day. This means that you can do trades while your principal is out to lunch.

927. **C. the same day as execution of the order**

Principals (managers) must approve trades on the same day as execution but not necessarily before execution. This would allow the order to be entered as quickly as possible. Principals must approve trades as soon as possible after execution but no later than the end of the day at the latest.

928. **C. 2 business days, and payment is due in 4 business days**

Corporate bonds settle in 2 business days, and payment is due in 4 business days.

929. **D. Thursday, October 9**

The stock settlement date for stock purchases is 2 business days, but the payment date is 4 business days after the trade date. Remember, Saturday and Sunday aren't business days, so the payment date would be Thursday, October 9.

930. **C. 2 business days after the trade date and payment is due in 2 business days after the trade date**

Municipal bonds settle 2 business days after the trade date (T+2), and payment is due in 2 business days after the trade date.

931. **A. 1 business day after the trade date**

The settlement date for U.S. government bonds is 1 business day after the trade date (T+1).

932. **A. 1**

Option trades settle in 1 business day after the trade date (T+1), and payment is due in 4 business days after the trade date.

933. **B. Friday, October 9, on a cash basis or Tuesday, October 13 regular way**

Cash trades always settle the same day as the trade date and regular way settlement is 2 business days after the trade date. Because there's a weekend in-between, regular way settlement is Tuesday, October 13.

934. **A. DK notice**

Occasionally, there might be a trade situation where there is some sort of discrepancy. Here are some examples: The purchasing dealer or selling dealer believed the trade was for a different number of shares. Or the trade was transacted for a different price, is not familiar with the trade at all, and so on. Sometimes, nefarious dealers will even DK a trade if the market goes in the wrong direction. DK notices are typically handled through the Automated Confirmation Transaction service (ACT), in which each dealer submits their version of the trade.

935. **D. All of the above**

An extension to pay for a trade may be granted by FINRA, the Fed, or any national securities exchange. The extension generally grants customers an extra 5 business days to pay for the trade.

936. **C. Sell out the stock and freeze the account for 90 days.**

If a client fails to pay for the trade by the payment date, the security is sold out and the account is frozen for 90 days. To apply for an extension with the FINRA, a customer must disclose a legitimate reason for needing the extension.

937. **A. They must deposit the full purchase price of the securities before the purchase order may be executed.**

A client's account would be frozen for 90 days if they failed to pay for securities they purchased or failed to deliver securities they sold. In this case, Mary must pay for the securities in full before any order would be entered or deliver securities before they will be sold.

938. **C. confirmation**

All member firms are required to send a trade confirmation to a customer at or prior to the completion of each transaction. The confirmation provides all the specifics of the trade, such as the trade date, whether the customer bought or sold, the amount of securities, the name of the security, the price of the security, and so on.

939. **D. I, II, III, and IV**

When a client receives a confirmation (receipt of trade), the confirmation has to include the trade and settlement date, the name and type of the security, how many shares were traded, and the amount of commission if traded on an agency basis. In the event that the trade was made on a principal basis, the amount of markup doesn't need to be disclosed.

940. **A. at or prior to the completion of the transaction**

For member-to-customer transactions, the member firm must send the trade confirmation at or prior to completion of the transaction (the settlement date). For member-to-member transactions, the firms must send each other confirmations no later than 1 business day after the trade date.

941. **C. II, III, and IV**

A confirmation must include the amount of commission charged for an agency trans-action, a description of the security purchased or sold, the registered representative's identification number, and so on. However, the markup or markdown doesn't need to be disclosed for principal transactions.

942. **D. whether the trade was executed on a dealer or agency basis**

MSRB (Municipal Securities Rulemaking Board) rules require that confirmations include whether a trade was executed on a principal (dealer) or agency (broker) basis. The amount of the commission on an agency trade does need to be disclosed, but the dealer's markup or markdown on a principal trade doesn't have to be disclosed. The trade date (the day the transaction was executed) would need to be disclosed but not the settlement date because that's assumed to be 3 business days after the trade date.

943. **A. whether the trade was solicited or unsolicited**

Whether an order is solicited or unsolicited is on an order ticket, not the confirmation. Order confirmations include items such as the customer's account number, the agent's ID number, the trade date, whether the security was bought (BOT) or sold (SLD), the number or par value of securities, the yield (if bonds), the CUSIP number (if any), the price of the security, the total amount paid, and the commission charged.

944. **B. 1 business day following the trade date**

Don't spend too much, or any, time remembering the rule number because it's extremely unlikely that you'll see the rule number on the exam. However, you should know that confirmations for trades between firms must be sent no later than 1 business day following the trade date. Confirmations to customers must be sent at or prior to the completion of the transaction.

945. **B. broker–dealer**

Brokerage firms cannot validate mutilated certificates.

946. **B. a change in the market price**

Securities can't be rejected due to a change in market price. Securities are rejected if the transfer agent doesn't follow the good delivery rules.

947. **A. 4 certificates for 150 shares each and 14 certificates for 5 shares each**

The number of shares on each stock certificate must be in multiples of 100 (100, 200, 300, and so on), divisors of 100 (1, 2, 4, 5, 10, 20, 25, 50), or in units that add up to 100 (70 + 30, 85 + 15, 60 + 40, and so on). Choice (A) is the exception because 150 isn't a multiple or divisor of 100. In addition, the odd-lot (less than 100 shares) portion of the trade is exempt from the rule. For example, in this case, you could have three certificates for 200 shares each and one certificate for 70 shares. Presently, the most common form of delivery is book entry, so I assume that sometime in the future questions like this will go by the wayside.

948. **C. 2 certificates for 200 shares each and 3 certificates for 80 shares each**

In order to be considered good delivery, the trade has to be in multiples of 100 shares (100, 200, 300, 400, and so on), divisors of 100 shares (1, 2, 4, 5, 10, 20, 25, 50, and so on), or shares that add up to 100 (20 +80, 35+65, 15+85, and so on). The odd-lot portion (the portion less than 100 shares) is exempt. The odd-lot portion in this case is 40 shares.

The answer choice that doesn't work in this question is Choice (C). The two certificates for 200 shares each is okay, but the three certificates for 80 shares isn't good because there's nothing to match up with the 80 shares to make it 100. Since most securities are now sold in book-entry form, questions like this will at some point not be included on the Series 7.

949. **A. reclamation**

Reclamation is the return of securities previously accepted. Rejection is the refusal of securities at the time of delivery.

950. **D. 10 business days after the settlement date**

If a client sold securities in their possession and failed to deliver them within 10 business days after the settlement date, your firm must buy them from another seller. Remember, once the order ticket is executed, your client's securities were sold. If your client fails to deliver them, your firm is still responsible for getting them to the purchaser. In this case, your client's account would be frozen for 90 days, and they wouldn't be able to purchase securities without paying first and wouldn't be able to sell securities in their possession without delivering them first.

951. **B. I and IV**

The buyer of a stock would receive a due bill from the seller if buying the stock before the ex-dividend date while the trade settles after record date due to delayed delivery.

952. **A. DRS**

The DRS (Direct Registration System) allows investors to maintain certificates in book entry form rather than receiving physical delivery of certificates.

953. **B. making sure that issued shares do not exceed authorized shares**

The registrar is responsible for making sure that the issued shares do not exceed authorized shares, not the transfer agent.

954. **B. Quarterly**

Whether an account is active or inactive, account statement must be sent out at least quarterly (once every three months).

955. B. quarterly

FINRA (Financial Industry Regulatory Authority) and the SEC (Securities and Exchange Commission) require member firms to send customer account statements at least quarterly (once every three months).

956. C. 4

If a question doesn't specify whether an account is active or inactive, assume that the client is inactive and will receive quarterly statements. If a customer places any trade orders in a particular month, they must receive an account statement that month.

957. C. semi-annually

Mutual funds must send investors account statements at least semi-annually.

958. D. II and IV

If trading was done during the month, the account is active. Account statements must be sent out at least quarterly (once every three months) for active or inactive accounts and semiannually (once every six months) for mutual funds.

959. C. Wednesday, September 16

The ex-dividend date (ex-date) is 1 business day before the record date.

960. A. 1 business day before the record date

The record date is the date the corporation checks its books to see who is entitled to the previously declared dividend. Since it takes 2 business days for stock transactions to settle, the ex-dividend date (the first day the buyer of the stock will not receive the dividend) is 1 business day before the record date.

961. D. IV, II, I, III

First, the corporation declares that a dividend will be paid. On the record date, the corporation will inspect its books to see who will get paid the dividend. However, the ex-dividend date is 1 business day before the record date. Then, at some time in the near future, the corporation will pay the dividend.

962. A. Monday, October 15

The last day that your investor client can buy the stock the "regular way" and still receive the dividend is on the business day before the ex-dividend date. The ex-dividend date is on Tuesday, October 16, so an investor must buy the stock no later than Monday, October 15, to receive the dividend.

963. D. II and IV

The record date is Thursday, August 15, so the ex-dividend date is Wednesday, August 14. If a regular-way trade is executed on the ex-dividend date, the seller of the stock receives the dividend. In a cash trade, the trade needs to be executed after the record date to receive the dividend.

964. B. accept the complaint and write down any action taken

After receiving Meisha's written complaint, the broker-dealer must accept the complaint and write down any action taken to resolve the complaint. All broker-dealers should keep a complaint file for each client and keep accurate records of any communications or actions taken regarding a complaint.

965. A. The customer decided to have it handled through COP, and any decision made by the court is appealable.

In the event that a brokerage firm didn't have the customer sign an arbitration agreement (most do), the customer decides whether to take a dispute to arbitration, mediation, or through code of procedure. In the event that either party is unhappy with the results, the decision can be appealed.

966. B. I and IV

Unless there is a signed arbitration agreement, the non-member decides whether the dispute is handled through arbitration or code of procedure. Arbitration decisions are binding and non-appealable.

967. A. members may take non-members to arbitration

Members can't force non-members to submit a dispute to arbitration. The non-member (customer) decides if the dispute is settled through arbitration or COP (Code of Procedure). However, many firms require customers to sign an arbitration agreement when opening an account that requires disputes to be settled through arbitration only.

968. C. $50,000

Simplified arbitration is used for member to non-member disputes not over $50,000. Simplified industry arbitration is used for member-to-member disputes not over $50,000. Most arbitration complaints are judged by a three-person panel, but simplified arbitration is decided by one person.

969. A. 15 days

The decisions in arbitration are binding and non-appealable, so they're less costly than court action. If a member firm or person associated with that member firm fails to comply with the terms of the arbitration (in the case of a loss) within 15 days of notification, FINRA reserves the right to suspend or cancel the firm's or person's membership.

970. B. I and IV

Arbitration decisions are binding and non-appealable. Mediation decisions are not binding and can be appealed.

971. B. NSCC

To process an ACAT (Automated Customer Account Transfer), a brokerage firm must be a member of the NSCC (National Securities Clearing Corporation). When a brokerage firm is a clearing firm, the firm is assuming financial responsibility if a customer doesn't pay for a trade or doesn't deliver certificates that are sold.

972. B. NSCC

To process an ACAT, a brokerage firm must be a member of the NSCC (National Securities Clearing Corporation). When a brokerage firm is a clearing firm, the firm is assuming financial responsibility if a customer does not pay for a trade or does not deliver certificates that are sold.

973. A. I and III

ACATs are account transfers from one brokerage firm to another. When a firm receives an ACAT notice, the firm must verify the customer's instructions within 1 business day and must transfer assets within 3 business days after verification.

974. A. Calls must be made after 8:00 a.m. and before 9:00 p.m. local time of the customer.

According to Rule G-39, all cold calls (calls to potential customers) must be made after 8:00 a.m. and before 9:00 p.m. based on the local time of the customer.

975. C. Five years

Individuals placed on a firm's do not call list can't be contacted for five years.

976. B. The price the dealer paid to purchase the security

The 5% markup policy (FINRA 5% policy) states that a brokerage firm may use all relevant factors of a trade to determine the markup or commission charged to a customer except dealer cost (the price that the firm paid to have the security in inventory).

977. D. The over-the-counter sale of outstanding non-exempt securities

The 5% markup policy doesn't apply to primary (new issue) offerings, mutual funds (continuous offering of new shares), or Regulation D (exempt) offerings.

978.

D. All of the above

The 5% markup policy is a guideline for broker-dealers to use when executing trades of outstanding securities for public customers. For a standard-sized trade of non-exempt securities, broker-dealers typically shouldn't charge a commission, markup, or markdown that is greater than 5%. However, some situations may warrant a charge more than 5%, such as a small trade or extra work involved in executing the trade. The 5% policy applies to both commission charges on agency transactions and to markups and markdowns on principal transactions, including proceeds transactions, and riskless (simultaneous) transactions.

979.

C. A dealer transaction of an OTC common stock

The 5% markup policy covers over-the-counter trades of outstanding (not new securities like IPOS, which require a prospectus), nonexempt securities with public customers. If securities are exempt from SEC registration, such as municipal bonds, they're exempt from the 5% policy. Under the Investment Company Act of 1940, mutual funds can charge up to 8-1/2% of the amount invested.

980.

C. hypothecation

Hypothecation isn't a violation. Hypothecation takes place when a brokerage firm lends money to a customer when purchasing securities or margin.

981.

A. combining fully paid and margined securities for use as collateral

If a brokerage firm does not segregate fully paid and margined securities, it is commingling securities of the customers. Commingling is a violation.

982.

C. bringing in a third party to execute a trade

Interpositioning is the violation of bringing in a third party to execute a trade without obtaining a better price.

983.

C. two years after the contribution is made

Under the Investment Advisers Act of 1940, investment advisers are prohibited from providing investment advisory services for a fee to a government client for two years after a contribution is made. This rule applies not only to the adviser, executives, and employees making contributions to certain elected officials, but also to candidates who may later be elected.

984. B. freeriding

Clients must pay for trades even if selling the securities at a profit shortly afterward. You can imagine the problems that would occur if clients never paid for trades and just waited to see whether there was a profit. In this case, the client's account would be frozen for 90 days, and she wouldn't be able to purchase securities without paying for them first.

985. B. backing away

Backing away is the failure on the part of a securities dealer to honor a firm quote.

986. A. the profit or loss

Churning is the excessive trading of a client's account for the sole purpose of generating commissions and is a violation. Yes, believe it or not, when FINRA (Financial Industry Regulatory Authority) is looking to see whether an account has been churned, the client's profit or loss doesn't come into play.

987. A. matching orders

Trading securities back and forth without any essential change of ownership is a violation known as matching orders. The idea behind it is to make it look like there's a large trading volume on a particular security to help drive the price up.

988. D. entering an at the open order

At the open orders are ones placed by investors so that their transaction will take place at the next opening price or it's canceled. However, there is a violation called marking at the open which could be done by a firm by placing a series of orders within minutes of the open to manipulate the price of a security.

989. D. the releasing of material, nonpublic information

The "FD" in Regulation FD stands for *fair disclosure*. Regulation FD is an SEC rule that covers the issuer releasing material, nonpublic information. Typically, issuers will want to release certain nonpublic information to certain individuals or entities such as securities market professionals, analysts, holders of the issuer's securities, and so on. Regulation FD requires the issuer to make that information available to the public at the same time to keep persons from being able to trade on insider information. The aim of Regulation FD is to promote full and fair disclosure.

990. **D. a lifetime**

Documents that establish the broker-dealer as a corporation or partnership must be kept for the firm's lifetime.

991. **A. I and III**

According to MSRB rules, records of blotters and complaints must be kept on record by brokerage firms for 6 years while confirmations and public communications must be kept on record for 4 years.

992. **C. 4 years**

According to FINRA rule 4513, complaints must be maintained by brokerage firms on their records for at least 4 years.

993. **D. six years**

According to MSRB rules, complaints must be kept by the brokerage firm for at least six years. FINRA requires complaints to be kept for four years.

994. **C. U-4 forms of terminated employees**

U-4 forms of terminated employees must be maintained by brokerage firms for 3 years. All other choices listed must be maintained by brokerage firms for 6 years.

995. **B. three years**

Records of customer powers of attorney must be kept for a minimum of three years and be kept easily accessible for two years.

996. **C. 2 years**

Whether the records have to be kept for 3 years, 6 years, or whatever, they have to be easily accessible for 2 years.

997. **A. At the time of the recommendation**

Control relationships must be disclosed to potential investors at the time of the recommendation verbally or in writing by a registered rep. If the first disclosure is verbal, disclosure must be made in writing at or prior to the completion of the transaction. Answer (D) would be correct if the question asked when written disclosure of the relationship is necessary.

998.
D. A brokerage firm must segregate a customer's cash and securities from the brokerage firm's cash and securities.

Under the Securities Exchange Act of 1934's Customer Protection Rule (Rule 15c3-3), broker-dealers must segregate customer securities and cash from the broker-dealers' securities and cash. Quite often, broker-dealers use their own securities and/or cash to execute trades. By forcing broker-dealers to segregate customers' cash and securities from the broker-dealer's transactions, the likelihood that customers' securities and cash will remain readily available to return to customers in the event of broker-dealer failure.

999.
C. II and III

The Uniform Practice Code regulates trades between members. The Rules of Fair Practice or Conduct Rules regulate trades between members and non-members. The Code of Procedure is a process of handling complaints.

1000.
D. Uniform Practice Code

The Uniform Practice Code regulates trades between members. The Rules of Fair Practice or Conduct Rules regulate trades between members and non-members. The Code of Procedure is a process of handling complaints.

1001.
A. I and III

Upon receiving a signed ACAT (account transfer) form, the delivering firm has 1 business day to validate the positions in the account. After validating the positions, the delivering firm must cancel any open orders and freeze the account. Then, the delivering firm must deliver the securities within 3 business days. Note that MSRB rules are different than Uniform Practice Code rules.

Index

A

ABLE accounts, 217
Account, 346
accounts, opening, 142–149
account statements, 339–340
account transfer form, 346
accredited investors, 252
accretion, 319–320
accrued interest, 191–192
accumulation units, 247
additional takedown, 168
ad valorem taxes, 205
advance refunding, 210
aggressive investing, 289, 292
all-in-one (AON) underwriting, 166, 167
all or none (AON) order, 215, 309
alpha, 291
alternative minimum tax (AMT), 315
alternative order, 310
American depository receipts (ADRs), 21–23, 181–182
amortization, 321
annual interest, 185
appreciation, 253, 316
arbitration, 222, 341–342
assumed interest rate (AIR), 247
at the close (market-on-close) order, 310
at-the-open (market-on-open) order, 310
auction-rate securities, 214
Automated Confirmation Transaction service (ACT), 336
Automated Customer Account Transfer Service (ACATS), 342, 346

B

backing away, 344
bankers' acceptance, 202
bankruptcy, 181
basis points, 185, 220
bearish call spread, 267
beta coefficient, 291
blind pool, 253

BLiSS (buy limit or sell stop) orders, 308–309
board of director, 249
bona fide quote, 222
bond anticipation notes (BANs):, 215, 216
Bond Buyer, The, 210, 225
Bond Buyer's Index, 226
bond counsel (attorney), 224
bond principal, 207
bond ratings, 220, 224, 225
bonds
  comparing, 31–34, 193–197
  general obligation, 40–42
  indenture, 185
  price and yield calculations, 29–31
  revenue, 42–44
  taxes, 314
  terms, 27–29, 184–188
  traits, 27–29, 184–188
  types, 27–29, 184–188
book-entry securities, 197
book value per share, 298
break-even point, 258, 260, 270, 277, 278
breakout, 301
broker-dealers, 121–122, 305, 334
build America bonds (BABs), 215
bullish indicator, 300
buy limit orders, 307, 308, 312
buy stop orders, 307, 308, 312

C

calamity call, 211
calendar spread, 271
callable bonds, 211
callable preferred stock, 180
call feature, 203
call options, 255, 256, 263, 277
call premium, 194
call protection, 194
call up, 260, 266
capital appreciation potential, 253

capital gains, 286, 287, 314, 316, 318

capital gains tax, 316

capital gains yield, 316–317

capital losses, 286, 318

capital preservation, 288

cash dividends, 174, 297, 315

cash flow, 298

cash withdrawals, 231

catastrophe (calamity) call, 211

certificate of limited partnership, 251

certificates of deposits (CDs), 200, 201

certificates of participation (COPs), 212

Chicago Board Options Exchange (CBOE), 304

churning, 331, 344

Class A (front-end load) shares, 244

Class C (level load) shares, 244

closed-end funds, 238–239

closing sale (option), 261

code of procedure (COP), 341

cold calls, 342

collateralized debt obligations (CDOs), 200–201

collateralized mortgage obligations (CMOs), 199–200

collateral trust bonds, 186

combinations, 263–273

combined equity, 231

commercial paper, 171, 202

commingling, 343

commissions, 305

common stock, 16–18, 174–178, 297

communication, 333

community property accounts, 330

companion tranches, 200

competitive offering, 209

complaints, 341, 344

concession, 167, 168

confirmations, 221, 337

consolidations, 177, 301

construction loan notes (CLNs), 215, 216

control relationship, 345

conversion ratio, 179–180, 195–197, 316

convertible bonds, 186, 195

convertible preferred stock, 179–180

cooling-off period, 164, 170

corporate and U.S. government debt securities
  answers and explanations, 184–202
    comparing, 31–34, 193–197

money market instruments, 37–38, 201–202

price and yield calculations, 29–31, 188–192

questions, 27–38

structured products, 38

types, 27–29

U.S. government securities, 34–37, 197–201

corporate charter, 163, 332

corporate resolution, 332

correspondence, 333

cost basis per share, 316

coterminous debt, 204

coupon date, 192

coupon rate, 186, 188

covenants, 207

Coverdell ESAs, 326

covered calls, 273, 277

credit agreement, 227

credit balance, 230

credit enhancer, 204

credit spread, 268

cum rights formula, 182

cumulative preferred stock, 179

cumulative voting, 175

currency risk, 292

current assets, 294, 296

current liabilities, 295

current market value (CMV), 236

current ratio, 296

current yield, 188

custodial accounts, 330, 331

customer identification programs (CIPs), 329

D

dated date, 191, 203

dealers, 305

debentures, 187

debit balance, 230

debit bull spread, 273

debit call spread, 270

debit put spread, 268

debit spread, 273

debt service coverage ratio, 208

debt-to-equity ratio, 298

deceased client's account, 332–333

default risk, 193, 204

defensive stocks, 292

defined benefit plans, 323

defined contribution plans, 323

depletion, 252

depletion deductions, 254, 255

designated beneficiaries, 248

designated market makers (DMMs), 126–128, 309, 310–313

developmental programs, 255

diagonal spread, 271

direct debt, 204

direct debt per capita, 208

direct participation programs (DPPs)

  answers and explanations, 249–255

  evaluating, 82–84, 252–255

  general partners, 80, 249–251

  investor recommendations, 294

  limited partners, 80, 249–251

  partnerships paperwork, 81, 251

  passive income and losses, 82, 252

  questions, 80–84

  types of offerings, 81–82, 252

Direct Registration System (DRS), 338

discount, 190

discount rate, 201

discretionary accounts, 331

diversification, 216–217, 289, 293

diversified investment companies, 249

dividend payout ratio (DPR), 299

dividends, 174

DK (don't know) notices, 336

dollar cost averaging (DCA), 242–243

double-barreled bonds, 186, 212, 245

Dow Jones Industrial Average (DJIA), 300

Dow Jones Transportation Average (DJTA), 300

Dow theory, 300

due diligence, 164

durable power of attorney, 332

E

earned (active) income, 314

earnings, 294

earnings per share (EPS), 298, 299

earnings trends, 294

effective date, 165, 170

electronic communications network (ECN), 303

electronic municipal market access (EMMA), 226

Employee Retirement Income Security Act (ERISA), 322–323

equipment leasing partnerships, 253

equipment trust bonds, 186

equipment trust certificates (ETCs), 186

equity REITs, 245–246

equity securities

  ADRs, 21–23

  answers and explanations, 174–184

  common stock, 16–18

  preferred stock, 19–21

  questions, 16–23

  rights, 21–23

  warrants, 21–23

escrow receipt, 273

estate taxes, 135–136, 322

Eurodollar bonds, 187, 189

Eurodollar deposits, 201

European-style options, 283

excess equity, 64, 231–234

exchanges, 120, 303–305

exchange-traded funds (ETFs), 73, 241, 245

exchange-traded notes (ETNs), 202

excise taxes, 211

ex-dividend date, 176, 312, 340–341

exempt securities, 171

exempt transactions, 171

exercise price, 258

expiration dates, 284

expiration months, 271–272, 285

ex-rights formula, 183

extraordinary call, 211

F

face-amount certificate companies, 73, 244

fair disclosure, 344

Fannie Mae (FNMA), 199

Farm Credit System, 199

feasibility study, 206

Federal Reserve Board (FRB)., 201, 227, 228

fiduciary accounts, 331

fill or kill (FOK) order, 309

final prospectus, 170

financial exploitation of specified adults, 333–334

Financial Industry Regulatory Authority (FINRA), 327, 340, 344

firm commitment underwriting, 166–167

first market, 302–303

Fitch, 193

529 plans, 326

5 percent markup policy, 342–343

fixed annuities, 74–76, 246–248

fixed assets, 294

fixed share averaging, 242

flexible premium variable life policies, 248

flow of funds, 203, 206

footnotes, 300

Form 144, 173

401(k) plans, 323

402(b) plans, 324

fourth market, 302–303

Freddie Mac (FNMA), 199

Freddie Macs (FHLMCs), 199

freeriding, 344

front-end loads, 244

fundamental analysis, 113–117, 294–300

G

general obligation (GO) bonds, 40–42, 202–203, 204, 216, 219

general partners, 80, 249–251

geographical diversification, 217

gifts, 222

gift taxes, 135–136, 322

Ginnie Maes (GNMAs), 199

good-til-canceled orders, 312

Gramm-Leach-Bliley Act, 334

grant anticipation notes (GANs):, 216

gross revenue pledge, 207

growth funds, 240

guaranteed bonds, 187

H

head and shoulders pattern, 302

hedge funds, 241

hedging, 278

highest bid price, 311

high-tech stocks, 240

high-yield bonds, 186, 293

horizontal spread, 271

hybrid REITs, 245–246

hypothecation, 227, 343

I

identified shares, 316

immediate or cancel (IOC) order, 309

income (adjustment) bonds, 186, 187

income bonds, 187, 293

income fund, 240

indenture, 185, 207, 224

index options, 282–283

individual retirement accounts (IRAs), 324–326

industrial development bonds, 213, 293

industrial development revenue (IDR) bonds, 212

inflation risk, 179, 292–293

initial margin requirements, 62

initial public offerings (IPOs), 170

insurance covenant, 207

insured municipal bond funds, 241

intangible assets, 295

intangible drilling costs (IDCs), 253, 254

interest rate risk, 292

interest rates, 179, 188, 194, 201

international fund, 241

interpositioning, 343

intrinsic value, 257

inventory, 294, 296

inverse ETFs, 241, 245

inverted head and shoulders pattern, 301

inverted saucer pattern, 302

investment advisers, 327, 343

Investment Advisers Act of 1940, 343

investment banking firm, 166

Investment Company Act of 1940, 249

investment grade bonds, 293

investment objectives, 240, 288

IPOs (initial public offerings), 170

IRAs (individual retirement accounts), 324–326

irrevocable trust, 330

J

joint accounts, 331

joint tenancy in common (TIC) account, 330

joint tenants with rights of survivorship (JTWROS), 329

jumbo CDs, 201

junk bonds, 186, 293

L

legislative risk, 292

letter of intent (LOI), 242

Level 3 halt, 313

level load, 244

liabilities, 297

liens, 186

life-cycle funds, 241

life income annuity, 247

limited partners, 80, 249–251

limited partnership, 294

limited partnership public offerings, 171

limited power of attorney (limited trading authorization), 332

limited tax general obligation bond (LTGO), 212

liquidity, 193, 289, 298

loan consent form, 227, 228

loan value, 231

local government investment pools (LGIPs), 217

long account calculations, 63

long combinations, 264

long coupon, 192

long market value (LMV), 230, 232, 233, 235

long straddles, 263

long-term bonds, 213

long-term capital gains, 316

long-term equity anticipation securities (LEAPS), 255, 280–281, 286

lowest ask price, 311

lowest interest cost, 209

M

make whole call provision, 210

management investment companies, 69–73, 238–244

manager's fee, 167, 168

mandatory redemption, 211

margin accounts

  answers and explanations, 227–237

  excess equity, 63, 64, 231–234

  FRB rules, 62, 228

  initial margin requirements, 62, 228–229

  long account calculations, 63, 230

  minimum maintenance, 65–66, 234–237

  paperwork, 61, 227–228

  questions, 61–66

  restricted accounts, 65–66, 234–237

  short account calculations, 63, 230–231

margin interest rate form, 227

marketability, 193, 203

market-on-close (at the close) order, 310

market-on-open (at the open) order, 310

market orders, 305, 311

market price, 188, 299, 338

market risk, 292

markup, 305

married put, 286

matching orders, 164, 344

maturity date, 206

member-to-customer transactions, 337

mini-max underwritings, 166

minimum maintenance, 65–66, 234–237

minimum yearly dividend payment, 181

money market funds, 240

money market instruments, 37–38, 201–202

Moody's, 193

Moody's investment grade (MIG) scale., 216

moonlighting, 334

moral obligation bond, 213

mortality guarantee, 248

mortgage bonds, 186

mortgage REITs, 245–246

municipal bond funds, 241–242

municipal bond insurance, 204

municipal bonds

  answers and explanations, 202–226

  bank-qualified, 205

  general obligation bonds, 40–42, 202–205

  information gathering, 55–57, 224–226

  marketability, 204

  municipal fund securities, 51

  municipal notes, 49–51, 215–217

  pension funds and, 323

  primary market, 44–46, 209–211

  questions, 40–57

  revenue bonds, 42–44, 205–208

  rules, 53–55, 220–223

  settlement date, 336

  short selling, 306

  as tax-advantaged investment, 289

  taxes, 51–53, 218–220, 315

  types of, 46–49, 211–215

municipal fund securities, 51, 217

municipal GO bonds, 218, 302

municipal notes, 49–51, 216

municipal securities dealers, 222–223

municipal securities principal, 221

Municipal Securities Rulemaking Board (MSRB), 222, 223, 327, 344, 345

mutual funds, 238–239, 289, 340

N

naked options, 259, 273

Nasdaq Levels I-IV, 304

NASDAQ OMX PHLX (Philadelphia Exchange), 283

Nasdaq PHLX, 303

National Securities Clearing Corporation (NSCC), 342

negotiated offering, 209

net asset value (NAV), 238, 242–243

net debt per assessed valuation, 208

net interest cost (NIC), 210, 225

net worth, 295, 297

new account form, 335

new housing authority (NHA) bonds, 213

new issues, 6–8, 163–166

New York Stock Exchange (NYSE), 313

NIC (net interest cost), 210, 225

nominal yield, 186, 188

non-discretionary accounts, 331

non-diversified investment companies, 249

non-equity options, 100–101, 282–284

non-exempt securities, 342

non-qualified retirement plans, 323

non-recourse debt, 250

non-systematic risk, 292

notice of sale, 225

notification, 165

numbered accounts, 328–329

NYSE ARCA, 303

NYSE Display Book, 312

NYSE Euronext, 303

O

odd-lot theory, 300

OEX options, 282–283

offering circular, 172

offering price, 170

Office of Foreign Asset Control (OFAC), 329

official notice of sale, 209–210

official statement, 224

oil and gas combination programs, 255

oil and gas exploratory programs, 254

oil and gas limited partnerships, 249, 251

open-end funds, 238–239

opening accounts, 142–149, 327–334

opening sale (option), 261

open order, 312

operating lease, 253

option account agreement (OAA), 102–104

optional call provision, 211

option premium, 255–256, 257, 278, 282, 284

options

  answers and explanations, 255–288

  basics of, 87–90, 255–262

  combinations, 90–96, 263–273

  non-equity, 100–101, 282–284

  option account agreement, 102–104, 284–287

  Options Clearing Corporation, 102–104, 284–287

  options risk disclosure documents, 102–104, 284–287

  questions, 87–105

  registered options principal, 102–104, 284–287

  rules, 104–105, 287–288

  settlement date, 336

  spreads, 90–96, 263–273

  stocks and, 96–100, 273–282

  straddles, 90–96, 263–273

options charts, 274–277, 279–280, 287

Options Clearing Corporation (OCC), 102–104, 284

options risk disclosure documents (ODDs), 102–104, 284–285

Order Audit Trail System (OATS), 312

orders and trades

  answers and explanations, 302–313

  broker-dealers, 121–122, 305

  designated market makers, 126–128, 310–313

  exchanges, 120–121, 303–305

  OTC (over-the-counter) market, 120–121

  primary and secondary markets, 120, 302–303

  questions, 120–128

  types of, 122–125, 305–310

order tickets, 335

original issue discount (OID) bonds, 214, 320

OTC Pink Market, 170, 303, 305

out of the money, 257
outstanding interest, 184
outstanding shares, 175
outstanding voting securities, 249
overlapping debt, 204
over-the-counter (OTC) market, 120–121, 303–305, 342–343
Over-the-Counter Bulletin Board (OTCBB), 170, 303

P
packaged securities
  answers and explanations, 238–249
  ETFs, 73
  exchange-traded funds, 245
  face-amount certificate companies, 73, 244
  fixed annuities, 74–76, 246–248
  investment company rules, 77
  management investment companies, 69–73, 238–244
  questions, 69–77
  real estate investment trusts, 74, 245
  UITs, 73
  unit investment trusts, 245
  variable annuities, 74–76, 246–248
  variable life insurance, 76, 248–249
  variable universal life insurance, 76, 248–249
parity, 310
par value, 176
passive income and losses, 82, 252, 315
payroll deduction plans, 323
penalty tax, 325
penny stocks, 177–178
periodic payment deferred annuity, 247
perpetual life, 249
Pink sheets, 305
placement ratio, 225
planned amortization class (PAC) tranche, 200
policyholders, 246
political risk, 292
portfolio and securities analysis
  answers and explanations, 287–288
  fundamental analysis, 113–117, 294–300
  portfolio analysis, 109–113, 288–294
  technical analysis, 117–118, 300–302
portfolio income, 314
portfolio margin accounts, 228
portfolio rebalancing, 291

positioning, 305
position limits, 288
power of attorney, 330, 331, 344
precedence, 310
preferred stock, 19–21, 178–181
preliminary official statement, 225
premium, 189
pre-refunding, 210
preservation of capital, 288
price-to-earnings (P/E) ratio, 299
primary market, 44–46, 120, 209–211, 302–303
principal (dealer) transactions, 305, 335–336
priority, 310
private pension plans, 323
private placement, 252
progressive taxes, 314
project notes (PNs), 216
property taxes, 205–206, 314
public housing authority (PHA) bonds, 212, 213
public offering price (POP), 238, 243–244
purchasing power risk, 292–293
put bonds, 194
put down, 260, 266
put options, 256, 259, 263

Q
qualification, 165
qualified dividends, 316
qualified legal opinion, 224
qualified retirement plans, 322–323
qualified salary deduction plans, 323
qualified tuition plans, 326
qualified tuition plans (QTPs), 217
quick assets, 296

R
RANs (revenue anticipation notes), 215
rate covenant, 207
rate covenants, 206
raw land, 253
real estate investment trusts (REITs), 74, 171, 245–246
reallowance, 167
Real-Time Reporting System (RTRS), 226
Real-Time Transaction Reporting System (RTRS), 313
reclamation, 339

record date, 340–341

red herring, 170

refunding, 210

registered options principal (ROP), 102–104, 284

registrar, 339

registration statement, 163

regressive taxes, 314

regulated investment companies (RICs), 239

Regulation A offerings, 172

Regulation D offerings, 172–173

Regulation S offerings, 172

Regulation T, 227, 229, 231, 232, 233

regulatory risk, 293

reinvestment risk, 292, 293

required beginning date (RBD), 325

resistance, 301

restricted accounts, 65–66, 234–237

restricted stock, 173

retail communications, 333

retirement plans

  answers and explanations, 322–326

  questions, 135–139

return of capital, 319

RevDex, 226

revenue anticipation notes (RANs), 215

revenue bonds, 42–44, 186, 203, 205–208

reverse stock splits, 312

revocable (living) trust, 330

rights, 21–23, 182–183

rights offering, 182–183

risk disclosure document, 177, 227

Roth 401(k) plans, 324

Roth IRAs, 325

Rule 144, 171, 173

Rule 147 offerings, 172

Rule 15g-1, 178

S

sales charge, 243

Sallie Mae (SLMA), 199

saucer pattern, 301

secondary market, 120, 302–303

second market, 302–303

Section 8 housing, 252

sector fund, 240

Securities Act of 1933, 166, 170

Securities and Exchange Commission (SEC), 163–164, 169, 170–173, 178, 187, 201–202, 246, 251, 326, 340

Securities Exchange Act of 1934, 346

securities regulatory organizations, 142, 326–327

selling group agreement, 167

selling groups, 164–165

sell limit orders, 307, 308, 312

sell stop orders, 307, 308, 312

SEP-IRAs, 326

serial bonds, 214

settlement date, 191–192, 220, 284, 336

75-5-10 test, 239

shelf registration, 163–164

short account calculations, 63

short combinations, 266

short market value (SMV), 230–231, 232, 235–236, 237

short sales against the box, 308

short sellers, 300, 306

short selling, 277, 278, 302, 316–317

short-term capital gains, 316

short-term debt securities, 201

short-term gain, 306

short-term notes, 215

SHO rules, 306

sideway markets, 301

single payment deferred annuity, 247

sinking fund provision, 211

SLoBS (sell limit or buy stop) orders, 308–309

sovereign bonds, 187

special assessment bonds, 211

specialized (sector) fund, 240

Specially Designated Nationals (SDNs) list, 327, 329

special memorandum accounts (SMAs), 230, 231, 233–234

special situation fund, 241

spreads, 223, 263–273

SPX options, 282

stabilization, 164

stabilizing bids, 167

Standard & Poor's, 193

standby underwritings, 167

statutory voting, 174

stock certificates, 338–339

stock dividends, 174, 176–177, 195, 281

stockholder's equity, 295, 297

stocks
  of new corporations, 289
  options, 96–100, 273–282
  settlement date, 336
stock splits, 176–177, 271, 315
stop orders, 306–307
straddles, 263–273
straight-life annuities, 248
strategic asset allocation, 290
street-name accounts, 227, 328–329
strike price, 256, 258, 272–273, 278
structured products, 38
subscription agreement, 251
Super Display Book (SDBK), 311
support, 301
sweeteners, 184
syndicate agreement, 166
syndicates, 210
systematic risk, 292

T

tactical asset allocation, 291
takedown, 167–168
tangible drilling costs (TDCs), 254
targeted amortization class (TAC), 200
taxable equivalent yield (TEY), 218
tax and revenue anticipation notes (TRANs), 216
tax anticipation notes (TANs), 215, 216
tax base, 206
taxes
  answers and explanations, 313–321
  estate, 135–136, 322
  gift, 135–136, 322
  on investments, 130–135, 313–321
  municipal bonds, 51–53
  questions, 130–136
tax-sheltered annuities (TSAs), 324
technical analysis, 117–118, 300–302
term bonds, 213
third market, 302–303
time value, 257
tombstone ad, 164–165
total dollar amount, 225
trade date, 228
Trade Reporting and Compliance Engine (TRACE), 312, 313

Trade Reporting Facility (TRF), 313
trading volume, 300
transfer agent, 339
Treasury bills (T-bills), 181, 197–198, 288, 292, 293
Treasury bonds (T-bonds), 198, 315
Treasury inflation-protected securities (TIPS), 198
Treasury securities, 198, 283
Treasury stock, 175–176, 198
Treasury STRIPS (T-STRIPS), 198, 293
trend lines, 300, 301
true interest cost (TIC), 210, 225
Trust Indenture Act of 1939, 166, 184
trust indentures, 166

U

U-4 forms, 344
uncovered calls, 257, 258
uncovered option, 259, 284
underlying securities, 255
underwriting securities
  agreement among underwriters, 8–11, 166–170
  answers and explanations, 163–174
  bringing new issues to market, 6–8, 163–166
  questions, 6–14
  reviewing exemptions, 11–14, 170–173
underwriting spread, 167
Uniform Gifts to Minors Act (UGMA) accounts, 330, 331
Uniform Practice Code (UPC), 346
Uniform Transfer to Minors Act (UTMA) accounts, 330, 331
unit investment trusts (UITs), 73, 245
unqualified legal opinion, 224
unsolicited order, 335
USA Patriot Act, 329
U.S. government securities, 34–37, 197–201

V

variable annuities, 74–76, 246–248
variable life insurance, 76, 248–249
variable rate municipal bonds, 214
vertical spread, 271
visible supply, 225
VIX options, 282
volatility, 291
voting rights, 184

W

warrants, 21–23, 183–184
wash sale rule, 319
wildcatting programs, 254
working capital, 295, 296, 297

Y

yield, 190
yield-based options, 283

Z

yield to call (YTC), 189–191, 220–221
yield to maturity (YTM), 188, 190, 221

zero-coupon bonds, 187, 214

About the Author

After earning a high score on the Series 7 Exam in the mid 1990s, **Steven M. Rice** began his career as a stockbroker for a broker dealership with offices in Nassau County, Long Island, and in New York City. In addition to his duties as a registered representative, he also gained invaluable experience about securities registration rules and regulations when he worked in the firm's compliance office. But it was only after Steve began tutoring others in the firm to help them pass the Series 7 Exam that he found his true calling as an instructor. Shortly thereafter, Steve became a founding partner and educator in Empire Stockbroker Training Institute (www.empirestockbroker.com).

In addition to writing the *Series 7 Exam For Dummies, Securities Industry Essentials Exam For Dummies,* and *SIE Exam: 1001 Practice Questions For Dummies,* Steve developed and designed the Empire Stockbroker Training Institute online (*Series 7, Securities Industry Essentials, Series 6, Series 63, Series 65, Series 24, and Series 66*) exams. Steve has also coauthored a complete library of securities training manuals for classroom use and for home study, including the *Securities Industry Essentials, Series 6, Series 7, Series 24, Series 63, Series 65,* and *Series 66.* Steve's popular and highly acclaimed classes, online courses, and training manuals have helped tens of thousands of people achieve their goals and begin their lucrative new careers in the securities industry.

Dedication

I dedicate this book to my beautiful wife, Melissa. Melissa was the love of my life, my joy, my inspiration, and my best friend. Unfortunately, Melissa lost her long battle with cancer and is no longer in my arms. She was the most joyous and loving person I've ever met. I will carry her love in my heart for the rest of my days.

Author's Acknowledgments

A phenomenal team over at Wiley made this book possible. I would like to start by thanking my acquisitions editor, Lindsay Lefevere, for setting up this project, putting together an awesome team, and providing guidance as needed. She is a professional through and through, and I appreciate all of her help.

A load of thanks also goes to my development editor, Tim Gallan, for his rapid-response emails, which provided guidance and helped to keep me moving in the right direction. Tim and I have worked on many projects together.

I would also like to thank my copy editor, Kelly Henthorne, for making suggestions and tweaking my writing to make it more in line with Dummies style. Her input ultimately made this book more fun to read for all of you.

Next, I would like to thank the entire composition team and the technical editor, David Lambert. Although I didn't get a chance to communicate with any of them directly, this book wouldn't be possible without every one of them. I sincerely appreciate all of their hard work.

Publisher's Acknowledgments

Executive Editor: Lindsey Lefevere
Development Editor: Tim Gallan
Copy Editor: Kelly D. Henthorne
Technical Editor: David Lambert

Managing Editor: Kristie Pyles
Production Editor: Pradesh Kumar